Baptist Sacramentalism 3

Baptist Sacramentalism 3

Edited by
Anthony R. Cross and Philip E. Thompson

Foreword by Alec Gilmore

PICKWICK *Publications* • Eugene, Oregon

BAPTIST SACRAMENTALISM 3

Pickwick
An Imprint of Wipf and Stock Publishers
199 W. 8th Ave., Suite 3
Eugene, OR 97401

www.wipfandstock.com

PAPERBACK ISBN: 978-1-7252-8608-5

HARDCOVER ISBN: 978-1-7252-8609-2

EBOOK ISBN: 978-1-7252-8610-8

Cataloguing-in-Publication data:

Names: Cross, Anthony R., editor. | Thompson, Philip E., editor. | Gilmore, Alec, foreword writer.

Title: Baptist sacramentalism 3 / Anthony R. Cross and Philip E. Thompson, with a foreword by Alec Gilmore.

Description: Eugene, OR: Pickwick, 2020 | Includes bibliographical references and index | 1 + 324 p.; 23 cm

Identifiers: ISBN 978-1-7252-8608-5 (paperback) | ISBN 978-1-7252-8609-2 (hardcover) | ISBN 978-1-7252-8610-8 (ebook)

Subjects: LCSH: Sacraments—Baptists. | Baptism—Baptists | Lord's Supper—Baptists | Baptists—Doctrines | Baptists—History

Classification: BX6338 C767 2020 (print) | BX6338 (ebook)

Typeset by Luna Seymour.   Manufactured in the U.S.A.

Contents

Practices

Contributors

Linda Aadne is a Baptist minister and church planter, and also a College Lecturer in Biblical Exegesis, New Testament Theology, and Baptist History and Identity at the Norwegian School of Leadership and Theology, Stabekk, Norway

Jan Martijn Abrahamse is Tutor Systematic Theology and Ethics, Ede University of Applied Sciences/Dutch Baptist Seminary, Amsterdam, The Netherlands

Henk Bakker is Professor at The James Wm McClendon Chair for Baptistic and Evangelical Theologies, Free University Amsterdam, The Netherlands

Faith Bowers is a Vice President of the Baptist Historical Society, and was a founder member and first convenor of BUild (Baptist Union Initiative with people with Learning Disabilities), UK

John E. Colwell is a retired Baptist Minister living in East Devon, who formerly was Tutor in Christian Doctrine and Ethics at Spurgeon's College, London, UK

Anthony R. Cross is an Adjunct Supervisor, The International Baptist Theological Study Centre, Amsterdam, The Netherlands

Joseph C. Delahunt is Pastor, First Baptist Church, New Haven, Connecticut, USA

Paul S. Fiddes is Professor of Systematic Theology, University of Oxford and Senior Research Fellow, Regent's Park College, Oxford, UK

Stanley K. Fowler is Professor Emeritus of Theology, Heritage Theological Seminary, Cambridge, Ontario, Canada

Alec Gilmore is a Baptist minister, ordained in 1952, and served two Baptist churches prior to becoming Editor of Lutterworth Press and Director of Feed the Minds, leading to recognition as a Senior Research Fellow at The International Baptist Theological Study Centre, Amsterdam, The Netherlands

Adam Glover is Associate Professor, Department of World Languages and Cultures, Winthrop University, Rock Hill, South Carolina, USA

Lon Graham is Pastor, The Woods Baptist Church, Tyler, Texas, USA

Brian Haymes is a Baptist Minister, ordained in 1965, served in two British Baptist Colleges and local pastorates the last being Bloomsbury Central Baptist Church, London, UK

Frank Rees is an Associate Professor and Chair of the Academic Board at the University of Divinity, Kew, Victoria, Australia

Sergiy Sannikov is Senior Research Fellow at The Center for the Study of Religions, National Pedagogical Dragomanov University, Kyiv, Ukraine, and Lecturer at the Odessa Theological Seminary, Odessa, Ukraine

Paul Sheppy was ordained in 1972, and is now retired from pastoral oversight in the UK

Philip E. Thompson is Professor of Systematic Theology and Christian Heritage, Sioux Falls Seminary, Sioux Falls, South, Dakota, and a Faculty Member of the Kairos Project, USA

Foreword
New Dimensions in Sacramentalism: A Baptist View

Alec Gilmore

Encouraged by a positive response to their two earlier volumes and a noticeable resurgence of sacramental theology among Baptists, it was a pleasure to learn that that Anthony and Philip had re-visited the territory, picking up the threads where the earlier volumes left off and introducing some new and younger writers with fresh ideas.

As I read the papers I was then further encouraged that they had avoided the normal entry through the foyer (sacraments as practiced in other churches) with a view to coming up with a Baptist alternative or adaptation, and instead had slipped round the back to enter by the stage door for a new angle. The result is a combination of academic objectivity with creativity and a degree of boldness (though not high risk), breaking new ground with what the editors fairly describe as "new dimensions of sacramentalism, and developments in sacramental thinking that are being explored." In my search for a lens through which to see the whole so as not to get lost in the detail, two images come to mind, one for the undertaking *per se* and the other for the presentation.

The undertaking strikes me as on a par with refurbishing a cathedral. The foundations are sacrosanct, every move must be handled with care, and the end product must still be recognizable as a cathedral and perform the basic functions for which it was created. The planners and construction workers are aware that some people never wanted cathedrals in the first place, preferring the local parish church with all its foibles, while others see cathedrals as a focal point, the *sine qua non* of a reputable church. Sacramentalism, for Baptists, enjoys a similar niche.

But to live is to change, to be alive is to address change, and the handling of change is everything. Some aspects were never quite right in the first place, some never completed, some no longer appropriate. Some have seen better days and simply need updating. Some "methods and treatments" are possible today which a few hundred years ago would have been inconceivable or impossible. Smyth and Helwys might have had a problem or two with cyberspace. So today's workforce must be sensitive to the past, fully aware of the present and have a clear vision for the future, always with a watchful eye on the fine line between change and continuity. In all respects, these contributors, with the benefit of Anthony R. Cross and Philip E. Thompson as architects and site managers, serve us well.

From Cathedral to Symphony

By the time I got to the end my second image came into play because what I see here is more than a refurbishment. The overall collection is more than the sum of its parts and casting around for a unifying element I sensed it had something of a symphony about it, subjecting familiar themes to fresh interpretation, fortifying the foundations for further development and, in common with a first movement, presented with vitality and freshness, forceful enough to demand attention but not shouting.

The first phrase that stood out when I read these papers was the editors' comment that it included "new dimensions of sacramentalism, and developments in sacramental thinking that are being explored." The second half of that sentence is as important as the first. These are not fanciful notions to entertain nor wild ideas to stir things up nor settled views to replace the thinking and practice of the past as if with papal authority, but all serious issues where positive participation would be more productive than conflict.

First Movement

The opening bars (Sheppy) are familiar: real presence, efficacy, sign and symbol, first in relation to sacraments in general, then specifically to baptism and eucharist, and each with a "novelty" or freshness for clarity, to assist memorability and to suggest a line for further thought. Examples are a challenge to the traditional description of a sacrament ("the outward and visible sign of an inward and spiritual grace"), sacraments which *effect* what they signify, and "Liturgy as Sacrament," intriguingly distinguishing text and performance, with an imaginative "vaudeville *versus* theatre" analogy, and finally a "gum-and-glue" approach to sign and symbol in such a way that never again can "just symbols" turn up with the same confidence in serious academic circles. Rich fare for slow digestion rather than immediate satisfaction.

If that seems heavy going the transition from "Liturgy and Sacrament" to liturgy as word (and preaching) is smooth, more familiar, acceptable and has its own thrust (Glover). Baptists have never questioned the power of the word and the capacity of preaching to effect change. Preaching indeed which fails to *effect* change is surely unworthy of the name, but to afford it the status of "sacrament" does not come naturally, challenging our ability to identify and evaluate significant change before deciding whether it is for us. Some, nevertheless, will give it a warm welcome, if only because it would have two significant spin-offs. One, bringing to an end the familiar "word and sacrament" dichotomy as if they were two different things. Two, give the lie to any suggestion that for Baptists it's preaching whereas for other churches it's sacraments, and as a bonus it could add depth to Baptist preaching which has mostly swung from bare-faced emotional appeals for converts at one extreme to little more than cerebral biblical instruction at the other.

But is all this truly Baptist or is it a distortion of Baptist identity? Instantly the knives are out, mainly extreme right wing evangelicals in the US—though another paper (Fowler) suggests that even there the tide is turning—responding aggressively to those who have spent time, energy and in some cases reputations establishing that it is, and that some of our Baptist forefathers were familiar with it. Brass, percussion and double bass weigh in, the music roughs up, at times unpleasant, and only calmed down by a skillful conductor (Graham) with the news that John Ryland apparently managed to embrace a memorialist approach and the real presence in the eucharist, not as the Roman Catholics understood it, but more in terms of a spiritual refreshment for the soul, and the first movement draws quietly to a close.

Second Movement (Adagio)

Second movements have a different tone and tempo. Softer, soothing, relaxing, and often rich in unforgettable melodies which people find themselves humming or whistling to sustain the soul long after the music has subsided, sometimes not even remembering where they first heard them. Two papers in particular have that quality, differing not only in tone and tempo from the rest but also differing markedly from each other.

In what reads like a personal discovery of sacramentalism, Brian Haymes describes it as "an exercise in ecumenical pastoral theology," seeking to explore the significance of first communion and the gifts of God in the eucharist. When I read it, give or take a detail, I felt as if I were reading my own story, a decade earlier and in the north of England, as I shared his experience. Like him, I learned the language of faith in the home, enriched by life in a community of faith and embodied care, with no recollection of childhood rebellion and proceeding smoothly to baptism, membership and ordination. Not surprisingly, therefore, I find much to welcome in his thinking.

Although, on the surface, it is very different from the "new dimensions" of the first movement, it is still a welcome one fortified partly by a reminder that within the New Testament itself there was no one pattern by which people came to be grasped by the gospel. But, more powerfully, in his email response to Faith Bowers, Haymes described her study as "a sacramental story through and through," adding "God uses flesh and blood to engage with us as we are." This I see as a crucial judgement and the heart of the adagio.

Further comment on the Faith Bowers story from me would be superfluous, like gilding the lily or taking all the petals off a flower one by one in order to appreciate its beauty, but both these contributions are not so much contributions *about* the sacraments as descriptions of a sacramental experience, and therein lies some of their newness, one aspect of which is language. So we have "real presence," memorable if not memorial, sacramentalism in the world of heart before head, experience before theory, reflection before proclamation,

Here is a door of opportunity for newness. It is slightly ajar and Brian
Haymes and Faith Bowers give it a push, opening *our* minds and hearts as
they open *theirs* for our benefit, bringing the adagio to a close with a tacit
reminder that sacraments are not all scholarship, doctrines, and dogmas. An
element not to be overlooked in sacramental discussions is that faith is
fundamentally about people and human experience with a message of hope
and encouragement as significant in the market place as in the cathedral or
central hall.

The change of language, however, or (to be more precise) vocabulary,
introduced intentionally or unintentionally but without comment, does not
stop there, and is significant because it crops up again indirectly in the scherzo
and more specifically in the final movement. Efficacy is not something to be
defined but experienced. It can vary from person to person, or even from day
to day for the same person. It can be acknowledged or denied but is not
debatable.

One open door then leads to another. "Real presence" becomes more like
"real presence (of Christ)," "means of grace" as an alternative to sacrament,
and you find yourself waiting for "communion," "ordinance," even "Lord's
supper" rather than eucharist, suggesting that re-thinking Anglo–Catholic
terminology might profitably be balanced by a re-examination of Baptist
practice.

While it would be difficult to deny sacramental status to such experiences
as Brian Haymes and Faith Bowers have described, more traditional
sacramental churches would presumably regard them at best as "true but
deficient" and would certainly hear alarm bells with any generalization
suggesting that all Christian practices are intrinsically sacramental; not only
baptism and communion, but also prayer, discernment, preaching and
teaching, and even the ministries of various prophetic gifts, hospitality,
healing and acts of mercy, counselling, and social engagement (Aadne). Then,
as if that were not enough we have the silence followed by the roar of the
crowd at the end of a musical performance. (Would it, I wondered, be the
same in Spain at the roar of the crowd with the death of the bull?) This was
the moment I found myself saying "Hang on, this is an adagio that thinks it's
a scherzo." Fortunately, Aadne backtracks in her penultimate paragraph,
distinguishing sacraments from "other elements of worship" deemed as
"sacramental in character" and the adagio comes thoughtfully to close.

Third Movement (Scherzo)

Usually lively and quick tempo. A jolt and a wake-up call after the more
pensive adagio, sometimes including a self-contained piece with no more than
a tangential link to the rest and occasionally a joke. Important to keep your
feet on the ground.

Suddenly, with a hint of "let's get on with it," we find ourselves in a different world with "cyberspace" and "virtual sacraments." Yet another new dimension, yet again a totally new context. Baptist sacramentalism is remarkable for its height, depth, length and breadth and a capacity for universal application.

Virtual sacraments (Fiddes) fall somewhere between church sacraments (bread and wine) and other sacramental media in the wider world. Some ("virtual scholars"?) have been too hasty in their dismissive approach and a few even objectionable, but no group today can claim exclusive copyright when it comes to language and meaning and with an eye on the issues of today (and tomorrow even more so) this comes across as a tonic of positive theological thinking meriting more attention than it has been given, while attempts to diminish or destroy it can only be seen as panic reaction to what may shortly come to be appreciated by others.

The link between a sacramental world and the world of Teilhard de Chardin resonates more with twentieth- than seventeenth-century theological thinking and resonates equally well with a relevant nineteenth-century link between sacrament and nature, expressed in familiar religious language by John Muir, naturalist and founder of the National Parks Movement in the USA.

Driven by a despotic father to reject all religions Muir chose the natural world in preference to creeds and doctrine, but he was by no means a neophyte when it came to religious language and knew a sacrament when he saw one. In one of his books he tells us that he saw every mountain as a cathedral, offering all the benefits of cathedrals made with hands, and that even a hundred miles away they held a "spiritual power" over him. With a capacity to transcend time and distance they were as near as a circle of friends. Sitting beneath pines more than two hundred feet high, he was thrilled, and as the sunbeams streamed through their feathery arches he walked beneath the radiant ceiling in devout subdued mood as if "in a grand cathedral with mellow light sifting through coloured windows", the whole landscape glowing "like the face of a god." Here was "heaven and the dwelling place of the angels . . . a new heaven and a new earth."[1]

Then, all at once, before we are carried off into the stratosphere up pops a "rather original phenomenon" from an Eastern European Perspective (Sannikov) with a friendly reminder that Russian eighteenth-century Baptist groups, based on *sola scriptura*, the independence and autonomy of the local church, rejecting ritualism and ceremonialism and stressing "the all-believers" priesthood, emerged long before they were aware of Baptists in the rest of Europe, surprised only to discover that what they had produced approximated very closely to what was happening elsewhere.

---

[1] John Muir, *The Eight Wilderness-Discovery Books*. London: Diadem Books, 2000, 491 and 268.

With that the Scherzo comes to an end and after the briefest of pauses for a gasp or a laugh we go straight into the final movement.

Final Movement

A final movement can fulfil several functions one of which is to make good anything that was missing or didn't easily fit with what was there already. "The Laying-on-of-hands" (Delahunt) and "Marriage" (Colwell) bid fair to redress the omission, one with an insistence on "convictions" that outweigh personal emotions and the other with a focus on mystery and divine joining as more than a human covenant or contract when put alongside the imagery of the church as "the body of Christ," all matters worthy of, and calling for, further consideration, and will no doubt get it.

A second function is to build a bridge between the heights just visited and the reality of the world they are about to re-enter, offering hope and excitement to send them out wanting more. The key to this transition is gradually to shift the emphasis to more familiar territory, first with "The priesthood of All the People" (Rees) followed by the gathered community (Bakker), relating to what has gone before and together providing the main thrust for the finale. Time to accept the given, recognize and locate the gaps, and encourage others to explore the issues further.

Rees, for example, suggests that the priesthood of all the people (or, if you prefer, the gathered church) might be described as "the primary sacrament," which while welcome to some will ring alarm bells for others, but it is imaginative, creative and merits serious consideration. At the same time, he is well aware that the consequential theological imperatives for church life (so different today from church life less than a century ago) may claim priority. Then "the church" was a religious institution living in a world "beyond religion" with its own professional management class. Today the trend is for the church to move from "*church* life" to the "*dispersed* life," relating to the lives and experiences of people when they are not gathered in church buildings, programmes and meetings.

Roughly in the same territory, Bakker picks up on McClendon's line that habits, practices and customs all predate theology which arrives later as clarification and justification for what we have already created and practiced. One consequence is that in a covenantal community the gap between sacramentalism and the "real presence" (a concept which has never had its due), will not be effectively communicated without first eradicating so much traditional "baggage" and widespread misunderstanding of "real presence," myths and perpetrations which too many Nonconformists have already got in their heads. That is a tough agenda, but without it little will be gained by offering anything approaching a Nonconformist alternative as we hark back to the unresolved linguistic issues in the second and third movements. The question still lying on the table is whether changing words or phrases will be enough. Is it vocabulary or language that is required, because they are very different. Language is more than the sum of its words. Stand by for a course in catachresis.

Finally comes the moment when you think you have got to the end, prepare to applaud but hold back until someone else begins, only to find that there is yet more to come, and our "symphony" is no exception. The *coup de grâce* falls to Abrahamse with a lighter touch of humanity with laughter and sacraments in the same breath. Laughter he sees as the sacramental sensation of hope in a weeping world, the tangible expression of another kingdom and the tragedy of life. Keeping firmly in the Baptist tradition this kind of laughter transcends the broken life, exploring the sacramental character within "the tragedy that is the Christian life." Now there *is* a new dimension. Fresh thinking. New doors. Unfamiliar pastures. As refreshing as a shower of rain, but beware. Having had my fingers burnt with a quite mild attempt to bring laughter and worship together in Lent I can only hope that Abrahamse will not have the same experience. Readers lacking a sense of humour who find the conjunction difficult to handle may reach for an umbrella as they leave the auditorium.

Acknowledgements

The editors are deeply grateful to the contributors to this volume, and for those who have encouraged us in putting it together. It is offered here in the hope, and with the prayer, that it might stimulate Baptists, those from the Free Churches/Believers Churches, and other traditions to explore God's gracious work in the church and in the world that he has created.

Especial thanks are due to the Rev. Dr Robin Parry of Wipf and Stock, Editor of their Cascade and Pickwick imprints, for his willingness to accept this and the following two volumes in this series of explorations of the sacraments and sacramentality.

And we offer profound thanks to the Rev. Alec Gilmore who graciously agreed to write the Foreword. This volume, and its two predecessors, and the two further volumes that are in progress, owe an enormous debt of gratitude to him and his colleagues who explored various forms of Baptist sacramentalism in the 1950s and 1960s. Their work inspired, and continues to inspire, Baptists in their theology and practice of the Christian life, personally and communally. Many of his colleagues were teachers of those who have written in these volumes. Through their theological research, teaching, ministries, and churchmanship, they have set examples of rigorous biblical, theological, historical, practical, and ecumenical scholarship which we seek to emulate. It is to Alec that this volume is dedicated with thanks from those who follow in his footsteps.

Anthony R. Cross and Philip E. Thompson
June 2020.

To
Alec Gilmore,
"a servant of Christ Jesus"

Introduction:
Sacramentalism Alive and Well

The last time Anthony R. Cross and his wife Jackie visited Neville Clark, his MTh supervisor at University College Cardiff and College Principal for two years at South Wales Baptist College, he remembers telling Clark, just before they left, that he and Philip E. Thompson were putting together a collection of essays on the subject of Baptist sacramentalism. In his customarily brief reply, Clark expressed a certain hopeful skepticism—more the latter to be honest, but in a kind way—as to whether it would ever see publication. But in 2003, a year after his death, that volume was published by the Paternoster Press in their newly founded Studies in Baptist History and Thought series. Mr Clark was never one for giving away much, but it's to be hoped that its publication would have pleased him.

The unimaginatively entitled *Baptist Sacramentalism* was followed five years later—reflecting the movie tradition of unimaginatively entitled sequels—by *Baptist Sacramentalism 2*. Together, these two volumes continued a tradition of collaborative essays in which Clark had himself been a participant,[1] and which has continued ever since.[2] Such work is in addition to the wealth of research that has been published throughout the twentieth century *and also* earlier work,[3] which can be traced right back to Baptist beginnings. Neither of these volumes initiated something new, for there have always been sacramentalists among the Baptists,[4] and the renaissance of sacramentalism,

---

[1] See Gilmore, ed., *Christian Baptism*; and Gilmore, ed., *Pattern of the Church*. See respectively Clark's chapters, "Theology of Baptism," and "Fulness of the Church of God."

[2] Walton's *Gathered Community* (though it is often mistaken for a solo work, see 8–10); Gilmore, ed., *Pattern of the Church*; Fiddes, ed. *Reflections on the Water*; and, in many ways, the two volumes edited by Porter and Cross, *Baptism, the New Testament and the Church*, and *Dimensions of Baptism*, though these include contributions by other baptists and Pedobaptists.

[3] For a survey of baptismal sacramentalism, which deals with Baptist pastor-theologians who elsewhere explore other sacraments, see Fowler, *More Than a Symbol*; Cross, *Baptism and the Baptists, passim*; the two "Introductions" by Porter and Cross in *Baptism, the New Testament and the Church*, 33–39, and *Dimensions of Baptism*, 1–6. On the sacrament of the Lord's supper among British Baptists in the nineteenth century, see, e.g., Walker, *Baptists at the Table, passim*.

[4] See, e.g., Fowler, *More Than a Symbol*, 10–88; Cross, "Myth of English Baptist Anti-Sacramentalism"; and Thompson, "New Question in Baptist History," 66–69, and "Practicing the Freedom of God," 128–31.

which began with the study of baptism in the early twentieth century,[5] is associated with the names of such eminent Baptists as H. Wheeler Robinson, A.C. Underwood, R.C. Walton, Alec Gilmore, Ernest A. Payne, Neville Clark, George R. Beasley-Murray, R.E.O. White, Paul S. Fiddes, John E. Colwell, and Christopher J. Ellis. However, what these two recent volumes appear to have done is to spark a resurgence in the exploration of sacramental theology, and also to provide what these earlier studies often lacked, and that is the retrieval of the over 400-year tradition of Baptist sacramentalism. It is appropriate at this point, then, to thank Alec Gilmore for his encouragement for the present volume in supplying the Foreword to it, and, thereby, setting this series of volumes in continuity to the work that has preceded it, in which he played such a prominent role, and from which it is so deeply indebted.

Back in 2003 and 2008, *Baptist Sacramentalism* volumes 1 and 2 included some of the scholars we have just mentioned, as well as some of the leading Baptist scholars at the time, and many "younger" scholars, all of whom were either North American, British or Australian. For this third volume, and the following two volumes, we are delighted to include contributions from many of the same theologians and historians, and also both from wider representation of the global Baptist community, and a new generation of "still younger" scholars whose formation was shaped by the budding renewal in Baptist sacramental thought. Sacramental thought among Baptists is more vigorous than ever. Comparison of the tables of contents between the first two and the later three volumes reveals that many of the same themes are still the focus of study, exploration, and discussion, but that there are also new dimensions of sacramentalism, and developments in sacramental thinking that are being explored.

The United Kingdom, United States, and Canada are still well represented. In more theologically oriented contributions, the leading British Baptist liturgist, Paul Sheppy, has contributed his mature reflections on years of the study of both liturgy and the sacraments, while John Colwell examines the concept of mystery and sacrament, and Adam Glover offers an argument for the sacramentality of scripture notable for its theological, historical, and philosophical breadth. Faith Bowers tackles the important though often neglected issue of sacraments and disability. Brian Haymes addresses the familiar subject of faith, but does so in dialogue with Thérèse of Lisieux, then, in characteristic fashion, Paul Fiddes approaches a subject which, to the best of our knowledge, has not been addressed before by a Baptist, that of virtual sacraments in cyberspace, while Frank Rees delves into the priesthood of "all the people. Taking a more historical approach, Stan Fowler returns to the study of baptism in face of some intense criticisms and frequent misreadings of his work. Joseph Delahunt examines the "fourth principle" and the laying

---

[5] See especially, Cross, *Baptism and the Baptists, passim*; and Fowler, *More Than a Symbol*, 89–155.

on of hands controversy of the seventeenth century,[6] while Lon Graham delves into the eucharistic theology of Dr John Ryland, whose work rarely explicitly uses the term sacrament, though whose theology clearly affirms God's use of the means of grace.

Further, what is often called the "Baptist sacramentalism movement" has spread beyond the English-speaking and European contexts, and is being examined by Baptists from across the globe, representing many different streams of the Baptist tradition. The gathered community provides the perspective from which Linda Aadne explores the sacramental practices from a Norwegian context, and Sergiy Sannikov offers us a detailed examination of water-baptism from an Eastern European context. Finally, two Dutch scholars round off this collection. Henk Bakker looks at "powerful practices" and how they address "the powers that be," while Jan Martijn Abrahamse creatively offers a view of sacraments through the lens of tragicomedy. All these essays, are a source of great encouragement, as they reflect the breadth and depth of Baptist engagement with the study of the ways of God in the past and the present, in the church and the world.

Readers will detect in some essays in this volume a response being made to critics. One of the signs of the strength of the sacramental recovery among Baptists is that it is deemed, even by some who do not agree with it, worthy of response. Another sign of strength is that robust answers can be given to the critiques. It is unfortunate that the arguments of Paul Fiddes and Stan Fowler have been subjected to what appear to be willful misreading and mischaracterization by persons who simply wish to discredit their ideas rather than to give reasoned responses. This is unfortunate for several reasons, perhaps especially because it can distract from serious questions and genuine concerns some Baptists have concerning sacramental thought. These are questions and concerns which need to be answered.

First, there are Baptists who in good faith are uneasy with it because the word has been associated more fully with more dominant churches in their contexts, even state churches, that are sacramental in their theology and against which Baptists have defined themselves. This is an undeniable aspect of Baptist sacramental thought historically, and needs to be taken seriously. To take but one, quite obvious, example, Baptists in England tended to move in a more non-sacramental direction in the first half of the nineteenth century in reaction to the Tractarian Movement.[7] Related to this, Baptist life was established in some contexts after the move away from sacramentalism, or emerged more "organically" rather than being "planted" by Baptists whose lineage stretched back to seventeenth-century England. We see both of these

---

[6] This study builds on Delahunt's doctoral research "Laying on of Hands Controversy."

[7] See, e.g., the discussion by Walker, *Baptists at the Table*, 84–120.

in the context of Philip Thompson, who serves in a seminary sponsored by
the North American Baptist Conference (NAB). The NAB emerged among
the German immigrant community in the United States in the first half of
nineteenth-century America (1839). The traditions from which it emerged
were Swiss Separatism and German Pietism, neither tradition being robustly
sacramentalist. Further, though the German Baptists soon became connected
with the American Baptist Home Mission Society, American Baptists had by
this time largely moved from sacramental beliefs. Hence sacramentalism was
never part of the German Baptist heritage as one could rightly say it is, for
example, for English Baptists.

Yet earlier Baptists in such contexts displayed very careful sacramental
thought, and even employed it critically.[8] The presence of an often-hostile
established church did not dissuade them from a sacramental stance even if it
may have affected their terminology. For instance, Lon Graham explores the
key late-eighteenth- and early-nineteenth-century British Particular Baptist,
Dr John Ryland, and the reasons for his limited explicit use of the term
"sacrament," while advancing a "sacramental" theology of the Lord's supper by
employing other terminology.[9]

And we see similar careful articulation in our time as well. In 2008, a
milestone in the Eastern European Baptist discussion of baptism came when
the journal *Theological Reflections* published two articles on the subject. The
first of these by Constantine Prokhorov, at the time researching his doctorate
while living in Omsk, Russia, had originally been submitted two years earlier.
However, because he argued for a sacramental understanding of water-
baptism among Russian Baptists, he adopted a position contrary to the
widespread Slavic view. The majority of Slavic Baptists had adopted Western
Baptists' antipathy towards sacramentalism and any suggestion that salvation
comes other than by faith in the triune God. Further, they advocated a form
of evangelicalism that rejected the ritualism associated with Roman
Catholicism and Eastern Orthodoxy.[10] It was for this reason, that publication
of Prokhorov's work was originally blocked because, it was argued, it was
contrary to the confession of faith of the Euro-Asian Accrediting Association,
though after two meetings of the EAAA Council, the article was finally
accepted on the condition that it appeared alongside an article presenting the
opposite point of view.[11]

---

[8] So Thompson, "Sacraments and Religious Liberty."

[9] This study has grown out of Graham's doctoral research, "'All Who Love Our
Blessed Redeemer.'"

[10] Prokhorov, "On Several Peculiarities," 89. See also Prokhorov's *Russian Baptists
and Orthodoxy*, 139–49, 166–70 and 366–73.

[11] For these details, see Sannikov, "An Holistic Approach to Water-Baptism,"
201–3.

In his study of the biblical theology of "What . . . happens in the spiritual realm at the moment of baptism," Prokhorov identifies salvation (1 Pet. 3.21), union with Christ in his death and resurrection (Rom. 6.3-11), incorporation into the church (1 Cor. 12.13), the clothing of believers with Christ (Gal. 3.27), renewal by the Spirit (Titus 3.5), the washing away of sins (Acts 22.16), and reception of the Spirit (Acts).[12] He also notes that, contrary to the still dominant position in Western interpretations, "the best" Eastern European Baptist authors adopt the mainstream Eastern tradition in which baptism is understood as a mystery and a sacrament—among them being N.P. Khrapov, N.A. Kolesnikov, M. Zhidkov, R. Vyzu, V. Kulikov, and S.V. Sannikov.[13] For Prokhorov and these writers, this sacramentalism is also found in some of the traditional songs sung in the churches, as well as accounts of baptismal services in the churches.[14] This leads Prokhorov to assert that "a formal ritual cannot possibly have such a far-reaching meaning"[15] as is clearly demanded by the biblical witness, and that this is why so many of the Russian Baptists believe that "the fullness of salvation is found in repentance *and* baptism, not in repentance only (and not in baptism only)."[16] Further, he explicates the closest connection between Spirit-baptism and water-baptism, the former being the indispensable element of regeneration.[17] In an authentic sacrament, he contends, "both spiritual and material beginnings are closely intertwined. It is while uniting the spiritual (faith) and material (water) worlds that God's grace is manifested and the Holy Spirit is bestowed (Acts 2:38; John 3:5; Titus 3:5)." Prokhorov seeks to maintain the "one baptism" of Ephesians 4.5 by arguing that "a single evangelical baptism has two aspects: water baptism (in the visible, material world) and baptism by the Holy Spirit (in the invisible, spiritual world) and these two constituents of one service can coincide in time as well as have a certain interval between them."[18]

Accompanying Prokhorov's essay was one by systematic and biblical theologian, Mark Saucy from Biola University in California, also a Russian-

---

[12] Prokhorov, "On Several Peculiarities," 90–92.

[13] See Prokhorov, "On Several Peculiarities," 91–92 and nn.13–18. Unable to speak Russian, the editors have, with the exception of Sannikov, been unable to access their writings, so take it that in this assertion Prokhorov's assessment of these writers' views is accurate.

[14] Prokhorov, "On Several Peculiarities," 92–94.

[15] Prokhorov, "On Several Peculiarities," 98.

[16] Prokhorov, "On Several Peculiarities," 99 (italics added). He illustrates this, 98–99, from the mysterious doctrinal "antimonies" evident in Mark 16.16, Acts 2.38, and John 3.5.

[17] Prokhorov, "On Several Peculiarities," 99–100.

[18] Prokhorov, "On Several Peculiarities," 100–101.

speaking missionary, at the time teaching in Kyiv. While Saucy's discussion of baptism is an illustration of his broader study of developing a national theology, he is aware that it is easy for Western approaches to dictate Eastern European theological thought, and acknowledges that Asian and Eurasian Evangelicals can embrace "historically Eastern approaches and intellectual categories" for the meaning of baptism, and that in practice this means they see it "within the more mystical, sacramental tradition" that is "historically characteristic" of Orthodoxy, in which baptism is understood as "the completion of the conversion process and the proper point at which the benefits of salvation are applied to the believer."[19] This said, in contrast to Prokhorov's Eastern evangelical study of baptism, Saucy's arguments read as presupposing "Western" evangelical anti-ritualism.

In order to make his case, Saucy examines the scriptural teaching on baptism, what he terms "Scripture's theological and salvation-historical concepts" regarding baptism, and how the church's history reveals the consequences of these viewpoints on baptism.[20] The result of this confirms his rejection of any suggestion that attaches salvific efficacy to the performance of a rite, that even in the presence of faith baptism "does not mark the moment of salvation, regeneration, or reception of the Holy Spirit," though he does concede that baptism is more than an empty symbol.[21] For Saucy, it is faith, and not baptism, in which saving power lies, which leads him to declare that "while baptism needs faith to work, faith does not in the same way need baptism to work."[22]

Among his concluding remarks, Saucy notes that sacramentalism does not follow East–West lines, but he doesn't stop there. Rather, he presumes to become the arbiter of the gospel when he pronounces that it does divide "along the eternal boundary of Gospel and Not-Gospel as a muting of the evangelium's demand of faith." However, he then makes a huge concession towards Prokhorov's sacramentalism when he recognizes "the uniform pattern in the apostolic church *not to separate baptism from the moment of belief*," adding the observation that "In the early church baptism was truly an initiatory rite."[23]

One positive outcome of these articles was that in 2006 and 2007 the faculties of the Kyiv and Odessa Seminaries, along with prominent members of the Ukrainian Baptist Union, explored together the theology of water-baptism.[24] A key figure in this was Dr Sergiy Sannikov, a leading churchman

---

[19] Saucy, "Baptism as a Test Case," 139–40.

[20] Saucy, "Baptism as a Test Case," 140–44, 144–47, and 147–53 respectively.

[21] Saucy, "Baptism as a Test Case," 140.

[22] Saucy, "Baptism as a Test Case," 142.

[23] Saucy, "Baptism as a Test Case," 156 (italics original).

[24] See Sannikov, "Discussions about Water Baptism in West and East," 140–41.

and scholar among European Baptists and contributor to the present volume. For over a decade he has continued to explore baptismal sacramentalism in a number of articles, and most significantly in his 2018 postdoctoral DSc,[25] which it can only be hoped might be translated into English and made more widely available, in a similar way that Prokhorov's research has been.[26]

In *The Phenomenon of Water Baptism*, Sannikov explores the relationship of the transcendent and the immanent in Baptist theology, and advocates an holistic approach in which he proposes that salvation be seen as a fact and, at the same time, as a way that begins when someone hears God's word and ends in the kingdom of God. Salvation is an holistic phenomenon comprising distinguishable elements which cannot be tied to a specific position in the process, and as such his views are fully in-line with the contemporary revival of Baptist sacramentalism. This is not to deny that there is a sequence of events, as is clearly seen in the Book of Acts, but that they are not rigidly prescribed.[27] As he says in a recent article, "From the human perspective salvation is the experience of all the major components of this drama, and its integrity is not destroyed if one of the parts is missed as a result of objective circumstances. The fact of the encounter between God and the human being is important."[28]

He also examines the disputed terms "ordinance," "sacrament," and "ritual," and sets out what Saucy so summarily dismissed, namely, the biblical context of sacramental theology, including Paul's sacramental language, in order to prepare the basis for a broader sacramental theology, which includes Christ as the primordial sacrament, and the church, scripture, and believers who, in certain circumstances, are themselves sacraments. Exploring baptism from various theological disciplines, Sannikov critically examines seven views commonly held by Baptists: baptism as a symbol; as initiation; as a covenant/promise; as a confession of faith; a sign of grace; as union with Christ in his death and resurrection; and as a sign of obedience. Together, these constitute an holistic understanding of baptism as a divine–human encounter.[29]

In February 2018, largely as a result of an invitation prompted by Sannikov, Cross was invited to present two lectures to the heads of the educational institutions of the All-Ukrainian Union of Evangelical Christians-Baptists

---

[25] Sannikov, *Phenomenon of Water Baptism.*

[26] Cf. Prokhorov's "On Several Peculiarities" of 2008, and his 2013 *Russian Baptists and Orthodoxy.*

[27] Sannikov, *Phenomenon of Water Baptism, passim.*

[28] Sannikov, "Discussions about Water Baptism in West and East," 142.

[29] Sannikov, *Phenomenon of Water Baptism, passim.* The originator of the term was Brunner, *Divine–Human Encounter.*

Churches, followed by another to the "Crucial Issues of Contemporary Theology: Recent Trends in the Development of Liturgical Theology" Conference, held at the National Dragomanov University, Kyiv.[30] An issue discussed at numerous points with the heads of the educational institutions, was the legitimacy of the Baptist use of the term "sacrament," primarily, in the Eastern European context, because of its Orthodox connotations. Ever since this time, Cross has found himself considering the many concerns raised, which have linked to his own ambivalence towards the term itself, for his is not attached to the word "sacrament," but finds it a useful term when used in a Baptist and evangelical way, a way that essentially defines sacrament as a "means of grace."

A similar reservation to that held by Ukrainian and Russian Baptists is evident among Norwegian Baptists, so it is particularly welcome to include in the present volume, not just an extensive essay by Sergiy Sannikov on an Eastern European Baptist perspective, but also Linda Aadne's discussion from within the Norwegian Baptist context.[31]

Second, there are those whose resistance to Baptist sacramental thought is grounded in their understanding of Baptist history, believing it can only arise from a departure from Baptist convictions. Because this is such a widely shared reason to question, not just the merit, but even the possibility, of Baptist sacramental thought, it must be taken seriously.

Numerous essays in the first two *Baptist Sacramentalism* volumes, as well as other works by scholars who contributed to them, have given well-documented evidence that such a historical concern can be answered. Still the view persists. For example, Tom Nettles, writing within a Southern Baptist milieu, explicitly condemns the sacramental "movement" among "some Baptist theologians, New Testament scholars, and historians," which he locates in "the early twentieth-century," for the way they emphasize "the sacramental power of the Lord's Supper and baptism." Nettles even states that their contention that such an understanding was "an early commitment embodied in seventeenth-century confessions and theologians," is wrong, and he initially cites the discussions of baptism by Stan Fowler, H. Wheeler

---

[30] One of the two papers presented to the heads of the Ukrainian Baptist educational institutions has been published as Cross, "Baptism, the New Testament, and the Baptist Tradition" (the other paper was on the importance of theology in ministerial training); while the conference paper, "Neville Clark and the Myth of Baptist Anti-Sacramentalism," will be published in Cross and Thompson, eds, *Baptist Sacramentalism 5* in 2022. Both Sannikov and Oleksandr Geychenko, President of the Odessa Theological Seminary, also interviewed Cross in "ВОССТАНОВЛЕНИЕ БАПТИСТСКОЙ САКРАМЕНТОЛОГИИ," which also includes a considerable amount of discussion on baptism.

[31] This is based on her doctoral research at The International Baptist Theological Study Centre Amsterdam, see Aadne, "Theology and Practice of Believers' Baptism."

Robinson, and George R. Beasley-Murray, as exemplars of this movement. It appears that his denunciation of their views justifies, as far as he is concerned, dismissing them as corruptors of Baptist ecclesiology and soteriology.[32] He claims that, "As to salvation, one's focus must now be divided between the historic work of Christ on the cross and the present event of baptism," adding, "This is real idolatry."[33]

A careful reading of Baptist sacramentalists quickly reveals that this is not what they are doing. None separates baptism from faith. On the contrary, they maintain this inseparable connection both explicitly and implicitly in their discussions of baptism, eucharist, and other sacraments. To suggest otherwise, as Nettles does, is, at best, simply to misread and, at worst, to misrepresent them. Nettles condemns Baptist sacramentalists, asserting that in their theology "the transforming event of human experience shifts from the hearing of the word of truth[34] under the efficacious and transforming power of the Spirit, to the doing of an event enacted by the church. In this scheme, the church changes from a transformed community, that receives other transformed sinners into the benefits of its fellowship and Spirit-granted gifts, into a community that grants transformation by its practice of sacraments, baptism and communion."[35]

What Baptist sacramentalists are contending for, however, is the same connection between faith and baptism that is found in the New Testament, and, as Paul so clearly expresses it in Romans 6.2–11, this *cannot* be separated from the work of Christ on the cross. John Colwell states the sacramentalist position clearly:

---

[32] Nettles, *Baptists*, 3:310–11, where his focus is on the following works: Fowler, *More Than a Symbol*, and "Is 'Baptist Sacramentalism' an Oxymoron?"; Robinson, "Place of Baptism in Baptist Churches of To-day"; and G.R. Beasley-Murray, "Baptism and the Sacramental View." Another anti-sacramentalist position is advanced by Moody, *American Baptismal Sacramentalism*.

[33] Nettles, *Baptists*, 3:311. See Nettles' more measured views as expressed in a more "ecumenical" setting, "Baptist View."

[34] When Nettles writes this it is difficult not to think of Rom. 10.8–10, and the baptismal context of Rom. 10.9–10, which is widely recognized by New Testament scholars. Among Baptists, see, e.g., White, *Biblical Doctrine of Initiation*, 146–48 and 151–53; G.R. Beasley-Murray, *Baptism*, 66, 87, 101, 272, 285 and 361; and Martin, *Worship in the Early Church*, 60, 99 and 108, and *Worship of God*, 93. Developing the theme of hearing, and, therefore, proclaiming the word, attention should also be drawn to the discussion below on the sacramental nature of preaching.

[35] Nettles, *Baptists*, 3:311.

xxviii   Introduction: Sacramentalism Alive and Well

We are not saved *by* faith anymore than we are saved *by* the sacraments; we are saved *by* God *through* faith and *through* the sacraments—and these instrumental means of salvation ought not to be opposed as rivals or alternatives.[36]

Against Nettles' implicit ecclesiology, shaped more by a legacy of American populism and republicanism than the New Testament which would make the church little more than an association of persons who choose to be baptized and then to unite on their own initiative, Colwell, answers:

the Church is to be defined in the first place (in every sense) in and through baptism; it is through the means of baptism that the Holy Spirit primarily gathers, shapes, and commissions the Church. Through baptism the Church is gathered to Christ and in Christ before the Father. Through baptism the Church is shaped by the Spirit in conformity with Christ. Through baptism the Church participates in the Son's mission to the world as commissioned by the Father . . . : suffice it for now to affirm baptism, not as a merely human ethical response to God's grace in Christ (as if any truly ethical response could ever be merely human), but as a means through which God has promised to mediate that grace in Christ to us by his Spirit. It is the promise of God (and nothing else) that establishes baptism as the primary defining sacrament of the Church. In and through baptism the Church shares in the baptism of Jesus and thereby comes to participate in his life, death, and resurrection; to participate through the mediation of the Spirit in the Son's relatedness to the Father. Baptism defines the Church and the individual Christian as being "in Christ". Baptism, therefore, defines the Church; the Church consists simply of those who are baptised.[37]

To this he adds, "baptism as defining of the Church, is neither a charade nor an empty ritual simply because God has promised to act by his Spirit in and through baptism and that action of God is a reality."[38] It is, therefore, the promises of God that ensure that faith-baptism—or any faith-sacrament—is effective.

Timothy George develops this further when he maintains that

It is the Holy Spirit who imparts faith to the believer and thus makes effective the *opus operatum* of the sacraments. The sacraments are thus seals of assurance and may not be dispensed with without spiritual detriment. But while we are bound to the sacraments, God is not. By no means should we disparage the external means of grace God has given to the church in its earthly pilgrimage,

---

[36] Colwell, *Promise and Presence*, 130 (italics original); cf. 131 n.72.

[37] Colwell, *Promise and Presence*, 72–73. See also Enns, "Believers Church Ecclesiology."

[38] Colwell, *Promise and Presence*, 73.

but neither should we be surprised when by his Spirit God works in ways that go beyond our understanding but a touch less—*etiam extra ecclesiam*!

He continues, noting that Baptists and Evangelicals protest against the kind of sacramental imperialism that endows sacraments with an importance which views salvation as impossible without them and the concomitant ecclesiology that regards the church as divine.[39] Nettles, on the other hand, makes human posture toward the sacraments more like God's. This, we believe, is what risks idolatry.[40]

Nettles strongly advocates Calvinism for Baptists.[41] This is ironic. Though he and many anti-sacramentalists are Reformed Baptists, yet their out-spoken opposition to the sacraments as sacraments comes at the expense of ignoring Calvin's own sacramental theology.[42] This is no small oversight. As Timothy George observes, in Calvin's theology the "maternal character of the church is seen especially in its dispensing of the sacraments,"[43] an observation that again shows how far Nettles' anti-sacramentalism has departed from Calvin. It is through their insistence on the priority of God's grace, the sovereign work of the Spirit, and that baptism is faith-baptism that prevents Baptist sacramentalists from falling into the position Nettles and others claim they do.

Even for careful historians, however, the suggestion that Baptists can legitimately be sacramentalists is a betrayal of historic Baptist convictions.[44] One of them, Southern Baptist historian Lloyd Harsch, asserts that it is "a commonly accepted belief that Baptists observe ordinances, not sacraments," and that it is only since the turn of the twentieth century that "some Baptists have questioned the historical accuracy of that belief and introduced a new perspective on the ordinances." He further claims that these "Baptist

---

[39] T. George, "Sacramentality of the Church," 29–30 (italics original).

[40] We are echoing William Kiffin's sacramentalist argument against John Bunyan. Bunyan accused Kiffin of making an idol of baptism. Kiffin said that to make one's own judgment superior to what God has commanded is a worse idolatry still. See Bunyan, *A Confession of My Faith*, 604, "It is possible to commit idolatry even with God's own appointments . . ." In response, Kiffin, *A Sober Discourse*, 42–43, indicated that matters of the highest importance were at stake. Those who cared not for "Christ sacramental," he maintained, cared not for "Christ God," for in the former the latter comes near. On this dispute, see Thompson, "Toward Baptist Ecclesiology," 110–12 n.124.

[41] See, e.g., Nettles, *By His Grace and for His Glory*.

[42] On his sacramental theology, particularly baptismal and eucharistic, see Calvin, *Institutes*, Book 4 chapters 14–19. On, e.g., Calvin's baptismal sacramentalism, see Cross, "Baptism in the Theology of Calvin and Barth," *passim*.

[43] T. George, *Theology of the Reformers*, 238

[44] E.g., Nettles, *Baptists*, 3:311; and Gay, *Baptist Sacramentalism*.

Sacramentalists" assert that seventeenth-century Baptists "were more sacramental in their understanding of baptism than has been commonly accepted," and that they also claim this view disappeared during the eighteenth and nineteenth centuries.[45]

Nettles seems convinced that neither seventeenth-century Baptists nor their confessions give evidence of Baptist sacramentalism.[46] Harsch concurs, claiming that "It seems clear that from their infancy, Baptists have been non-sacramental in their understanding of baptism,"[47] adding, "the evidence currently suggests, that even the earliest Baptists espoused a non-sacramental view."[48] Yet the early writings show something much different.

What we actually find from a study of the original writings of the first Baptists—John Smyth, Thomas Helwys, John Murton, Richard Overton, an anonymous Baptist, Leonard Busher, and Elias Tookey—is that, at times, the earliest Baptists do adopt both sacramental terminology and sacramental theology in their explication and defence of believers' baptism. Even when the word or its cognates are not explicitly present, there is sacramental theology, or there is a sufficient amount of material that is not inconsistent with a sacramental view. There were tensions within sacramental thought, no question. Yet to call the early Baptists non- or anti-sacramentalist as many of their twenty-first century descendants are, is the anachronistic projection of later distinctions and sensibilities which the first Baptists simply wouldn't have understood. Indeed, the tension led them not to reject sacramentalism, but to a very careful one. Granted, their sacramental thought needed fuller development at numerous points. As often persecuted Dissenters, they lacked the luxury of the tranquility needed for theological elaboration. This explains why their sacramental theologies evince, at times, contradictions, and, at others, tensions with which Baptists have wrestled for four centuries. What the first Baptists exemplify is the desire to restore the true church, a position at which they arrived through their reading of scripture and their commitment to be faithful to it in both belief and practice. We must also recognize that the views of these earliest Baptists are not normative for Baptists who are heirs of the tradition they pioneered; but then neither should we regard our views as normative either for our Baptist forebears or those Baptists in different countries.[49]

Given that those who argue for a more sacramental position amongst early Baptists have more than adequately demonstrated from Baptist history the

---

[45] Harsch, "Were the First Baptists Sacramentalists?" 25.

[46] Cf. Nettles, *Baptists*, 3:310.

[47] Harsch, "Were the First Baptists Sacramentalists?" 40.

[48] Harsch, "Were the First Baptists Sacramentalists?" 41.

[49] Cross, "Sacrament of Baptism among the first Baptists," 210.

warrant for their claims, we need to ask how those who, like Nettles and Harsch, reject the idea can do so. Such a question demands a fuller answer than is possible here, so we merely offer possible directions of an answer. One could argue that the only way such positions can be maintained is because they have either relied on secondary sources which have simply stated and then repeated this to be so, or they have not read the sources, or they have ignored what those sources say. We would urge circumspection in suggesting this. Harsch, for instance, is a thorough scholar and has produced excellent work. That, however, makes his claims on this topic more mystifying. Philip Thompson has argued that much Baptist thought, theological and historical, since the nineteenth century has been guided by a certain form of dogmatic norms derived not from doctrine, but from a certain reading of history through the lens of "Baptist distinctives."[50] We may apply to Baptists an observation by Ernst Cassirer, "It is not by its history that the mythology of a nation is determined but, conversely, its history is determined by its mythology."[51] Thus it may be that many are simply rendered incapable of receiving the testimony of the historical record because it runs so counter to the positions required by the reigning mythology. For example, we see in the words of a former colleague of Harsch's, R. Stanton Norman, a certain tension, and ambivalence in the face of clear evidence: "Evidence does exist," he admits, "that a few Baptists on occasion have used the term sacrament, but the vast majority of Baptists commonly use the word ordinance to refer to baptism or the Lord's Supper."[52] In one sense, this is incontrovertible. Over the course of Baptist history, more have used the term "ordinance," and in a non- or even anti-sacramental way. Yet it is a truth that conceals as much as it discloses, because sacramental language and, even more importantly, thought were far more prevalent among the early Baptists than he and others indicate.

While it may seem futile to seek remedy by appeal to the sources, we must start there. Baptist scholars need to return to the original sources, and to read them historically, not dogmatically or ideologically.[53] This has been done *par excellence* by Stan Fowler, who demonstrates that "In the 17th century in England, the foundational period of Baptist life and thought, those Baptists who directly addressed the question often spoke of baptism in a way that was both verbally and conceptually sacramental."[54] He concludes, "At both verbal

---

[50] Thompson has explored this in his unpublished paper, "Defining Identity in Unsettled Times."

[51] Quoted in Kammen *Mystic Chords of Memory*, 30. The point is not limited by the original referent, "nation."

[52] Norman, *Baptist Way*, 129 (italics original).

[53] On the latter, see Cross, "Sacrament of Baptism among the first Baptists," 211.

[54] Fowler, *More Than a Symbol*, 87.

and conceptual levels, Reformed sacramentalism was the essence of the mainstream baptismal theology of 17th-century English Baptists."[55] In this he is not alone.[56] For instance, Stephen Holmes states categorically that "Baptists, in their origin, were sacramentalists."[57] It needs to be reiterated that this is not to suggest that the theology and practices of seventeenth-century Baptists is normative for contemporary Baptists; only that it is indicative and informative. It is the latter of these which connects those exploring Baptist sacramentalism with the study of Baptist retrieval and Baptist catholicity. On the latter, the leading figure in the Baptist catholicity movement, Steven R. Harmon, has demonstrated that sacramental theology is one of seven identifying marks of the theology of catholic Baptists.[58]

There is a third category of persons who reject a more sacramentalist position among Baptists. These have reservations of a more a theological or theo-political nature. Joshua Searle would fit this, though his work has significant problems of its own. The problem is that he's so badly off base. In reality, early Baptists both resisted Constantinianism and were sacramamental. That alone undoes his argument that the two are of a piece. Further, in the US at least, as Baptists became more bound up in Constantinian habits, they became less—not more—sacramentalist in their theology. Thus, his argument is off base in more than one way.

Searle has recently summarily dismissed Baptist sacramentalism as a waste of time. In a book appearing in the "After Christendom" series, under the general editorship of Stuart Murray (Murray Williams), whose antipathy towards Christendom and predilection for Anabaptism[59] are shared by Searle,[60] Searle makes claims without nuance that "For reasons that will be

---

[55] Fowler, *More Than a Symbol*, 249.

[56] See, e.g., Thompson, "New Question in Baptist History," and "Practicing the Freedom of God"; and Cross, "Myth of English Baptist Anti-Sacramentalism."

[57] Holmes, *Tradition and Renewal in Baptist Life*, 29.

[58] Harmon, *Towards Baptist Catholicity*, 13–14, and his wider discussion of the seven features, 6–17. In addition, see his "'Catholic Baptists' and the New Horizon of Tradition," "*Dei Verbum* § 9," "Scripture in the Life of the Baptist Churches," "Why Baptist Catholicity?" and "Free Church Theology"; and also, e.g., Harvey, *Can These Bones Live?*; Freeman, *Contesting Catholicity*, and "Confession for Catholic Baptists"; and Jorgenson, "Bapto–Catholicism."

[59] See, e.g., Murray, *Church After Christendom*, *Post-Christendom*, and *Naked Anabaptist*. Murray was also chair of the UK Anabaptist Network, and editor of *Anabaptism Today*.

[60] E.g., for Searle, *Theology after Christendom*, 9, Anabaptism made a lasting impression on him, and he lauds the faith of many of its leaders, including Felix Manz, Balthasar Hubmaier, Jakob Hutter, Dirk Willems. However, he overlooks that many

apparent from my argument throughout this book, I regard this approach as a road to nowhere."[61] Baptists rightly should be interested in such efforts, given both their history of protests against Constantinianism and their more recent, in some contexts, seduction by it.[62] Yet Searle's critique displays a weakness at precisely this point that leads one to wonder how trustworthy his whole project is. He has clearly not engaged the Baptist sacramental thought with any scholarly rigor.[63]

It is within Searle's onslaught against Christendom and all that he associates with it, that he repeatedly repudiates sacramentalism. Doubtless, Searle's rejection of Christendom drives his rejection of sacramental thought. But with the one exception of a footnoted reference to Fowler, all Searle's discussions of sacramentalism are of its non-Baptist expressions, and he even fails to define what he means by sacramentalism. So, for example, he sweepingly announces that Christendom was the cause for the ossification of "the dynamic vitality of living faith in Christ," replacing it with "a sterile sacramentalism and rigid systems of sound doctrine."[64] He issues "a summons" to post-Christendom theologians "to pioneer a new trail *out of the morass of sacramentalism.*"[65] Later, he declares that "The sacramental interpretation of Christianity, which prevails in Christendom-minded churches, is inimical to the spirit of biblical prophecy."[66] Further on, he opines that post-Christendom is at a crossroads, and calls for it to plot "a course of renewal and new life" which will require "bold and prophetic theologians who can unshackle theological endeavor from the dead weight of dogma and sacramentalism."[67]

---

of the leading Anabaptists were sacramentalists, see, e.g., Rempel, *Lord's Supper in Anabaptism*, and *Recapturing an Enchanted World*; and Siegrist, *Participating Witness*.

[61] Searle, *Theology after Christendom*, 163 n.29.

[62] On which, see, e.g., Harvey, *Another City*.

[63] The only Baptist sacramental volume Searle consults is Fowler's *More Than a Symbol*, see Searle, *Theology after Christendom*, 163 n.29 and 199, and he cites Fowler as illustrating "a sacramentalist understanding of ministry," which it does not. Searle does cite Kreitzer, *Gospel According to John*, and McClendon's *Doctrine* and *Ethics*, but he does not do so in relation to Baptist sacramentalism, see 202 and 203 and *passim*.

[64] Searle, *Theology after Christendom*, 20,

[65] Searle, *Theology after Christendom*, 132 (italics added). A similar sentiment is expressed by Southern Baptist theologians, Kenneth Keathley and Mark Deaver, which is ironic given that Southern Baptists are perhaps the most consistent of all Baptists both in their rejection of sacramentalism and their embrace of a Christendom model. See Keathley, "Word of God: Salvation"; and Dever, "Church."

[66] Searle, *Theology after Christendom*, 29.

[67] Searle, *Theology after Christendom*, 133.

These are nothing more than sweeping assertions, made without supporting evidence. They are reminiscent of contemporary political statements which, if repeated often enough, tend to be accepted by the uncritical as if they had been demonstrated to be so. Searle believes that, as charismata, "all Christians" should be, and even are, prophets.[68] This raises the question why, since prophecy is proclamation,[69] it doesn't follow that God uses proclamation (preaching) as a means of working in the lives of believers and non-believers (cf. Rom. 10.14–17).[70]

The post-Christendom rejection of Baptist theology,[71] sacramental or otherwise, loses force as soon as it is pointed out that Baptists are not a product of Christendom, and that the sacramentalists are among the most forceful critics of Christendom. Conversely, and ironically, it is the Baptists who are most adamant in rejecting sacramental theology who are also most in thrall to Christendom.[72] Historically, Baptist christology emphasizes Christ above the state and/or nation; their pneumatology is grounded in the work of the Spirit in the believer's life in regeneration, sanctification, and discipleship; their soteriology is by grace through faith in what has been termed the divine–human encounter; their ecclesiology is of the gathered church of believers; while their sacramentalism is always and only of faith-sacraments.

Any merit of his brief notwithstanding, Searle's critique appears to be grounded more in personal taste than in rigorous scholarship. In a candid series of autobiographical statements, Searle admits that his academic training is in modern history, and his forays into theological studies were self-directed, and accompanied by reading in literature, philosophy, and the study of modern languages. These were followed by postgraduate study in applied theology, and doctoral studies on the hermeneutics of crisis in the Northern Irish troubles.[73] He even openly admits to an "enduring suspicion towards

---

[68] Searle, *Theology after Christendom*, 32. See his fuller discussion of prophecy, 26–32. Cf., however, 1 Cor. 12.10 and 29.

[69] See, e.g., Martin, *Spirit and the Congregation*, 65–68.

[70] See, e.g., Haymes, "Towards a Sacramental Understanding of Preaching"; and Quicke, *360–Degree Preaching*, 57 and 60, and "Further Reflections on a Sacramental Understanding of Preaching."

[71] Cf., e.g., Murray, *Post-Christendom*, 302; cf. 300–302.

[72] See Harvey, *Another City*, 85–93. Harvey, 87–88, quotes the Southern Baptist theologian E.Y. Mullins as an exemplar of an (unwitting?) embrace of a Christendom model. See Mullins' *Axioms of Religion*, 274. In this same work, Mullins categorically rejects a sacramental understanding of church rites, see 60 and 100–104.

[73] Searle, *Theology after Christendom*, 3, 5 and 9–10. For his doctorate, see "Hermeneutics of Crisis."

biblical studies,"[74] and an aversion to clericalism, Christendom, and sacramentalism, the latter antipathy he imbibes from the nineteenth-century Danish, Lutheran philosopher, Søren Kierkegaard. Of particular concern to us is when Searle announces that he has "never felt any affinity for the sacramental elements of church life."[75] He exhorts Christendom theologians to abandon their preoccupation with "the internal affairs of the church" and navel gazing "on parochial issues such as the meaning of the sacraments and so-called apostolic succession."[76] He doesn't believe that God is "necessarily" to be found in church sacraments,[77] which appears to leave the door open to occasions when he can be found in them? He appears to admit that he is not only anti-sacramental, but also anti-liturgical, anti-ritual, and anti-dogma.[78] In short, he is dispositionally against much that has given the church its identity. Searle even finds in a passage from David Hume justification for consigning to the flames any library books which, among other things, attempt "to assign a sacred or sacramental character to church institutions," even though the passage makes *no* reference at all to "sacred or sacramental institutions."[79]

---

[74] Searle, *Theology after Christendom*, 8.

[75] Searle, *Theology after Christendom*, 6. Cf. also 56. He evens states, 22, that "the very concept of post-Christendom is an implicit critique of the validity of the whole concept of 'church,' as the term is often used in everyday Christian discourse—i.e., as a special or sacramental institution, set apart for a special mission," a view at odds with Jesus' intention to build his church (Matt. 16.18), Paul's declaration that all those baptized by the Spirit enter the one body, Christ's church (1 Cor. 12.13), and are commissioned by Christ to continue his mission (Matt. 28.19 and John 17.18). In a passage in which Searle focuses on Jesus' teaching, 61–62, he selects only those aspects of it that fit his argument, and fails to mention that Jesus taught about baptism, Matt. 28.19, and John 3.5, and the Lord's supper, Mark 14.12–25 and par., and 1 Cor. 11.23–26.

[76] E.g., Searle, *Theology after Christendom*, 61.

[77] Searle, *Theology after Christendom*, 134.

[78] Searle, *Theology after Christendom*, 102; cf. 160. However, in his promotion of the Northumbria Community, an example of a new monastic community, Searle, 185, changes his views when he speaks of "ritual and symbol as a means of conferring a sense of common identity among its Friends and Companions," and "the potential of story as mediated through ritual, as a way of giving members a metanarrative which would confer meaning and identity within a Christian framework." Cf. 186 (see also 187), where he cites the Community's *Rule of Life*, "The human spirit requires ritual. The stories we tell, the myths that shape us and give us meaning need to be acted out.'"

[79] Searle, *Theology after Christendom*, 127, citing, 127 n.38, David Hume's *An Enquiry concerning Human Understanding* (Oxford: Oxford University Press, 2007), 120.

Thus he seems merely to be seeking material that might confirm him in his prejudices.

In spite of all his claims to the contrary, however, Searle does not escape sacramental thinking. He believes God is alive, and is a God of love, irresistible grace, and "active in the world in wondrous and mysterious ways."[80] He also believes that in a post-Christendom society that is materialistic, pragmatic, and relativistic, it is still possible for theology to "become spiritual, mystical and evangelical."[81] On the spiritual dimension he cites James K.A. Smith that Christendom has tended to subordinate spirituality to doctrine, and also failed to understand that people are both embodied and material, as well as formed by material, daily liturgies, thus seeming to signal agreement with Smith.[82] This is not Smith's argument, however. While he does contend that Western Christians, particularly Evangelicals, need to attend more carefully to the formative power of ritual, his is not an argument against Christendom, but what he will later call "liturgical capture" that leads to malformation through alternative regimes of moral formation such as consumerism. Further, this argument by Smith is most forceful in the first volume of his Cultural Liturgies series, *Desiring the Kingdom*. He maintains this same emphasis on formation in the third volume, *Awaiting the King*, though in that volume he argues for a form of Christendom. Again Searle's argument is undercut.

Clearly, Searle is comfortable with the notion of mystery, as are so many Baptist sacramentalists.[83] He writes, "Living in the reality of God's Kingdom means to exhibit a profound awareness of the world as a place pulsating with the mysterious presence of God."[84] He is also willing to speak of how post-Christendom "can affirm science as an instrument for learning about God's

---

[80] Searle, *Theology after Christendom*, 4–5. Later, also 5, he happily talks of the "beauty and mystery of life," and how the Holy Spirit expanded the horizons of his imagination, perception, and compassion, yet throughout this book he excludes the Spirit's work, so clearly stated in scripture (cf., e.g., John 3.5; Acts 2.38; 11.15–16; 1 Cor. 12.13; Titus 3.5), in baptism or the eucharist, or any other means through which God might chose to work.

[81] Searle, *Theology after Christendom*, 23.

[82] Searle, *Theology after Christendom*, 44, quoting James K.A. Smith, *Desiring the Kingdom: Worship, Worldview, and Cultural Formation* (Grand Rapids: Baker, 2009), 33. For the importance Searle attaches to "embodied spirituality that transforms material reality"—though he still implicitly excludes sacraments—see *Theology after Christendom*, 191.

[83] Searle, *Theology after Christendom*, 82, where he maintains that there is a spiritual dimension to life and not just an organic side to it, and theology's aim is to "raise awareness of the depth, mystery and beauty of life."

[84] Searle, *Theology after Christendom*, 126.

world"[85] in terms that could easily be read as sacramental. He contends that spiritual formation, by which he means growing in Christlikeness, "is attainable only by responding actively to the initiatives of divine grace. Such a response," he continues, "is made by applying the 'vision, intention and means,' which are necessary to make such a transformation possible."[86] Searle accepts the world as being "not only symbolical but sacramental."[87] In his critique of fundamentalism, he attacks their fixation with the Bible as an academic text book "that details facts about God," and argues that in doing so they thereby fail "to discover and experience the depth, beauty, mystery and sacrament of life."[88] Thus Searle denies ecclesial sacraments in order to posit a pan-sacramental reality. Thus, if everything is sacramental generally, nothing is particularly. It seems, then, that his primary animus is not against Christendom, but the church.

We will leave it to the reader to decide whether Searle's arguments have merit. We will content ourselves with saying that when it comes to the life of Baptist churches, and other Believers Churches, what we actually find is that this "road to nowhere" is being widely traversed and by those who are, like the early Baptists, profoundly critical of a Christendom model,[89] and is the theme of the Free Church Sacramentalism conference arranged for the autumn of 2022 in Amsterdam, planned by John D. Rempel, Anthony R. Cross, Henk A. Bakker, and Philip E. Thompson. The original plan was for a third *Baptist Sacramentalism* volume, so the editors wrote to those they thought might be interested in participating, thinking that one in three might accept. What happened, however, was that only several people declined the invitation and there were enough contributors to put together three volumes in this informal, and unplanned, series. Our project is not the only evidence. In addition, at the invitation of the President of the Baptist World Alliance, Dr Neville Callam, Anthony R. Cross was invited to present a special "Forum on Baptism" at the annual meeting of the BWA in Bangkok, Thailand, on Tuesday 4 July 2017.[90]

---

[85] Searle, *Theology after Christendom*, 72.

[86] Searle, *Theology after Christendom*, 44.

[87] Searle, *Theology after Christendom*, 112.

[88] Searle, *Theology after Christendom*, 148.

[89] See, e.g., from the from the Stone-Campbell Movement, Hicks, *Enter the Water, Come to the Table*; the Pentecostal, Green, *Toward a Pentecostal Theology of the Lord's Supper*; the Christian and Missionary Alliance, Smith, *Evangelical, Sacramental and Pentecostal*; and from Newfrontiers, Wilson, *Spirit and Sacrament*. See also the Free Church essays in Heath and Dvorak, eds, *Baptism*.

[90] See the programme, Baptist World Alliance, *BWA Annual Gathering*, 14. Cross' invitation came on the back of his two major works on the subject, *Baptism and the Baptists* and *Recovering the Evangelical Sacrament*, see Baptist World Alliance press release, 20 March 2017.

The forum comprised two lectures, both of which have been subsequently published.[91] This was followed by the meeting and conference in Kyiv in 2018 that have already been mentioned. In addition, there has been a considerable number of studies published in the last three decades.[92] In addition to those already mentioned, and those which continue to explore baptism and the Lord's supper,[93] there have been an array of books and articles on two or more of the sacraments, authors, again, coming from across the world.[94] The reasons for this are varied, adoption of a Christendom mindset and model not being among them. One quite potent reason is a recovery of, and subsequent constructive building upon, the past, both Baptist and catholic.

On the Baptist retrieval of tradition, Daniel H. Williams has led the way in seeking to bridge the gap that is often evident between Baptists and the past in his work on retrieving Christian tradition, and, in particular, the patristic tradition.[95] Such work has also been undertaken by Paul Fiddes, Brian Haymes, and Richard Kidd on the communion of saints.[96] Such studies haven't originated, but certainly have encouraged, the active exploration of the Christian past for sources which can enrich, inform, renew, and even transform contemporary Baptist thought and practice. Leading scholars in this

---

[91] The first lecture was published in the *American Baptist Quarterly* as Cross, "Baptism in Recent Baptist Thought"; while an academic and also more popular version of the second paper were published by South Korean Baptists, Cross, "Guwonkwa Chimrye," and "구원과 침례: 침례교적인 성례주의적 침례관."

[92] See the overview of such baptismal studies by Cross, "Baptism in Recent Baptist Thought."

[93] On baptism, see, e.g., and Callam, "Multi-lateral Discussion on Baptism," 282–85, "Baptists and the Subject of Baptism," and "On Baptism"; Jones, *Waters of Promise*; Carter, "Recovery of a Sacramental Ontology"; Newman, "Baptism: Substance and the Sign"; Nelson, "'Water Buries Like a Tomb'"; Nalls, *Bombshell in the Baptistery*; and the blog post by P. Beasley-Murray, "The ordinance can be a sacrament." On the eucharist, see, e.g., James, *Analogous Uses of Language*; and Ellis, *Approaching God*, 127–28.

[94] See, e.g., Ellis and Blyth, eds, *Gathering for Worship, passim*; Stackhouse, *Gospel-Driven Church*, 125–62; Haymes, Gouldbourne and Cross, *On Being*, 63–73; Gouldbourne, "Story-telling, Sacraments, and Sexuality"; Freeman, *Contesting Catholicity*, 311–83; Harmon, *Baptist Identity and the Ecumenical Future, passim*; and Deverell, *Bonds of Freedom*.

[95] See D.H. Williams, *Retrieving the Tradition*, and *Evangelicals and Tradition*; as well as D.H. Williams, ed., *Free Church and the Early Church*.

[96] Fiddes, Haymes, and Kidd, *Baptists and the Communion of Saints*, and its follow-up volume, *Communion, Covenant, and Creativity*. See also Haymes' "Communion of Saints."

movement are Steven R. Harmon,[97] Stephen Holmes,[98] and also Glenn Hinson.[99] A theological term for this retrieval is *réssourcement* in which the past is used as a source for the renewal of contemporary ecclesial life and thought,[100] and it stands in marked contrast with the conviction that the inherited church is detrimental to contemporary Christianity.[101]

Some of the greatest vigor in recent Baptist theology has arisen from this creative engagement with, and appropriation of, the past. Baptist scholars have especially examined their confessions of faith,[102] and have also examined baptism and the creeds,[103] including the volume *Evangelicals and the Nicene Faith*, edited by Timothy George, which includes essays by eight Baptists.[104] More recently, Anne Klose's research has included the study of covenant and sacrament.[105] Other North American Baptists, such as Philip Thompson and Steven Harmon, have also examined Baptist confessions respectively within their seventeenth-century context, and also in relation to the patristic

---

[97] Harmon, *Towards Baptist Catholicity*, and *Baptist Identity and the Ecumenical Future.*

[98] Holmes, *Tradition and Renewal in Baptist Life*, and "Baptism: Patristic Resources."

[99] Hinson, "Authority of Tradition."

[100] Cf. T. George's front cover endorsement of Haykin, ed., *"At the Pure Fountain of Thy Word,"* which he calls "A stellar example of Baptist réssourcement!" On this réssourcement, Freeman, "Back to the Future of Trinitarianism?" discusses it with particular reference to trinitarianism, and also the patristic tradition. See also Harmon, *Towards Baptist Catholicity*; Jorgenson, "Bapto-Catholicism"; and Bullard, *Remembering the Body, passim.*

[101] See, e.g., Murray, *Post-Christendom, Church After Christendom*, and *Naked Anabaptist*, 71–91; and Searle, *Theology after Christendom*. The late Methodist theologian, Thomas C. Oden, *After Modernity . . . What?*, 35–36, called this the attitude "modern chauvinists," "whose historical perspective, loyalties, and attachments are so strictly limited to modern values that they impulsively denigrate all premodern wisdoms."

[102] Lumpkin and Leonard, eds, *Baptist Confessions of Faith*; T. George and D. George, *Baptist Confessions, Covenants, and Catechisms*; and Kidd, *Something to Declare*

[103] E.g., Cross, "Baptism, Christology and the Creeds."

[104] Harmon, "Nicene Faith and the Catholicity of the Church"; Pinson, "Confessional, Baptist, and Arminian"; Freeman, "Toward a Generous Orthodoxy"; Newman, "Practicing the Nicene Faith"; D.P. Nelson, "Nicene Faith and Evangelical Worship"; DeVine, "Can the Church Emerge"; Wood, "Life after Life after Death"; and T. George, "Delighted by Doctrine."

[105] Klose, *Covenantal Priesthood.*

tradition.[106] Unsurprisingly, fruitful research has been carried out on the Anabaptists, including work by Ruth Gouldbourne, Brian Brewer, and Graeme Chatfield.[107]

One usually neglected area of study which deserves to be mentioned is that of the spirituality of the sacraments. Christopher Ellis explores both the spirituality of the Lord's table and the baptismal pool, on the latter concluding that it is a sacrament of grace and community, "a divinely ordained means of human response to the saving work and call of Christ," and shows the character of that response as "whole-hearted consecration."[108] Michael Haykin examines the baptismal spirituality of Particular Baptists, Cross provides a broader discussion, while Elizabeth Newman enters dialogue with Teresa of Ávila, and Molly Marshall sets sacraments within her discussion of discipleship.[109] This list is by no means exhaustive.

While much of this "Introduction" has revolved around challenges to Baptist sacramental thought, the following essays in this volume, and the succeeding two volumes, are not defensive, but are sterling examples of Baptist scholars taking seriously the truths and questions inherent in sacraments and sacramental thought. They are offered in the hope that they will stimulate further reflection and study of God and his ways in the world, that they will honour him, and help the church in its worship and mission in the world to be faithful disciples and witnesses to the gospel of our Lord Jesus Christ.

Anthony R. Cross and Philip E. Thompson
June 2020.

Bibliography

Aadne, Linda. "The Theology and Practice of Believers' Baptism within the Norwegian Baptist Union: Tradition, Revision and Renewal." PhD diss., The International Baptist Theological Study Centre Amsterdam/The Free University, Amsterdam, in progress.

---

[106] Thompson, "Seventeenth-Century Baptist Confessions in Context"; and Harmon, "Baptist Confessions of Faith and the Patristic."

[107] Gouldbourne, *Flesh and the Feminine*; Brewer, *A Pledge of Love*, and "Free Church Sacramentalism"; and Chatfield, *Balthasar Hubmaier*. In addition to these Anabaptist studies, see also: Gouldbourne's "Encountering Christ"; and Brewer's "'Signs of the Covenant'."

[108] Ellis, *Gathering*, 200–221.

[109] Haykin, "'Hazarding all for God at a clap'"; Cross, '*Sapientia Experimentalis*'; Newman, *Attending to the Wounds on Christ's Body*; and Marshall, "Changing Face of Baptist Discipleship."

Akin, Daniel L., ed. *A Theology for the Church*. Nashville, TN: B&H, 2007.

Baptist World Alliance. *BWA Annual Gathering. July 2–7, 2017, Bangkok, Thailand*. s.l.: s.n., 2017.

Barker, David G., Michael A.G. Haykin, and Barry H. Howson, eds. *Ecclesia semper reformanda est. The Church Is Always Reforming. A Festschrift on Ecclesiology in Honour of Stanley K. Fowler on His Seventieth Birthday*. Kitchener, ON: Joshua, 2016.

Beasley-Murray, George R. "Baptism and the Sacramental View." *Baptist Times* 11 February 1960, 9–10.

———. *Baptism in the New Testament*. Exeter: Paternoster, 1972 [1962].

Beasley-Murray, Paul. "The ordinance can be a sacrament." 26 May 2016, http://paulbeasleymurray.com/blog/2016/05/ordinance-can-be-sacrament/

Brewer, Brian C. "Free Church Sacramentalism: A Surprising Connection between Baptists and Anabaptists." In *Interfaces, Baptists and Others: International Baptist Studies*, edited by David Bebbington and Martin Sutherland, 3–28. Milton Keynes: Paternoster, 2013.

———. *A Pledge of Love: The Anabaptist Sacramental Theology of Balthasar Hubmaier*. Studies in Christian History and Thought. Milton Keynes: Paternoster, 2012.

———. "'Signs of the Covenant': The Development of Sacramental Thought in Baptist Circles." *Perspective in Religious Studies* 36.4 (2009) 407–20.

Brunner, Emil. *The Divine–Human Encounter*. London: SCM Press, 1944.

Bullard, Scott W. *Re-membering the Body: The Lord's Supper and Ecclesial Unity in the Free Church Traditions*. Free Church, Catholic Tradition. Eugene, OR: Cascade, 2013.

Bunyan, John. *A Confession of My Faith and A Reason of My Practice—or—With Who, And Who Not, I Can Hold Church Fellowship*. In *The Works of John Bunyan:* Volume 2. *Experimental, Doctrinal, and Practical*, edited by George Offer, 593–616. Glasgow: Blackie and Son, 1853.

———. *Peaceable Principles and True*. In *The Works of John Bunyan:* Volume 2, edited by George Offer. Glasgow: Blackie and Son, 1853.

Callam, Neville. "Baptists and the Subject of Baptism: Any Real Progress during the Last 25 Years?" *The Ecumenical Review* 67.3 (2015) 334–61.

———. "The Multi-lateral Discussion on Baptism: Where Are We Today?" In *Baptist Faith & Witness. Book 4*, edited by Vasconcelos, 279–89.

———. "On Baptism." Baptist World Alliance General Secretary's Blog, 1 June 2016, https://www.bwanet.org/dialogue/entry/on-baptism

Calvin, John. *Institutes of the Christian Religion*. Translated by H. Beveridge; 2 vols. London: James Clarke, 1949.

Carter, Craig A. "The Recovery of a Sacramental Ontology as the Basis for Developing a Sacramental Theology of Baptism." In *Ecclesia semper reformanda est*, edited by Barker, Haykin and Howson, 115–36.

Chatfield, Graeme R. *Balthasar Hubmaier and the Clarity of Scripture: A Critical Reformation Issue*. Eugene, OR: Pickwick, 2013.

Clark, Neville. "The Fulness of the Church of God." In *Pattern of the Church*, edited by Gilmore, 79–113.

———. "The Theology of Baptism." In *Christian Baptism*, edited by Gilmore, 306–26.

Colwell, John E. *Promise and Presence: An Exploration of Sacramental Theology*. Milton Keynes: Paternoster, 2005.

Cross, Anthony R. *Baptism and the Baptists: Theology and Practice in Twentieth-Century Britain*. Carlisle: Paternoster, 2000.

———. "Baptism, Christology and the Creeds in the Early Church: Implications for Ecumenical Dialogue." In *Ecumenism and History: Studies in Honour of John H.Y. Briggs*, edited by Anthony R. Cross, 23–49. Carlisle: Paternoster, 2002.

———. "Baptism in Recent Baptist Thought." *American Baptist Quarterly* 37.2 (2018) 175–97.

———. "Baptism in the Theology of John Calvin and Karl Barth." In *Calvin, Barth, and Reformed Theology*, edited by Neil B. MacDonald and Carl Trueman, 57–87. Paternoster Theological Monographs. Milton Keynes: Paternoster, 2008.

———. "Baptism, the New Testament, and the Baptist Tradition: Towards a Baptist Sacramental Theology and Practice of Baptism/Крещение в Новом Завете и баптистская традиция: на пути к баптистской сакраментальной теологии и практике крещения." *Theological Reflections* 22 (2019) 27-50.

———. "Guwonkwa Chimrye: Chimryekojukin Seongryejooeuijuk Chimryekwan (Saved through Baptism: A Sacramental Baptist View)', *The Baptist* [Journal of the Korea Baptist Convention] 150 (January and February 2018) 94–114.

———. "The Myth of English Baptist Anti-Sacramentalism." In *Recycling the Past*, edited by Thompson and Cross, 128–62.

———. "Neville Clark and the Myth of Baptist Anti-Sacramentalism." In *Baptist Sacramentalism 5*, edited by Cross and Thompson, forthcoming.

———. *Recovering the Evangelical Sacrament: Baptisma Semper Reformandum*. Eugene, OR: Pickwick, 2013.

———. "The Sacrament of Baptism among the First Baptists." In *Ecclesia semper reformanda est*, edited by Barker, Haykin, and Howson, 189–211.

———. "*Sapientia Experimentalis*: 'Knowledge by experience'—Aspects of a Baptist Baptismal Spirituality." In *Grounded in Grace: Essays to Honour Ian M. Randall*, edited by Pieter J. Lalleman, Peter J. Morden and Anthony R. Cross, 235–59. London: Spurgeon's College and The Baptist Historical Society, 2013.

———. "구원과 침례: 침례교적인 성례주의적 침례관 (Saved through baptism: A Sacramental Baptist View)." Korea Baptist Convention website, 2018: http://www.korea baptist.or.kr/공지사항/자유게시판/.

Cross, Anthony R., and Philip E. Thompson, eds. *Baptist Sacramentalism*. Studies in Baptist History and Thought, 5. Carlisle: Paternoster, 2003.

———. *Baptist Sacramentalism 2*. Studies in Baptist History and Thought, 25. Milton Keynes: Paternoster, 2008.

———. *Baptist Sacramentalism 3*. Eugene, OR: Pickwick, 2020.

———. *Baptist Sacramentalism 4*. Eugene, OR: Pickwick, forthcoming 2021.

———. *Baptist Sacramentalism 5*. Eugene, OR: Pickwick, forthcoming 2022.

Cross, Anthony R., and Ruth Gouldbourne, eds. *Questions of Identity: Studies in Honour of Brian Haymes*. Centre for Baptist History and Heritage, 6. Oxford: Regent's Park College, 2011.

Delahunt, Joseph C. "The Laying on of Hands Controversy among Seventeenth-Century English Baptists." PhD diss., The International Baptist Theological Study Centre Amsterdam/The Free University, Amsterdam, in progress.

Deverell, Garry J. *The Bonds of Freedom: Vows, Sacraments and the Formation of the Christian Self*. Paternoster Theological Monographs; Milton Keynes: Paternoster, 2008.

Dever, Mark. "The Church." In *Theology for the Church*, edited by Akin, 766–856.

DeVine, Mark. "Can the Church Emerge without or with Only the Nicene Creed?" In *Evangelicals and Nicene Faith*, edited by T. George, 179–95.

Ellis, Christopher J. *Approaching God: A Guide for Worship Leaders and Worshippers*. Norwich: Canterbury, 2009.

———. *Gathering: A Theology and Spirituality of Worship in Free Church Tradition*. London: SCM, 2004.

Ellis, Christopher J., and Myra Blyth, eds. *Gathering for Worship: Patterns and Prayers for the Community of Disciples*. Norwich: Canterbury Press for The Baptist Union of Great Britain, 2005.

Enns, Fernando. "Believers Church Ecclesiology: A Trinitarian Foundation and Its Implications." In *New Perspectives in Believers Church Ecclesiology*, edited by Abe Dueck, Helmut Harder, and Karl Koop, 179–98. Winnepeg, MB: CMU Press, 2010.

Fiddes, Paul S., Brian Haymes, and Richard L. Kidd. *Baptists and the Communion of Saints: A Theology of Covenanted Disciples*. Waco, TX: Baylor University Press, 2014.

———. *Communion, Covenant, and Creativity: An Approach to the Communion of Saints through the Arts*. Eugene, OR: Cascade, 2020.

Fowler, Stanley K. "Is 'Baptist Sacramentalism' an Oxymoron?", Reactions in Britain to *Christian Baptism* (1959)." In *Baptist Sacramentalism*, edited by Cross and Thompson, 129–50.

———. *More Than a Symbol: The British Baptist Recovery of Baptismal Sacramentalism*. Studies in Baptist History and Thought, 2. Carlisle: Paternoster, 2002.

Freeman, Curtis W. "Back to the Future of Trinitarianism?" In *Theology in the Service of the Church: Essays Presented to Fisher H. Humphreys*, edited by Timothy George and Eric F. Mason, 36–61. Macon, GA: Mercer University Press, 2008.

———. *Contesting Catholicity: Theology for Other Baptists*. Waco, TX: Baylor University Press, 2014.

———. "Toward a Generous Orthodoxy." In *Evangelicals and Nicene Faith*, edited by T. George, 116–29.

Gay, David H.J. *Baptist Sacramentalism: A Warning to Baptists*. Biggleswade: Brachus, 2011.

George, Timothy. "Delighted by Doctrine: *A Tribute to Jaroslav Pelikan*." In *Evangelicals and Nicene Faith*, edited by T. George, 202–6.

———, ed. *Evangelicals and Nicene Faith: Reclaiming the Apostolic Witness*. Beeson Divinity Studies. Grand Rapids: Baker Academic, 2011.

———. "The Sacramentality of the Church: An Evangelical Baptist Perspective." In *Baptist Sacramentalism*, edited by Cross and Thompson, 21–35.

———. *Theology of the Reformers*. Leicester: Apollos, 1988.

George, Timothy, and Denise George. *Baptist Confessions, Covenants, and Catechisms*. Nashville, TN: B&H, 1999 [1996].

Gilmore, Alec, ed. *Christian Baptism: A Fresh Attempt to Understand the Rite in Terms of Scripture, History, and Theology*. London: Lutterworth, 1959.

———, ed. *The Pattern of the Church: A Baptist View*. London: Lutterworth, 1963.

Gouldbourne, Ruth. "Encountering Christ: Zwingli, Signs and Baptists around the Table." In *For the Sake of the Church: Essays in Honour of Paul S. Fiddes*, edited by Anthony Clarke, 78–90. Centre for Baptist History and Heritage Studies, 3. Oxford: Regent's Park Collee, 2014.

———. *The Flesh and the Feminine: Gender and Theology in the Writings of Caspar Schwenckfeld*. Studies in Christian History and Thought; Milton Keynes: Paternoster, 2006.

———. "Story-telling, Sacraments, and Sexuality." In *Questions of Identity*, edited by Cross and Gouldbourne, 239–52.

Graham, Lon. "'All Who Love Our Blessed Redeemer:' The Catholicity of John Ryland Jr." PhD diss., The International Baptist Theological Study Centre Amsterdam/The Free University, Amsterdam, forthcoming.

Green, Chris E.W. *Toward a Pentecostal Theology of the Lord's Supper: Foretasting the Kingdom*. Cleveland, TN: CPT, 2012.

Harmon, Steven R. "Baptist Confessions of Faith and the Patristic Tradition." *Perspectives in Religious Studies* 29.4 (2002) 349–58.

———. *Baptist Identity and the Ecumenical Future: Story, Tradition, and the Recovery of Community*. Waco, TX: Baylor University Press, 2016.

————. "'Catholic Baptists' and the New Horizon of Tradition in Baptist Theology." In *New Horizons in Theology*, edited by Terrence W. Tilley, 117–43. Maryknoll, NY: Orbis Books, 2005.

————. "*Dei Verbum* § 9 in Baptist Perspective." *Ecclesiology* 5 (2009) 299–321.

————. "Free Church Theology, The Pilgrim Church, and the Ecumenical Future." *Journal of Ecumenical Studies* 49.3 (2014) 420–42.

————. "The Nicene Faith and the Catholicity of the Church: *Evangelical Retrieval and the Problem of Magisterium*." In *Evangelicals and Nicene Faith*, edited by T. George, 74–92.

————. "Scripture in the Life of the Baptist Churches: Openings for a Differentiated Catholic-Baptist Consensus on Sacred Scripture." *Pro Ecclesia* 18.2 (2009) 187–215.

————. *Towards Baptist Catholicity: Essays on Tradition and the Baptist Vision.* Studies in Baptist History and Thought, 27. Milton Keynes: Paternoster, 2006.

————. "Why Baptist Catholicity, and By What Authority?" *Pro Ecclesia* 18.4 (2009) 386–92.

Harsch, Lloyd. "Were the First Baptists Sacramentalists?" *The Journal for Baptist Theology and Ministry* 6.1 (2009) 25–43.

Harvey, Barry. *Another City: An Ecclesiological Primer for a Post-Christian World*. Christian Mission and Modern Culture. Harrisburg, PA: Trinity, 1999.

————. *Can These Bones Live? A Catholic Baptist Engagement with Ecclesiology, Hermeneutics, and Social Theory*. Grand Rapids: Brazos, 2008.

Haykin, Michael A.G., ed. *"At the Pure Fountain of Thy Word": Andrew Fuller as an Apologist*. Studies in Baptist History and Thought, 6. Carlisle: Paternoster, 2004.

————. "'Hazarding All for God at a Clap': The Spirituality of Baptism among British Calvinistic Baptists." *Baptist Quarterly* 38.4 (1999) 185–95.

Haymes, Brian. "The Communion of Saints." *Baptist Quarterly* 49.2 (2018) 50–60.

————. "Towards a Sacramental Understanding of Preaching." In *Baptist Sacramentalism*, edited by Cross and Thompson, 263–70.

Haymes, Brian, Ruth Gouldbourne, and Anthony R. Cross. *On Being the Church: Revisioning Baptist Identity*. Studies in Baptist History and Thought, 21. Milton Keynes: Paternoster, 2008.

Heath, Gordon L., and James D. Dvorak, eds. *Baptism: Historical, Theological, and Pastoral Perspectives*. Eugene, OR: Pickwick, 2011.

Hicks, John Mark. *Enter the Water, Come to the Table: Baptism and the Lord's Supper in the Bible's Story of New Creation*. Abilene, TX: Abilene Christian University Press, 2014.

Hinson, E. Glenn. "The Authority of Tradition: A Baptist View." In *Free Church and the Early Church*, edited by D.H. Williams, 141–61.

Holmes, Stephen R. "Baptism: Patristic Resources for Ecumenical Dialogue." In *Dimensions of Baptism*, edited by Porter and Cross, 253–67.

———. *Tradition and Renewal in Baptist Life*. The Whitley Lecture 2003. Oxford: Whitley, 2003.

James, Aaron B. *Analogous Uses of Language: Eucharistic Identity, and the "Baptist" Vision*. Studies in Baptist History and Thought. Milton Keynes: Paternoster, 2014.

Jones, Brandon C. *Waters of Promise: Finding Meaning in Believer Baptism*. Eugene, OR: Pickwick, 2012.

Jorgenson, Cameron H. "Bapto-Catholicism: Recovering Tradition and Reconsidering Baptist Identity." PhD diss., Baylor University, 2008.

Kammen Michael G. *Mystic Chords of Memory: The Transformation of Tradition in American Culture*. New York, NY: Knopf, 1991.

Keathley, Kenneth. "The Word of God: Salvation." In *Theology for the Church*, edited by Akin, 686–764.

Kidd, Richard L. *Something to Declare: A Study of the Declaration of Principle*. Oxford: Whitley, 1996.

Kiffin, William. *A Sober Discourse of Right to Church-Communion*. London: George Larkin, 1681.

Klose, Anne. *Covenantal Priesthood: A Narrative of Community for Baptist Churches*. Studies in Baptist History and Thought. Milton Keynes: Paternoster, 2018.

Kreitzer, Larry. *The Gospel according to John*. Regent's Study Guides, 1. Oxford: Regent's Park College, 1990.

Lumpkin, William L., and Bill J. Leonard, eds. *Baptist Confessions of Faith*. 2nd ed. Valley Forge, PA: Judson, 2011.

Marshall, Molly T. "The Changing Face of Baptist Discipleship." *Review and Expositor* 95.1 (Winter 1998) 59–73.

Martin, Ralph P. *The Spirit and the Congregation: Studies in 1 Corinthians 12–15*. Grand Rapids: Eerdmans, 1984.

———. *Worship in the Early Church*. Grand Rapids: Eerdmans, 1974 [1964].

———. *The Worship of God: Some Theological, Pastoral, and Practical Reflections*. Grand Rapids: Eerdmans, 1982.

McClendon, James W. *Doctrine: Volume 2. Systematic Theology*. Nashville, TN: Abingdon, 1994.

———. *Ethics: Volume 1. Systematic Theology*. 2nd ed., rev. and enlarged. Nashville, TN: Abingdon, 2002.

Moody, Christopher. *American Baptismal Sacramentalism? Toward a Sacred Theology of Baptism in the Context of Transatlantic Baptist Disagreement*. Saarbrücken: VDM Verlag Dr. Müller Aktiengesellschaft, 2009.

Mullins, Edgar Young. *The Axioms of Religion: A New Interpretation of the Baptist Faith*. Philadelphia: American Baptist Publication Society, 1908.

Murray, Stuart. *Church After Christendom*. After Christendom. Milton Keynes: Paternoster, 2004.

————. *The Naked Anabaptist: The Bare Essentials of a Radical Faith.* Scottdale, PA/ Waterloo, ON: Herald, 2010.

————. *Post-Christendom: Church and Mission in a Strange New World.* After Christendom. Milton Keynes: Paternoster, 2004.

Nalls, Justin. *A Bombshell in the Baptistery: An Examination of the Influence of George Beasley-Murray on the Baptismal Writings of Select Southern Baptist and Baptist Union of Great Britain Scholars.* Eugene, OR: Pickwick, 2019.

Nelson, David P. "The Nicene Faith and Evangelical Worship." In *Evangelicals and Nicene Faith,* edited by T. George, 147–58.

Nelson, Sally. "'The Water Buries Like a Tomb': Baptists and Baptism." In *Gathering Disciples: Essays in Honor of Christopher J. Ellis,* edited by Myra Blyth and Andy Goodliff, 112–27. Eugene, OR: Pickwick, 2017.

Nettles, Thomas J. *The Baptists: Key People Involved in Forming a Baptist Identity.* 3 vols. Fearn, Ross-shire: Mentor, 2005–7.

————. "Baptist View: Baptism as a Symbol of Christ's Saving Work." In *Understanding Four Views on Baptism,* by Thomas J. Nettles, Richard L. Pratt Jr, Robert Kolb and John D. Castelein, 25–41. Counterpoints; Grand Rapids: Zondervan, 2007.

————. *By His Grace and for His Glory: A Historical Theological, and Practical Study of the Doctrines of Grace in Baptist Life.* Rev. and expanded ed. Cape Coral, FL: Founders, 2007.

Newman, Elizabeth. *Attending to the Wounds on Christ's Body: Teresa's Scriptural Vision.* Cambridge: James Clarke, 2013 [2012].

————. "Baptism: The Substance and the Sign." In *Gathering Together: Baptists at Work in Worship,* edited by Rodney Wallace Kennedy and Derek C. Hatch, 110–24. Eugene, OR: Pickwick, 2013.

————. "Practicing the Nicene Faith." In *Evangelicals and Nicene Faith,* edited by T. George, 133–46.

Norman, R. Stanton. *The Baptist Way: Distinctives of a Baptist Church.* Nashville, TN: Broadman and Holman, 2005.

Oden, Thomas C. *After Modernity . . . What?", Agenda for Theology.* Grand Rapids: Zondervan Academic, 1990.

Pinson, J. Matthew. "Confessional, Baptist, and Arminian: *The General-Free Will Baptist Tradition and the Nicene Faith.*" In *Evangelicals and Nicene Faith,* edited by T. George, 100–115.

Porter, Stanley E., and Anthony R. Cross, eds. *Baptism, the New Testament and the Church: Historical and Contemporary Studies in Honour of R.E.O. White. Journal for the Study of the New Testament* Supplement Series, 171. Sheffield: Sheffield Academic, 1999.

————. eds. *Dimensions of Baptism: Biblical and Theological Studies. Journal for the Study of the New Testament* Supplement Series, 234. Sheffield: Sheffield Academic, 2002.

Prokhorov, Constantine. "On Several Peculiarities of the Understanding of Baptism in the Russian Baptist Church." *Theological Reflections* 8 (2007) 89–105.

———. *Russian Baptists and Orthodoxy, 1960–1990*. Carlisle: Langham Partnership, 2013.

Quicke, Michael J. *360-Degree Preaching: Hearing, Speaking, and Living the Word*. Grand Rapids: Baker Academic, 2003.

———. "Further Reflections on a Sacramental Understanding of Preaching." In *Questions of Identity*, edited by Cross and Gouldbourne, 18–33.

Rempel, John D. *The Lord's Supper in Anabaptism: A Study in the Christology of Balthasar Hubmaier, Pilgram Marpeck, and Dirk Philips*. Studies in Anabaptist and Mennonite History, 33. Scottdale, PA: Herald, 1993.

———. *Recapturing an Enchanted World: Ritual and Sacrament in the Free Church Tradition*. Dynamics of Christian Worship. Downers Grove, IL: IVP Academic, 2020.

Robinson, H. Wheeler. "The Place of Baptism in Baptist Churches of To-day." *Baptist Quarterly* 1.5 (1923) 209–18.

Sannikov, Sergiy. "Discussions about Water Baptism in West and East." *European Journal of Theology* 28.2 (2019) 136–43.

———. "An Holistic Approach to Water-Baptism: An Eastern European Perspective." In *Baptist Sacramentalism 3*, edited by Cross and Thompson, 198–242.

———. *The Phenomenon of Water Baptism in the Context of Contemporary Baptist Sacramentology*. DSc diss., The National Pedagogical Dragomanov University, Kyiv, Ukraine, 2018/Rovno: Diatlik M., 2018.

Sannikov, Sergiy, and Oleksandr Geychenko. "ВОССТАНОВЛЕНИЕ БАПТИСТСКОЙ САКРАМЕНТОЛОГИИ. Интервью с британским богословом Энтони Кроссом"/"Anthony Cross, Interview (15.02.2018)." *Богомыслия/Bogomyslie* 24 (2019), 58–80.

Saucy, Mark. "Baptism as a Test Case for the Nature and Limits of National Theology." *Theological Reflections* 8 (2007) 135–59.

Searle, Joshua. "The Hermeneutics of Crisis: Evangelicals, Apocalypse and Conflict in Northern Ireland Troubles." PhD diss., Trinity College Dublin, 2012.

———. *Theology After Christendom: Forming Prophets for a Post-Christian World*. After Christendom. Eugene, OR: Cascade, 2018.

Siegrist, Anthony G. *Participating Witness: An Anabaptist Theology of Baptism and the Sacramental Character of the Church*. Princeton Theological Monograph Series. Eugene, OR: Pickwick, 2013.

Smith, Gordon T. *Evangelical, Sacramental and Pentecostal: Why the Church Should be All Three*. Downers Grove, IL: IVP Academic, 2017.

Stackhouse, Ian. *The Gospel-Driven Church: Retrieving Classical Ministries for Contemporary Revivalism*. Deep Church. Milton Keynes: Paternoster, 2004.

Thompson, Philip E. "Defining Identity in Unsettled Times: The Union of History and Dogmatics in Baptist Life and Thought." Unpublished paper presented to the Young Scholars in the Baptist Academy, 25–30 July 2011 International Baptist Seminary, Prague, Czech Republic.

———. "New Question in Baptist History: Seeking a Catholic Spirit among Early Baptists." *Pro Ecclesia* 8.1 (1999) 51–72.

———. "Practicing the Freedom of God: Formation in Early Baptist Life." In *Theology and Lived Christianity*, edited by David M. Hammond, 119–38. The Annual Publication of the College Theology Society, 45. Mystic, CT: Twenty-Third, 2000.

———. "Sacraments and Religious Liberty: From Critical Practice to Rejected Infringement." In *Baptist Sacramentalism*, edited by Cross and Thompson, 36–54.

———. "Seventeenth-Century Baptist Confessions in Context." *Perspectives in Religious Studies* 29.4 (Winter 2002) 335–48.

———. "Toward Baptist Ecclesiology in Pneumatological Perspective." PhD diss., Emory University, 1995.

Thompson, Philip E., and Anthony R. Cross, eds. *Recycling the Past or Researching History?", Studies in Baptist Historiography and Myths*. Studies in Baptist History and Thought, 11. Milton Keynes: Paternoster, 2005.

Vasconcelos, Fausto A., ed. *Baptist Faith & Witness. Book 4: Papers of the Study and Research Division of the Baptist World Alliance 2005–2010*. Falls Church, VA: Baptist World Alliance, 2011.

Walker, Michael J. *Baptists at the Table: The Theology of the Lord's Supper amongst English Baptists in the Nineteenth Century*. Didcot: The Baptist Historical Society, 1992.

White, R.E.O. *The Biblical Doctrine of Initiation*. London: Hodder & Stoughton, 1960.

Williams, Daniel H. *Evangelicals and Tradition: The Formative Influences of the Early Church*. Deep Church. Milton Keynes: Paternoster, 2005.

———. *Retrieving the Tradition and Renewing Evangelicalism: A Primer for Suspicious Protestants*. Grand Rapids: Eerdmans, 1999.

Williams, D.H., ed. *The Free Church and the Early Church: Bridging the Historical and Theological Divide*. Grand Rapids: Eerdmans, 2002.

Wilson, Andrew. *Spirit and Sacrament: An Invitation to Eucharistic Worship*. Grand Rapids: Zondervan, 2018.

Wood, Ralph C. "Life after Life after Death: *A Sermon on the Final Phrase of the Nicene Creed*." In *Evangelicals and Nicene Faith*, edited by T. George, 196–201.

Sacramentality

CHAPTER 1

Liturgy and Sacrament

Paul Sheppy

Introduction

In a previous collection of essays, I argued that the category of sacrament required an element of efficacy; beyond the outward and visible sign of an inward and spiritual grace, sacraments effect what they signify.[1] In what follows, I shall take that point as given. My concern here is to consider how liturgical performance in our tradition expresses the sacraments of baptism and eucharist.

Among liturgists one of the perennial debates asks whether liturgy is text or performance. The same question may be asked of a play or a film, or a song and its text, script, or lyric. As with many either-or questions, to pick one alternative over the other is to make a choice that cannot be properly made. Yet, in the academy, it is the textual critics who have predominated for centuries.[2]

For Baptists, who have traditionally eschewed written texts (apart from hymns) and the use of liturgical books prescribing what is to be done and said, the question scarcely arises.[3] Liturgy is usually simply called "worship" and—despite the much rehearsed ecclesiology of the priesthood of all believers—the conduct of worship has generally been left in the hands (and the control) of the few: at one period, the minister alone; more recently, the worship group. Baptists, it might be said, simply do not do liturgy as text.

---

[1] Sheppy, "Penance," 118–20.

[2] It is interesting to note that more recently, cultural studies professionals have begun to make an increasing contribution, using observations (rather than questionnaires) to establish what is happening in worship. One very interesting example has used video to record body posture as a marker of how members of different congregations and traditions stood and moved in community intercessions.

[3] It is worth noting that many ministers used the orders provided for the pastoral offices and for baptism and supper in the various manuals and handbooks which were available, of which the best known was probably Payne and Winward, *Orders and Prayers*.

In Britain, this assertion cannot be too seriously pressed. Even if we were only to take a view from the twentieth century onwards, we would have to note the successive manuals and worship books containing suggested orders of service published by the Baptist Union (see n.3). Moreover, when in 1963 the ecumenical Joint Liturgical Group of Great Britain (JLG) was founded, the Baptist Union appointed two of its most distinguished ministers, Neville Clark and Stephen Winward, as its members and representatives. They and their successors on the JLG always had an official status, even if most Baptists did not really see liturgy as their thing.

Moreover, despite this reserve, much Baptist worship was shaped by a discernible pattern—the "hymn sandwich." A call to worship (perhaps with a sung introit by a choir) was followed by a hymn and prayers of thanksgiving and confession. This we might call the gathering rite. In the morning, when children were present, a special short address would be made to them and an appropriate hymn was sung. Scripture was read and a hymn sung.[4] The sermon was preached, and intercessory prayer was offered (the order of these two items might be reversed) and a hymn was sung. This we might call a liturgy of the word. The dismissal rite was little more than a hymn and a final benediction.[5]

The Lord's supper was in many places added as a separate service after the dismissal of those who would not be staying. Holy communion was frequently reserved for church members only and was a remembrance rather than a celebration. The mood carried a strong penitential note and there was a primary emphasis on remembering "the Lord's death until he come." Any note of resurrection was subsumed into a future parousia.[6] My overwhelming memory of this service in my home church was of its mournfulness. Reverence was sombre and wore dark clothes.

As with any description of what Baptists do, the autonomy of the local congregation meant that there would always be a degree of variation among different worshipping communities. However, the foregoing picture gives a general summary of what was the norm for most British Baptists.

---

[4] Scripture reading might be limited to just one extended passage, which would be (or would contain) the text for the sermon. A Psalm might be read or chanted. Provision was made for the latter in various Baptist hymnbooks.

[5] Attentive readers will notice that I have somehow omitted the collection (sometimes called "the offertory"), which provided for the upkeep, mission and ministry of the local congregation. It was not an insignificant act; many tithed their incomes and saw in the collection of these offerings a serious response to the gospel. It should be added that in other traditions, "the offertory" refers to the bringing forward of bread and wine as the eucharistic table is prepared.

[6] In some churches, if Easter did not fall on the appropriate Sunday of the month (often first and/or third), then the supper would not be kept on Easter Day.

Few would have talked of "sacraments." The more commonly used word in connection with baptism and the Lord's supper was "ordinance." The two actions were ordained by the Lord: baptism because of Jesus' baptism by John in the Jordan and the Great Commission of Matthew 28.16–20; the supper because of Jesus's command to "do this in memory of me."

Sacraments, for Baptists, were "Catholic"—and therefore, let's be blunt, not something we did. The notion of a *sacramentum* as the oath of allegiance a soldier took when he joined up had been lost. At the very least, this idea might have been retained in relation to baptism.[7] However, the word "sacrament" had become tainted by association and strong arguments were rehearsed to rebut any notion of *ex opera operato*.

To some extent, in congregations where a strong covenantal theology held sway, baptism and the supper were seen as signs of the new covenant—and indeed that language was frequently used at the table: "This is the cup of the new covenant of my blood shed for you." However, they remained at best "outward and visible signs of an inward and spiritual grace." To suggest that they might effect what they signified was never an option.

Liturgy as Patterned Performance

Leaving to one side, for the moment, the matter of text, worship is not simply words. There has to be an action—even if only of the heart. It is the contrite heart which makes the offering acceptable (Ps. 51.17). In private devotion, we are free to order our prayer as we will and as the Spirit directs. In public worship, the several limbs become one body and no one member may monopolize the worshipping assembly.

Public worship is different from private devotion because it is the common action of the body of Christ gathered in the Spirit. As St Paul remarks, while each may bring a contribution, there has to be order. The Spirit, after all, is the breath which transforms the dust into the living Adam. The Spirit broods over the chaos so as to produce order. The Spirit shapes us into the likeness of Christ.

The inevitable question arises: How does this order come to be? Is it from books and scripts, or is it a sort of controlled spontaneity?[8] Those who reject external control and opt for spontaneity may be surprised to discover that recording what happens week by week reveals that the extemporaneous

---

[7] Tertullian, *De Corona* (ch. 11, 99–100), argued that Christians should not take the military oath, since the *sacramentum* that bound them was baptism.

[8] This is not to displace the Holy Spirit, who may as surely work in the hearts and minds of those who write texts as in the hearts and minds of those who never use those texts. It is another question as to why the Spirit should, having inspired those who wrote the texts, be required to act again in those who have rejected her previous activity.

gradually becomes patterned both in the ordering of various elements that recur and in words and phrases which gain currency and even normative status. Even songs and hymns settle into regular choices which gradually form a central core. The old joke "How many liturgists does it take to change a light bulb?"—"Change?!!" may equally apply to any worshipping community after a few years. As my church history tutor remarked, "Anything can be a tradition if you do it twice."

Inevitably, an established pattern emerges, and it broadly follows what worship leaders (whether a central body or a local group) decide. There is nothing sinister about this. It is how groups operate.

What can be discerned is how discrete items (songs, prayers, readings, processions, dances) are put together. To look, for a moment, at the world of entertainment, we have two major models: music hall (vaudeville) and theatre.

In vaudeville, the ordering is determined by the popularity of the act. A young singer who is the second act in the first half at the beginning of the tour has a worldwide hit. Suddenly, she is top of the bill (or very close to it). The magician who had been in the second half is now relegated to the first. The aim of vaudeville is to send the audience away happy.

In the theatre, we cannot move the Act I scene ii to a later point in the play simply because it's doing well. Its position is determined by its place in the drama. Julius Caesar dies in Act II; and, no matter how great the actor, Brutus will not slay Caesar in Act V.[9] The aim of theatre is to send the audience away changed.

Liturgy as Converting

If the musical postlude is seen as the climax of worship and the silence of taking bread and wine is lost, then we are perilously close to vaudeville. This is not to say that we cannot have great or thrilling music as we leave the house of prayer. Indeed, it may send us into the world in joyful mission. However, if our parting is simply an emotional "high" without any sense of conversion, something has gone wrong. We came to the assembly where God waited to encounter us, yet we left unchanged, unconverted. So who was it that we met and why did we remain the same?

We are beginning to see how worship needs to be shaped so that we are re-shaped into the image of Christ. This is not something that we can achieve. The preacher who answers the question "How many conversions did you get?" by saying "None" has it right. The wind blows as it will, bringing order from chaos, new life from the dead. We know not how.

In those two ordinances (which henceforth I will call "sacraments") of baptism and supper (which I will call "eucharist"), we come to the primary liturgical actions of the church. How do these signs become effective?

---

[9] I refer to the eponymous tragedy, written by William Shakespeare.

More than forty years ago, I had the great privilege of private conversation with Metropolitan Anthony Bloom. Our talk began with some discussion about worship in the Orthodox tradition. However, after a while, I began to see that I was wasting time and I made my confession to him.

Readers will have to content themselves with the earlier part of my conversation with Metropolitan Anthony. At one point I asked how he felt about people who seemed to arrive very late for worship and those who appeared to leave very early.[10] He answered first with a pastoral concern. Some people came from far away and might not be able to arrive as the liturgy began; others had to leave before its conclusion in order to return home or to get to work. He then added, "But the first to arrive is late in coming, and the last to go leaves early. We are simply dropping in on the ceaseless activity of heaven." I have never forgotten the admonition.

Baptism

In worship, the Holy Spirit precedes human activity. So, in baptism, when we swear our *sacramentum* to become Christ's soldiers in the fight against sin and death, it is the Sovereign Lord, enthroned upon the cherubim and the seraphim, who hears our vows and descends upon us in seven-fold energy and nine-fold harvest. It is I AM, I AM who seals us and transforms us and adopts us as daughters and sons.

The word of the Lord does not return empty; it is not fruitless. The One who said, "Let there be light" and there was light, says "Yes and Amen" to us in Christ Jesus. His word is effective. To this let all say, "Aye" and none "Nay."

When we make of baptism an arrival point ("Now you have arrived"), we lose its sacramental power. It is more than an arrival point; it is also a departure point—or, better, it is a mission point. To be baptized into Christ is to be baptized into the mission of God. The Spirit drives us into that desert where God will feed us and where we will meet Christ in the hungry, the thirsty, the stranger, the naked, the sick, the imprisoned. These are not the people I normally mix with. To meet them I must be converted. In my baptism, everything changes. If anyone is in Christ, there is a new creation.

The way we order this rite must enable us to see the outward and visible sign through which God effects an inward and spiritual (literally "of the Spirit") grace. Clothe the candidate in white; give her an alb as a sign of the birthing pool where new life begins. Anoint him with oil and declare Ephphatha to eyes and ears, mouth, heart, hands and feet. See Christ in all you meet; listen for Christ in all you do; speak for Christ as you are led; open your heart to the unloved Christ; open your hand to receive him and your

---

[10] The divine liturgy seldom takes less than two hours, and I had witnessed those that lasted nearly four.

arms to embrace him; in his footmarks place yours. Then, lead her to the table, and feed her with bread and wine; feed him with the body and blood of the Lord. How feeble much of our baptismal liturgy is!

Eucharist

I am not concerned here about the frequency of the celebration, but about how our liturgy provides the framework for sacramental encounter.[11] Once again, we need to remember that God comes before we do. I shall always remember the prayer of one dear brother at the table, "Lord, we invite you to come among us . . ." I understood the sentiment, but I wondered whether we were presuming too much. It is the Lord who does the inviting and we are the guests. I have always preferred the gathering formula which declares:

> The Lord is here:
> his Spirit is with us.

Similarly the versicle and response,

> Lord, open our lips:
> and our mouth shall proclaim your praise[,]

seems to me to get the emphasis right. It all begins with the presence and the call of God.

The old term "The Lord's Supper" reminded us that what we did was not at our bidding or invention but at the gracious invitation of the crucified, risen and ascended Lord. And it is for this reason that the prayer as bread and wine are placed on the table "Send your Spirit on these gifts . . ." is so appropriate. It is that same crucified, risen and ascended Lord who bestows the Spirit upon his people.

If the gestures at baptism (even if the only one we use is immersion) are grand in scale, those used at the eucharist frequently seem rather hole-in-the-corner. "Lift up your hearts!" we cry as though some great event were about to happen and then we hand out tiny cubes of bread and plastic cups of wine-substitute. Jesus made gallons of wine for a country wedding where people had drunk the place dry. His feast of bread and fish left twelve baskets full of leftovers.

---

[11] I advocate a eucharistic celebration each Sunday and on the great dominical feasts—Easter, obviously, and at least in addition Ascension, Pentecost and Transfiguration. Not all will agree. However, most people see the need for regular physical food, and it might be argued that the same considerations apply when we meet together to celebrate. We offer visitors to our homes refreshment, but refuse it when offered by Christ in his house. It's odd.

We, on the other hand, offer the hospitality of the poorhouse. We would not treat dinner guests so. Yet at this rehearsal for the messianic banquet, we become almost miserly. At the very least, we should hold high the bread and the cup, just as we lift high our hearts. The outward and visible signs we make do not suggest any great riches in the inward and spiritual grace to be bestowed—"Just a nibble for you, Carole; just a sip for you, Ahmed."[12] We can never match the generosity of grace, but we might make more of an effort!

In the great eucharistic prayer we give thanks for the gifts of creation, for salvation won for us by Christ, for the life of the Spirit. Sometimes, the mood may be darker. In Lent, we may want to reflect on being hungry for nourishment. In times of natural disaster, we may want to reflect on the fragility of our planet and its place on the edge of things rather than being at the centre (which is where God is).[13] Times and seasons bring their own opportunities to express our thanksgiving in different ways.

Occasionally, it might be good to have a setting of the eucharistic prayer which the congregation could sing (rather like Bland Tucker's hymn based on the *Didache*).[14] There is plenty for the enterprising liturgist to do.[15] The problem, of course, is inertia and our resistance to change. This comes strangely from people who affirm their faith in the One who declares, "Behold, I make all things new."

Conclusion

Sacraments are effective signs. Their effectiveness is wrought by God, who is not limited to the smallness of our thought. However, in our baptism we are given a full measure of the Spirit and we quench the Spirit when we do not live in and by the divine energy granted to us. At the table, we take bread and wine (which are more than bread and wine) to nourish our life in the Spirit. If it does not nourish us, why eat, why drink?

---

[12] A friend of mine, a Catholic priest, commented of the eucharistic wafer used in his tradition, "Of course, the great miracle is to believe that this little white disc is actually bread . . ."

[13] Sometimes, the language of the church makes it sound as though we live in a pre-Copernican universe where everything revolves around planet earth. Such an implied worldview simply confirms to many that we are "unreal."

[14] "Father, we thank Thee who hast planted / Thy holy name within our hearts."

[15] I offer an example that I have written as an appendix to this essay. It is set to the tune Thaxted, "I vow to thee, my country." (Permission is given herewith for local congregational use on the condition that authorship is acknowledged: Paul P.J. Sheppy. If publication rights are sought, specific permission must be obtained from the author at sheppyliturgy @gmail.com.)

When we say that these things are "just symbols," the word "just" might as well read "not" (they are "not symbols"), for a symbol is a form of metaphor. It is more than its surface meaning. It points to a reality beyond itself and contains depths and resonances far beyond our grasp.

Without that depth, that resonance, it is like a song with neither words nor melody. When a symbol is no more than its surface, when the sacrament has no effect, it is not the sound of one hand clapping.[16] It is a nothingness.

We thank you, mighty Maker, for all you have unfurled,
the variety of nature, the glories of our world,
the treasures of our planet, the vastnesses of space,
the gift of our discoveries in every time and place,
for all that has inspired us, for all that's yet to be:
and we pray that all creation shall at the last be free.

We thank you, loving Saviour, for all that you have won,
the rescue of the lost and sad, the outcast, those we shun,
the healing of the broken, the gifts of hope and trust,
in days when all our golden dreams had faded into dust,
for love that stayed unconquered when we had done our worst:
and we pray for that new dawning when the last shall be the first.

We thank you, guiding Spirit, for all that you have shown
of energy and insight into what was yet unknown,
the paths of understanding, of learning and of skill
in healing mind and body, in girding heart and will.
Breathe now upon this people, upon this bread and wine,
as we pray that in our day and world we may be of Christ the sign.

© Paul Sheppy
September 2019

Bibliography

Cross, Anthony R., and Philip E. Thompson, eds. *Baptist Sacramentalism 2*. Milton Keynes: Paternoster, 2008.
Payne, Ernest A., and Stephen F. Winward, comp. *Orders and Prayers for Church Worship: A Manual for Ministers*. London: The Carey Kingsgate Press, 1960.

---

[16] "What is the sound of one hand clapping?" is an old Buddhist riddle. The answer is variously explained; but the common strand appears to be that when what is sought and the intense quest for it become one, that is the sound of one hand clapping. The saying of Jesus, "I am the way, the truth, the life" is the Christian sound of one hand clapping: the journey and the goal are one.

Sheppy, Paul. "Penance." In *Baptist Sacramentalism 2*, edited by Cross and Thompson, 117–34.

Tertullian. *The Chaplet, or De Corona*. In *The Ante-Nicene Fathers*: Vol. 3, edited by Alexander Roberts, James Donaldson, and revised by A. Cleveland Coxe; translated by S. Thelwall, 93–103. Edinburgh: T. & T. Clark, 1997 [1885].

CHAPTER 2

The Presence of the Kingdom:
On the Sacramentality of Scripture

Adam Glover

Introduction

In certain critical respects, the history of sacramental theology in the Latin
West is the history of a narrowing.[1] Whereas the New Testament μυστήριον
(Lat. *sacramentum*) referred to God's comprehensive plan, now revealed in
Christ, to reconcile the world to himself, subsequent theologians came to
associate the sacraments less with the mystery of redemption itself than with
the various rites and rituals whereby the church both re-presented that
mystery and made its effects (i.e., divine grace) available to the faithful.[2] In the
later Middle Ages, this already narrow focus on the ritualistic transmission of
grace gave rise to a series of questions that narrowed matters further still. Thus
medieval theologians debated the precise number of sacraments, the necessity
of explicit dominical institution, the nature of sacramental efficacy, and the
conditions of sacramental validity—all within a set of legal and juridical
categories that encouraged an understanding of sacraments as discrete,
autonomous "things" that could be extracted not only from their liturgical
contexts, but also from their place within the broader revelation of the
musterion of God in the person of Christ.[3] Unsurprisingly, the Reformers
objected to these developments, but even their efforts to return the church to
an ostensibly purer, more biblical sacramental system paid ambiguous
dividends. By insisting that the sacraments were two and two alone, the
Reformers not only abetted the late medieval tendency to isolate
sacramentality from other aspects of Christian worship. They also paved the
way for the rather more aggressive anti-sacramentalism of certain forms of
"low church" Protestantism, where to call the sacraments even an "appendix to
worship" would be nothing so much as an insult to actual appendices.

---

[1] Forrester *et al.*, *Encounter with God*, 68–72.

[2] Forrester *et al.*, *Encounter with God*, 70–71.

[3] Forrester *et al.*, *Encounter with God*, 72; see also Vorgrimler, *Sacramental Theology*,
54–56.

This way of telling the story is, of course, far too broad and sketchy to be applicable in every case, but it does catch the general drift of a concern that has animated some of the best and most influential theology of the past 100 years. In the middle third of the twentieth century, a group of Catholic thinkers loosely associated with the so-called *nouvelle théologie* sought to recover an older and more expansive vision of sacramentality, one that saw the incarnate Christ as the "primordial sacrament" and the whole economy of salvation as sacramental in character.[4] This move was hardly novel, of course, and one finds versions of it scattered throughout the history of theology.[5] Nor was the goal to denigrate the named sacraments. The point, rather, was to see sacraments less as autonomous, stand-alone rites than as elements within the broader economy of God's offer of salvation, and thereby to open up a space for thinking about the sacramental dimensions of Christian experience as a whole. Baptists have not been absent from these conversations, and in the past two decades Baptist theologians have made important contributions to a sacramental understanding not only of eucharist and baptism, but also of preaching, ordination, the church, penance, and scripture.[6]

It is within the space opened up by this renewed interest in sacramentalism among Baptist scholars that I would like to situate my own reflections on the sacramental character of scripture.[7] At first blush, a Baptist argument for the sacramentality of scripture might look like an easy sell. Baptists have always had a high view of the Bible, and the Reformation in general took as its starting point an understanding of scripture as the sole source of authority on questions of faith and morals. And yet, as Alister McGrath has pointed out, many within the Protestant tradition, especially those who followed Zwingli, came to view scriptural revelation primarily as a "form of information," a set of propositions aimed at disclosing the "great foundational truths of Christianity" or "the moral duties of believers."[8] The Reformed theologian Edward J. Young (1907–68), for instance, defines revelation in the "biblical sense of the term" as "the communication of information."[9] The enormously influential

---

[4] See, e.g., de Lubac, *Corpus mysticum*, and Schillebeeckx, *Christ the Sacrament*, 13–20. See also Vorgrimler, *Sacramental Theology*, 30–32; Boersma, *Nouvelle Théologie*; and Osborne, *Christian Sacraments*, 5–40.

[5] For a good discussion with a host of examples, see Genig, *Viva Vox*, 1–106. On the Reformers in particular, see Beaton, *Embodied Word, Spoken Signs*, 51–106.

[6] See the various essays collected in Cross and Thompson, eds, *Baptist Sacramentalism* and Cross and Thompson, eds, *Baptist Sacramentalism 2*.

[7] This essay was inspired by Harmon, "Sacramentality of the Word," 239–53, though our approaches are finally very different.

[8] McGrath, *Twilight of Atheism*, 202–3.

[9] Young, *Thy Word is Truth*, 41.

evangelical theologian Carl F.H. Henry (1913–2003) argues along similar lines that divine revelation "contain[s] a body of divinely given information actually expressed or capable of being expressed in propositions" and hence that the Bible itself ought to be understood primarily as an "inspired literary deposit of divinely revealed truths."[10] Something of this view persists in the various permutations of the *Baptist Faith and Message*, where we learn that scripture is, among other things, the "perfect treasure of divine instruction" and "the supreme standard by which all human conduct, creeds, and religious opinions should be tried."[11]

I have no interest in denying this view in all its particulars, not least because whatever else the Bible might be, it is surely also a "deposit of divinely revealed truths." And yet I wonder whether an excessive emphasis on the informational character of scripture might tempt us into the same narrowing tendency that has characterized the history of sacramentalism. What I would like to argue in particular is that a conception of the Bible as primarily a source of propositional truths risks obscuring a somewhat more ancient view of divine revelation, one which, without rejecting the importance of propositional revelation, also saw the scriptural text as a kind of sacrament in which the divine Logos takes on "real presence" in the *logoi* of the sacred page. I borrow the language of "real presence" from Catholic eucharistic theology, and although I do not mean to push a full-blooded, transubstantiational model of scriptural sacramentalism, I do wish to urge a conception of scripture according to which the words of the sacred page make Christ present to us in something like the way the eucharist does. Making sense of the slightly handwavy expression "something like" in the previous sentence will be the central task of this essay.

Scripture, Incarnation, and Eucharist

The idea that scripture is more than information is deeply rooted in the history of Christian theology, and it is often treated within the context of the incarnation. In his *Letter to the Philadelphians*, for instance, Ignatius of Antioch (d.c. 107) writes that we must "flee to the Gospel [τῷ εὐαγγελίῳ] as to the flesh of Jesus [ὡς σαρκὶ Ἰησοῦ]."[12] Subsequent theologians would develop Ignatius' insight, but perhaps none quite so forcefully as Origen of Alexandria (184–253), whose incarnational exegesis sits at the heart of a vast and deeply influential program of biblical interpretation.[13] In his now classic

---

[10] Henry, *God, Revelation, and Authority*, 452–53.

[11] Hobbs, *Baptist Faith and Message*, 18.

[12] Ignatius of Antioch, *Letter to the Philadelphians*, 5.1.

[13] For a good account of sacramental or incarnational exegesis in the early patristic period, see Weinrich, "Patristic Exegesis as Ecclesial and Sacramental," 21–38.

study of patristic scriptural exegesis, Henri de Lubac argues that for Origen "the Word of God that is Scripture . . . is none other, in his essence, than the Logos, the One 'who was in the beginning with God'."[14] Henri Crouzel suggests along similar lines that Origen's identification of the scriptural *logoi* and the divine Logos is so absolute that one can speak of "an incarnation of the Word into the letter analogous to the other incarnation into the flesh."[15] This feature of Origen's exegesis is evident throughout his scriptural commentaries. In the commentary on Matthew, for instance, he remarks that "just as Christ came veiled [*celatus*] in a body," so "all divine scripture is likewise incorporated [*incorporata*] . . . since the spiritual and prophetic sense of scripture is veiled [*celatus*] in the history of the subject proposed."[16] Here Origen's reference to the incarnation serves primarily to illustrate the relationship between the literal and spiritual senses of the biblical text, but in other places the analogy carries significantly more theological weight. In the commentary on Matthew, for example, Origen argues that while the divine Logos is "invisible according to its proper nature," it becomes visible when it is "written and, as it were, incarnate [οἱονεὶ σωματωθῇ] in the Bible."[17] A passage from the *Philocalia* is even more explicit: "we see the Word of God on earth ever since he became human because eternally in the Scriptures [ἀεὶ ἐν ταῖς γραφαῖς] the Word became flesh that he might dwell among us."[18]

Origen's conviction that the Logos of God is "incarnate" in scripture in a manner analogous to the historical incarnation would prove decisively influential, and one finds echoes of it in a variety of later thinkers. In his third *Homily on the Song of Songs*, for instance, Gregory of Nyssa explicitly associates the word of God as scripture (ὁ νῦν λόγος) with the Word of God as the Second Person of the Trinity. John Chrysostom's doctrine of συγκατάβασις (*attemperatio*, accommodation) likewise takes the historical incarnation as the paradigm of scriptural inspiration, while Augustine's account of linguistic signification leans heavily on an analogy between human speech and the incarnation of the divine Word.[19] Nor was the idea confined to patristic

---

[14] de Lubac, *History and Spirit*, 385.

[15] Crouzel, *Origen*, 70. See also Hanson, *Allegory and Event*, 194–95.

[16] Origen, *Series in Matthaeum*, 27 (*PG* 13:1633). Cf. Origen, *In Leviticum Homilia I* (*PG* 12:405).

[17] Origen, *Comm. in Matthaeum*, frag. 11, in *Die griechischen christlichen Schriftsteller der ersten drei Jahrhunderte* 40.1 (Leipzig: Hinrichs, 1935), 19.

[18] Origen, *Philocalia*, 15.19.

[19] See Gregory of Nyssa, *Homilies on the Song of Songs* 3 (*PG* 44:808); John of Chrysostom, *In Gen. 3:8. Homily* 17.1 (*PG* 53:134). For more on this aspect of Chrysostom's exegesis, see Naidu, *Transformed in Christ*, 80–82. On Augustine, see Burris *et al.*, *Seducing Augustine*, 34–37.

exegesis. One finds versions of it in Bonaventure's famous triad of the "threefold word" (*Verbum increatum, Verbum incarnatum,* and *Verbum inspiratum*), and also in Aquinas' claim that because Christ is the "natural word of God," "every word inspired by God is a certain participated similitude in him."[20] By the mid-twentieth century, an intimate connection between scripture and incarnation had become something like the official position of the Catholic Church. Drawing on Pope Pius XII's *Divino Afflante Spiritu* (1943), the framers of *Dei Verbum* (1965), the Second Vatican Council's statement on divine revelation, write that "just as the Word [*Verbum*] of the eternal Father . . . was in every way made like human beings," so likewise "the words of God [*dei verba*], expressed in human language, have been made like human discourse."[21] In time, Baptists got in on the game as well. In fact, nearly a century before *Dei Verbum*, the great Baptist preacher Charles Haddon Spurgeon (1834–92) made an even stronger version of the same point. In an 1887 sermon called "The Word a Sword," Spurgeon argues that the phrase "the Word of God" in Hebrews 4.12 refers simultaneously to the "Word of God Incarnate" and the "Word of God Inspired." "Weave the two into one thought," he writes, for

> the Word of God, namely, this revelation of Himself in Holy Scripture, is all it is here described to be because Jesus, the incarnate Word of God, is in it. He does, as it were, incarnate Himself as the divine truth in this visible and manifest revelation . . . As the Christ reveals God, so this Book reveals Christ, and therefore it partakes, as the Word of God, in all the attributes of the Incarnate Word . . . In fact, they are now so linked together that it would be impossible to divide them.[22]

Spurgeon's "as it were," like Origen's οἱονεί, is designed to preserve a degree of analogical distance, but his identification of scripture and incarnation is otherwise as strict as the diversity of the media (text and flesh) will allow. In each case, the point is the same: because scripture is not simply a repository of divinely revealed information, the point of reading scripture is likewise not simply to learn about Christ but to "commune" with Christ and thereby to experience, in and through the *logoi* of the biblical text, the presence of the same divine Logos who took on flesh in the person of Jesus of Nazareth.

The incarnational vision of scripture common to Origen, Bonaventure, and Spurgeon finds its natural home within the church's sacramental life, specifically in the celebration of the eucharist. This should not be surprising.

---

[20] Bonaventure, *Itinerarium mentis in Deum*, IV, 3, in *Opera omnia*, 5:306; Aquinas, *Super Evangelium Sancti Ioannis lectura*, cap. 5, lectio 6.

[21] *Dei Verbum*, 13; Pius XII, *Divino Afflante Spiritu*, 37. Both available online at www.vatican.va. See also Mary Healy, "Inspiration," 27–41.

[22] Spurgeon, "The Word a Sword," 40.

For most of its history, Christian thought has construed incarnation and eucharist as two sides of the same christological coin, and theologians as early as Irenaeus of Lyons (d.c. 202) drew parallels between Christ's presence in the eucharistic loaf and his presence in the words of scripture. In the *Adversus Haereses*, for instance, Irenaeus writes that the "perfect bread of the Father" revealed himself to us in human form, so that by "eating and drinking the Word of God" we might be prepared to receive the "bread of immortality."[23] Origen picks up the same theme in his commentary on Numbers, suggesting that we "drink the blood of Christ not only in the rite of the sacraments [*sacramentorum ritu*] but also when we receive his words [*sermones*], in which life consists."[24] A somewhat stronger version of this idea appears in the *Peri Pascha*, where Origen remarks that "his [Christ's] flesh, his bones, his blood are the divine Scriptures, and when we eat them, we have Christ."[25] The Middle Ages witnessed a proliferation of such images. In his *Meditatio de redemptione humana*, Anselm likens scriptural interpretation to a process of chewing, sucking, and swallowing, while in his commentary on the Gospel of John, the Benedictine exegete Rupert of Deutz (c. 1080–c. 1129) describes the bread with which Jesus feeds the 5,000 (John 6.1–15) as the "loaves of scripture" (*scripturarum panes*).[26] Nor was the connection lost on Protestants, least of all Spurgeon, who devoted an 1890 sermon to the importance of "feeding on the word" as on the "living bread which comes down from heaven."[27] Luther was even more explicit. In *The Adoration of the Sacrament* (1523), he argued that "the body you receive [in the Lord's Supper] and the word you hear [in preaching] are the body and Word of him who holds the whole world in his hands and inhabits it from beginning to end."[28] Despite certain obvious differences of language and emphasis, the consistent witness of the Christian tradition points to a strikingly similar conclusion: it is possible to speak of Christ as "present" in scripture—indeed as "incarnate" in scripture—because scripture itself is a kind of sacrament, a "visible and manifest revelation" (Spurgeon) of the divine Logos who took on flesh in the person of Jesus of Nazareth and who is present whenever the community of believers gathers to hear the Word of God in the proclamation of scripture and to consume the Word of God in the bread and wine of the Lord's table.

---

[23] Irenaeus, *Adversus Haereses*, IV, 38 (*PG* 7:1106).

[24] Origen, *In Numeros Homilia*, 16.9 (*PG* 12:701).

[25] Origen, *Sur la Pâque*, 133.

[26] Anselm, *Meditatio de redemptione humana* (*PL* 158:763); Rupert, *In Evangelium S. Ioannis*, bk. IV (*PL* 169:443). For other examples, see Magrassi, *Praying the Bible*, 51–54.

[27] Spurgeon, "Feeding on the Word," 497.

[28] Luther, *Adoration of the Sacrament*, 298.

For all its apparent ecumenical tidiness, however, this way of stating the point is rather less a conclusion than a provocation. The problems are at least twofold. The first has to do with the difficulty of making sense of the idea that Christ is somehow "present" in the scriptural text. What could it mean, after all, to claim that a person is "present" in a text? The second difficulty has to do with the suggestion that Christ is present in scripture "as in the eucharist." What exactly does "as in the eucharist" add to our understanding? Does this not amount to illuminating one mystery by appealing to another? And, in any event, wouldn't any argument of this form depend upon some prior agreement about the nature of eucharistic presence itself? The answer to each of these questions must certainly be "yes"; and while I very much doubt that any single account of the sacramentality of scripture could be rendered consistent with the dogmatic commitments of the various Christian confessions, I would like in the rest of this essay to sketch an account of scriptural sacramentalism which, though it draws on the insights of Catholic eucharistic theology, may nonetheless prove useful, if not to all Baptists, then at least to those Baptists already predisposed to a sacramental understanding of faith and practice. Perhaps we can get some traction on this issue by stepping back and looking more closely at the first of the two problems I mentioned earlier: the difficulty of making sense of the idea that a person could be "present" in a text.

Language and Presence

I take it as uncontroversial that one of the purposes of language is to state propositional truths, and I take it as equally uncontroversial that this is not its only purpose. Ever since J.L. Austin's *How to Do Things with Words* (1962), we are comfortable with the idea of "performative utterances" and so also with the idea that language, in addition to describing reality, can change, modify, or otherwise influence it. To take a common example, the utterance "I now pronounce you husband and wife" does not merely describe an existing state of affairs, but brings a new state of affairs into existence by rendering the couple in question husband and wife. Other instances of language use also seem to go beyond the strictly constative, albeit in somewhat different ways. Take, as one example among many, that most beautiful line in all of Dante: *in la sua volontade è nostra pace* ("in his will is our peace").[29] This sentence communicates a certain kind of propositional content, and it will count as a true sentence if the content it expresses turns out to be true (i.e., if our peace is indeed in God's will). but to imagine that the point of Dante's line is simply to transmit a bit of propositional content is to miss more than half the point. It is to miss, in the first place, that *in la sua volontade è nostra pace* is a line of poetry and that part of the joy of poetic language lies in the sheer physical process of articulating it: the feel of the last two syllables of *volontade* as the

[29] Dante, *Paradiso*, 3.85.

tongue taps gently against the teeth, the tension in *pace* as the delicacy of the initial 'p' gives way to the breathy openness of the 'a', which in turn is first slowly constricted, then halted altogether, and finally released again as the affricate 'c' rushes over tongue and palate, softly grazing the lips as it exits the mouth. Here one almost senses the presence of Dante himself, as if one were participating bodily in the same range of physical articulations as the poet when, in a study in Ravenna nearly 700 years ago, he first mumbled the words under his breath. Perhaps even more importantly, to see Dante's line primarily as a vehicle for the transmission of propositional content would be to miss what the line is trying to *do* to us. In one sense, of course, Dante is trying to convince us that our peace is indeed in God's will, but he is also, it seems to me, attempting to induce that peace in us, to make it present to us both as a lived reality and as a foretaste of the perfect peace of the eschatological kingdom.

To get a clearer sense of why this might be relevant to the question of the sacramentality of scripture, consider a rather more mundane example. Suppose that during her journey home after a long absence my wife posts a letter telling me, "I will see you tomorrow" (call this sentence P_1). In one sense, P_1 expresses a bit of propositional content, and if future contingents have truth values, it too will have a truth value. I do not wish to minimize the importance of that propositional content, since everything else I want to say depends upon my ability to grasp it. What I want to emphasize, however, is that P_1 creates a further set of effects quite in addition to its propositional content. First, and most basically, it has the effect of reconfiguring my sense of the meaning of certain words. From one angle, for instance, the verb "see" means "perceive with the eyes," and while this is certainly part of what my wife intends, it cannot be all she has in mind. In this basic, utility sense, after all, she will also see lots of other things tomorrow (our kitchen stove, for instance), but she will not see any of them in the same sense she will see me. And this is simply because, when applied to me, the word "see" does not simply mean—perhaps does not even primarily mean—"perceive with the eyes." It means instead that my wife and I will "be together" and hence that we will resume the life we have shared together in the past and hope to share together in the future.

But if my wife's letter indeed inflects my sense of the meaning of certain words, it also has the far more important effect of reconfiguring my experience of time. When my wife tells me that she will see me "tomorrow," the word "tomorrow" ceases to refer merely to a date on a calendar and comes instead to function as what I would like to call a "moment": a point in time whose significance transcends the proportions of its immediate chronological referent. In a purely chronological sense, the difference between "today" and "tomorrow" is a mechanical measure of the interval required for a clock to tick and tock a certain number of times. Understood as a "moment," by contrast, "tomorrow" is neither a mechanical measure nor a point on a timeline. It is instead what we might think of as a "reality anticipated." To anticipate something is, of course, to "expect" or "look forward" to it; but it is also, and somewhat more literally, to "take hold of it beforehand" (*ante capere*), to reach forward into the future and draw it back into the present. In some cases, this posture of anticipation draws the future so thoroughly into the present that we experience the present not as a "now" that stands at some definite temporal remove from the future, but as a present that is partly *constituted* by its relationship to the future. Among children anxiously awaiting the arrival of Santa Claus, for example, the evening of 24 December derives its meaning and intelligibility from its anticipation of Christmas morning. For lovers of Beethoven, the sequence of three G eighth notes followed by one E-flat half note in the opening statement of the *Fifth Symphony* derives its meaning and intelligibility from its anticipation of the subsequent sequence of three F eighth notes and one D half note. In each of these cases, the future is already implicit in the present in such a way and to such an extent that the present itself is what it is partly in virtue of what the future *will be*. If, for instance, while listening to what I took to be the opening statement of the *Fifth Symphony*, I were suddenly to learn that something other than three F eighth notes and one D half note would follow the initial sequence of three G eighth notes and one E-flat half, the very character of my present experience (i.e., the experience of hearing three G eighth notes followed by one E-flat half) would change fundamentally.

Something similar, I think, goes for my wife's letter. Because our relationship constitutes my identity at the deepest level, the expectation that I will see her tomorrow so thoroughly determines the character of the present that part of what it means for me to exist *now* is to live in anticipation of her promised return. And this suggests that one of the effects of the letter is not simply to provide information about the future, but also to "pre-realize" the future, to make it available to me in advance of its arrival. I do not mean to suggest, of course, that my wife's letter makes her present to me as she will be present tomorrow, since tomorrow she will be present in a rather different sort of way (i.e., locally present, present as a body is present in a place). but it is to say that while she is most certainly not present in *that* sense, she is not simply absent either. Rather, to borrow a set of helpful phrases from Louis Mackey, she is "absent in the mode of presence" and "present in the mode of absence."[30] These are not gratuitous oxymorons. Nor do I intend by them anything especially spooky or mysterious. They are simply ways of making sense of an experience to which the categories of simple presence and simple absence apply only imperfectly. And such categories apply only imperfectly because while my wife is no doubt absent in one sense (i.e., spatially absent), to say that she is *merely* absent obscures the extent to which she nonetheless exercises genuine causal influence on the present. It obscures, in other words, the extent to which, in virtue of inducing in me an anticipation of her future

---

[30] Mackey, *Peregrinations of the Word*, 111.

presence, she in some sense causes the present to be what it is (i.e., a present partly constituted by its anticipation of that future). Further, if my wife is indeed present in this sense, it would appear that she is also "really present," for surely "being present enough to cause an effect" is a sufficient condition for "being really present." Even more critically, because she brings about the relevant effect by writing and posting a letter, it likewise seems to follow that, if my wife is indeed "really present" in the sense just specified, she is really present in and through her words. It is precisely her words, after all, that activate my anticipation and hence "pre-realize" the future. To the extent that she is present at all, it is her language that makes her so.

Eucharist and Presence

As should perhaps now be clear, the point of the last section was to suggest a way of articulating the idea that language can make something really present even under conditions of local absence. I have lingered over this point because, as we shall see in a moment, the notion of "present under conditions of local absence" is central to sacramentality as I wish to understand it. For whatever else a sacrament may be or do, it is also a *sign*, and whatever else a sign may be or do, it always signifies something other than itself. And this means that sacraments are always and irreducibly symbolic—that is, they function *as* sacraments only to the extent that the divine presence to which they point remains imperfectly realized. In fact, even in those traditions that emphasize sacramental efficacy and "real presence," the eucharist itself is nonetheless also a sacrament of absence: one celebrates the Lord's supper because Christ has not yet come and because the kingdom of heaven is not yet fully at hand.[31] Sacraments therefore always imply both presence *and* absence. Seeing how these terms jointly constitute a sacrament *as* a sacrament is critical to grasping the nature of sacramentality more generally.

Until about the ninth century, the church had a reasonably firm hold on this issue as broadly realistic and broadly symbolic approaches to the eucharist coexisted peacefully on the basis of a conception of symbols not as entities independent of the reality they signify but as means of participating in it.[32] As this unity dissolved, however, it became possible not only to oppose symbol to reality, but also to see the one as inversely proportional to the other. As a result, and especially in the wake of the eucharist controversies of the ninth and eleventh centuries, Catholic eucharistic theology began an unmistakable drift toward increasingly physicalist conceptions of the Lord's table.[33] To take

---

[31] Hence Aquinas' claim that there will be no sacraments in heaven (*Summa theologiae* 3a, q. 61, a. 4 ad 1).

[32] Crockett, *Eucharist*, 106.

[33] Rempel, "Anabaptist Theologies of the Eucharist," 117.

just one especially telling example, in the eleventh century, Berengar of Tours (999–1088) was accused of heresy for denying Christ's real presence in the eucharist and thereafter compelled by Pope Nicholas II to sign a confession according to which Christ's body is "broken by the hands of the priest and crushed by the teeth of the faithful in a sensory fashion, not only as a sacrament but in truth."[34] The vulgar realism of the oath imposed on Berengar does not represent the mature opinion of medieval Catholic theology, and in any event it seems unlikely that Nicholas II was genuinely interested in propounding a theory of eucharistic presence that a second-century pagan might well have been justified in calling cannibalism. There can be little doubt, however, that the reaction to Berengar revealed both an appetite for aggressively realistic accounts of eucharistic presence and a sense that the best way to safeguard such accounts was to downplay the sacrament's symbolic connotations.

Unsurprisingly, this drift toward a rather extreme form of sacramental realism prompted an equally extreme anti-realist backlash in some quarters of the Protestant Reformation. Among the major Reformers, the most thoroughgoing rejection of Christ's bodily presence in the eucharist probably belongs to the Swiss theologian Huldrych Zwingli. In his polemical tract *On the Lord's Supper* (1525), Zwingli premises a memorialist or "symbolic" account of the Lord's supper on the observation that because a sacrament is "a sign and nothing more," and because "the sign and the thing signified cannot be one and the same," it follows that "the sacrament of the body of Christ cannot be the body itself."[35] Zwingli accepts this view of signs for reasons which, on their face, look intuitively plausible. Appealing to John 16.5–11, he argues that if Christ "has left the world" and now sits at the right hand of the Father, "the body and blood of Christ cannot be present in the sacrament."[36] The argument is simple and plausible: because the creed demands that Christ be seated at the right hand of the Father, and because bodies cannot simultaneously occupy multiple spatial locations, it follows as a matter of straightforward logical deduction that Christ cannot be present in the sacrament.

Everything depends, however, upon what Zwingli means by "present in the sacrament." And what he must mean, of course, is that Christ cannot be *locally* present, where being "locally present" means being present as I am present in my study, as you are present wherever you are, as bodies are present in a place. The problem is that, with a few minor exceptions, Zwingli would get no real

---

[34] Available in Denzinger, ed., *Enchiridion symbolorum et definitionum*, 690: "sensualiter, non solum in sacramento, sed in veritate, manibus sacerdotum tractari et frangi et fidelium dentibus atteri." The translation is mine.

[35] Zwingli, *On the Lord's Supper*, 188.

[36] Zwingli, *On the Lord's Supper*, 214–15.

objection from Catholics on this point. In his *Mysterium Fidei* (1965), for instance, Pope Paul VI writes that while Christ is indeed "bodily present" in the eucharist, he is not present "in the way bodies are present in a place [*in loco*]."[37] Nor is this a twentieth-century innovation. In the *Breviloquium*, Bonaventure argues that Christ is present in the eucharist species "totally" (*totaliter*) but not "circumscribably" (*circumscriptibiliter*);[38] and Aquinas insists in various places that Christ is neither present in the eucharist "as in place" nor comes to be present in the eucharist "by local motion" (*per motum locale*). In fact, in his commentary on the *Sentences*, Aquinas strikes an audibly Zwinglian tone when he argues that because a body is said to be "in a place [*in loco*] when its spatial dimensions are commensurate with the dimensions of the place," it follows that Christ "is present in only one place, namely, heaven."[39] The same line of thought reappears near the end of the *Summa*, where Aquinas notes that Christ cannot be present in the eucharist "as in a place" (*sicut in loco*) since this would imply that he "ceased to be present in heaven."[40] At this point, however, the agreement with Zwingli ends. Zwingli, on the one hand, thinks (a) that Christ is present in the eucharist as a sign, (b) that presence as sign implies local absence, and (c) that local absence excludes bodily presence. Aquinas accepts the inference from (a) to (b) but rejects the inference from (b) to (c). He agrees, in other words, that presence as sign implies local absence, but he sees no reason to suppose that local absence should exclude bodily presence.

Aquinas' way of putting this point is to say that Christ is present in the eucharist not *sicut in loco* but *sicut in sacramento*—not "locally" but "sacramentally."[41] This only deepens the mystery, however, since it means that we shall have to find a sense for "bodily presence" that is consistent with "local absence." Near the end of the *Summa*, Aquinas hints at an answer. There he argues that the eucharist has a "threefold significance." In one sense, it refers to the past as the memorial of Christ's passion and death. In another sense, it refers to the present and signifies the *unitas* or *communio* of the pilgrim church. In yet a third sense it refers to the future insofar as it foreshadows or prefigures the *fruitio Dei*: the full revelation of Christ's presence in the eschaton.[42] The key point to notice here is that for Aquinas eucharistic

---

[37] Paul VI, *Mysterium Fidei*, para. 36. Available online at www.vatican.va.

[38] Bonaventure, *Breviloquium*, VI, 9, in *Opera omnia*, vol. 5, 273.

[39] Aquinas, *De sententiis*, lib. 4 d. 10 q. 1 a. 1 ad 5.

[40] Aquinas, *Summa theologiae*, 3a, q. 75, a. 2, ad 2.

[41] Aquinas, *Summa theologiae*, 3a, q. 75, a. 1, ad 3. Although I begin these reflections on eucharistic presence with Aquinas, I do not mean to suggest that he would accept everything I shall say.

[42] Aquinas, *Summa theologiae*, 3a, q. 75, a. 1.

presence is always conditioned by a double absence: if Christ is indeed "really present" on the altar, he is present neither as he was to the disciples 2,000 years ago, nor as he will be in the eschatological kingdom. It is precisely this double absence, moreover, that constitutes the eucharist *as* a sacrament. Sacraments, after all, exist only in what Denys Turner has called the "times between": that is, in the historical interval that separates the resurrection from the *parousia*.[43] By its very nature, then, the eucharistic sign is always caught up in a kind of two-sided temporal ecstasy. As a memorial, on the one hand, it looks back to Christ's death and resurrection as past events. And yet, as St Paul makes clear, because we are to celebrate the memorial of Christ's death "until he comes" (1 Cor. 11.26), the memorial itself is not only a recollection of the past but also a pledge of the future—a promise of the eschatological kingdom that was inaugurated by the resurrection but which still awaits its final consummation in the eschaton. Further, insofar as the eucharist points ahead to an eschatological reality that has been announced but not fulfilled, what it enacts is not the kingdom itself but the "not yet" of the kingdom, not the future itself but the *future as anticipated*. Put another way, if the eucharist indeed makes Christ bodily present to us, it does so only to the extent that a resurrected and glorified kingdom-body can be made present to unresurrected, fallen bodies. We do not know what that "extent" is, of course, since we no more know how raised bodies are related to unraised bodies than we know how to measure the difference between the present and the kingdom (cf. 1 Cor. 2.9). What we must say, however, is that because the kingdom is not yet fully at hand, Christ's real presence in the eucharist is always and necessarily interpenetrated by a "real absence."[44] And yet this absence is not Zwinglian absence, not absence as opposed to presence. Nor is it simply absence as the future is absent from the present because separated from it by a definite temporal interval. Rather, as in the case of my wife's letter, it is absence as anticipation and promise, absence as the partial and fragmentary advent of an eschatological future that still awaits its full and final realization. Or, to put the point another way, what the eucharist realizes, or "makes real," is the future kingdom, and the mode in which it makes the future kingdom present is the mode of absence. Like my wife's letter, moreover, it makes the kingdom present in this sense by constituting our present experience as so thoroughly eschatological, so thoroughly determined by its anticipation of God's future reign that, in the words of Jean-Luc Marion, the present itself "occurs entirely as this anticipation concretely lived."[45] Just as my wife's words have the effect of drawing the future into the present and thus of making her

---

[43] Turner, "Darkness of God," 152. The rest of this paragraph is deeply indebted to Turner's analysis of eucharistic presence.

[44] Turner, "Darkness of God," 157.

[45] Marion, *God Without Being*, 174.

present to me even under conditions of local absence, so the eucharistic sign likewise draws the eschatological future into the present and thus makes Christ present to us as both a present absence and the absence of a presence to come.

Scripture and Real Presence

I do not know whether the account of sacramental presence sketched in the previous section will persuade all (or any) Baptists, but if it is convincing even in general outline, it may open up a way of navigating some of the impasses that often attend ecumenical discussions of the eucharist. On the one hand, it suggests that certain "realistic" accounts of eucharistic presence err not by making Christ too present, but by putting the presence in the wrong place—that is, by encouraging us to imagine that bodily presence depends upon a kind of reified, localizing presence rather than upon the eucharist's mysterious power to draw the absent and future kingdom into the midst of the community of believers. And, conversely, it suggests that certain "merely symbolic" approaches to the eucharist err not by making Christ too absent but by putting the absence in the wrong place—that is, by encouraging us to see eucharistic absence as a function of the distinction between sign and reality rather than as a function of the difference between raised bodies and unraised bodies, between the present and the kingdom.

I mention these points only in passing, and I do not intend to pursue them further. What I would like to suggest in the final section of this essay is that this same eschatological conception of eucharistic presence may also provide a workable model of the sacramental character of scripture. Rather than pursue this argument in the abstract, however, I propose to look closely at a single New Testament passage that seems to hint at just such a model.

Matthew 8.5–13 tells the story of Jesus' encounter at Capernaum with a centurion whose servant "lies at home paralyzed, in great distress" (8.6; cf. Luke 7.1–10; John 4.43–54). Because this passage follows the Sermon on the Mount (Matt. 5–7) and introduces an extended set of healing narratives (Matt. 8–9), it seems clearly designed to highlight the continuity between Jesus's work as teacher and healer; and indeed it is precisely this relationship between the power of Christ's words and the power of his deeds that will frame the encounter as a whole. Initially at least, the accent falls squarely on the latter: Jesus no sooner hears the centurion's story than declares that he will "come and heal" his servant (ἐγώ ἐλθὼν θεραπεύσω αὐτόν, v. 7). These words set in motion a series of conceptual and linguistic leitmotivs that will prove crucial to the overall effect of the passage. Notice, in the first place, that the future tense θεραπεύσω ("I shall heal") lends the scene a mildly eschatological character and thus situates it within the broader "logic of promise" that Jürgen

Moltmann has identified as characteristic of scriptural rhetoric in general.[46] Second, and more critically, Jesus associates the fulfillment of this promise with his own spatial or local presence: only after "having come" (ἐλθὼν) will Christ heal the servant. At this, however, the centurion famously balks: "I am not worthy that you should come in under my roof, but only declare it by a word [μόνον εἰπὲ λόγῳ] and my servant will be healed [ἰαθήσεται]" (v. 8). The centurion's response works two important modifications on Christ's original offer. First, while the future-tense ἰαθήσεται ("will be healed") preserves the eschatological or promissory character of Christ's θεραπεύσω ("I will heal"), the shift from active (θεραπεύσω) to passive (ἰαθήσεται) voice installs a degree of distance between the healing and its cause (Christ). Second, and far more significantly, this shift in grammatical voice echoes the broader contours of the centurion's response, which effectively severs the link between the fulfilment of Christ's promise and his local or spatial presence. For the centurion, Christ need not come in person. He need only speak.

Unsurprisingly, the commentary tradition, or at least the premodern commentary tradition, made much of this response, especially the phrase μόνον εἰπὲ λόγῳ. Peter Chrysologus (c. 380–c. 450), for instance, the fifth-century bishop of Ravenna, takes the phrase as a reference to language's capacity to "do" or "create" (*virtus faciendi*), and proceeds on this basis to link the creative power of Christ's word to the act of creation itself.[47] John Chrysostom (c. 349–407) makes a similar point: "Do you not think," he asks in his sermon *In centurionem*, "that the one who says, 'Declare it only by a word', knows clearly that the heavens and all their power were established by the word of the Lord (λόγῳ κυρίου), and that by the word everything that exists is held together and governed?"[48] The sixteenth-century Carmelite theologian and commentator Johannes Maria Verratus (1496–1567) carries the point further still, associating the centurion's λόγῳ (*verbo* in Verratus' Latin) both with the *Verbum* through whom all things were made and with the *Verbum* who "was in the beginning with God."[49] Other commentators would develop a similar line of thought in a different but related direction. In his *Catena aurea* on Matthew 8, for instance, Aquinas cites Jerome to the effect that it is precisely the centurion's recognition of the "divinity hidden behind the covering of [Christ's] body" that prompts him both to reject the offer to visit the servant in person and to insist that Christ's "word" alone is sufficient.[50] Origen is even more explicit: "Come only in word," he writes,

---

[46] See Moltmann, *Experiences in Theology*, 87–113.

[47] Chrysologus, *Sermo XV*, in *Opera Omnia*, 234.

[48] Chysostom, *In centurionem* (*PG* 10:994).

[49] Verratus, *Homeliae*, 57.

[50] Aquinas, *Catena aurea in Matthaeum*, cap. 8, lect. 1. Cf. Paul the Deacon, *Homilia LIV: In dominica III post Epiphaniam* (*PG* 95:1193).

paraphrasing the centurion: "your word is your face; your presence is everywhere unfailing; your face is everywhere present."[51] In each of these cases, at least two points are worth noting. First, the commentators in question presume an intimate connection between two otherwise distinct realities: on the one hand, the *logoi* articulated by Christ in Capernaum sometime around AD 30 and recorded by Matthew sometime thereafter; and, on the other hand, the eternal Logos who was in the beginning with God and through whom all things came into being. Second, and more critically, each presumes that the eternal and omnipresent Logos inheres so thoroughly in the *logoi* of Jesus of Nazareth that the Logos himself is capable of operating in and through those *logoi* even in the absence of Christ's physical, human body. Or, to state the point in the language of my broader argument of this essay, each presumes that Christ's words have a kind of sacramental power, a capacity to make Christ present—really, efficaciously present—even under conditions of local absence.

It is within this context that I suggest we interpret the rest of the passage. After the centurion's initial demurral, an astonished Christ responds:

> "Truly I tell you, in no one in Israel have I found such faith. I tell you, many will come from east and west and will recline at table with Abraham and Isaac and Jacob in the kingdom of heaven, but the sons of the kingdom will be cast out into the darkness outside, where there will be weeping and gnashing of teeth." (Matt. 8.10–12.)

Here Jesus picks up the eschatological motif mentioned earlier by describing the future kingdom in terms reminiscent of the so-called "Messianic Banquet," the great eschatological meal described in Isaiah 25.6–8 and 53.13–14, among other places, in which the "Lord of hosts will make for all peoples a feast of rich food," "wipe away the tears from all faces," and "swallow up death forever" (Isa. 25.6–8).[52] For Christ, moreover, this banquet functions simultaneously as blessing and curse. Many, including faithful Gentiles like the centurion, will come and recline with Abraham, Isaac, and Jacob, while others, including the "sons of the kingdom," will be "cast out [ἐκβληθήσονται] into the darkness outside" (v. 12). Clearly Jesus means here to mark some sort of contrast between "faithful" Gentiles and "faithless" Israel, but because the precise relationship between these two groups is so vexed and controversial, and because nothing in my argument depends upon settling it, I do not wish to pursue the question further.[53] What I would like to point out, however, is

---

[51] Origen, *Homily* II, 5, in Klostermann and Benz, *Origenes Werke*, 252.

[52] For a helpful discussion see Pitre, "Jesus," 133–62 (see especially 141 n.32 for additional references).

[53] For a careful and illuminating discussion, see Pitre, "Jesus," 141–43 (with references).

that in his description of those who will be "cast out [ἐκβληθήσονται] into the darkness outside" (v. 12), the Gospel writer uses a form of the same verb (ἐκβάλλω) he had employed earlier to describe the centurion's servant (βέβληται παραλυτικός—"lies paralyzed," the perfect middle passive of βάλλω, v. 6). Strikingly, then, the servant's illness serves here as a kind of counterimage of the kingdom, a present sign of the future that awaits those who will be "cast out" (ἐκβληθήσονται) from the messianic banquet. It is, so to speak, an *anti-sacrament*, the sign of a kingdom lost. but if the servant's illness is indeed a foretaste of the future that awaits those excluded from the kingdom, the transition from "lies paralyzed" (βέβληται, v. 6) to "healed" (ἰάθη, v. 13) is precisely the opposite. It is a *sacrament* of the kingdom, a physical healing which, by reversing the "casting out" of v. 12, also points ahead to the eschatological healing of the messianic banquet itself.

Seen from this angle, then, the centurion's reference to the power of Christ's *logos* works in two different but complementary ways. First, because it proceeds from the divine Logos through whom all things were made, the word spoken by Christ on a dusty road in Capernaum in AD 30 transmits the real, efficacious, healing presence of the Son of God even under conditions of local absence. Second, and more importantly, the presence transmitted by Christ's word is also and at the same time the presence of the eschatological kingdom itself. This is not, of course, the kingdom as it will be in the future. It is, rather, the kingdom as pledge and promise, the kingdom as inaugurated and previewed in a physical healing that both symbolizes and pre-realizes the eschatological restoration of all things in Christ. It is in precisely this sense, moreover, that Christ's word to the centurion has a sacramental character. Like my wife's letter, and like the eucharist itself, the word spoken to the centurion in Capernaum not only makes a locally absent Christ sufficiently present to heal the ailing servant; it is also draws the "not yet" of the absent kingdom into the present and thus offers a dim, "pre-realized" intimation of the eschatological future that awaits those who "will recline with Abraham and Isaac and Jacob" in the full glory of God's presence at the banquet of the ages.

Conclusion

My goals in this essay were two. The first was to sketch what I have called an "eschatological" account of sacramental real presence. Although it is inspired by certain strands of Catholic eucharistic theology, I hope this account may prove useful to Baptists who, rightly or not, remain suspicious of some of the alleged extravagances of the Catholic sacramental system. To that end, I have scrupulously avoided both the language of transubstantiation and the attendant idea that Christ comes to be present in the eucharist when the bread and wine are "converted" into his body and blood. I have also attempted, albeit somewhat less scrupulously, to avoid the language of "bodily presence," though I am inclined to think that the picture of real presence sketched in section three and reprised in section four entails bodily presence as well. My second goal was to propose that this account of sacramental presence might provide a useful way of thinking about the sacramental character of scripture. Here the suggestion was that, like the eucharist itself, the scriptural *logoi*, as participations in the eternal Logos, have the effect of drawing the future eschatological kingdom into the midst of the community of believers. My reading of Matthew 8.5–13 is significant in this context not only because it strikes me as a paradigmatic scriptural case of the power of Christ's "word alone" to pre-realize the eschatological kingdom, but also because it offers us the opportunity to see ourselves reflected in the biblical narrative. As readers 2,000 years removed from Christ's local presence on earth, we are in a position significantly analogous to that of the servant himself. We are wounded, sick, sinful, and fallen, and so we are always in perpetual need of Christ's healing presence. And yet in these "times between," in the temporal middle that separates the ascension from the *parousia*, Christ is present to us only in the mode of absence. As I have insisted throughout this essay, however, "presence in the mode of absence" is not simple absence, not absence as godforsakenness. It is, rather, absence as pledge and promise, an absence that so thoroughly constitutes the present as an anticipation of the future that it makes that future present to us here and now. What produces this effect, moreover, is the Logos of God in its two primary manifestations this side of the general resurrection: the Logos spoken in the reading and proclamation of scripture, and the Logos consumed in the sacrament of the Lord's table. On this point, as on so many others, the Rite of the Roman Mass gets it exactly right. Near the end, just before receiving communion, the congregation recites the so-called Prayer of Humble Access: "Lord, I am not worthy that you should enter under my roof, but only say the word and my soul shall be healed." This modified version of the centurion's words to Christ gives voice to a beautiful and messy ambiguity that makes exactly the point I want to make. In one sense, the "word" in question is the word of Christ spoken in Capernaum nearly 2,000 years ago, and when we hear it spoken in the liturgy, we, like the servant himself, experience Christ's healing presence both as a present reality and as an anticipation of the absent and future kingdom made mysteriously available to us in advance of its arrival. In another sense, however, the "word" in question is the eucharist itself, the Logos of God which, as Saint Athanasius (296–373) puts it, "descends upon the bread and the cup" and "becomes Christ's body."[54] At this moment of highest dramatic and liturgical intensity, then, word and sacrament are bound together so indissolubly that the one is practically indistinguishable from the other. The word *is* sacrament, and the sacrament *is* word, and together they work to usher

---

[54] Athanasius, *Orations to the Baptized* (PG 26:1325): καταβαίνει ὁ λόγος εἰς τὸν ἄρτον καὶ τὸ ποτήριον, καὶ γίνεται αὐτοῦ σῶμα. The translation is mine.

us into the presence of the divine and eternal Logos in whom all things hold together and with whom we are invited to dwell *in saecula saeculorum*.

Abbreviations

PG   *Patrologia graeca*. Edited by J.-P. Migne. 162 vols. Paris, 1857–86.
PL   *Patrologia Latina*. Edited by J.-P. Migne. 217 vols. Paris, 1844–64.

Bibliography

Aquinas, Thomas. *Summa theologiae. Corpus Thomisticum*. http://www.corpusthomis ticum.org.
———. *Catena aurea in Matthaeum. Corpus Thomisticum*. http://www.corpusthomis ticum.org.
———. *Super Evangelium Sancti Ioannis lectura. Corpus Thomisticum*. http://www. corpusthomisticum.org
———. *Scriptum super sententiis. Corpus Thomisticum*. http://www.corpusthomis ticum.org.
Austin, J.L. *How to Do Things with Words*. Edited by J.O. Urmson. Oxford: Oxford University Press, 1962.
Beaton, Rhodora. *Embodied Word, Spoken Signs: Sacramentality and the Word in Rahner and Chauvet*. Minneapolis, MN: Fortress, 2014.
Boersma, Hans. *Nouvelle Théologie and Sacramental Ontology: A Return to Mystery*. Oxford: Oxford University Press, 2012.
Bonaventure. *Doctoris seraphici S. Bonaventurae Opera omnia*. 10 vols. Quaracchi: Collegium S. Bonaventurae, 1883–1901.
Burris, Virginia, Mark D. Jordan, and Karmen Mackendrick. *Seducing Augustine: Bodies, Desires, Confessions*. New York: Fordham University Press, 2010.
Chrysologus, Peter. *Sancti Petri Chrysologi Opera Omnia*. Petit-Montrouge: J.-P. Migne, 1846.
Constitutio dogmatica de divina revelatione: Dei verbum. Firenze: Vallecchi, 1969.
Crockett, William. *Eucharist: Symbol of Transformation*. Collegeville, MN: Liturgical, 1999.
Cross, Anthony R., and Philip E. Thompson, eds. *Baptist Sacramentalism*. Eugene, OR: Wipf & Stock, 2006.
———, eds. *Baptist Sacramentalism 2*. Eugene, OR: Wipf & Stock, 2009.
Crouzel, Henri. *Origen*. Translated by A.S. Worrall. Edinburgh: T. & T. Clark, 1989.
Dante. *The Divine Comedy of Dante Alighieri*. Volume 3. *Paradiso*. Edited and translated by Robert M. Durling and Ronald L. Martinez. Oxford: Oxford University Press, 2011.

Denzinger, Heinrich, ed. *Enchiridion symbolorum et definitionum quae de rebus fidei et morum a conciliis oecumenicis summis pontificibus.* Rome: Fridericus Pustet, 1909.

Forrester, Duncan, Ian McDonald, and Gian Tellini. *Encounter with God: An Introduction to Christian Worship and Practice.* 2nd ed. London: T. & T. Clark, 1996.

Genig, Joshua. *Viva Vox: Rediscovering the Sacramentality of the Word through the Annunciation.* Minneapolis, MN: Fortress, 2015.

Hanson, R.P.C. *Allegory and Event: A Study of the Sources and Significance of Origen's Interpretation of Scripture.* Louisville, KY: Westminster John Knox, 2003.

Harmon, Stephen R. "The Sacramentality of the Word in Gregory of Nyssa Catechetical Orations: Implications for a Baptist Sacramental Theology." In *Baptist Sacramentalism 2*, edited by Cross and Thompson, 239–53.

Healy, Mary. "Inspiration and Incarnation: The Christological Analogy and the Hermeneutics of Faith." *Letter & Spirit* 2 (2006) 27–41.

Henry, Carl F.H. *God, Revelation, and Authority*: Vol. 3. Waco, TX: Word, 1979.

Hobbs, Herschel H. *The Baptist Faith and Message.* Nashville, TN: Convention, 1971.

Ignatius of Antioch. *To the Philadelphians.* In *The Apostolic Fathers*, 3rd ed., edited and translated by Michael W. Holmes. Grand Rapids: Baker, 2008.

de Lubac, Henri. *Corpus mysticum: l'eucharistie et l'Église au moyen âge.* Paris: Aubier, 1949.

———. *History and Spirit: The Understanding of Scripture according to Origen.* Translated by Anne Englund Nash. San Francisco: Ignatius, 2007.

Luther, Martin. *The Adoration of the Sacrament.* In *Luther's Works*: Vol. 36, edited by Helmut Lehmann and Jaroslav Pelikan, 275–305. Saint Louis, MO: Concordia, 1955.

Mackey, Louis. *Peregrinations of the Word: Essays in Medieval Philosophy.* Ann Arbor, MI: University of Michigan Press 2000.

Magrassi, Mariano. *Praying the Bible: An Introduction to Lectio Divina.* Collegeville, MN: Liturgical, 1998.

Marion, Jean-Luc. *God Without Being: hors-texte.* Translated by Thomas A. Carlson. Chicago: University of Chicago Press, 1991.

McGrath, Alister. *The Twilight of Atheism: The Rise and Fall of Disbelief in the Modern World.* New York: Doubleday, 2008.

Moltmann, Jürgen. *Experiences in Theology: Ways and Forms of Christian Theology.* Translated by Margaret Kohl. Minneapolis, MN: Fortress, 2000.

Naidu, Ashish. *Transformed in Christ: Christology and the Christian Life in John Chrysostom.* Eugene, OR: Pickwick, 2012.

Origen. *Origenes Werke, Zwölfter Band: Matthäuserklärung III: Fragmente und Indices, Erste Hälfte.* Edited by Erich Klostermann and Ernst Benz. Leipzig: J.C. Hinrichs Verlag, 1941.

———. *Commentarium in evangelium. in Matthaei*. In *Die griechischen christlichen Schriftsteller der ersten drei Jahrhunderte*, 40.1. Leipzig: Hinrichs, 1935.

———. *Philocalia*. Edited by J.A. Robinson. Cambridge: Cambridge University Press, 1893.

———. *Sur la Pâque*. Edited by Octave Guéraud Octave and Pierre Nautin. Paris: Beauchesne, 1979.

Osborne, Kenan B. *Christian Sacraments in a Postmodern World: A Theology for the Third Millennium*. New York: Paulist, 1999.

Paul VI. *On the Holy Eucharist: Mysterium Fidei*. Washington, DC: National Catholic Welfare Conference, 1965.

Pius XII. *Divino afflante Spiritu: Encyclical Letter of Pope Pius XII on Promotion of Biblical Studies*. Washington, DC: National Catholic Welfare Conference, 1943.

Pitre, Brant Pitre. "Jesus, the Messianic Banquet, and the Kingdom of God." *Letter & Spirit* 5 (2009) 133–62.

Rempel, John D. "Anabaptist Theologies of the Eucharist." In *A Companion to the Eucharist in the Reformation*, edited by Lee Wandel and E.J. Brill, 115–38. Boston: Brill, 2014.

Schillebeeckx, Edward. *Christ the Sacrament of the Encounter with God*. New York: Rowan and Littlefield, 1963.

Spurgeon, Charles. "Feeding on the Word." *The Metropolitan Tabernacle Pulpit* 38 (1890) 493–501. London: Passmore and Alabaster, 1855–1917.

———. "The Word a Sword." In *Classic Sermons on the Word of God*, edited by Warren W. Wiersbe, 39–58. Grand Rapids: Kregel, 1997.

Turner, Denys Turner. "The Darkness of God and the Light of Christ: Negative Theology and Eucharistic Presence." *Modern Theology* 15 (1999) 144–58.

Verratus, Johannes Maria. *Homeliae, sive commentaria, in omnia quae ab Adventu Domini usque ad dominicam Resurrectionis legi solent Evangelia*. Venice: s.n., 1571.

Vorgrimler, Herbert. *Sacramental Theology*. Translated by Linda M. Maloney. Collegeville, MN: Liturgical, 1992.

Weinrich, William C. "Patristic Exegesis as Ecclesial and Sacramental." *Concordia Theological Quarterly* 64 (2000) 21–38.

Young, Edward J. *Thy Word Is Truth: Some Thoughts on Biblical Inspiration*. Grand Rapids: Eerdmans, 1957.

Zwingli, Huldrych. *On the Lord's Supper*. In *Zwingli and Bullinger*, edited by G.W. Bromiley, 185–238. London: SCM, 1953.

CHAPTER 3

Some Fallacies of Baptist Anti-Sacramentalism

Stanley K. Fowler

In the twentieth century, Baptists in Great Britain reformulated their baptismal theology in a sacramental direction, and more recently this move has had some effect in North America. The British trend began a century ago in the work of H. Wheeler Robinson, was continued by writers like A.C. Underwood and Robert Walton, and became a focus of public discussion with the publication of *Christian Baptism* in 1959. That book was a multi-author publication, and two of those authors subsequently authored major works of their own: R.E.O. White with his *The Biblical Doctrine of Initiation* in 1960, and G.R. Beasley-Murray with his magisterial *Baptism in the New Testament* in 1962. By the time Beasley-Murray published his smaller book *Baptism Today and Tomorrow* in 1966, the British reformulation was essentially fully developed, although later publications reflected on that theme and pondered its implications. The whole process was described by Anthony R. Cross in his *Baptism and the Baptists* (2000), and the conclusions were given a fresh and sustained defense by Cross in his *Recovering the Evangelical Sacrament* (2013).

Although this movement has never been as prominent in North America, it has been growing in significance. The transatlantic nature of the movement is displayed in two books published in the Paternoster Studies in Baptist History and Thought series, *Baptist Sacramentalism* (2003) and *Baptist Sacramentalism 2* (2008), and this volume continues that process. North American contributors to the previous volumes include Philip E. Thompson, Clark H. Pinnock, Stanley J. Grenz, Steven R. Harmon, Timothy George, Barry Harvey, Stanley E. Porter, Michael A.G. Haykin, Curtis W. Freeman, and Elizabeth Newman. Most of these North Americans can be located within what is often called a "moderate" tradition, but there are evidences of this theology among Baptists who are self-consciously conservative evangelical in orientation. In the list above, both Timothy George and Michael Haykin would be in this category along with me, and they are not alone. Brandon C. Jones has articulated a sacramental theology of baptism with a focus on covenant theology in his *Waters of Promise* (2012), recognizing the influence of the British tradition, but also arguing that Cross and others have overstated the efficacy of baptism. In a similar way, the Center for Baptist Renewal, founded by Lucas Stamps and Matthew Emerson, exists in part to call evangelical Baptists to affirm a catholicity that understands baptism and the Lord's supper as sacramental means of grace, although the Center's foundational documents explicitly reject the British tradition as a paradigm.[1]

The Paternoster volumes explore sacramentality as a more comprehensive concept, but my focus in this study (as also in my contributions to the previous volumes) is specifically on baptism. A sacramental theology of baptism has solid roots in early Baptist thought, as I have argued in my book *More Than a Symbol* (2002) and will argue again later in this study, but for various reasons that tradition largely disappeared, so that a Baptist-sacramental view of baptism is widely thought to be wrong-headed or worse, especially in North America. It is not hard to find negative comments in passing about such a concept, but it is more difficult to find a serious and sustained engagement with the relevant literature. That changed, however, in 2011 when an English Baptist, David H.J. Gay, published his book, *Baptist Sacramentalism: A Warning to Baptists*. In a unique way this book captures and articulates with passion the typical Baptist reasons for rejecting a sacramental understanding of baptism, so this study will be essentially a response to Gay's arguments, with some references to other Baptist critics. As it happens, I am a recurring target of Gay's criticisms, and that will explain the personal nature of this study and the frequent use of first-person singular pronouns.

What I propose to show here is that Baptist anti-sacramental arguments are invalid, often displaying a misunderstanding of the case for sacramentalism, making false assumptions about the meaning and history of sacramentalism, and drawing false inferences from the exegetical and theological aspects of baptismal sacramentalism. I turn now to the identification of the most common fallacies of this anti-sacramentalism as displayed in Gay's book.

Fallacy #1: "Ordinance" and "sacrament" are mutually exclusive terms

In North America at least, one frequently hears it said that, "Baptism is an ordinance, not a sacrament." If such assertions are repeated often enough, they come to be seen as self-evident, but constant repetition does not make an assertion true, and this one deserves close scrutiny. This idea is clearly important for Gay, in that the heading for a major section in his introductory chapter is, "Baptism is an ordinance, not a sacrament."[2] He develops this idea in this way:

> . . . this question of "ordinances" brings us to the heart of the issue. Ordinances. Here we come to a great divide. It is not merely a question of words. I, and

---

[1] http://www.centerforbaptistrenewal.com/bibliography. See the annotation for my book, *More Than a Symbol*.

[2] Gay, *Sacramentalism*, 47.

> people like me, take baptism and the Lord's supper as Christ's two ordinances, symbolic acts which Christ commanded his people to do in order to represent and demonstrate, by the physical, the spiritual realities they have already experienced. Sacramentalists, on the other hand, claim that God is at work in these two ordinances, actually conveying effective grace to those undertaking the acts.[3]

At some points Gay describes "ordinance" as simply equivalent to "command,"[4] which would extend the concept so broadly as to negate any special reference to the ritual signs of the gospel, but for present purposes I will accept his more specific definition above, noting that for him the crucial question is (rightly) whether the sign of baptism leads in some sense to the thing signified or whether it points only backward to a prior experience of the spiritual reality.

One challenge we face in this discussion is the fact that neither "ordinance" nor "sacrament" is an explicitly biblical term describing a category of sacred rituals. So, in one sense, this is a matter of definition of terms, and the debate at hand is a diversion from the conceptual issue, but the debate about terminology must be addressed, because it continually arises in Baptist life. I am encouraged to note that some contemporary Baptist theologians recognize the fallacy of this focus on terminology, for example, John Hammett in his influential textbook, *Biblical Foundations for Baptist Churches*.[5] Nevertheless, Gay's confident dismissal of sacramental terminology is still a recurring theme that demands an answer. We are talking here about theological terms that have acquired meaning over time, so a bit of history may be helpful.

In early Baptist usage, both "ordinance" and "sacrament" were used to describe baptism, but they were not simply synonyms. The term "ordinance" was often used to describe actions in addition to baptism and the Lord's supper that were ordained by Christ for spiritual benefit. For example, the catechism prepared to be used in conjunction with the *Second London Confession* referred to "his Ordinances, especially the Word, Baptism, the Lord's Supper, and Prayer."[6] When the catechism uses the term "especially" it indicates that the category of "ordinances" is actually broader than the four mentioned above, perhaps alluding to those Baptists who considered the laying on of hands after baptism as an ordinance (as expressed, for example, in the *Standard Confession* of General Baptists in 1660).[7] Contemporary Baptists often argue that one Baptist distinctive is an affirmation of only two

---

[3] Gay, *Sacramentalism*, 48.

[4] E.g., Gay, *Sacramentalism*, 47.

[5] Hammett, *Biblical Foundations*, 294–96.

[6] Anon., *Baptist Catechism*, 26.

[7] Lumpkin, ed., *Confessions*, 220–35.

ordinances, but that use of terms is obviously a later development. The earlier Baptist usage understood "ordinance" as the broader term and "sacrament" as the narrower term describing baptism and the Lord's supper in particular. Thus, early Baptist writers could speak of "word and Sacrament"[8] to describe the proclamation of the gospel in verbal and ritual modes, and the authors of confessions that referred to baptism as an ordinance could also describe it as "this holy Sacrament."[9]

This evidence shows that when early Baptists used the term "ordinance" to describe baptism, there was no intention to say that baptism was not a sacramental means of grace. To refer to the *Baptist Catechism* again, the ordinances are described as "the outward means whereby Christ communicates to us the benefits of redemption . . . all which means are made effectual to the elect, through faith, for salvation."[10] Although the term "sacrament" is absent from that question and answer in the *Catechism*, it is clear that the *Catechism* affirms that in some sense the experience of salvation is mediated through baptism, which is to say, that baptism is sacramental. The debate about the relationship between baptism and the experience of saving union with Christ cannot be settled by a simplistic appeal to terminology.

Fallacy #2: A sacramental view of baptism implies baptismal regeneration (in an unacceptable sense)

It is, of course, true that notable forms of sacramental theology do affirm baptismal regeneration without apology, the Roman Catholic tradition in an *ex opere operato* form[11] and the Lutheran tradition in a form that grounds the efficacy in a meeting of baptism and faith,[12] however difficult it may be to link that to infant baptism. It is also not difficult to see how this can be grounded in biblical language, given that both John 3.5 and Titus 3.5 use the image of water in connection with regeneration, and Acts 2.38 envisions the gift of the Spirit who gives new life as the effect of baptism. David Gay argues that if John 3.5 and Titus 3.5 do in fact refer to water-baptism, then baptismal regeneration is true, and Baptist sacramentalists ought to admit that.[13] For Gay, and most Baptists (certainly in North America), that would be perhaps

---

[8] Lawrence, *Of Baptism*, 47.

[9] Keach, *Gold Refin'd*, 78.

[10] Anon., *Baptist Catechism*, 26.

[11] Anon., *Catechism of the Catholic Church*, 1127–28.

[12] *Augsburg Confession*, IX, and Martin Luther, *Small Catechism*, both in Schaff and Schaff, eds, *Creeds of Christendom, passim*.

[13] Gay, *Sacramentalism*, 191, 206.

the most damning thing that could be said about a sacramental theology of baptism. but there is much more to be said.

To say that baptism is sacramental is to say that in some sense the sign leads to the thing signified, which implies that in some sense baptism leads to regeneration, but that sense is defined in diverse ways in the various Christian traditions. Most Baptist sacramentalists have been understandably nervous about an unqualified affirmation of baptismal regeneration, due to the typically pejorative way in which the term is used by their fellow Baptists, but some have pushed back by asserting that the concept is both biblical and evangelical. Two chapters in *Baptist Sacramentalism 2* fall into this latter category. Anthony R. Cross argues that the concept is deeply rooted in both scripture and the history of Christian thought (including the Baptist tradition), and so it should be reclaimed without embarrassment.[14] Paul Fiddes goes one step further and argues that much of the Baptist rhetoric about the Catholic phrase *ex opere operato* ("by the work done") is overstated and betrays a misunderstanding of the Catholic concept.[15] Fiddes' chapter rightly calls Baptists to understand what Catholics mean and do not mean by the phrase in question, but his argument assumes more than defends the link between baptism and regeneration, and it is, therefore, not directly relevant for my present concern.

Cross' argument, though, is especially relevant as a response to Gay's criticism, because it shares Gay's concern for both the biblical text and Baptist identity. The argument works backward, showing that the connection between baptism and spiritual rebirth has been present in the Baptist tradition, then showing the roots of that in history from Justin Martyr to John Calvin, then showing its biblical roots. Baptist examples include Thomas Grantham, Benjamin Keach, and William Mitchill (later Mitchell) from the seventeenth century, Baptist W. Noel from the nineteenth century, and Neville Clark, R.E.O. White, Stephen Winward, and Johannes Schneider from the twentieth century.[16] Given the significance of Beasley-Murray's work, it is somewhat surprising to see that he is omitted from this list, but that may be strategically effective. Gay and others would not deny that Beasley-Murray belongs in this list—in fact, Gay asserts that and claims it as a reason to reject his baptismal theology. What is crucial is to show that Beasley-Murray is exceptional only in the sense that he is an exceptionally articulate and convincing proponent of a view with strong roots in the Baptist tradition. An early proponent like Benjamin Keach referred to baptism as the

---

[14] Cross, "Baptismal Regeneration: Rehabilitating a Lost Dimension of New Testament Baptism," in *Baptist Sacramentalism 2*, 149–74. See also his development of his argument in *Recovering the Evangelical Sacrament*, 194–213.

[15] Fiddes, "*Ex Opere Operato*."

[16] Cross, "Baptismal Regeneration," 154–59.

"Sacrament of Regeneration,"[17] with appropriate clarification, which should make clear that connecting the words "baptism" and "regeneration" is *not* alien to Baptist theology.

At the heart of Cross' argument in his many articles and books is that baptism in biblical terms is conversion-baptism or faith-baptism, and it is the failure to grasp this that underlies the excessively negative response to the idea of baptismal regeneration. On the one hand, pedobaptists affirm regeneration in the case of baptized infants, thus affirming a divine action in the ritual itself. but on the other hand, anti-sacramental Baptists separate baptism from conversion, treating it as simply a backward-looking symbol of a conversion validated by other means, so that in that construct regeneration via baptism would be a divine action through the ritual itself disconnected from response to the gospel. If baptism is understood as an integral part of conversion, that is, the formal and embodied way in which the repentant person says yes to the gospel and confesses faith in Christ, then to say that spiritual rebirth normatively comes through baptism is essentially to say that it comes through faith. In the experience of Baptists, baptism has often been disconnected from conversion by months or even years, and while that is evidence that regeneration can and does occur apart from baptism, that should be considered an anomaly and not the biblical-theological norm.

In Cross' survey of the history of Christian thought on baptismal regeneration, he claims Calvin as an example of the idea that he is defending,[18] and that may provide a useful clarification that avoids some of the negative connotations of "baptismal regeneration." What I mean is that the Baptist idea is very much like the Reformed concept of baptism as a sacramental seal or a moderately stated form of Stone-Campbell theology,[19] that is, baptism as a means that God uses to confirm salvific union with Christ at the level of conscious experience. Viewed that way, baptism normatively conveys the assurance of regeneration rather than regeneration *per se*. What is crucial to the sacramental view of this baptism is that it conveys the assurance of present entrance into the benefits of Christ, not an assurance that the benefits were entered into at some point in the past. This can be and has been argued in the context of various interpretive approaches to John 3.5 and Titus 3.5, and it should be noted that some Baptists understand at least Titus 3.5 as an allusion to baptism while expressing misgivings about the term sacrament. Exhibit A here would be Thomas Schreiner's treatment of the text in his

---

[17] Keach, *Gold Refin'd*, 129.

[18] Cross, "Baptismal Regeneration," 163–65.

[19] As found, e.g., in John Mark Hicks, *Enter the Water, Come to the Table*, and, with Greg Taylor, *Down in the River to Pray*. Hicks describes his view as "Calvinian." Cf. Fowler, "Baptists and Churches of Christ."

chapter in the book, *Believer's Baptism*.[20] I suggest that this is just one example of several authors in that fine book who interpret baptism in a way that is conceptually sacramental even though they reject the term.[21]

When reading Baptist attacks on baptismal regeneration, it is crucial to note what exactly is being attacked. Normally what is being rejected is the idea that in baptism regeneration occurs apart from faith (as in infant baptism) and/or the idea that baptism is absolutely necessary for regeneration/forgiveness/salvation (as in some streams of Stone-Campbell theology). Many anti-sacramental Baptists look to Charles Haddon Spurgeon as an exemplar of Baptist identity, and they point to his famous sermon of 1864, "Baptismal Regeneration," as evidence for their view. There is no question about Spurgeon's rejection of the term "baptismal regeneration," but it needs to be noted that his critical focus is on the *Prayer Book* rubric for infant baptism, and his illustrations all relate to pedobaptism. When he does talk about the baptism of believers, he admits the following:

> Brethren, the baptism here meant is a baptism connected with faith, and to this baptism I will admit there is very much ascribed in Scripture. Into that question I am not going; but I do find some very remarkable passages in which baptism is spoken of very strongly ... Used by faith, had God commanded it, miracles might be wrought, but without faith or even consciousness, as in the case of babies, how can spiritual benefit be connected necessarily with the sprinkling of water?[22]

It should be noted that the announced text for his sermon is Mark 16.15–16, which includes the statement, "He who believes and is baptized will be saved," giving Spurgeon the opportunity to explain the sense in which baptism points forward to salvation in some sense. Unfortunately for our present purposes, he resolutely focused his sermon on the errors of the *Prayer Book* and did not pursue a positive statement of baptismal theology. In any case, it needs to be noted that his words are directed at errors associated with pedobaptism, not at the idea of faith-baptism espoused by Baptist sacramentalists.[23]

With regard to the second concern, the idea that salvation is impossible apart from baptism, those who are the targets of Gay's criticism have made it perfectly clear that they do not affirm the idea that he rejects. As Beasley-

---

[20] Schreiner, "Baptism in the Epistles," 85.

[21] I am thinking especially of the chapters by Robert Stein, Jonathan Rainbow, and Ardel Caneday in addition to Schreiner. Cross notes this also, "Baptismal Regeneration," 173–74.

[22] Spurgeon, "Baptismal Regeneration," 318, 326.

[23] See Fowler, *More Than a Symbol*, 79–83; Grass and Randall, "Spurgeon on the Sacraments"; and Morden, "C.H. Spurgeon and Baptism," especially "Part 1."

Murray said decades ago, we are trying to think clearly about baptism as
scripture describes it, not baptism as it is practiced in the average Baptist
church. So, if asked whether salvation can occur apart from baptism, the
answer is emphatically positive, because the freedom of God's grace is not
thwarted by our baptismal confusion. but to ask that question is to ask the
wrong question. We ought not be asking how we can dispense with baptism,
but rather how God intends baptism to function for our benefit, and if we ask
that question, we will take the first step toward the baptismal reform that will
allow us to connect the biblical picture of baptism with our experience.[24]

Is it fair to say that Baptist sacramentalists see a connection between
baptism and regeneration? Yes, of course, but not in the traditional Roman
Catholic sense or any other sense in which baptism is powerful *in itself*. It is
the Holy Spirit who regenerates, not baptism and not faith, both of which are
signs accompanying regeneration, faith as necessary and baptism as relatively
necessary.

Fallacy #3: A sacramental view of baptism denies justification by grace alone through faith alone

This assertion makes Baptist sacramentalism not only anti-Baptist but also
anti-Protestant, at least implicitly a denial of two *solas* of the Reformation.
This argument is implicit, I think, in Gay's book, but he does not tend to use
the language of justification. However, this argument is used by Brandon
Jones in his critique of Cross' baptismal theology specifically. Jones develops a
case for what he calls covenantal sacramentalism, which he distinguishes from
faith-baptism as described by Cross. Jones writes,

> There are roughly two understandings of baptism's meaning among
> sacramentalists. One view, shared by Cross and others, holds to faith-baptism, in
> which baptism (understood as one's expression of faith) is rightly part of the
> conversion process as a proper response to the gospel. The Spirit normatively
> conveys some of Christ's benefits, namely remission of sins and the gift of the
> Spirit, to the believer through baptism. Another view, shared by Fowler and
> covenantal sacramentalists, holds to a different understanding of baptism's
> meaning, in which the Spirit normatively confirms one's consciousness of
> salvation (including remission of sins and the gift of the Spirit) through baptism,
> but it is not part of God's justifying work.[25]

As I have indicated above, I share Cross' view that faith and baptism are
conjoined in biblical thought in a way that forbids any temporal division

---

[24] See Beasley-Murray's articulation of this relative-but-not absolute necessity in
Baptism, 296–305. See also Fowler, *Rethinking Baptism*, 34–35.

[25] Jones, *Waters of Promise*, 144.

between the two, so that the benefits promised to faith and the benefits promised to baptism are the same benefits. But both Cross and I agree that in common, though anomalous, practice the two are often divided in a way that denies the biblical paradigm. We are both arguing for baptismal reform that seeks to rehabilitate the biblical paradigm, and, if that is achieved, then the temporal distinction between the fact of salvation and the knowledge of salvation is effectively nullified. Therefore, I am not convinced that Cross and I are offering two different varieties of sacramentalism. I do not have space here to engage Jones' covenantal proposal in detail, but I suggest that his construct is not ultimately distinct from that of Cross and myself. Jones interprets baptism as the normative means of initiation into the new covenant,[26] but at the heart of the new covenant (Jer. 31.31–34) is the promise of a full and final forgiveness of sins, which is the essence of justification. If baptism initiates the baptizand into that covenant, then baptism in some sense conveys justification.

I conclude, then, that this criticism is easy to understand, but it is in fact off target. Superficially it seems to be a cogent argument against the idea that the benefits of union with Christ, including justification, are conveyed through baptism. If we are justified by faith alone, then how can we coherently speak of the forgiveness of sins that is inherent in justification as something sought by baptism? Does that not make justification a matter of faith plus baptism, not faith alone? but when we press a bit further, the argument is not so compelling. Does faith alone imply that repentance is not necessary? The two are related, but not simply equivalent. When Paul says that entrance into salvation comes through calling on the name of the Lord, does that add an action to the attitude of faith, thus denying *sola fide*? The act of turning to Christ requires more than one term to capture its full essence, and that means that we need to think carefully about what we mean by "faith alone."

We need to understand that Paul's argument in Romans and Galatians is very much about faith versus a wrong way of thinking about works of the law, one might say, about Christ versus misuse of Torah. Nowhere does Paul set faith over against repentance or baptism, as if they were somehow meritorious works. In fact, the culmination of his argument in Galatians 3 includes the affirmation that we are all sons of God through faith in verse 26, followed immediately by a description of that reality in terms of being baptized into Christ in verse 27. Baptism is simply not a "work" in Paul's sense as expressed in Galatians or Romans.[27] Indeed, the baptizand is in one sense passive and not "working" at all, allowing a divinely prescribed sacred ritual to be performed and accepting that as a marker of faith and acceptance by God.

---

[26] Jones develops this theme and compares it to what he calls ordinance-only and faith-baptism views in *Waters of Promise*, 132–46.

[27] Fowler, *Rethinking Baptism*, 32–34.

There is nothing meritorious about the act, even though the person chooses to accept the sacrament. Choosing to be baptized is no more a meritorious work than choosing to pray "the sinner's prayer." Further evidence that Paul understands saving faith as inclusive of more than the bare attitude is found in Galatians 5.6, where he indicates that the heart of the matter is "faith working through love."

Beyond this clarification of Paul's teaching about faith and works, it is useful to think about the history of the Reformation and the theology of the Reformers. Both the Lutheran and the Reformed streams of the Reformation affirmed that justification is bestowed *sola gratia* and *sola fide*, but both streams also affirmed that baptism is instrumental in the gracious application of Christ's work to believers. The idea that a sacramental view of baptism is contrary to the theology of the Reformation is at least historical nonsense.

Fallacy #4: A sacramental view of baptism logically and inevitably leads to an affirmation of infant baptism

Ironically, David Gay agrees with many pedobaptists when he argues that Baptist sacramentalists will inevitably follow the logic of their baptismal theology to the practice of infant baptism. Gay writes,

> Sacramental Baptists are not at all embarrassed to acknowledge that they can see it coming. Fowler: "Does genuine sacramentalism demand infant baptism?" Quite a thought, is it not? Even though, at present, they clearly feel the need to fend off infant baptism, sacramental Baptists have no illusions: "The conclusion [of many contemporary infant baptisers] is that if Baptists are going to take seriously the divine action in baptism, then they will have to surrender their opposition to the baptism of infants."
>
> Whatever else it is, that's clear enough. It is all very well for Fowler to say in reply that "Baptist sacramentalists are neither unbiblical nor incoherent in their assertion that the grace which is active in baptism is the grace of applied redemption, a grace which has effects that cannot realistically be posited of any but confessing believers", but this, I am sure, will come to be seen as whistling in the dark. Once sacramentalism is granted, comparison or contrast of "prevenient" (in the baptism of infants) and "applied" grace (in the baptism of believers) will fade away.[28]

I admit that I asked the question whether sacramentalism implies pedobaptism, but Gay ignores the fact that I spent the next eight pages answering "No" to the question.[29] Ultimately, the question revolves around the definition of the sense in which baptism is a means of grace. If, as I and others have argued, baptism is intended to mediate saving union with Christ at the

---

[28] Gay, *Sacramentalism*, 108.

[29] Fowler, *More Than a Symbol*, 211–19.

level of conscious experience, that is, to be a sacramental seal of conversion, then there is no coherent way to defend the baptism of infants.

At this point I do have to admit that some of the British Baptists who were part of the twentieth-century reformulation did argue that, although baptism ought not be applied to infants, an already accomplished infant baptism ought to be counted as a valid baptism. but it is crucial to note the reason given for this conclusion by Robert Walton, Alec Gilmore, and Neville Clark.[30] They each argued that to deny the validity of the infant baptism is to deny that the church doing the baptism is a true church, and this is an argument grounded in broader issues of ecclesiology, not in their theology of baptism developed elsewhere. Frankly, their reasoning is far from convincing, because it assumes that any action by a true church must be accepted as theologically appropriate. It must be emphasized that these writers argued for the acceptance of infant baptism as valid in spite of its irregularity, but they did not argue that infant baptism should be practiced. Late in his life, some three decades after publishing his *magnum opus*, Beasley-Murray expressed a tentative openness to the possibility of accepting infant baptism followed by confirmation as an alternative path of Christian initiation,[31] but this still involved no desire to practice infant baptism. Open membership, in which Baptist churches admit to membership people baptized as infants without requiring their rebaptism as believers, has been common in the British tradition, but essentially as an act of Christian charity and not as an affirmation of the validity of infant baptism.[32] Perhaps a case can be made for open membership by prioritizing Christian unity over baptismal regularity, but that would have to be argued in spite of Baptist sacramental theology and not because of it.

Fallacy #5: The biblical texts that refer to baptismal efficacy all refer to baptism in the Spirit, not baptism in water

This way to avoid the apparently sacramental texts occurs occasionally among Baptists, but it occupies a prominent place in the argument of David Gay. He identifies five texts that speak of baptismal efficacy: Romans 6.1–11; 1 Corinthians 12.13; Galatians 3.27; Colossians 2.11–12; and 1 Peter 3.21. He then describes three possible approaches to these texts: (1) the Baptist non-sacramental approach that interprets the texts as a figure of speech, understanding the baptism there as referring to water-baptism, but only as a symbol of a previously completed conversion; (2) the sacramental approach (Baptist or otherwise) that reads them straightforwardly and concludes that

---

[30] Walton, *Gathered Community*, 166; Clark, "Theology of Baptism," 326; Gilmore, *Baptism and Christian Unity*, 81.

[31] Beasley-Murray, "Problem."

[32] As affirmed by Beasley-Murray, *Baptism*, 391–92.

baptism conveys salvific union with Christ; and (3) the Baptist non-sacramental approach that reads these texts as references to baptism in the Spirit, not water. Building on John the Baptist's assertion that there are two baptisms, one in water and one in the Spirit, he chides his fellow Baptists (probably the majority of Baptists) who refuse to face up to the language of the texts and choose to explain away their obvious force, while avoiding the solution provided by the Baptist at the Jordan River.[33]

Gay argues that the parallel texts in Romans 6 and Colossians 2 do not say explicitly that baptism pictures anything, but rather that both texts are talking about spiritual reality in their language of burial and resurrection.[34] One of the ironies in the Baptist community is the tendency to say that Romans 6 may actually be a reference to Spirit-baptism because it predicates an efficacy inapplicable to water-baptism, but at the same time to employ the text as a proof for immersion as the mode of water-baptism. Gay would say, rightly, that we can't have it both ways. The Corinthian text is low hanging fruit, because there Paul speaks of baptism *en pneumati*, putting the Spirit in the grammatical location where water would be if that were the referent.[35] He argues that it is unthinkable that Paul would talk in Galatians about any ritual act that might rival faith as the means of union with Christ.[36] And finally, he points out that in 1 Peter 3, baptism is not a typological representation of some other reality, but is in fact the antitype of the Flood, thus reality and not ritual.[37]

1 Corinthians 12.13 is unique among these texts, in that it is the only one in which the Spirit is named, and Gay may well be right to limit Paul's point to the Spirit. In view of the connection between water-baptism and the gift of the Spirit as two parts of the normative conversion experience described in Acts, it is hard to imagine first-century readers not thinking of that connection here, but in fact only the Spirit is named.[38] but the other texts are not so easily explained away. In 1 Peter 3, it is, after all, the great Flood that is said to typologically point to baptism, and it is hard to see how the antitype could be dry. Furthermore, Peter feels the need to carefully explain that the heart of the matter is the inner attitude of the person baptized and not the washing of the physical body, a clarification that makes good sense if ritual baptism is in view.

---

[33] Gay, *Sacramentalism*, 166–69.

[34] Gay, *Sacramentalism*, 205–15 and 226–28.

[35] Gay, *Sacramentalism*, 217–23.

[36] Gay, *Sacramentalism*, 223–26.

[37] Gay, *Sacramentalism*, 234–37.

[38] See Fowler, *More Than a Symbol*, 172–74.

The Pauline statements about being baptized "into Christ" make better sense if referred to water-baptism. In the image of Spirit-baptism as described by John, Christ is the baptizer, but in Romans 6 and Galatians 3 that is not the grammatical structure. The language of baptism into Christ calls to mind the language of Matthew 28, that is, being baptized "into the name" of the triune God. In the typical biblical language, the name generally denotes the person, as in "calling upon the name of the Lord." So, baptism "into the name" of the triune God is essentially baptism into union or fellowship with the triune God. All of this indicates that the natural reading of Paul's language is that we come to be "in Christ" via baptism in some sense.[39]

If this realistic reading of Romans and Galatians seems contrary to what Paul argues elsewhere in those Epistles and seems to overstate the significance of baptism, one must recall how Paul described his own conversion in Acts 22. He indicates that while he submitted to Christ in one way on the road to Damascus, the instruction of Ananias was that he should be baptized in order to call on the Lord and be cleansed of his sins. In Paul's own experience, the formally definitive moment of his conversion was his baptism.

Fallacy #6: The apostle Paul refutes sacramentalism by his comments in 1 Corinthians 1.13–17

It is not hard to see why this text might be taken to minimize the significance of baptism and thus to challenge the idea that it is instrumental in the experience of salvation. Paul actually expresses his relief that he baptized so few in Corinth, and he opposes baptizing to preaching the gospel. Others have made the point, but here are the strong words of David Gay concluding his treatment of the passage:

> Let me summarise: 1 Corinthians 1:13–17 is the only major passage in Paul's letters which deals with water baptism as far as it concerns the subject in hand. As such, it must play a very important role—indeed, the all-important role—in determining how we view the ordinance. From this passage, it is quite clear that preaching—not baptism—is that which God has established as the means of calling sinners to Christ. A huge, unbridgeable chasm yawns between Paul and the sacramentalists here. Sacramentalism is bound to reverse the roles of preaching and baptism. It is logically bound to reverse their order, too. but the reversal of the priority—let alone the order—of preaching and baptism, is fatal to sacramentalism in that it so plainly contradicts the apostle in this passage. Baptism, therefore, whatever else it is, cannot be sacramental. The sacramentalists must be wrong. 1 Corinthians 1:13–17 is conclusive. It is, indeed, the clinching passage.[40]

---

[39] Fowler, *More Than a Symbol*, 186–89.

[40] Gay, *Sacramentalism*, 259–60.

There is surely some major overstatement in these comments. Gay is able to assert that this is the only major Pauline text that addresses the sacramental question only because he has previously argued that the apparently sacramental texts are actually talking about Spirit-baptism. It should also be noted that the subject of this text is disunity in Corinth, and baptism is referred to only insofar as it is relevant for that question. This is not what could be called a development of baptismal theology.

Although a superficial reading of this text seems to minimize the significance of baptism, that inference is not clearly justified. The problem addressed by Paul is factionalism rooted in attachment to particular preachers, in this case Paul, Apollos, and Peter plus a super-spiritual Christ party. Paul counters this by reminding his readers that they were not baptized into the name of Paul (or any other preacher, for that matter). Now, why would Paul bring up baptism to deal with this disunity? Perhaps this may indicate that some of the factions were defined by the name of the person who baptized the members of the faction, and that would point to the significance of baptism, not to its insignificance. Paul is, then, grateful that he left most of the baptizing to other members of his team, so that he avoided any basis for creating a Pauline faction based on his involvement in their baptism into the name of Christ. There is no doubt that Paul here subordinates baptizing to preaching the gospel, but that is simply a reminder that baptism has no power in itself, but only as the formal way to say yes to the gospel.[41] However one might describe the efficacy of baptism, if it is designed to be the sacramental form of response to the gospel, then communication of the gospel clearly is prior to baptism temporally, and baptism is effective only because the gospel is effective. And that is Paul's point.[42]

Fallacy #7: Baptist sacramentalism is an oxymoron, because Baptists have always denied that baptism is a sacrament

Gay states this criticism explicitly and presses it vigorously. On the second page of his introductory chapter, he says,

> A Baptist baptises only those who profess (and give evidence of) inward spiritual grace, and does so to represent that grace. A sacramentalist baptises to produce or convey the grace. To me, therefore, a Baptist cannot be a sacramentalist; as I have said, "Baptist sacramentalism" is an oxymoron.[43]

---

[41] I agree here with Schreiner, "Baptism in the Epistles," 80.

[42] See also Fowler, *Rethinking Baptism*, 30, and *More Than a Symbol*, 162.

[43] Gay, *Sacramentalism*, 23.

In response to William Brackney's Foreword to my book *More Than a Symbol*, Gay says,

> Let me translate: British Baptist sacramentalists have an agenda. They want to introduce (not "restore", let me stress with as much force as I can—"introduce") sacramentalism among Baptists. They want to tackle (and overcome) the arguments of those Baptists who, the sacramentalists allege, have no appetite for fresh light (which, of course, goes to prove that sacramentalism is a novelty among Baptists) . . .[44]

I admit in *More Than a Symbol* that the British reformulators of the last century failed to show that their view had strong connections to the Baptist literature of the seventeenth century, and I fault them for this. If they had taken the time to show that connection, they could have blunted the force of some of the criticism of their work. Gay's explanation of all that is to assert that "There was no such 'early Baptist tradition' of sacramentalism." His description of the historical survey in my book is that it is "tortuous" argumentation that amounts to "Fowler whistling in the dark."[45]

Now, what can be said in response to such confident claims? First, we must all remember that Baptists are committed to the principle of *sola scriptura*, so even if a given doctrine is generally absent from Baptist thought of the past, that may be a reason to repent and bow to the uniquely final authority of scripture. Gay and I agree that the ultimate appeal is to scripture, and historical questions are secondary.

But it is also true that the evidence reveals the error of Gay's assertions. Repeating the mantra, "Baptists are not sacramentalists," does not make it true. One problem in reading the evidence is the issue of terminology that I have mentioned earlier, that is, the mistaken notion that describing baptism as an ordinance is equivalent to saying that it is merely an ordinance. The fact that early Baptists describe baptism as an ordinance cannot be taken to prove anything about the issue at hand. One must also look at the way Baptists describe the function of baptism in texts where neither "ordinance" nor "sacrament" appears as a descriptor. And when we do that, we see them describing it as an act not of a confirmed disciple, but of a penitent sinner turning to Christ to experience salvation. I offer just two examples, the first from Thomas Grantham, the most significant theologian of the General Baptists.

> . . . Baptiſm in the ordinary way of Gods communicating the graces of the Goſpel is antecedent to the reception thereof, & is propounded as a means wherein not only the Remiſſion of our ſins ſhall be granted to us, but as a

---

[44] Gay, *Sacramentalism*, 43.

[45] Gay, *Sacramentalism*, 58–59.

condition whereupon we fhall receive the gift of the Holy Ghoft ... [It] was fore-ordained to fignifie and Sacramentally to confer the grace of the pardon of fin, and the inward wafhing of the Confcience by Faith in the Bloud of Jefus Chrift.[46]

The second example is from Benjamin Keach, one of the leading theologians of the Particular Baptists.

Confider the great Promifes made to thofe who are obedient to it, amongft other things, Lo, I am with you always, even to the end of the World. And again, He that believeth, and is baptized, fhall be faved. If a Prince fhall offer a Rebel his Life in doing two things, would he neglect one of them, and fay this I will do, but the other is a trivial thing, I'll not do that? Surely no, he would not run the hazard of his Life so foolifhly.

And then in Acts 2.38. Repent, and be baptized every one of you for Remiffion of Sin, and ye shall receive the Gift of the Holy Spirit: See what great Promifes are made to Believers in Baptifm.[47]

Elsewhere Keach understands the "washing of regeneration" in Titus 3.5 as a reference to baptism, and he refers to baptism as the "Sacrament of Regeneration," not in terms of physical causality but as the "means of God's Appointment" by which faith reaches out to Christ.[48]

Gay devotes an appendix of his book to Thomas Helwys on baptism, and there he tries to counter the claim of Philip E. Thompson that Helwys thought in sacramental terms.[49] What he proposes is "to let Helwys speak for himself," and then he provides an extended quote from Helwys including the following:

If you follow not Christ in the way of regeneration; that is, if you be "born again of water and of the Spirit, and so enter the kingdom of heaven", all is nothing ... And Cornelius (Acts 10), if he had not been baptised "with the Holy Ghost and with water", for all his prayers and alms, he had not, nor could not have entered into the kingdom of heaven ... No other way of salvation has Christ appointed but that they first believe and be baptised (Mark 16:16).

Unbelievers ... and ... all infidels ... there was, nor is, any way for you to join unto Christ, but to "amend your lives [repent] and be baptized", and by "baptism to put on Christ" ... Our Saviour Christ ... gives likewise a general

---

[46] Grantham, *A Sigh for Peace*, 87–88.

[47] Keach, *Gold Refin'd*, 173 (italics removed).

[48] Keach, *Gold Refin'd*, 82–83 and 128–29.

[49] See Thompson, "Sacraments and Religious Liberty," 48. Thompson's conclusion is further demonstrated by Cross, "Sacrament of Baptism among the first Baptists," especially 197–200 on Helwys.

direction, what all unbelievers must do, if they will be saved. "They must believe and be baptized".[50]

Granted, the word "sacrament" does not appear in this passage, but to claim that this language is not conceptually sacramental is to deny the obvious force of the words. In fact, it is quite astonishing that Gay thinks that these comments by Helwys somehow support his view. For Helwys, baptism is clearly more than a backward-looking testimony to an already completed conversion. It is not the obedient act of a previously confirmed disciple, but rather the act of a repentant sinner who says yes to the gospel in the way that Christ commanded, that is, by repentance and faith given tangible expression in baptism.

Conclusion

In summary, although there are forms of sacramentalism that Baptists cannot coherently affirm, the idea that baptism is more than human obedience pointing backward to a completed conversion, that it is in fact a sacred ritual in which God is at work conveying union with Christ at an experiential level, is both historically and theologically at home in Baptist thought, not to mention exegetically defensible as a natural way to read the New Testament. Baptist sacramentalism is not an oxymoron.[51]

Bibliography

Anon. *Catechism of the Catholic Church.* New York: Doubleday, 1995.

Anon. *The Baptist Catechism: Commonly Called Keach's Catechism: Or, A Brief Instruction in the Principles of the Christian Religion.* Philadelphia: American Baptist Publication Society, 1851.

Barker, David G., Michael A.G. Haykin, and Barry H. Howson, eds. *Ecclesia semper reformanda est. The Church Is Always Reforming. A Festschrift on Ecclesiology in Honour of Stanley K. Fowler on His Seventieth Birthday.* Kitchener, ON: Joshua, 2016.

Beasley-Murray, G.R. *Baptism in the New Testament.* Grand Rapids: Eerdmans, 1962.

———. *Baptism Today and Tomorrow.* London: Macmillan, 1966.

———. "The Problem of Infant Baptism: An Exercise in Possibilities." In *Festschrift Günter Wagner*, edited by Faculty of Baptist Theological Seminary Rüschlikon, 1–14. International Theological Studies: Contributions of Baptist Scholars, 1. Berne: Lang, 1994.

---

[50] Gay, *Sacramentalism*, 280 and 287.

[51] Cf. Fowler, "Is 'Baptist Sacramentalism' an Oxymoron?"

Caneday, A.B. "Baptism in the Stone-Campbell Restoration Movement." In *Believer's Baptism*, edited by Schreiner and Wright, 285–328.

Clark, Neville. "The Theology of Baptism." In *Christian Baptism*, edited by Gilmore, 306–26.

Cross, Anthony R. "Baptismal Regeneration: Rehabilitating a Lost Dimension of New Testament Baptism." In *Baptist Sacramentalism 2*, edited by Cross and Thompson, 149–74.

———. *Baptism and the Baptists: Theology and Practice in Twentieth-Century Britain*. Carlisle: Paternoster, 2000.

———. *Recovering the Evangelical Sacrament: Baptisma Semper Reformandum*. Eugene, OR: Pickwick, 2013.

———. "The Sacrament of Baptism among the first Baptists." In *Ecclesia semper reformanda est*, edited by Barker, Haykin and Howson, 189–211.

Cross, Anthony R., and Philip E. Thompson, eds. *Baptist Sacramentalism*. Studies in Baptist History and Thought, 5. Carlisle: Paternoster, 2003.

———, eds. *Baptist Sacramentalism 2*. Studies in Baptist History and Thought, 25. Milton Keynes: Paternoster, 2008.

Fiddes, Paul S. "*Ex Opere Operato*: Re-thinking a Historic Baptist Rejection." In *Baptist Sacramentalism 2*, edited by Cross and Thompson, 219–38.

Fowler, Stanley K. "Baptists and Churches of Christ in Search of a Common Theology of Baptism." In *Baptist Sacramentalism 2*, edited by Cross and Thompson, 254–69.

———. "Is 'Baptist Sacramentalism' an Oxymoron?" Reactions in Britain to *Christian Baptism* (1959)." In *Baptist Sacramentalism*, edited by Cross and Thompson, 129–50.

———. *More Than a Symbol: The British Baptist Recovery of Baptismal Sacramentalism*. Studies in Baptist History and Thought, 2. Carlisle: Paternoster, 2002.

———. *Rethinking Baptism: Some Baptist Reflections*. Eugene, OR: Wipf & Stock, 2015.

Gay, David H. J. *Baptist Sacramentalism: A Warning to Baptists*. Biggleswade, UK: Brachus, 2011.

Gilmore, Alec, ed. *Christian Baptism: A Fresh Attempt to Understand the Rite in Terms of Scripture, History, and Theology*. London: Lutterworth, 1959.

Gilmore, Alec. *Baptism and Christian Unity*. Valley Forge, PA: Judson, 1966.

Grantham, Thomas. *A Sigh for Peace: or the Cause of Division Discovered*. London: Printed for the Author, 1671.

Grass, Tim, and Ian Randall. "C.H. Spurgeon on the Sacraments." In *Baptist Sacramentalism*, edited by Cross and Thompson, 55–75.

Hammett, John S. *Biblical Foundations for Baptist Churches: A Contemporary Ecclesiology*. 2nd ed. Grand Rapids: Kregel, 2019.

Hicks, John Mark. *Enter the Water, Come to the Table*. Abilene, TX: Abilene Christian University Press, 2014.

Hicks, John Mark, and Greg Taylor. *Down in the River to Pray: Revisioning Baptism as God's Transformative Work*. Siloam Springs, AR: Leafwood, 2004.

Jones, Brandon C. *Waters of Promise: Finding Meaning in Believer Baptism*. Eugene, OR: Pickwick, 2012.

Keach, Benjamin. *Gold Refin'd; or Baptism in its Primitive Purity*. London: Nathaniel Crouch, 1689.

Lawrence, Henry. *Of Baptisme*. London: F. Macock, 1659.

Lumpkin, William L., ed. *Baptist Confessions of Faith*. Philadelphia: Judson, 1959.

Morden, Peter, J. "C.H. Spurgeon and Baptism: [Part 2] The Importance of Baptism." *Baptist Quarterly* 43.7 (2010) 388–409.

———. "C.H. Spurgeon and Baptism: Part 1: The Question of Baptismal Sacramentalism." *Baptist Quarterly* 43.4 (2009) 196–220.

Rainbow, Jonathan H. "'Confessor Baptism': The Baptismal Doctrine of the Early Anabaptists." In *Believer's Baptism*, edited by Schreiner and Wright, 189–206.

Schaff, Philip, and David S. Schaff, eds. *The Creeds of Christendom: With a History and Critical Notes*. Volume III. *The Evangelical Protestant Creeds*. Grand Rapids: Baker Books, 1983 [1931].

Schreiner, Thomas R. "Baptism in the Epistles: An Initiation Rite for Believers." In *Believer's Baptism*, edited by Schreiner and Wright, 67–96.

Schreiner, Thomas R. and Shawn D. Wright, eds. *Believer's Baptism: Sign of the New Covenant in Christ*. NAC Studies in Bible & Theology. Nashville, TN: B&H Academic, 2006.

Spurgeon, Charles Haddon. "Baptismal Regeneration." In *Metropolitan Tabernacle Pulpit* 10, 313–28. Pasadena, TX: Pilgrim, 1981.

Stein, Robert H. "Baptism in Luke-Acts." In *Believer's Baptism*, edited by Schreiner and Wright, 35–66.

Thompson, Philip E. "Sacraments and Religious Liberty: From Critical Practice to Rejected Infringement." In *Baptist Sacramentalism*, edited by Cross and Thompson, 36–54.

Walton, Robert C. *The Gathered Community*. London: Carey, 1946.

CHAPTER 4

"... a profound mystery":
The Real, the Mystical, and the Sacramental

John E. Colwell

"For this reason a man will leave his father and mother and be united to his wife, and the two will become one flesh." This is a profound mystery—but I am talking about Christ and the church. (Eph. 5.31–32.)

One doesn't need to be married for long for the designation of marriage as a "mystery" to prompt any number of cheap quips; moreover our familiarity with the text probably blinds us to the truly mysterious nature of the claim that to be married is to become "one flesh." If something more profound than mere sexual intimacy is being affirmed (and surely it is) then this deeper oneness is something more than is immediately and simply apparent. Perhaps in its primary context as the climax of the second creation story in Genesis the claim may be less problematic: a rib has been taken from Adam from which the woman has been formed; the male and female here truly are portrayed as bone of bone and flesh of flesh; their coming together is simply a joining again of what was previously single (Gen. 2.21–25). Far more problematic, however, is the wider context in which this Genesis story occurs: a text from which present day readers infer the highest ideal of monogamy occurs in a context of polygamy, concubinage, and prostitution—are we to conclude that the earliest readers of this text were oblivious to the tension between this ideal and the other stories that were formative for their faith and identity?

Assuming that Paul's Letters predate the Gospels, at least in their final written form, the next reference to the text occurs in the first Corinthian letter and only serves to compound the problem: here the Apostle seems to be suggesting that mere sexual union may not be merely sexual union at all; that to be joined sexually to a prostitute is to be joined precisely in this "one flesh" sense (1 Cor. 6.15–17). It is reasonable to assume that what Paul is suggesting is as surprising to his original Corinthian readers as it is to us—the passage suggests that they did not realize that, as members of Christ, they were joining Christ to a prostitute—but here, as in Ephesians, this more profound oneness is assumed rather than explained. Only in the Gospel accounts of Jesus' response to the Pharisees on the issue of divorce do we find what may be an explanatory comment: ". . . what God has joined together, let no-one separate" (ὃ οὖν ὁ θεὸς συνέζευξεν ἄνθρωπος μὴ χωριζέτω; Matt. 19.6; cf. Mark 10.9). The man and the woman are "one flesh" not just because, as in the Genesis story, they were one flesh originally, nor just because they have joined together sexually; they are one flesh because they have been joined together by God. Something is what it is simply because God says that it is what it is. Hence, beyond any physical, tangible, observable joining, there is a joining by God that is unseen and perhaps even unfelt; a joining that is nonetheless real; a joining that, therefore, is "mystery." The joining of a man and a woman is "mystery" simply because something more is the reality here than meets the eye—and that something more is a decision (or perhaps a promise) of God.[1]

If the notion of marriage as a divine joining poses a challenge to our present context of same-sex relationships, casual sex, prostitution, and divorce we should remind ourselves that the context into which Paul was writing and Jesus was speaking was really not that different. Moreover, if we want to affirm marriage as a divine joining, rather than merely a human covenant or contract, perhaps we ought not to be so hastily dismissive of the Catholic claim that marriage is a sacrament[2]—not least because in the Vulgate translation of the New Testament this is the only sacrament of the church that is explicitly named as "sacrament" within the text. The term "mystery" (μυστήριον) is used six times in this Epistle, usually (as in other Pauline letters[3]) with reference to the hidden purposes of God now revealed through the gospel. A "mystery" therefore, here and elsewhere, is simply something hidden from ordinary sight and understanding. Hence, in this specific, that two instances of "flesh" are in fact one instance of "flesh," is something hidden from common sight and understanding, something determined by God.

What can only remain a further mystery is why Jerome should sometimes (as here) translate the Greek word μυστήριον with the Latin word *sacramentum* and, on other occasions, translate the Greek word with the Latin word *mysterium*. For instance, in Daniel 2.47 Jerome translates the twice occurring Hebrew word רז (translated as μυστήριον in the Septuagint) first

---

[1] For a fuller discussion of the sacramental nature of marriage, see chapter 11 of my *Promise and Presence*.

[2] As elsewhere, I use the term "Catholic" (capitalized) to refer to the Roman Catholic communion and the term "catholic" (uncapitalized) in its broader sense of the connectedness and continuity of the church throughout the world and throughout the ages.

[3] It is irrelevant to the purposes of this paper to engage in the debate over the authorship of Ephesians: I use the term "Pauline" without prejudice to the question of actual authorship.

with the word *mysterium* and then with the word *sacramentum*.[4] One could conclude in this instance that Jerome uses the word *mysterium* in a general sense of mystery and the word *sacramentum* of a particular example of mystery. However, in Ephesians 3.3–4, where again the Greek word μυστήριον occurs twice,[5] Jerome translates the first occurrence with the Latin *sacramentum* and the second occurrence with the Latin *mysterium*[6]—and here no such distinction between the general and the particular would seem to pertain. The only other occasion in Ephesians where Jerome translates the Greek μυστήριον with the Latin *mysterium* is at 6.19 where the reference (as is usual) is to the mystery of the gospel. Reams of paper and gallons of ink could be spent (and probably have been spent) speculating on the motivations for Jerome's decisions of translation—but such can only be speculation.[7] What we can affirm is that the habit of rendering the Greek word μυστήριον with the Latin *sacramentum* long predates Jerome and may even predate its first extant occurrence in Tertullian.[8] And, as I have argued elsewhere,[9] while in common use the term *sacramentum* may have signified an oath or a deposit, that it became accepted as a translation of μυστήριον enhances its significance: a sacrament may be a promise by God (or by us in response to God), a sign or seal of a promise by God or by us (as in the sense of a deposit), but it surely must now include this significance of "mystery", of that which is hidden from common sight and understanding.

But while all this undoubtedly is of momentous significance to an understanding of marriage, the text interrupts this train of thought with a "mystery" that is perhaps even more surprising: ". . . but I am talking about Christ and the church."[10] The imagery of the church as the "body of Christ" (το σῶμα Χριστοῦ) is common to Paul—but the notion of the church and Christ being "one flesh" is extraordinary in a number of respects.

In the first place (and perhaps least problematically), we should note that, while the imagery of the church as "the bride of Christ" has become

---

[4] loquens ergo rex ait Daniheli vere Deus vester Deus deorum est et Dominus regum et revelans mysteria quoniam potuisti aperire sacramentum hoc.

[5] κατὰ ἀποκάλυψιν ἐγνωρίσθη μοι τὸ μυστήριον, καθὼς προέγραψα ἐν ὀλίγῳ, πρὸς ὃ δύνασθε ἀναγινώσκοντες νοῆσαι τὴν σύνεσίν μου ἐν τῷ μυστηρίῳ τοῦ Χριστοῦ.

[6] quoniam secundum revelationem notum mihi factum est sacramentum sicut supra scripsi in brevi prout potestis legentes intellegere prudentiam meam in mysterio Christi.

[7] See, for instance, Foster, "'Mysterium' and 'Sacramentum'."

[8] Tertullian, *On Baptism*.

[9] Colwell, *Promise and Presence*, 4–5.

[10] ἐγὼ δὲ λέγω εἰς Χριστὸν καὶ εἰς τὴν ἐκκλησίαν.

commonplace in the Christian tradition, other than by implication in this single text, it is entirely absent within the Pauline corpus—it is Johannine rather than Pauline imagery (John 3.29; Rev. 21.2–9; 22.17). Throughout the Pauline corpus Christian disciples are identified as those who are "in Christ" and the church is repeatedly depicted as Christ's body (Rom. 12.3–8; 1 Cor. 10.14–22; 12.12–31; Eph. 1.23; 2.16; 4.4; 4.11–16; 5.23; 5.30; Col. 1.18; 1.24; 2.19). Perhaps most significantly in 1 Corinthians 10.16b–17 Paul links the sense in which the bread of the Lord's supper is the body of Christ with the identity of the church as the body of Christ:[11] there is an intriguing ambiguity in the text—is the church's participation in a single loaf a sign that they are a single body or is the participation in a single loaf that which constitutes the church as a single body—whichever the case (and the tradition strongly affirms the church and the supper as mutually constituting) the imagery of the church as the body of Christ is unquestionably a key Pauline theme.

But, though this imagery of the church as Christ's body informs the discussion of marriage in this passage, the imagery in this text is that of "flesh" rather than that of "body" and, with the possible exception of the passage in 1 Corinthians 6.15–16 where "flesh" and "body" appear to be interchangeable, the imagery of "flesh" in relation to the church occurs nowhere else in the Pauline corpus.

And the imagery of "flesh" is problematic. The Hebrew word בָּשָׂר (generally translated with the Greek word σάρξ in the Septuagint) seems to signify no more than the stuff of the body (the meat you buy in a butcher's) and, thereby, could be taken as synonymous with body—indeed, there are occasions when the Hebrew בָּשָׂר is translated by the Greek word σῶμα ("body"; e.g., Lev. 6.10). However, there are passages within the New Testament where the word "flesh" (σάρξ) seems to have more negative connotations: for instance in Romans 8 where the possibility of living according to the Spirit is contrasted with the possibility of living according to the flesh; or Galatians 5.16–26 where the fruit of the Spirit is contrasted with the works of the flesh; or (and more pertinently) here in Ephesians 2.1–8 where our following the desires of the flesh is contrasted and superseded by the life that we now have through grace alone. It is surely not unreasonable to conclude that the imagery of flesh carries connotations of frailty that are not necessarily present in the imagery of body and that, just as the male and the female being one "flesh" conveys something more stark than if they were affirmed as one "body," the same is similarly true when this imagery of one "flesh" is applied to Christ and his church. Both in the parallel with the husband and the wife and in the utilizing of this imagery of one "flesh" the

---

[11] τὸν ἄρτον ὃν κλῶμεν, οὐχὶ κοινωνία τοῦ σώματος τοῦ Χριστοῦ ἐστιν; ὅτι εἷς ἄρτος, ἓν σῶμα οἱ πολλοί ἐσμεν, οἱ γὰρ πάντες ἐκ τοῦ ἑνὸς ἄρτου μετέχομεν.

text can be taken as suggesting an identity between Christ and the church that is both real and (for want of a better term) earthy.[12]

Of course, this fleshly rootedness of the union between Christ and the church is qualified within the text by the word "mystery": that which is being affirmed, though real (and even earthily real) is not apparent to common sight and understanding—and it is the tension between the reality that is being affirmed here and its qualifying mysterious character that will be the focus for the remainder of this paper.

In 1944, Henri de Lubac published the first edition of his exploration of the term *corpus mysticum* as it developed within the Western Church through the Middle Ages—the work was republished in a second edition in 1949. The book is easy to summarize and difficult to evaluate. It demonstrates a quite extraordinary scholarly familiarity with the early medieval discussions of the Western Church, especially with those usually dubbed the Carolingian theologians, but even in this detail the text is less than clearly ordered (as is admitted in the Editors' Preface)[13] and at least some of the distinctions de Lubac draws between different authors can be explained by differing nuances of the terms in question—terms on their way to technical use rather than already having arrived at such. However, de Lubac's conclusions are clear, they caused significant controversy at the time, and they proved potent in the discussions at the Second Vatican Council: from early medieval uses of the term *corpus mysticum*, that generally held Christ's body to be at the Father's right hand, in the elements on the altar, and as the church (the latter forms of Christ's body being both mystical and real), the debates moved (largely in response to the denials of Berengar of Tours) to a point where the bread on the altar was dogmatically affirmed as the true (*verum*) body while the church came increasingly to be viewed as the mystical body (*corpus mysticum*) in a rather less than real sense.

> Against *mystically, not truly*, was set, in no less exclusive a sense, *truly, not mystically*. Perhaps orthodoxy was safeguarded, but on the other hand, doctrine was certainly impoverished.[14]

---

[12] Commenting on this passage in his generally excellent commentary on Ephesians Andrew Lincoln focuses almost entirely on the significance of the passage for the marriage relationship with little reference to the considerable ecclesiological consequences of the text. Lincoln, *Ephesians*, 385–94.

[13] "De Lubac's text in many ways reflects the confusions of the age in which it was written. His preparation and the editing of the book are often erratic and inconsistent: authors are given differing titles or descriptions across various points, the use of parentheses does not always reflect a clear purpose, and at times the referencing is confusing." Editors' Preface in de Lubac, *Corpus Mysticum*, ix (ix–xx).

[14] de Lubac, *Corpus Mysticum*, 223.

Commenting on de Lubac's conclusions, William Cavanaugh writes,

> . . . de Lubac shows how the dynamic relationship between the liturgical action of the Eucharist and the formation of the church community was gradually reduced until the community-forming power of the sacrament was borrowed by the nascent state and the Eucharist became an individualized, miraculous spectacle that served to reinforce clerical power. Whereas the early church saw Christ's *corpus mysticum* as the sacrament on the altar that gathered Christ's *corpus verum*, the church, by the twelfth century the terms had been inverted, so that the real body was the miracle on the altar, and the community became the mystical body, where "mystical" indicated something less than real. The mystical as corporative fiction then made its way into the legitimation of the modern state.[15]

What de Lubac applauds in the earlier period and considers to have been lost subsequently is the power of the symbol to present the real:

> But a temptation developed here, in the case of the Church, precisely as in that of Scripture: the temptation of no longer seeing anything in this metaphor except the metaphor itself, and of considering "mystical" as a watering-down of "real" or of "true".[16]

Two further questions arise, however, in the light of the Ephesians text cited at the head of this paper. In the first place, what might be the relationship (both in early medieval thought and in the later "dialectic" tendencies that displaced such) between the Latin terms *mysticum* and the Latin term *mysterium*; whatever the distinctions between the terms may or may not have been in classical Latin what prompted these medieval writers to employ the former term and not the latter term (not least when the former term does not occur, as far as I am aware, in Jerome's Vulgate)? And in the second place (and especially in the light of its earthily real connotations), why was the term "flesh" employed so little in these debates when, in this Ephesians text, it is used specifically to speak of the unity of Christ and his church? In this latter respect, de Lubac argues (understandably) that the term "flesh" came more readily to be applied to the bread on the altar, but, here again, this scriptural text appears to have been overlooked:

---

[15] Cavanaugh, *Field Hospital*, 114.

[16] de Lubac, *Corpus Mysticum*, 249. Again Cavanaugh comments: "De Lubac . . . is trying to move behind the modern inversion in order to recapture a sense of the mystical that is not opposed to the real, to overcome 'the temptation of no longer seeing anything in this metaphor except the metaphor itself, and of considering "mystical" as a watering-down of 'real' or of 'true'." Cavanaugh, *Field Hospital*, 116.

We have seen that, from the beginning, *flesh* was used more specifically of the Eucharist than *body*. This can easily be understood, because since Saint Paul the word *body* had a further dogmatic function of supreme importance to which *flesh* could not aspire. There is indeed, in the current acceptance of the word "body", an idea of totality which is both unified and diversified, and which is essential in the Pauline concept of the Church. A "body" is an organism, it is the exchange between members whose functions simultaneously differ and work together. It also represents plenitude. The theologians of the thirteenth century would not fail to observe that, if the Eucharist were to be considered by itself alone, independently of its significance, it would be more proper to call it *flesh of Christ*. Furthermore *flesh* was the word used for the sacrifices of the ancient law where the bodies of animal victims prefigured the flesh of the divine Victim.[17]

Leaving aside for a moment the questions this Ephesians text raises in relation to this Catholic debate, one must concede, with de Lubac, that the "less than real" (or less than physically actual) connotations of the church as the "mystical" body of Christ were compounded at the time of the Reformation. As de Lubac earlier comments,

> . . . the objections of the likes of Wycliffe, Jan Huss, Luther or Calvin would assail Catholicism itself, and the inverted excesses of their "spiritualist" reaction would lead to the total dissociation of the mystical body of Christ from the visible body of the Church.[18]

Notwithstanding the expressed intention of early Reformers to reform rather than to break away, nor the contrary and sectarian intention of some Radicals and some Anabaptists to dismiss all else as apostate and to identify themselves as a new and true beginning, the divisions consequent on the Reformation and the subsequent multiplication of denominations encourage the notion that the true church is "mystical" in the sense of being invisible, not to be identified too simply with the earthly, fleshly, physical actuality of the visible church. That "The Lord knows those who are his" may be a cry of desperation where it occurs in 2 Timothy 2.19, but it becomes a reassuring and self-justifying affirmation in the context of a deeply divided church. And, to our shame, this notion of the true church as invisible is not uncommonly expressed amongst Baptists—and it is *to our shame* since, notwithstanding the sectarian assumptions of at least some of the early Anabaptists, Baptists (together with Congregationalists) surely ought to be able to bring a particular and realist contribution to this debate.

I have argued elsewhere and at some length that merely to define the church as gathered with respect to the text of Matthew 18.20 ("For where two or three come together in my name, there am I with them") is insufficient as

---

[17] de Lubac, *Corpus Mysticum*, 123.

[18] de Lubac, *Corpus Mysticum*, 116–17.

an ecclesial definition—for the church to be truly gathered to Christ is for the church to be gathered through baptism, around holy scripture and holy communion, and (I would argue) with appropriately recognised and separated ministry.[19] Similarly, the creedal affirmation that the church is one, holy, catholic, and apostolic must qualify the manner of gathering that identifies such gathering as truly church. Nonetheless, the Baptist and Congregationalist affirmation of the church as gathered commits such communions to an ecclesial realism in all its fleshly, physical, this worldly, actuality.

A further expansion and development of de Lubac's thesis could explore the degree to which this move from the real to the mystical (and invisible) was paralleled by a move from the particular to the general, from an affirmation of the local church as truly the body of Christ to the reservation of that designation for the universal church (if not the eschatological revelation of that universal church). Paul has no hesitation in declaring to the church at Rome or the church at Corinth that they, in particular and in all their earthy and fleshly actuality, are the "body of Christ," and this without prejudice to the universality of the church as Christ's body. That this affirmation of the local (without prejudice to the universal) continued within the early medieval period is strongly suggested (though not expanded) in de Lubac's analysis. Indeed, in a context where the eucharist and the church were mutually defining, a context where both were affirmed as both mystical and real, we would expect such: if Christ is truly and wholly present in each celebration of the eucharist, he surely similarly is truly and wholly present in each particular gathering of the church. Later medieval writers were clear that, to receive Christ truly in the eucharist was to receive the totality of Christ[20]—by virtue of the same mysterious dynamic each locally gathered church must be affirmed as *totus Christus*, the locally gathered church can no more be a "part" of Christ than can the bread of the eucharist; Christ, who is bodily present at the Father's right hand, is wholly but mysteriously present in the bread and wine of every eucharist and in every particular gathering of his church. Nor perhaps is the term "present" sufficient here. Certainly the promise of Jesus in Matthew 18.20 is a promise of presence, but the designation of the church as Christ's body, together with the text of Ephesians 5.31–32, affirm an identification: the ascended Christ is identified with the bread and wine of every eucharist and with every gathering of his church; they are "one flesh," albeit in this "mysterious" sense.

---

[19] Colwell, "Church as Sacrament," 48–60; cf. *Promise and Presence*, especially chapters 3, 5, 7 and 10.

[20] For instance: ". . . the whole substance of the bread is changed into the whole substance of Christ's body, and the whole substance of the wine into the whole substance of Christ's blood." Aquinas, *Summa Theologica*, III.75.4.

At this point one can only puzzle with regret at the medieval (and contemporary) use of the term *mysticum* in preference to the term *mysterium* particularly with the latter's associations with the term *sacramentum*: in practice, this preference for the term *mysticum* seems to have obscured the sacramental dynamic from which both the eucharist and the church derive their identity. For Thomas Aquinas, Christ's presence in the eucharist is sacramental, that specific dynamic whereby he, though bodily (physically?) present at the Father's right hand, can be truly identified with the bread and wine of the eucharist without the accidents (physicality?) of the bread and wine being annulled.[21] Neither is it difficult to argue that what Thomas designates a sacramental presence corresponds to that which John Calvin designates a Spiritual presence[22]—though perhaps the term "spiritual" (uncapitalized) lends itself in subsequent thought to similar "unreal" connotations as does the term "mystical." One can only ponder whether, had Thomas continued with his *Summa*, he might have applied the same sacramental dynamic to each particular gathering of Christ's church: Christ, bodily present at the Father's right hand, is truly and wholly identified with every authentic gathering of his church notwithstanding the continuing earthy and fleshly actuality of those ecclesial gatherings.

The Ephesians text that stands at the head of this paper affirms the union of Christ and his church as "mystery," as that which is not commonly accessible to sight or understanding, as that which is what it is simply because God has determined and promised such. but the same text affirms this unity in the starkest, most real, most fleshly, terms. And somehow we must hold these two apparently conflicting affirmations together. Just as a man and a woman, though appearing to be two instances of flesh, are but one, so too the church, both in its universality and its gathered particularity, notwithstanding its all too apparent distinction from Christ, is truly one with Christ precisely in these most fleshly terms.

I have written elsewhere of the dangers of ecclesiological Docetism or Nestorianism:[23] the beguiling attraction of the *corpus mysticum* when marginalized to the general, the universal, the invisible, is that it alleviates the necessity of grappling with the stark fleshliness of the particular. but for Baptists and Congregationalists such a temptation ought not to gain purchase. The distinct contribution of Baptists and Congregationalists to the universal and catholic church is their entirely catholic witness to the integrity of the locally gathered congregation as truly the body of Christ, as gathered together

---

[21] Aquinas, *Summa Theologica*, III.73–83.

[22] Smallwood, "A comparison of Thomas Aquinas' and John Calvin's understanding of the Eucharist"; cf. Colwell, *Promise and Presence*, 168–71; and Gerrish, *Grace and Gratitude*.

[23] Colwell, "Provisionality and Promise."

under the promise of his presence, albeit a presence mediated by the Spirit. When the church is gathered something more is the reality than that which immediately and commonly meets the eye; the Lord Jesus is present here simply because he has promised to be present here; the reality of the gathered church is simply and precisely that which God says it is whether or not this presence is recognized or felt. And more particularly, since the church is gathered through baptism around the word and the sacrament of the Lord's supper, the bread and wine of communion, themselves a means of participating in the body of Christ (1 Cor. 10.16), establish and confirm the church as the reality in which they are participating:

> Eucharistic realism and ecclesial realism: these two realisms support one another, each is the guarantee of the other. Ecclesial realism safeguards Eucharistic realism and the latter confirms the former. The same unity of the Word is reflected in both.[24]

The issue here is not just an assured promise of presence but a corresponding affirmation of identity: the gathered church *is* the body of Christ. And it is not a huge step from this distinctive (but, I would argue, wholly catholic) affirmation of the particular and gathered as Christ's true body, albeit in this mysterious or sacramental sense, to a confession and affirmation of the fleshly character of this identity. Just as the continuing dual fleshly identity of a husband and wife distracts us from their divinely declared fleshly oneness so also the all too apparent fleshly character of the gathered congregation militates against any unequivocal affirmation of their identity as truly Christ's body—yet, if we are to take this Ephesians text seriously, it is precisely in this stark fleshliness that Christ chooses to own them and identify himself with them. Perhaps it is no coincidence that the First Epistle to the Corinthians, that depicts a church at its most frail fleshliness, includes the clearest affirmation of that particular church's identity as Christ's body. Indeed, perhaps the most remarkable passage in that letter, a passage already alluded to within this paper, has Paul affirming the Corinthians' identity in Christ even in the act of exploiting prostitutes. In identifying with his church, the Lord Jesus does not disown or disregard our fleshly frailty but, in grace and mercy, chooses to identify himself with us precisely in that fleshly frailty. Truly this is "a profound mystery," but its mysterious character establishes

---

[24] de Lubac, *Corpus Mysticum*, Conclusion, 251. Compare the following from William Cavanaugh: ". . . in the Eucharist, we receive the gift of Christ not as mere passive recipients, but by being incorporated into the gift itself, the Body of Christ. As members of the Body, we then become nourishment for others—including those not part of the visible Body—in the unending trinitarian economy of gratuitous giving and joyful reception. Property and dominium are thus reconfigured." Cavanaugh, *Theopolitical Imagination*, 48–49.

rather than detracts from its reality. The church in all its fleshly frailty is the body of Christ, both mysteriously and truly (*corpus Christi mysterium et verum*):

> The Church is a mystery; that is to say that she is also a sacrament. She is "the total locus of the Christian sacraments", and she is herself the great sacrament which contains and vitalizes all the others. In this world she is the sacrament of Christ, as Christ Himself, in His humanity, is for us the sacrament of God.[25]

Bibliography

Cavanaugh, Williams T. *Field Hospital: The Church's Engagement with a Wounded World*. Grand Rapids: Eerdmans, 2016.

———. *Theopolitical Imagination: Discovering the Liturgy as a Political Act in an Age of Global Consumerism*. London: T. & T. Clark Continuum, 2002.

Colwell, John E. "The Church as Sacrament: A Mediating Presence." In *Baptist Sacramentalism 2*, edited by Anthony R. Cross and Philip E. Thompson, 48–60. Milton Keynes: Paternoster, 2008.

———. *Promise and Presence: An Exploration of Sacramental Theology*. Eugene, OR: Wipf and Stock, 2011 [2005].

———. "Provisionality and Promise: Avoiding Ecclesiastical Nestorianism?" In *The Theology of Colin Gunton*, edited by Lincoln Harvey, 100–115. London: T. & T. Clark, 2010.

Foster, Theodore B. "'Mysterium' and 'Sacramentum' in the Vulgate and Old Latin Versions." *American Journal of Theology* 19.3 (1915) 402–15.

Gerrish, B. A., *Grace and Gratitude: The Eucharistic Theology of John Calvin*. Edinburgh: T. & T. Clark, 1993.

Lincoln, Andrew T., *Ephesians*. Nashville, TN: Thomas Nelson, 1990.

de Lubac, Henri. *Corpus Mysticum: The Eucharist and the Church in the Middle Ages*. Translated Gemma Simmonds CJ with Richard Price and Christopher Stephens; edited by Laurence Paul Hemming and Susan Frank Parsons. London: SCM, 2006.

———. *The Splendour of the Church*. Translated Michael Mason; New York: Sheed and Ward, 1956.

Smallwood, Varujan Richard. "A Comparison of Thomas Aquinas' and John Calvin's Understanding of the Eucharist." Unpublished BD dissertation, Spurgeon's College, the University of Wales, 2003.

Tertullian, *On Baptism*. In *The Ante-Nicene Fathers of the Christian Church*: Vol. 3, edited by Alexander Roberts and James Donaldson, 669–79. Edinburgh: T. & T. Clark/Grand Rapids: Eerdmans, 1989.

Thomas Aquinas, *Summa Theologica*. Translated by Fathers of the English Dominican Province; Westminster, MD: Christian Classics, 1981.

---

[25] de Lubac, *Splendour of the Church*, 147.

CHAPTER 5

First Communion:
Reflecting with St Thérèse of Lisieux

Brian Haymes

Our lives are a continuous engagement with time; hour follows hour, day after day, year by year. but some days in our lives take on special significance because they are "firsts," crucial moments in our personal story; our birthday; our first day at school; first "date"; first day at work; the first day we met that one who would become the "significant other." What someone considers a significant "first" might tell us quite a lot about their life and self-understanding. Such days may well turn out to be special because they reveal a trajectory, an event which provides a key to the fundamental explanation and meaning of that person's life. There is no understanding of them without knowing of this aspect of their days.

This essay, an exercise in ecumenical pastoral theology, seeks to explore the significance of first communion, the first receiving of the gifts of God in the eucharist. The approach will be by way of telling two stories, describing two different personal experiences. They reflect two contrasting ecclesiologies. The lifetimes are lived in different centuries and the stories reveal distinguishable understandings of holy communion for which people from both "sides" have killed one another. An attempt will be made to draw out the significance of the sacrament for the life of Christian discipleship in a Roman Catholic and Protestant tradition and, then, to reflect more particularly on the present British Baptist situation with regard to the seriousness or otherwise with which the sacraments are taken. The two persons whose experiences will be contrasted are St Thérèse of Lisieux and myself, ordained as a Baptist minister in 1965.

St Thérèse of Lisieux

Thérèse of Lisieux is one of the most popular and much-loved saints of the twentieth century, yet her short life was lived in a geographically small compass in the last quarter of the nineteenth century. At the age of fifteen she entered the local Carmelite monastery and remained there enclosed until her death aged twenty-four. However, within a short time of her death her reputation, teachings, and influence on many grew and grew. This was largely as a result of her published writings, notably her life story which she wrote in the carmel under obedience. Her autobiography was widely read, had, and continues to have, considerable impact and was a major factor in her early canonization.[1] She is considered one of the most significant saints of modern times.

Marie-Françoise-Thérèse Martin was born on 2 January 1873 in Alençon, France. Her parents were Louis and Zélie Martin, a deeply devout couple who both had sought the monastic life prior to their marriage. Together they went to early mass each morning. They were to offer the most careful nurturing of their children in the faith.[2] Thérèse's baptism took place two days after her birth with an older sister, Marie, being her godmother. In August 1877, Zelie Martin died. Louis moved the family to Lisieux by the end of that year to be near other family members. The older sisters, all of whom were to enter the religious life, took care of the instruction of the younger ones, Celine and Thérèse. They lived an economically and socially comfortable life with their father. Often he and Thérèse would go for afternoon walks, calling in at local churches and spending time in adoration before the blessed sacrament. From her father she learned the responsibility of giving alms.

Thérèse developed a sensitive conscience. She became scrupulously self-critical. These were days in France when the remaining effects of Jansenism were still in the air. Jansenism emphasized our fallenness, the human tendency to sin. Divine justice was enacted by a wrathful God. In particular, Jansenism taught that coming to communion in any but a Jansenist moral state was itself to commit sin. Here was a breeding ground for enervating scrupulosity and Thérèse's family, in keeping with many Roman Catholic bourgeois families, was not free from its effects.[3]

Thérèse attended a boarding school, as did all her sisters. She did not find this a happy experience. It was while she was at school that she was formally prepared for her first communion, although her sisters Marie and Pauline were very influential in this respect. She was present when Céline, four years older than her young sister, received her first communion, a day to which Thérèse came with great excitement. She was to say, "I believe I received great graces that day and I consider it one of the most *beautiful* days of my life."[4] All these children grew up in a context in which first communion was of great significance in their spiritual life.

---

[1] Thérèse, *Story of a Soul*. Hereafter referenced as *SS* with page number.

[2] Nine children were born to Zélie and Louis Martin, but four of the children, two boys and two girls, did not survive infancy. Thérèse was the last to be born to the couple, the first married couple to be canonized by the Roman Catholic Church in October 2015.

[3] See the discussion by Foley, *Context of Holiness*, 90.

[4] *SS* 57.

Thérèse had already made first confession, but now began preparation for first communion. Marie and Pauline encouraged her to keep a notebook in which she could record sacrifices and good moral acts she had undertaken during the day. This was a not uncommon practice with children at the time although the dangers of Jansenism are obvious, stressing that good deeds will be rewarded. Thérèse was not unaware of this since for all of her self-conscious life she had lived with the desire to please God. In these days she became conscious of her weaknesses and tendency towards self-centredness. However, her fundamental conviction was her deep confidence in God's love for her. Some have later interpreted Thérèse's life as the Holy Spirit's answer to Jansenism in the church.

The preparation at school included four days of retreat in silence and prayer. Thérèse delighted in this as all the retreatants shared the life of the Bendictine community. She imagined herself living like a nun, and during this time she said she made a spectacle of herself by wearing a large crucifix, the gift of another of her sisters, Léonie. She listened carefully to the instructions Father Domin gave as he led the retreat. He was the long-serving school chaplain. His talks have been described as not far in spirit from Jansenism. He focused on the children's ability of making sacrilegious communions, their possible committing of mortal sin and thereby being damned.[5] Thérèse kept her own thoughts to herself, aware that what the chaplain taught was frightening as he stressed how much God hated a soul steeped in sin. but Thérèse described the retreat as a "sweet memory" because in spite of the sufferings of boarding school there came "the ineffable happiness of those few days spent in waiting for Jesus."[6] This is a revealing quotation, showing how Thérèse understood the coming encounter. First communion would mean the first direct meeting with the living Jesus in his eucharistic presence.

Thérèse's First Communion

There were careful final preparations for this "beautiful day of days."[7] Special greetings from the teachers and older pupils were received. Then there were the dresses, "white as snow"; how people dress tells something of the kind of event they are attending.[8] This was very special. Then the procession into chapel as the first communicants approached the altar of God with high expectation.

---

[5] Schmidt, *Everything is Grace*, 98.

[6] *SS* 75.

[7] *SS* 77.

[8] *SS* 77.

At this point in her autobiography, Thérèse almost becomes silent, restraining herself in recognition that there are some things that cannot be fully expressed in words. They are too wonderful in their intimate and heavenly meaning. In May 1883 she received an appearance of the Virgin Mary at a time of healing. Under some pressure she was made to talk about this to the sisters in the monastery. She did this very reluctantly, sensing that in doing so she failed to convey the wonder at the heart of the gift. Now she realized that this first communion on 8 May 1884 is beyond words, unspeakable, divine. but then she writes,

> Ah! how sweet was that first kiss of Jesus! It was a kiss of love; I felt that I was loved, and I said, "I love You, and I give myself to You forever!" There were no demands made, no struggles, no sacrifices; for a long time now Jesus and poor little Thérèse looked at and understood each other. That day, it was no longer simply a look, it was a fusion, they were no longer two. Thérèse had vanished as a drop of water is lost in the immensity of the ocean. Jesus alone remained. He was the Master, the King. Had not Thérèse asked Him to take away her liberty, for her liberty frightened her? She felt so feeble and fragile that she wanted to be united forever to the divine Strength! Her joy was too great, too deep for her to contain, and tears of consolation soon flowed, to the great consternation of her companions. They asked one another; "Why was she crying? Was there something bothering her?"—"No, it was because her mother was not there or her sister whom she loves so much, her sister the Carmelite." They did not understand that all the joy of Heaven having entered my heart, this exiled heart was unable to hear it without shedding tears. Oh! No, the absence of Mama didn't cause me any sorrow on the day of my First Communion. Wasn't Heaven itself in my soul, and hadn't Mama taken her place there a long time ago? Thus in receiving Jesus' visit, I received also Mama's. She blessed me and rejoiced at my happiness. I was not crying because of Pauline's absence. I would have been happy to see her by my side, but for a long time I had accepted my sacrifice of her. On that day, joy alone filled my heart and I united myself to her who gave herself irrevocably to Him who gave Himself so longingly to me.[9]

This special day was marked in other ways. In the afternoon Thérèse made an act of consecration to the Virgin Mary during which she particularly remembered and prayed for an elderly man to whom she had once offered alms, only to have them refused, but she promised herself to remember him on her first communion day. She made three resolutions; first, not to be discouraged, a particular tendency of hers, a result of Jansenism. She affirmed her desire to please Jesus in all things. She already knew how easily she could give in to self-doubt and confusion so she knew that this was no easy resolution to make and to keep. Second, to say the "Memorae," a familiar prayer to Mary, every day. Third, she knew herself well enough to resolve to try to be humble, to control her self-love, for the nature of true love for Jesus

---

[9] SS 77–78.

involves humbling oneself even as he humbled himself. It was her understanding that in the eucharist Jesus perpetuates his incarnation, lowering himself and becoming one with her.[10] She had received an unspeakable gift. It was the most beautiful of days.

In this respect it was all the family had hoped it might be. In their understanding of faith and the life of faith this moment, this first receiving, was a defining moment, a singular step in the journey of faith. It was not a matter of having specially intense feelings, but living a truth revealed to her. Moreover, it was little Thérèse's sharing in the heart of the matter. She was united with Jesus in this sacrament, and with all those who lived, died and lived again in him. Here was a taste of salvation. Jesus had come to her in his living presence. Her desire to share communion, to receive Jesus in the mass remained with her and provided a living description of the trajectory of her whole life. She would live eucharistically, participating in the life of God, centred on the Jesus who shared everything he had heard from the Father, and who gave himself away in love.

My Own Story

I was born in 1940 and, like Thérèse, the home in which I grew up was Christian. From the first I was taught to say my prayers. Every Sunday we would all go to church. We "said grace" at meals and simply by living in this family community, talking together, reading and hearing the stories of the Bible, I learned the language of faith. Not the least, I was given a sense of privilege in learning of Jesus. I cannot recall any childhood rebellion against this religion which possessed an inherent joyfulness and love. This early childhood was lived through the war years, in a large house belonging to my grandparents, the home of an extended family with children and grandchildren present. It was a community of faith and embodied care. I cannot remember any serious moments of anxiety even when the bombs were dropping on the local Poole harbour. Later, we were to move to south London when my father returned from the war. Now we were a smaller family of four, my sister being born after the war. I missed the larger community but my parents were careful of their responsibility as Christian parents, and so my developing faith was broadened as I entered upon a very different church experience in a very different congregation to those of the local evangelical chapels I had known in Dorset.

Sutton Baptist Church was quite definitely in what has come to be called the baptist-catholic way of being church. There was an implicit sacramentality about its life, reflected in its building, its music and careful liturgies, its engagement with the life of the wider community and, most especially, in the importance given to baptism in the ever open baptistry and the regular

---

[10] Schmidt, *Everything is Grace*, 103.

eucharist. The building, designed and built in the early 1930s, had a very obvious pulpit to one side, the lectern on the other and the solid table in the center. Soaring arches, concealed lighting and eye capturing stained glass windows all added to the sense of wonder. Upon entering I knew, as a teenager, that this was a special place.

Sutton Baptist Church

In an architectural note written at the opening of the church building in 1934, reference was made to the separate chancel, unusual in a Free Church building, but adding greatly "to the sense of remoteness that is part of the atmosphere of worship."[11] The Lord's table or communion table is described as "unusual in that the 'mensa' or upper surface projects beyond the supporting structure beneath—a practice now universal in Catholic altars. The position of the Minister's seat behind the Table, facing the congregation stems ultimately from the 'Ambrosian Rite' of Milan . . . The flanking seats of the Deacons are arranged on a curve, as in the apse of an Early Christian Basilica."[12]

Perhaps unexpectedly, the church was of the "open membership" tradition among Baptists, that is, membership was open to all professed disciples of the Lord Jesus Christ.[13]

---

[11] The note appears as an Appendix to the brief history, Pettman and Kingsford, *Sutton Baptist Church 1869–1969*. The Appendix, "An Architectural History," 44–46, was written by H.V. Molesworth Roberts.

[12] Pettman and Kingsford, *Sutton Baptist Church 1869–1969*, 46.

[13] The next two paragraphs are a direct quotation from the small membership booklet given to each new member upon joining the church, published and printed by

Membership

The membership of the Church is open to all professed disciples of the Lord Jesus Christ. Application is made to the Minister, and if he is satisfied that the candidates fulfil this essential condition, messengers are appointed to visit them. The messengers report to a Church meeting, and if their report be satisfactory the candidates are accepted by vote of the Church, and at the following Communion Service are given the right hand of fellowship.

The Sacrament of Believer's Baptism is administered by the Minister to those who profess repentance towards God and faith in our Lord Jesus Christ. Baptism is not an essential condition of membership, but it is regarded as the normal mode of admission to the Church, and is believed to be morally binding on all who accept the New Testament as their authority. Infants may, at the request of their parents, be dedicated to God.

Communion Services are normally held on the first Sunday evening and the third Sunday morning of each month. All members are expected to be present and to place a Communion Card in the offertory bag, and they are furnished with an annual supply of tickets for this purpose. The contributions received at this Service, after deducting the necessary expenses, are devoted to the relief of needy members of the Church and congregation.

My First Communion

My first sharing in holy communion came on Sunday 4 July 1954 at the evening service when I was received into membership at Cheam Road Baptist Church, Sutton, Surrey. On the previous Sunday I had been baptized in the name of the triune God by total immersion and so became a member of the church catholic, a member of the body of Christ. I had been present at services of communion before with my parents, but only after baptism did I receive the gifts from the table myself. I have no recollection of being formally taught that this was the proper order of things and, in fact, as I have said above, the church was in the "open membership" tradition, but it was the church's and my parents' practice that sharing the feast followed baptism. Being baptized I came to share the meal for disciples, people committed to Christ in and by covenant love and calling. I can still recall the thrill when, for the first time, with many others I was offered and shared the bread and wine, seated in the front pew with others being welcomed into membership. I received the bread and wine and so was feeding on Christ with thanksgiving; I was part of that company that no one could number, the church in heaven and earth. My memory is that the language of the Fourth Gospel and Paul predominated in such services, especially the themes of feeding on Christ, abiding in Christ and Christ in us. There was also, in sermons and hymns, an engagement with the Exodus story of the people of God; answering a call, beginning a journey,

---

the church. Communion cards were common in those days of congregations numbered in their hundreds, and served an important role in maintaining pastoral care.

crossing the Jordan river, into wilderness years with temptations but being sustained with the wonder of the bread of heaven as we headed for the Land of Promise.

I cannot say what the congregation of those days expected as they came to the table; I can only speak for myself. There was no doubt that the service of worship was approached and shared with great care. Nothing informal, casual or superficial was there. For me, this was *holy* communion. It was a meeting place with Christ. The literalness of the language and action made a deep impression as we fed upon Christ's body and drank his blood. Here was the real presence of Christ, in bread and wine, in this people, in this one indivisible action as he had promised. I don't ever recall any special feelings, no moments of ecstasy, save an intensity of what was true of all life in, through, by and with Christ. The table proclaimed what was true about every place and time, a total immersion as affirmed in baptism in the form of sacrificial love for the world of God's creating and saving in Christ.

Unforgettably, at the evening services with communion, the lights were dimmed apart from one clear light focused on the table. After our receiving there was a time of deep quietness until a single note on the organ led us all unannounced and unaccompanied into a singing of the *Nunc Dimittis,* "Lord, now lettest Thou thy servant depart in peace, according to Thy Word." In these early formative years of my Christian life I knew, without it ever being spelled out intellectually that pool, table and pulpit all belonged together. Word without sacrament was word incomplete, as was sacrament without word.

Holding the Two Pictures Together

There are clear differences concerning communion in these two accounts of first communion, such as issues of priesthood, presence, ecclesiology and authority. However, for all such important differences I believe that all but the most narrowly sighted in vision will recognize important similarities. In both Roman Catholic and Baptist congregations, communion is an act of worship. The focus is on God, the One who by grace has gathered this congregation. The story of scripture is read and shapes the action. Prayers affirm the gracious presence of God, an offering of praise, confession, intercession and thanksgiving, all this in company with the saints. There is a table with bread and wine. Themes of tradition, presence, sacrifice, love, grace, giving and receiving, hope, abound with an invitation to share God's life of communion. That there are important theological differences is undeniable and that these differences wound us individually and together as the body of Christ is sadly true. but there is an essential unity here in the triune life and love of God, a vision of hope and salvation of all things in Christ. It is in the light of this conviction that I continue a conversation with Thérèse, recognizing what will become increasingly evident, namely that the eucharist set the whole direction for her life. Jesus was the One who called and sustained her in life, not least her dying. Her continuing story reveals more of her understanding of what it was to share the sacrament.

Christ at the Center

Christ was at the center of Thérèse's life. The union with Jesus known at first communion was the truth in which she trusted and hoped. Every day she made offerings to Christ of her joys and sorrows. She loved even the most difficult and unloving of her sisters in carmel because she loved Jesus in them and them for his sake. Not that her life was one of untroubled pleasant joy in the convent. There were difficult relationships to be negotiated, humiliations to be born, a tongue to be held and her own weaknesses to be faced. However, all her life was lived *coram deo*, before the triune God whose Son loved us and gave himself for us. The first communion confirmed the direction and gave the meaning to her existence.

After returning from midnight mass on 25 December 1886 she received an experience which she understood as the leaving behind of her childhood as she began a new period of her life. Jesus called her, and "I experienced a great desire to work for the conversion of sinners, a desire I hadn't felt so intensely before."[14] She heard continually in her heart Jesus' cry "I thirst," a cry which ignited within her an unknown and very living fire, this before she entered carmel. She set about praying for sinners. All this is a direct line from the first communion, the fusion with Jesus. She had no spiritual director, but rather speaks of a directness with Jesus. "Because I was little and weak He lowered Himself to me, and He instructed me secretly in the *things* of His *love*."[15]

On 9 April 1888, Thérèse entered the carmel at Lisieux. In 1890, she discovered the biblical texts in Isaiah which speak of "the Suffering Servant." Here she read of one disfigured, despised and rejected, one who had no form or likeness that meant he was undesired and passed by. She read and reread St John of the Cross, works which along with *The Imitation of Christ* she came to know intimately along with the Gospels. She was in the carmel, sacrificing her life for Jesus, sharing his longing for the salvation of others. Her body was in the cloister, but her prayers reached out all over the world, longing for Jesus to be known. She believed that Jesus knew the harshest physical pain on the cross and he fundamentally died of love for all, for the Father and for that humanity forever the focus of the Father's love. His thirst was deep, his desire that no one be lost. In June 1895, Thérèse wrote and made with Celine *An Act of Oblation to Merciful Love*. It is difficult not to see the deep eucharistic themes of the mass shaping this desire to share in Jesus' sacrificial death. A recent

---

[14] *SS* 99.

[15] *SS* 105 (italics original).

paraphrase expresses her desire this way,[16] *"Father, I understand that many people will not allow you to love them as you wish. There is an infinite ocean of merciful love pent up in your heart. Pour out that love on me. Love me for those who do not allow you to love them. Consume me with this love as you have consumed your Son in his passion. May this love overflow in me to draw many into the embrace of your love. Father, through my love, spare your son Jesus the pain of the loss of even one man or woman for whom he suffered. In the end, may I, with him, die of love."*[17]

Then on the night between Holy Thursday and Good Friday, 2–3 April 1896, Thérèse coughed up blood for the first time. She was not alarmed but rather delighted because she saw this as a sign of the immanent coming of the Bridegroom.[18] It happened again on Good Friday evening. Then on Easter Day, Sunday 5 April she experienced a sudden entrance into the night of faith, a trial that lasted until her death. She was in physical agony, but that was not all. She had been deeply touched by Jesus' thirst for souls, and this only intensified, except that she was in the dark, a fog, as in a tunnel devoid of light. She came to reflect more deeply on Jesus and the cross, the crucified God who longs to draw people into his life and love. Easter Day 1896 she entered a time of unrelieved darkness.

The teaching on the love and mercy of God she had received was what she trusted although there was plenty of evidence as to its truthfulness to the contrary. She persisted in hope of God, trusting that Jesus was her Saviour and that of all the world, but the darkness became very deep, shutting out the stars. The pain of tuberculosis was intense. She warned Mother Prioress not to leave tablets which might be used for suicide near those who suffered as she did. She began to wonder if her faith in life after death, the meaning of all those sacrifices in her life of faith, were not in the end in vain. The thought of heaven became nightmarish. The words "trial" and "suffering" appear more and more especially in her letters. The night of faith became the night of nothingness. The darkness was not penetrated and this she accepted. She realized that there really are people who do not know of God, believe in God. She prayed for atheists, shared their table, in some sense became one with them. The France in which she lived was increasingly secular and aggressive towards the church. In her trial of physical illness and agony she embraced also the sins and sinners of her time, sharing their life and table of nothingness. Living eucharistically, she understood this as a sharing in the passion of Christ, her part in his thirst and longing of love.

Thérèse did not require to develop a doctrine of the eucharist, or a theology of atonement. She lived it. The life centered on Jesus meant, for her, a true

---

[16] Miller, "St Thérèse of Lisieux," 23.

[17] Cf. *SS* 276–77 (italics original).

[18] *SS* 211.

surrender to his will in love and for love. She had long desired to be a saint, a martyr for the faith. Now she saw that martyrdom was not necessarily one great act of sacrifice, but could also take the form of the daily offering of love, for the unlovely, in the way and will of Jesus. She gave herself in the darkness to share Jesus' passion, he who died on the cross when there was darkness over all the earth (Matt. 27.45). She learned to die to herself and live for God. She did not parade any of this, longing instead to be hidden. She believed that in some way she was sharing the passion of Christ in a life hid with Christ in God (Col. 3.3), but this passion was, like the sacrifice of Jesus, for the church and for the world. Here, as at first communion, the Lover and the beloved are one in the saving action and purposes of the triune God.

Back to My Story

In keeping with the way of "open membership" the invitation to the table given early in the Baptist service of worship did not specify baptism, but the invitation was to all who sincerely love our Lord Jesus Christ. My memory also includes that of a regular reading, following always the words of institution, of Paul's warning in 1 Corinthians 11.27–32. We, who might come so easily, were called to examine ourselves. Earlier in the service of worship, we would have confessed our sins in trust of God's forgiveness. My recollection is that coming to the table was at Christ's invitation and that meant it was no light matter. It was the Lord's table, not the possession of the church. Something serious, a kind of solemn joyfulness, was going on in the eucharist. We were being brought into the life of the loving, suffering, sacrificing, saving God. It was and is all a great privilege as grace abounds.

Christ was present in word and sacrament. I recall being introduced even before theological college days to the meaning of *anamnesis*. This was, and is usually translated as, "remembrance," leaving a sense of the recollection of a past event. *Anamnesis,* the biblical word is more about the present, so recalling "the past event . . . that it becomes operative in the present."[19] The action at the table represented not just the upper room as a preface to the crucifixion but rather the total redemptive work of God, the new Exodus in the life, death, resurrection, ascension and high priestly rule of Christ in his perpetual intercession and offering to the Father. Christ was present as the Living One, not located in the bread and wine but in the whole event, the movement, in the gathered people of God, those becoming one body sharing the one loaf. Thus, the church is made a sacramental fellowship, entered by baptism and ever sustained by its shared participation in the sacrificial life of the Lord, risen from the dead. At the eucharist, *anamnesis,* that work of the Holy Spirit,

---

[19] Winward, "Church in the New Testament," 70. This was an important book for Baptists of that time. One of the contributors, Neville Clark, had also been a member at Sutton Baptist Church.

taking the things of Christ and showing them to us, made and makes Christ present, really present in the past, present and future nature of God's saving work, and so makes the church.

For myself, here was comfort in confusing teenage years when there seemed to be particular difficulties in living in love and charity with some neighbors. In days of seemingly constant school examinations and other more subtle but difficult social tests, such as the seemingly ever-present question of what I would do with my life, sharing in Christ at the table became a secure focus. Here I came not to remember a dead hero whom I might admire and even emulate in my self-dedication, but to receive, to be affirmed and welcomed among the people of God, to receive grace upon grace, the life and love of God in Trinity.

Admittedly there were occasions when, with sincerity of heart and mind, I shared the sacrament only to leave with the feeling that nothing had happened, there was no meaning or consequence to what we all had done. At such times, when I was very tired, low spirited, when bitterness of spirit and various other matters dominated, there was a sense of darkness and emptiness. I had yet to learn that in the darkness faith is deepened. In such moments, not always consciously, I was grateful for what I had been taught and come to believe as the faith of the church. Christ kept coming, present, as the gift beyond words. Such things were true regardless of my feelings, so I kept coming to the table. Some contemporary forms of celebration, all too casual, unshaped by the story, individual to the point of privacy, memorialistic, disembodied, left and still leave me feeling angry and cheated. Not every gathering at the table is a building up the body of Christ by feeding on his body and so becoming one with him. Yet, I still believe that even in such circumstance Christ keeps his promise. However, Paul's warning stands, that it is all too easy for us to eat and drink unworthily, not discerning the body.

Do I then have faith in the sacrament? The question is not the right one. My faith is in God, a God-given faith, and so I trust that Christ keeps his word, meets me and all of us gathered in his name, giving himself. It is not in the action, *ex opere operato,* that I believe as though the words and actions might conjure up something mystical, but it is in the promised Word made flesh that I put my trust.[20] Communion has nothing to do with what I feel, or how strong my faith is on any particular occasion. It has to do with God, the promised action of God in Trinity. My faith is in God, Father, Son, and Holy Spirit, who called and keeps on calling, who blessed and keeps on blessing, who gave and keeps on giving. Any service of Christian worship offered to God in Trinity that is of word only falls short of the full diet of God-given Christian worship, word and sacrament. In 1965 I was ordained to the ministry of word and sacrament.

---

[20] But see Fiddes, *"Ex Opere Operato."* I have much sympathy with the argument advanced here.

I can recognize the story Thérèse tells. Would she recognize mine? There are differences, some relatively trivial, but some critical. It is not my desire now in this essay to major on them, but rather to try to understand her convictions as well as my own. So, rather than yet another discussion of transubstantiation, priesthood and the liturgy, all of which would seriously matter to Thérèse, I want to focus on four inter-related issues which arise significantly in her life and mine. After all, if it really is the case that anyone wanting to know what Christians really believe should look at the way they live, and particularly how they worship, then the importance of communion is one of the keys to understanding Thérèse and Baptists.

Before moving to these issues, however, I need to point out one factor should it not already be obvious. Thérèse was nurtured, remained loyal to, and was declared to be a Doctor of the Church, the Roman Catholic Church, with its long tradition of authority. What the church believes and teaches is publicly declared in such documents as the *Catechism of the Catholic Church* for all to read.[21] Here we learn what Roman Catholic Christians believe. There is no such document for the Baptists.[22] Baptists have always been a varied lot. So I recognize that my description of first communion might only be acknowledged by a few older Baptists in England. I certainly cannot claim it is the "Baptist way." Indeed, to my dismay, I have to record that I would not expect to find such a shape and discipline in many British Baptist congregations today. Now, to the first of the four issues.

Presence

Both Thérèse and myself would affirm the presence of Christ in the eucharist, but our affirmations would be supported by different explanations. For Thérèse, Christ's presence is always with us but, as the *Catechism* teaches, "he is present . . . most *especially in the Eucharistic species*."[23] It is by this *conversion* of the bread and wine into Christ's body and blood that Christ becomes present in this sacrament.[24] This is the doctrine called "transubstantiation." This is why Thérèse could worship before the blessed sacrament for Christ was truly there, body, blood, soul and divinity, as she had been taught, for her and all the world. But, "Ecclesial communities derived from the Reformation and separated from the Catholic church 'have not preserved the proper reality of the Eucharistic mystery in its fulness, *especially because of the absence of the*

---

[21] A revised edition was published by the Catholic Truth Society in 2016, hereinafter cited as *CoCC* with paragraph number.

[22] See the discussion by Holmes, *Baptist Theology*, 1–9.

[23] *CoCC*, 1373 (italics original).

[24] *CoCC*, 1375.

sacrament of Holy Orders.'"[25] This is familiar and painful ground. There are
sharp questions I would want to put to this position, largely relating to just
how we understand the Christ-like God's engagement with us.

Rather than that debate again, I want to focus on the theme of presence. I,
too, want to affirm, even without the Catholic explanation, the real presence
of Christ when we are called to the table of the Lord. This holy presence is
sheer gift, the work of God. It is not localized in the elements specifically, nor
in the celebrant, but in the totality of the living event of remembering at the
table. It begins with God's word, calling us together in and through Christ by
the Spirit. It involves God's gathering of the people whom God has promised
to meet in the story of scripture, the fellowship of the church with all the
saints, the action of breaking, giving and sharing, the embodiment of faith and
hope and love by the grace of God. I am not appealing to a particular kind of
feeling which might be called "presence," but rather trusting the keeping of a
promise and the gift made in freedom. From all this, it makes no sense to
suggest that God is absent! Forms of ecclesiastical legalism do not set the
rules, not for the freedom of God, a point I shall develop later. At the table,
we feast on Christ with thanksgiving. By grace, we abide in him as he abides
in us. Relating, participating, promising and trusting, this is the movement
into which both God and the people are caught up in holy communion. God
speaks his word and is sacramentally present, as he promised.

Nurture, Teaching and Preparation

Both Thérèse and I thank God for the careful teaching and nurture in the
faith that we received. We found this at home, church and school, but what
was once so common is no longer to be assumed. The privilege that was ours
is now available only to a minority. France and England know the influence of
secularism and the ignorance of the basic Christian story of God is alarming.

In some ways we might think of ourselves as nearer to the early church,
those first Christians who had good news to proclaim, but which involved
time and explanation fully to enter into. Most of our fellow citizens live by
other faiths or no faith in God at all.

As the early church grew and spread the message of Jesus, it is clear, within
the New Testament itself, that there was no one pattern by which people
came to be grasped by the gospel. We have stories of instant conversion (Acts
9, Paul and the voice of the living Christ), stories of instant baptism (Acts 8,
Philip teaches the Ethiopian eunuch from Isaiah and baptizes him then and
there), and stories of Paul finding disciples who had never heard of the Holy
Spirit (Acts 19). There are strenuous arguments about the significance of the
Jewish Torah now that Christ has come (Galatians). It seems that conversion,
baptism and receiving the Holy Spirit are all aspects of the process of

---

[25] *CoCC* 1400 (italics added).

becoming a Christian, but there is no special order for this to happen in a person's life. The first Christians had to work this out, and local differences emerged. What becomes clear is that in those first three centuries the teaching and modelling of the faith in life became crucial. The time spent as catechumens could last years.[26] Much care was taken before baptism and the first communion. It is this old tradition of pastoral care in the church to which Thérèse and myself, in admittedly different ways, are grateful heirs. It needs recovering and reinstating.

This theologically careful proclamation and preparation has almost totally disappeared from among contemporary English Baptists. As I mentioned above, the pattern of my experience of first communion would be hard to find. It is currently said to belong to the inherited church with its traditional ways of doing things which can put people off and make it hard for them to come and worship. Certainly, whether this is true or not, the move has been towards informality and inclusiveness, especially with regard to holy communion. The most usual invitation to the Lord's table is to all who love the Lord, all who wish to come may come. This may reflect a common mood in churches, anxious about declining numbers and wary of anything which may look and sound like judgementalism and exclusivism. There is almost certainly a desire underlying such an approach for people to come and know Jesus Christ. What has been inherited is good and a gift, and I wish to affirm it and see it recovered, but it should not be turned into a new law. Baptism is a response to the gracious call of God who is rich in mercy and loving kindness. It is not a hoop to be jumped through. So attention is properly drawn to those stories of Jesus sharing table fellowship with sinners and outcasts, those actions which scandalized the religiously righteous, as told for example in Luke 7.36–50 and 14.1–14. For all that there is the closest of links between the last supper and the eucharist, is it possible that these meals tell us something about the presence of Christ in all forms of table fellowship?

Present day English Baptists have become undisciplined in this respect, perhaps for good reasons.[27] We chose the congregation of our choice, not first the one to which God has brought us. The basis of fellowship can turn into common enjoyment of a certain kind of song, again something of our choosing. I have no desire to press for a return to the practices even of my childhood much as I remember them with gratitude for such tradition can become slavish legalism. but we are vulnerable in the kind of theology, common in our churches, to individualism and a failure to recognize our one life in Christ, the fellowship of believers in Christ. Some hard thinking about the meaning of what it is to share communion, to discern the body, is long overdue even if it does go against the spirit of the age, and may have more to do with the renewal of the church than we realize.

---

[26] See Kreider, *Patient Ferment*, 176–77.

[27] See the helpful essay by Clarke, "A Feast for All?"

Sacraments and the Challenge to Dualism

Both Thérèse and myself share a sacramental view of life, the result of our teaching in the faith. Again, we do not agree on what this means and implies, but there are important consequences that we share. The Christian faith affirms creation and new creation which find expression in embodiment.[28] Such an affirmation challenges the simplistic, unbiblical dualisms found among Baptists, dualisms that separate spirit and matter, body and soul. Such dualisms are prone to appearing in some services of communion where the emphasis is on the death of Jesus, the forgiveness of sins and a (mis)understanding of atonement, which is primarily about going to heaven. Such unsacramental views limit the promise of salvation as new creation, and require somebody less than the Cosmic Christ, the Word by whom all that is is made and redeemed.

The dualism of matter and spirit linked with the individualism that rejoices only in "my personal Savior" is going miss the urgent ecological and economic implications of holy communion. If "The earth is the Lord's and all this is in it, the world, and those who live in it,"[29] then how we treat the world and care for all its inhabitants is no small matter. Living eucharistically, in trust of the God who became incarnate, who is forever using the things of earth to make his presence and purpose known, is the calling of the people of God.

Thérèse found great pleasure in the natural world of flowers and birds. She was creative, writing plays and poetry. She did not long for some separated spiritual existence safe away in heaven, but famously hoped that she could spend her heaven on earth doing good. For both of us, the heart of our faith is trust in God in Trinity, which means the essential presence of the incarnate God who redeems in flesh and blood. Communion keeps bringing us back to this God and his ways to which we are called. He who made us, became flesh for us, was raised by the Spirit and remains present in the world as he promised. He calls us to be the new humanity in Christ, the new creation, the coming time when God is all in all. This is part of what it is to be on the way of salvation and it finds focus and strength in the eucharist, in word and sacrament.

The Corporate Christ

Communion affirms scriptural tradition, *paradidōmi*, the handing on of what has been received from the Lord (1 Cor. 11.23–26). These words are often referred to as "The Institution," the passage often read in narrative form in Baptist communion services. The early Christians did not make this up; the meal came as a gift grounded in the history of the embodied Son of God. So,

---

[28] See Fiddes, Haymes and Kidd, *Communion, Covenant and Creativity*.

[29] Psalm 24.1.

through the centuries, Christians have come to the table, to remember and be remembered.

Thérèse's response to her first communion reveals how it set the trajectory for her whole life. She received more than she could ever give, indeed she discovered that such was the nature of the divine love in Jesus that no sacrifice was required. Yet her life was one grateful sacrifice, one act of martyrdom coming to a climax during those months of unrelieved darkness which she offered to Jesus in the hope that others in darkness might know him too. She loved Jesus and lived out a great desire to make Jesus' love known. Here was faith in the crucified God, calling disciples to carry the cross, participating in the life of God. All this before God and so possessed of wonderful hope, leading to apostolic boldness. She lived as a witness to the Cosmic Christ of God who is never anyone's individual possession, but is to be found as he gives himself in his body.

For this Baptist, Thérèse remains an inspiration and challenge. Our tendency to individualism, our stress on independent congregations, these features of our inheritance as Baptists have also become signs of our weakness, our limited ecclesial calling, our diminished notions of discipleship. We keep longing for renewal, that we might be more the church of Jesus Christ. I have come to agree with Stephen Holmes who, after a lecture concerned with Baptist demands for renewal in acknowledgement of hungry, hurting people jumping on one bandwagon after another, argued that we might have to face this truth. He says, "If we are to be faithful to the Scriptures, and to our Baptist tradition: if we are to be theologically orthodox and pastorally wise, might I suggest one thing, and one thing only;

Come to this sacred table, not because you must, but because you may.[30]

To which I say a hearty "AMEN." And yet, is there not a crucial sense in which we *must* come to the table of Christ to remember and be re-membered? Lord, to whom else can we go? (John 6.68)

Bibliography

Catholic Truth Society. *Catechism of the Catholic Church*. London: Catholic Truth Society, 2016.

Clarke, Anthony. "A Feast for All? Reflecting on Open Communion for the Contemporary Church." In *Baptist Sacramentalism 2*, edited by Cross and Thompson, 92–116.

Cross, Anthony R., and Philip E. Thompson, eds. *Baptist Sacramentalism 2*. Studies in Baptist History and Thought, 25; Milton Keynes: Paternoster, 2008.

---

[30] Holmes, *Tradition and Renewal*.

Fiddes, Paul S. "*Ex Opere Operato*: Re-thinking a Historic Baptist Rejection." In *Baptist Sacramentalism 2*, edited by Cross and Thompson, 219–38.

Fiddes, Paul S., Brian Haymes, and Richard Kidd. *Communion, Covenant and Creativity*. Eugene, OR: Wipf and Stock, forthcoming 2020.

Foley, Marc. *The Context of Holiness; Psychological and Spiritual Reflections on the Life of St Thérèse of Lisieux*. Washington, DC: ICS, 2008.

Holmes, Stephen R. *Baptist Theology*. Doing Theology. London: T. & T. Clark International, 2012.

———. *Tradition and Renewal in Baptist Life*. The Whitley Lecture 2003. Oxford: Whitley, 2003.

Kreider, Alan, *The Patient Ferment of the Early Church: The Improbable Rise of Christianity in the Roman Empire*. Grand Rapids: Baker Academic, 2016.

Miller, Frederick, L. "St Thérèse of Lisieux: Doctor of Divine Love." *Mount Carmel* 67.4 (2010) 8–16.

Pettman, K., and H. Kingsford. *Sutton Baptist Church 1869–1969*. s.l.: Privately published, 1969.

Schmidt, Joseph F. *Everything is Grace: The Life and Way of Thérèse of Lisieux*. Ijamsville, MD: The Word among Us, 2007.

Thérèse of Lisieux. *Story of a Soul: The Autobiography of St Thérèse of Lisieux*. 3rd ed. Translated by John Clarke. Institute of Carmelite Studies. Washington, DC: ICS, 1996.

Winward, S.F. "The Church in the New Testament." In *The Pattern of the Church: A Baptist View*, edited by A. Gilmore, 54–78. London: Lutterworth, 1963.

CHAPTER 6

Sacraments in a Virtual World:
A Baptist Approach

Paul S. Fiddes

A Cautionary Tale

In June 2009 I received a request from Mark Brown, who was then the CEO of the New Zealand Bible Society, to write a brief paper on whether it was possible to have sacraments in services of worship in a virtual world in cyberspace.[1] Brown was one of the founders of the Anglican Cathedral established in the online virtual world of "Second Life,"[2] and later I was to be drawn in for a short while—and gladly—to the life of the Cathedral when I agreed to the request of Bishop Christopher Hill[3] to be a theological consultant on several issues that had arisen, though not that of virtual sacraments.[4] The Bishop was at the time the presiding chaplain overseeing the Cathedral. I did not, however, know that the writer of a liturgical blog, an Anglican priest named Bosco Peters, would be asked by Second Life Cathedral (SLC) in 2009 to comment on my paper.[5] In fact, I remained blissfully unaware of his response, together with an extensive online correspondence it generated, until 2018. I also did not know that Bishop Christopher had commented on my paper in one he had written himself called

---

[1] Fiddes, "Sacraments in a Virtual World." This is no longer available online.

[2] "Second Life" is developed and owned by the San Francisco-based firm Linden Lab and launched on 23 June 2003. By 2013, Second Life had approximately one million regular users, but by the end of 2017 the count had dropped to between 800,000 and 900,000. Land can be bought and property erected; the Anglican Cathedral was built in June 2007 on Epiphany Island.

[3] Christopher Hill was Bishop of Guildford 2003–14, and has been continuously involved in ecumenical relations throughout his ministry.

[4] Two issues were whether animal and fabulous-beast avatars, dragons, for example, were welcome to worship in the Cathedral; and whether it was proper for a man to offer counselling using the avatar of a woman. The consultancy group advised respectively in the positive and negative.

[5] Peters, "Virtual Eucharist."

"Second Life and Sacraments," offering a set of guidelines for the Cathedral.[6]
I have, further, been interested to find a number of recent books and articles
on the subject which comment on my all-too brief paper. This general
ignorance of a debate raging in cyberspace and book-space, to which I have
apparently made a small contribution, seems to call for a written follow-up
which I am glad to provide for the present volume.[7]

In my paper of 2009, I argued that "The key theological question is
whether the triune God is present . . . within the virtual world. If the answer is
yes, then one can conceive of the mediation of grace through the materials of
that world, i.e. through digital representations." The result of reading some of
the material generated by this piece since 2009 is to discover, to my
astonishment, that it has largely ignored a key point that I made in my paper,
a point in fact occupying about a third of its small space. Since I want to
concentrate on this same aspect in my chapter here, I shall repeat part of what
I wrote earlier:

> There can be an "extension" of the sacraments from the church sacraments of
> bread and wine into the sacramentality of the whole world, since the world is
> held in the life of the triune God; for an expression of this, see Teilhard de
> Chardin's *Mass on the World*. Many physical objects in the world can become a
> focus of mediated grace in continuity with the church sacraments, while
> remaining dependent upon the sacraments of dominical institution for their
> meaning. My suggestion about virtual sacraments thus falls somewhere into the
> spectrum between church sacraments of bread and wine and other sacramental
> media in the world. I do not want to suggest that virtual sacraments would be
> simply *identical* with the church sacraments, though given the context of a
> "virtual church" I suggest they would be closer on the spectrum than—say—the
> sacraments of sand and light in RS Thomas' poem "In Great Waters."[8] It might
> be said that the stuff of a virtual sacrament includes both sand (silicon) and light
> (photons)! Is there any less sand and light in a virtual world than in Thomas'
> experience of the sea off the coast of Wales?

I want to return to the question of "stuff" later, but for the moment I want to
underline that what interested me then—and still does—was the *particular*
place on a spectrum of "sacramentality" occupied by pixels in a computer
program, in which human persons could be deeply involved, emotionally,
aesthetically and intellectually. I was not arguing for a simple equivalence
between sacraments in cyberspace and sacraments in a church located in a
specific, geographical place. I am glad to say that Bishop Christopher in his

---

[6] Hill, "Second Life and Sacraments."

[7] Based on my symposium paper on "Virtual Body of Christ?"

[8] Thomas, *Collected Poems*, 351. Thomas observes that the sand is like crumbs of
bread, and the light is like wine lying in a chalice.

"guidelines" saw the point, welcoming my affirmation that "God is present in a virtual world in a way that is suitable for its inhabitants," and writing that "Fiddes argues, again in a manner entirely coherent with traditional (Catholic and Anglican) sacramental theology that grace can be mediated through the material world—including the silica chip and light photons."[9] Bishop Christopher prefers, however, to call these kind of mediations "sacramentals" rather than "sacraments," to make the distinction clearer from sacraments received in a non-virtual church.[10] Again he writes,

> My use of an extended traditional concept of "sacramentals" is consistent with Fiddes' conclusion that his suggestion about virtual sacraments falls into a spectrum between sacraments proper "and other sacramental media in the world."[11]

Thus he warns, "respect would need to be paid to Fiddes' careful use of the term 'virtual sacraments', implying, to my mind, a proper distinction between a virtual sacrament [and a sacrament] in the 'real', ie nonvirtual, world where physical, human presence is necessary."[12]

We notice that the Bishop places "real" in inverted commas, and immediately clarifies this as meaning "non-virtual." Thereby he flags up a problem in language. He seems reluctant to make a simple distinction between "real" and "virtual," and I sympathize with him in this. We might say that an online world is real in its own right, and so to call it "unreal" would be misleading. It is also in a sense, physical, and so "virtual" and "physical" are not absolute contrasts either.[13] In my paper I refer to non-virtual sacraments as "church sacraments," but this is not really satisfactory since a virtual church is certainly a kind of church. In this paper I will use the word "local-church sacrament" as distinct from a virtual sacrament, since this indicates that it is a sacrament received in a congregation which is gathered in a single place that can be *located* in the world, as distinct from a virtual place that (while being, in a sense, physical) has no particular location as it exists dispersed in many computers. A local-church sacrament is, of course, at the same time a

---

[9] Hill, "Second Life and Sacraments," 6.

[10] Hill, "Second Life and Sacraments," 1 and 6.

[11] Hill, "Second Life and Sacraments," 6.

[12] Hill, "Second Life and Sacraments," 6.

[13] Bennett and Schmidt note that the situation is further complicated by the fact that the Catholic Church, living by the sacraments and other symbols, is anyway a kind of "virtual church," making what is absent present: Bennett, "Key Issues in Digital Theology"; and Schmidt, "Virtual Communion," 81–126.

sacrament of the church universal, as local and universal exist in what Walter Kasper names as a relationship of *perichoresis*, or co-inherence.[14]

The cautionary nature of the tale I am telling is that what the Bishop calls "respect" for the distinction I make has not in fact been paid, and I was over-naive to think it *would* be in the age of online networking. The immediate response by Bosco Peters ignored the distinction I had carefully made, and attacked me mercilessly for the supposed absurdity of treating an online sacrament as equivalent to a sacrament in bread and wine received in a local congregation, or—as he put it—"a parodying in the virtual world of that which is particular to Real Life."[15] The multiple responders to his blog did not trouble to read my paper, but simply assumed Peters had given an accurate account of it. At one point, for instance, Peters makes a sarcastic refutation of virtual baptism, along the lines that "we cannot pour a jar of jelly beans over someone and say they are baptized." In fact, I never proposed virtual *baptism* in my original paper, and in this chapter I want to give reasons, within the logic of a virtual world, why this is not possible.[16]

A careful master's thesis, written by Kate Lord out of her experience of working with Second Life Cathedral and published on the SLC website in 2012, again makes no mention of the distinction I make between the virtual and the local, although she does write that "I admit myself disappointed with the paper recently released by Bishop Christopher Hill regarding this issue of sacraments in Second Life, and the extent to which he agrees with Fiddes."[17] By contrast, I should say that a recent book by Teresa Berger does entirely see the point of the distinction I make between different kinds of sacrament, and underlines the significance of it.[18]

But enough of a cautionary tale. Let us now proceed to the really interesting theme of the place occupied on a sacramental "spectrum" by the creation of a eucharistic sacrament in cyberspace—I mean a sacrament within the logic of a virtual world, involving virtual elements which represent bread and wine, and administered by an avatar to avatars. The Catholic theologian Jana Bennett, in her book *Aquinas on the Web?* comments that my approach here—which she found cited favorably in an article by Thomas Locke[19]—at first "made sense" to her, and on that basis she embarked on a tour of virtual

---

[14] Kasper, "On the Church," 927–30.

[15] Peters, "Virtual Eucharist."

[16] Hutchings, *Creating Church Online*, assumes that I am arguing for a virtual baptism on the basis of Peters' account, and maintains wrongly therefore that Christopher Hill must disagree with me: see ch. 2, section "Ritual."

[17] Lord, "Can Eucharist be administered in a virtual world?" 16.

[18] Berger, *@Worship*, 87–88.

[19] Locke, "Virtual World Churches," 60–61.

churches built in the world of Second Life; however, she reported that unfortunately she could find no instances of such a digital sacrament. She records that she visited the Holy Angels' Chapel, and listened there "virtually" to Thomas Aquinas' *Tantum Ergo*, but "found that oddly disconcerting, since the hymn is about adoring Christ in the Body and Blood of the Eucharist, but there was no Blessed Sacrament before which to fall."[20] My proposal probably remains at this moment unactualized, but this is no reason why it should not be explored for coherence and for the spiritual gain it *might* offer, especially if we consider the nature of a sacrament from the perspective of the Baptist tradition.

A Sacramental World

Perhaps I was unwise to place a summary at the head of my original paper in which I began "An avatar can receive the bread and wine of *the Eucharist* within the logic of the virtual world." The specific reference to "the" Eucharist may have fostered the view that I was proposing a substitute eucharist, a form of worship equivalent to eucharist in a local congregation. This danger was probably in Bishop Christopher's mind when he preferred the term "a sacramental." However, I deliberately used the word "eucharist" in order to assert a definite *continuity* with what I am calling a "local-church sacrament." In viewing the whole world as "sacramental" (an adjective) I want to conceive of many objects within the world as having potential to be "sacraments" (noun) though they will all be dependent on the local-church sacraments. I prefer then to call these wider means of grace "various *kinds* of sacrament" rather than "sacramentals."

This seems also be the strategy of Teilhard de Chardin, who does not hesitate to use the word "mass" in considering the sacramental consecration of the whole world. He speaks of "prolongations" and "extensions" of the eucharist as celebrated by a priest in a church. He writes, "from the particular cosmic element into which he has entered, the Word goes forth to subdue and to draw into himself all the rest."[21] So, when Teilhard was on a geological field trip in the bitter-cold mountains of Northern China in 1923, he wrote his piece called *Mass on the World*, and begins,

> Since once again, Lord—though this time not in the forests of the Aisne but in the steppes of Asia—I have neither bread, nor wine, nor altar, I will raise myself beyond these symbols, up to the pure majesty of the real itself; I, your priest, will make the whole earth my altar and on it will offer all the labours and sufferings of the world . . . I will place on my paten, O God, the harvest to be won by this

---

[20] Bennett, *Aquinas on the Web?* 121–22.

[21] Teilhard de Chardin, *Hymn of the Universe*, 14.

renewal of labour. Into my chalice I shall pour all the sap which is to be pressed out this day from the earth's fruits . . .[22]

For Teilhard, this is not merely a playful simile. He believes he is *actually* celebrating the mass, praying "Do you now therefore, speaking through my lips, pronounce over this earthly travail your twofold efficacious word . . . This is my Body . . . This is my Blood."[23] but he can make this universal celebration, *only because* bread and wine are consecrated in the eucharist of the local church.

Just as Teilhard celebrates a mass in which the elements are the whole world, so it should be possible to have a "eucharistic" celebration in which the elements are pixels, although this cannot be regarded as the *same* as a "local-church" eucharist. Any such act of worship would be dependent for its meaning and reality on the fact that elements of bread and wine are consecrated in local churches. Again, we may appeal to the reflections of Teilhard when, one day in the trenches of the First World War, he had a vision of the consecrated host that he had been carrying in his pocket. Each time he thought he had grasped the surface of the host, he found that what he was holding was "not the host at all, but one or other of the thousand entities which make up our lives: a suffering, a joy, a task, a friend to have or console." There was a breaking down of the barrier between the communion bread and all the bodies of the world and the result, he testified, was "[a] feeling of rapture produced in me by this revelation of the universe placed between Christ and myself."[24]

Poets such as Gerard Manley Hopkins have testified to the same rapture of finding Christ present in a eucharistic form in the world—that is, present in the mode of sacrifice. Hopkins watches a Windhover, or hawk, which has been soaring masterfully on the currents of air, suddenly "buckle" or plummet to the earth; and there he finds the presence of Christ in the world of nature, showing his lovely majesty in his descent to the death of the cross. He writes,

My heart in hiding
Stirred for a bird,—the achieve of, the mastery of the thing!
Brute beauty and valour and act, oh, air, pride, plume, here
       Buckle ! AND the fire that breaks from thee then, a billion
Times told lovelier, more dangerous, O my chevalier![25]

---

[22] Teilhard de Chardin, *Hymn of the Universe*, 19.

[23] Teilhard de Chardin, *Hymn of the Universe*, 23.

[24] Teilhard de Chardin, *Hymn of the Universe*, 51–53.

[25] Hopkins, "Windhover," in *Poems*, 69.

The world of cyberspace can be also part of this sacramental universe for at least two reasons. The first is the willingness of God to enter and inhabit all worlds, and the second is the complex relation between the person and his or her avatar. Both these factors I included in my earlier paper of 2009.

First, the combination of the doctrines of the incarnation and the resurrection of Jesus encourages us to think that God is present in a virtual world in a way that is suitable for its inhabitants. In Christ, God becomes flesh. Then the risen Christ continues to inhabit the world in a universal lordship, unhindered by any one space and time, though taking special opportunities to be visible through a particular form of his body, the church.[26] Taking a trinitarian perspective, we may say that the whole universe lives within the interweaving relations of the triune God, and through Christ God deepens God's own reciprocal living in us. The world of cyberspace cannot be excluded from this mutual habitation.

I was first brought to think this because of an analogy with the world which is inhabited by a schizophrenic. Living closely to a schizophrenic son for a number of years, I became familiar with his experience that the world in which he was living appeared completely real to him, though alien to others. The theological question was whether he could meet Christ in *his* world, and I came to say that Christ walked its streets. I was glad to see that Teresa Berger underlined that analogy—only an analogy, of course, in her comment on my original paper.[27]

If we, through our avatars, can meet Christ in a *virtual* world, then we can receive grace through sacraments created in that world. Grace is, of course, not a substance but the gracious presence of God, coming to transform personality and society. In sacrament, God takes the occasion of bodies in creation to be present in an intense or "focused"[28] way to renew life. There seems no reason to deny that God can take the materials of a virtual world, that is, digital representations, in the same way, and that the risen Christ can take visible form in that world through a virtual church.

The second reason for thinking that the world of cyberspace is part of a sacramental and eucharistic universe is the unique relation between the person entering this world and his or her avatar, or the *persona* that is being adopted. Within the logic of the virtual world, a virtual church such as the Anglican Cathedral in *Second Life* is a place where avatars worship God and avatars minister to avatars. If a eucharist were offered, the "person" could thus only receive a virtual sacrament *indirectly* through relation to the avatar. My

---

[26] I make clear elsewhere that the church is not the only form of the body of Christ in the world, see Fiddes, *Seeing the World and Knowing God,* 344–46.

[27] Berger, *@Worship,* 87.

[28] The term is used by Macquarrie, *Principles of Christian Theology.* 449.

argument is that the grace of God received by an avatar through a virtual means of grace, can be shared with the person whose avatar it is.[29]

This is because there is a mysterious and complex interaction between the person and the *persona* projected (avatar), and this is also the case between a person and his/her *personae* (self-presentations to others) in everyday life. There is what the Christian psychotherapist, Paul Tournier, calls the relation between the "person" and the "personage."[30] The "personage" is Tournier's word, as a doctor, for the mask or the image which we project when we present ourselves to others. We have, he observes, many masks that we wear, according to occasion and our needs for acceptance. We might find a vivid example of this phenomenon in a story told by the biographer of the film-star Judy Garland, writing of his first interview with her in a hotel room in 1968. She had kept him waiting for four hours, and when she finally allowed him to come up, he found she had prepared for the meeting by putting on a circus clown's makeup. He realized immediately that she was coping with a potentially painful meeting by presenting an image of herself as the helpless victim everyone pities, "seizing on this way out, to hide behind this façade— the wistful, loveable little clown whom no one would dare to hurt."[31]

Less dramatically than this example we have a repertoire of personages with which we play the game of life and society. We take on the role, and ask people to see us in a certain way. It would be quite wrong to say that these "personages" are false and artificial, and must be stripped away to find the real person underneath. Of course, they must not be *confused* with the person, of whom we can suddenly catch a glimpse, or find ourselves meeting at an intuitive level. We can experience communication with the person at his or her core of being in an I–Thou encounter; we know when it happens. but the masks (which belong to the "it" world) cannot be simply removed like a coat

---

[29] Bosco Peters remarks, "Virtual Eucharist," that "The concept of an avatar being the receiver of God's grace is astonishing from an Oxford Professor of Systematic Theology," but it appears that he is working with the idea of grace as some kind of substance, when he asks, "does all of the grace received by the avatar automatically get transferred to the person behind the avatar? Or in some . . . cases is only some of the grace transferred, with the avatar retaining grace that was originally given by God to the avatar? . . . What happens to this grace when the computers fail and the virtual world ceases?" Such questions of quantity of grace are themselves absurd when we understand grace here as God's graciously relating God's self to the avatar and at the same time to the person through it. The idea of an avatar receiving grace is, we notice, accepted quite readily by a Bishop of the Church of England, see Hill, "Second Life and Sacraments," 6, urging a sincere relationship between person and avatar. Similarly, Neal Locke has approved my proposal of receiving grace through an avatar in "Virtual World Churches," 62.

[30] Tournier, *Meaning of Persons*, 71–83.

[31] Gardiner, "Interview."

or suit of armor. We are wedded to them and can never be divided from them. When we ask "who am I?" we ourselves have to search among the personages for the mystery of our person as much as *others* do when they ask who we are. The sociologist Erving Goffman has stressed that these images have their part to play in making us who we are. Without them, we would not be social beings but mere individuals.[32]

Admittedly Goffman's analysis is *reductionist*; the person for him is not much more than the sum of the roles she plays or is accorded. Society is the games people play, or a sacred theatre of ritual. but if we accept his basic point that the masks we wear are part of us, a Christian pastor will seek to enable someone to live in the interaction between person and personage, to become aware of the way that he or she is using masks, to live in harmony between self and presentation. The problem is not the personage itself, the roles and the rituals, but *discord* between the personage and the person. I would like then to refine Bishop Christopher's point that an avatar can transmit grace to the person who owns it only if the person is using the avatar *sincerely*.[33] Rather, we need to learn, by God's grace and pastoral help, to bring *all* our masks or personages into a whole.

Integrating our two reasons for thinking a virtual world can be sacramental—the presence of God and relation to an avatar—we should observe that avatars in a virtual church are not worshipping merely an avatar-God. There *is* only one God, for whom person and persona are identical, and in whom "all things live and move and have their being" (Acts 17.28), including the beings of virtual worlds. The question now is *which* sacramental actions in this world can be means of grace. In his guidelines, Bishop Christopher suggests a range of "sacramentals" to which he thinks my proposal can apply; these include renewal of baptismal and confirmation vows, services of penitence, acts of healing, and renewal of marriage vows. They do not include anything that looks eucharistic, as he is obviously anxious to prevent confusion with local-church eucharist, which requires the presence in one place of elements, presiding priest and congregation. I, however, suggest that taking seriously our two factors of the presence of God in a virtual world and intimate involvement of the person with an avatar, it ought to be possible to have the same kind of eucharistic celebration as Teilhard found with his mass on the world, and Hopkins found in the watching of a bird in flight. It seems impossible to separate a sacramental world from a eucharistic world, if we take the sacrifice of Christ as basic to creation and redemption.[34] Dangers of confusion are evidently to be taken seriously, but I would like to explore

[32] Goffman, *Presentation of the Self*, 19–25, and *Interaction Ritual*, 5–8, 42–44 and 82–84.

[33] Hill, "Second Life and Sacraments," 6.

[34] See Balthasar, *Studies in Theological Style*, 381–83.

possibilities of eucharistic celebration which are not simply equivalent to eucharist in a local church, but have their own reality. In a moment I will make a practical suggestion, but first I want to consider the theological issue of:

Real Presence in the Eucharist

In his ironic attack, Peters presumes to guess what kind of sacramental theology I have as a Baptist theologian. He writes about a "minority position" in the Christian tradition that "the bread and wine are [merely] reminders to the faithful person receiving them," and goes on, "Fiddes, an ordained Baptist minister, is faithful to the Baptist foundations of Regent's Park College in his sacramental ideas about an individual receiving grace by being [merely] mentally involved in a computer simulation." In fact, my whole argument of a relation between person and avatar depends on a eucharistic theology of the "real presence" of Christ, though with many theologians, and with the Articles of Religion of the Church of England, I do not regard this as identical with transubstantiation.[35] That would indeed make any kind of eucharistic celebration with computer simulations of the elements impossible. With a large number of Christian thinkers, I understand the real presence of Christ to be an action of Christ in making *himself* present through the whole drama of the eucharist, through the elements and through the bodies of the disciples who are participating. While God is always present to the world, and the created world is present to God through being involved in the life of the Trinity, in the moment of the eucharist this presence is deepened, focused and intensified. It is not the materials of the eucharist that make Christ present in this special way, but always Christ who presences himself. As a Baptist writer on the sacraments, John Colwell insists a sacrament is a means of grace because "only God is the efficient cause of grace within a sacrament." Instrumentality (the elements) and "agency" are not to be confused.[36]

This is, I suggest, a distinctively Baptist approach to the eucharist—which is not, as Peters supposes, a purely mental memory of Christ, but a discernment of the body of Christ in the action of the meal and in the disciples who gather. A movement of thought away from the localized containment of the body within the bread and wine, and towards the agency of God through Christ, helps to avoid a static notion of presence, and allows for a more dynamic kind of presence-as-encounter throughout the whole drama of the supper. Indeed, modern ecumenical consensus on the eucharist has moved in this direction, away from a restriction of presence within the

---

[35] See the Church of England, *Articles of Religion of the Church of England*, XXVIII, "Of the Lord's Supper," C4.

[36] Colwell, *Promise and Presence*, 60.

substance of the elements to encounter with Christ through the whole action of the rite.[37]

Thus, both General and Particular Baptist theologies in the first two centuries of Baptist life witness to the supper as an occasion for "communion" with Christ, for receiving the "benefits" of his atoning work on the cross, and for spiritual feeding and nourishment of the soul. For example, an English Particular Baptist of the late sixteenth century, Hercules Collins, recognizes that "as the Bread and Wine fuſtain the Life of the Body, ſo alſo his crucified Body, and Blood ſhed, are indeed the Meat and Drink of our Souls" so that "we are Fleſh of his Fleſh, and Bone of his Bones."[38] Here, though a Calvinist, he echoes the thinking of Huldrich Zwingli about the community of disciples, that "We eat bread so that we are made into one bread . . . What we become by this eating . . . is the body of Christ."[39] In the same period the General Baptist writer Thomas Grantham speaks of "Gods preſence in his Ordinances," so that in the supper "by faith we herein eat the Fleſh of the Son of God and drink his blood."[40] At the same time he affirms encounter: Christ crucified is "held forth" and "an offer [is] made" in the elements in a way that calls for us to make an "approach nigh to God with the whole heart."[41] Another Particular Baptist stresses this element of true meeting, writing that "There is a myſtical Conveyance or Communication of all Chriſt's bleſſed Merits to our Souls through Faith held forth hereby, and in a glorious manner received, in the right participation of it."[42]

A recent Catholic writer on digital theology, Catherine Schmidt, draws on the similar thought of Henri de Lubac, maintaining that the sociality and unity of the church are expressed and formed through the celebration of the eucharist.[43] Using the language of "symbolic exchange" she affirms that the symbols of the eucharist are the location where human subjectivities interact in the presence of Christ. She then finds the same kind of "symbolic exchange" happening in cyberspace, but tends to detach these exchanges from the eucharist itself, regarding the internet as offering what she calls "ancillary

---

[37] E.g., *Agreed Statement on the Eucharist*, 7.

[38] Collins, *Orthodox Catechism*, 41–42 and 39.

[39] Zwingli, Letter to Matthew Alber, 16 November 1524, in Pipkin, *Huldrych Zwingli*, vol. 2, 141.

[40] Grantham, *Christianismus Primitivus*, 91, 93.

[41] Grantham, *Christianismus Primitivus*, 88, 92.

[42] Keach, *Tropologia*, IV, 45.

[43] De Lubac, *Catholicism*, 18, 92–99 and 225. Schmidt, "Virtual Communion," 82–90, is also critical of de Lubac, however, finding that he allows ecclesiology to supplant the sacramentality of the body of Christ.

spaces" to the eucharistic community.[44] I am going further in suggesting that a
Baptist theology of "real presence" will find that the essential conditions of
eucharistic communion can be met in the virtual reality of the web—there can
be the drama of the meal, in breaking bread and pouring wine, symbols representing the sacrifice of Christ, and the gathering of those in whom Christ
takes bodily form. Through all these Christ can presence himself. Digital
sacraments are thus not only a "visible signs" to be received by the sense of
sight, as Neal Locke suggests is characteristic of Reformed thought. While he
believes that my proposal of avatars receiving grace at the hands of other
avatars fits with this Reformed emphasis,[45] I am in fact arguing for a more
embodied grace.

One ought not to assume that cyberspace is a disembodied world. The net
is composed of a form of energy, just as is the familiar physical world in which
we operate every day. Moreover, the persons behind the avatars are in physical
connection with the virtual world—through many of the senses (sight,
hearing, touch—i.e., keyboard, mouse). Anyway, mental activity always has a
physical base in the brain. Studies have shown that people feel a bodily
connection with those with whom they are communicating over the net. In
one book, the author interviews a number of people who have "virtual
relationships" with other net-users. These are people who meet, talk and
even—it seems—find love in cyberspace. What fascinated the author was the
way that these relationships were not just a matter of words (or rather
duodecimal digits), but seem to have taken over the whole person, including
the body. Although one net-user gave the author permission to communicate
with his "virtual partner," he became increasingly agitated, abruptly took the
keyboard back, and could hardly type because his hands were shaking so
much. He felt that this had been an intrusion on an intimate relationship.
Other people the author talked to felt strongly that they were being unfaithful
to their married partners by having such relationships, and that they had—
virtually—committed adultery. His conclusion was that the cyberspace
personality had taken on a "surprising substance."[46]

Alternative Forms of Online Eucharist

There remains the urgent question as to how, practically, a eucharistic
celebration in cyberspace can avoid confusion with a "local-church" eucharist,
and occupy a place on the sacramental spectrum somewhere *between* local-
church and the general sacramentality of the world—the latter as experienced,

---

[44] Schmidt, "Virtual Communion," 187–92 and 194–95.

[45] Locke, "Virtual World Churches," 59–61.

[46] Slouka, *War of the Worlds*, 52–55.

for example, through a painting as a means of grace.[47] My own proposal has been that the elements of the eucharist may be represented digitally—with bread and wine created from the material reality of digits and pixels. Two people who have been closely connected with the Second Life Cathedral who think this cannot be eucharistic are Kate Lord and Bishop Christopher Hill. Lord proposes eucharist by an extension: it may be celebrated by worshippers bringing their own bread and wine to the computer screen for an ordained priest conducting the service online to consecrate in a general prayer of consecration.[48] Hill proposes that the priest in the virtual church should be conducting a eucharist in a local church at the same time as broadcasting over the net, and that participants in the virtual congregation should make a purely spiritual communion.[49] Even if they eat bread and drink wine they have provided (and he would prefer not), it remains a spiritual event.

Whatever may be said for and against these proposals (and each proponent finds the other approach inadequate),[50] I observe that they are aiming to make the online eucharist *equivalent* to a local-church eucharist. My own proposal is within the logic of a virtual world that is also sacramental and eucharistic. It suggests that there can be a virtual form of eucharist which is a means of grace while not being the same as the local-church sacrament. However, experience of participating in worship in a "lock-down" at home resulting from the Covid-19 pandemic in 2020, when it was impossible to attend worship in a local-church situation, has persuaded me that something more should be said about putting a local-church eucharist online.

By exploring the logic of a virtual eucharist, I am not ruling out something like "extended communion" in particular circumstances. In Baptist sacramental theology, it is good order for the minister called by a local church to be its pastor to preside at the holy table—among other reasons, by her or his ordination (s)he represents the universal church in the local assembly. However, Baptists do not see this as a legal exclusiveness. In Baptist tradition, a church meeting may, in particular circumstances, call others of its members to preside at the table, usually a deacon, while nobody should take this privilege upon themselves.[51] In a situation of "lock-down," it seems proper for the church meeting to give consent for all members to "co-celebrate" with the minister. The minister will still preside at a service which is taking the form of a digital meeting, but members of the church who wish may have bread and wine at home with them, and may share in saying the words of institution and

---

[47] So Brown, *God and Enchantment of Place*, 5–25.

[48] Lord, "Can Eucharist be administered in a virtual world?" 22.

[49] Hill, "Second Life and Sacraments," 11.

[50] Lord, "Can Eucharist be administered in a virtual world?" 16–17; and Hill, "Second Life and Sacraments," 11.

[51] Fiddes, *Tracks and Traces*, 178.

consecration with the minister. In this way, the dramatic action of breaking and pouring comes together in each place with the word spoken. This is therefore not consecration "from a distance," such as is proposed by Kate Lord, and will not be possible with an Anglican, Catholic, or Orthodox theology of ordained ministry. From a Baptist perspective, I believe this is a true re-membering (coming into one) of the body of Christ, especially since in Baptist tradition Christ is understood to be present not only through the elements and the whole action of the Lord's supper, but in the bodies of the disciples who are sharing in the bread and wine. Their faces may well be presented on the screen in a kind of montage program such as "Zoom," so that Christ becomes visible in a new way through all the members of his body.

In his book *SimChurch*, Douglas Estes suggests that sacraments in cyberspace might take four forms.[52] He calls these respectively: symbolic virtual communion, avatar-administered virtual communion, extensional virtual communion, and outsourced virtual communion. The first of these correspond roughly to the proposal of Christopher Hill. The second concerns the consumption of digitized bread and wine, which is my main focus in this paper. The disadvantages that Estes finds with this are: the danger of trivialization, and an over-spiritualization due to lack of physical elements. However, he is considering only an attempt at *equivalence* with a local-church eucharist, and so does not consider whether the physicality of the web might be sufficient for the kind of virtual sacrament I am proposing, and whether this would render it non-trivial.[53]

It may be impossible to achieve this without confusion, and it may remain simply an abstract concept that *ought* to be possible, but in practice is not. but I am encouraged to think it possible through a phenomenon that happens constantly in the kind of real world represented by a local church, and which is experienced by Baptists. I mean that in, for example, a Local Ecumenical Partnership which contains Baptists and Anglicans, a service of holy communion may take place presided over by a Baptist minister. The Church of England does not, at present, recognize Baptist ministerial orders, and so, in its official theology, Baptist ministers cannot have a eucharistic ministry. Yet, by sponsoring the LEP, it encourages the Anglican worshippers present to regard the sacrament they receive as a means of grace. Rather than making the negative judgement that such a communion is "not" a eucharist, the general Anglican approach is simply to make clear that it is "not an *Anglican* communion" but it is (say) a "Baptist Lord's supper." The relevant canon

---

[52] Estes, *SimChurch*, 118–23.

[53] The fourth model he suggests is less obvious: it envisages a group from an online church being given hospitality in a local church, and participating in an online eucharist in that situation. Estes judges that this "outsourcing" would seem to undermine the value of the virtual community in itself.

states that "the service is not to be held out or taken as being a celebration of the Holy Communion according to the use of the Church of England."[54] Yet such services still take a eucharistic form, and are presumably occasions for Christ to presence himself and give grace in a special way that nourishes the Anglican faithful. Is there an analogy here? Might mainstream Christian confessions simply say of a virtual eucharist, using virtual sacraments, that "this is not an Anglican eucharist" or it is "not a Baptist Lord's supper" but that it is "a eucharistic celebration in a virtual world"?

An alternative approach from a Catholic perspective to distinguishing between eucharist in the local church and on the web has recently been (tentatively) made by Jana Bennett, in an unpublished lecture.[55] She suggests that the host, consecrated in a local church, might be presented in a digitized form on the web and so be available to be adored. There is, of course, an established liturgy of adoration in the Catholic Church, through which the body and blood of Christ, present under the appearance of the sacramental bread, is the focus of devotion by the faithful. Thus, adoration might be a suitable activity for a web-user, as an alternative to participation in the eucharist through either virtual eating and drinking or communion by extension. Bennett appears to have in mind the transmission on the web of a local eucharistic celebration with consequent exposition of the host, and then its subsequent repetition on an online video-sharing channel like YouTube.

If a viewer is adoring the body of Christ in the host in a broadcast *simultaneous* to that of a local church service, then it could be claimed that what is being adored is the body of Christ as shown to the faithful in its original ecclesial context, "behind" the digitized image. but as soon as the scene is repeated on demand by the user (as Bennett is envisaging), that particular host is being stored in a digital form and is only available in a display of pixels of light. There seems then, I suggest, to be no greater "reality" in such digital storage and re-creation than in the creation of a consecrated host by a computer program in the first place. The advantage that the kind of eucharistic event in a virtual world I am commending has over "adoration" is that the presence of Christ is not being restricted to a particular collection of pixels, but "happens" there and then through the action depicted and through the whole community of users who are sharing in it.

Conclusion: Virtual Eucharist but not Virtual Baptism

I only include the eucharist in this virtual celebration of sacrament, and not baptism, and finally explaining why will—I hope—underline the internal logic

---

[54] Church of England, *Canons*, B43, 11(2)(b).

[55] Bennett, "Key Issues in Digital Theology."

of a virtual sacramental world.[56] Baptism must take place in a local church, because my argument depends on virtual eucharist being on a point on the sacramental spectrum somewhere *between* local church and the general "sacramentality" of the universe. It cannot *replace* communion in a local church, but is a means of grace that can give depth and meaning to communion in a local congregation. It is good then that, as far as possible, members of a virtual church should—from time to time—worship with fellow-Christians in a local church, each enriching the experience of the other. Baptism, however, simply *is* a local church sacrament. By its nature it is a once-for-all initiating event to be practiced in non-virtual water in a church gathered locally which is nevertheless part of the church catholic. Just as online eucharist cannot *replace* local church eucharist, by the same logic there can be no *replacement* for local church baptism. Any sacramental action that by its nature is non-repeatable will, if practiced in cyberspace, be bound to attempt to replace its local-church form; this would, in addition to baptism, include ordination and marriage which are therefore also to be excluded from virtual celebration.

In fact, there is already a "baptismal" sacrament which *can* be practiced in cyberspace parallel to virtual eucharist, and which similarly occupies a place on the spectrum between "local church" and "universal" sacramentality. This is not baptism, but renewal of baptismal vows. Baptism is an initiating immersion into the death of Christ so that we may share in his resurrection, yet every day is a continuing experience of dying and rising with Christ for those who are baptized. This may be expressed sacramentally from time to time in renewal, through water, of vows made either personally by a disciple ("believers' baptism"), or made on his or her behalf by sponsors and the gathered church ("infant baptism"). There has always been liturgical provision in some churches for this renewal by asperging, or sprinkling with water, especially at the Easter season, and the Liturgical Commission of the Church of England in 2006 allowed for this to be expressed through immersion.[57] Bishop Christopher Hill has argued that both sprinkling and immersing for renewal of baptismal vows may also be represented in a virtual world, and avatars may administer them to avatars. He writes,

> If in Second Life an authorized minister (lay or ordained in accordance with
> Anglican law) were to conduct such a service of Renewal of Baptismal Vows in

---

[56] Estes, *SimChurch*, 126–27, discusses "Avatar-mediated virtual baptism," and suggests that it might be a solution in parts of the world where baptism in water and a local community is highly dangerous for candidates.

[57] The Commission allows that candidates for "Affirmation of Baptismal Faith" might "use significant amounts of water with which to sign themselves (or even dip themselves)," see commentary by the Liturgical Commission in Church of England, *Christian Initiation*, 349–50.

the Epiphany Cathedral, it is my view that providing the person "behind" the avatar sincerely taking part in such a service had been really baptised, they would be really renewing their baptismal vows.[58]

Hill, as I have already observed, opts to call this and other digital rites "sacramentals" rather than "sacraments," but as with eucharistic worship on the web I prefer the term "sacrament" in order to preserve continuity with the "local-church" sacraments, as long as they are understand as *depending* on the local-church form to give them validity and meaning. As with local and internet forms of the eucharist, the common element between baptism and renewal of vows is encounter with Christ. Again, this encounter is clearly seen in a Baptist understanding of sacramentality which distinguishes between the "instrumentality" of water, bread and wine and the "agency" of God; God uses created instruments to act in a transformative way.

Baptism is an interplay between the human act of faith and the active grace of God, understood as the gracious coming of the triune God, or the immersion of a believing disciple in the gracious communion of the triune God through the death and resurrection of Christ. While some Baptists have understood baptism only as a witness of faith to a salvation already received, there is a strong current in the Baptist tradition[59] which understands baptism as a "sacrament of regeneration" (the phrase is from the Baptist Thomas Grantham);[60] this is because in the baptismal pool God uses the created material of water as a place of meeting between a disciple who comes with faith and God's own self, whose coming must be a force to change human life. The Baptist requirement that it should be (normatively) already believing disciples who come for baptism may appear to conflict with the affirmation that such a meeting, or "rendez-vouz,"[61] with God in Christ is salvific or "regenerative"; but the solution is to realize that salvation is not a single point, but a process that begins in the intention of God and ends in the final glorified body of resurrection. Baptism is thus not the beginning of God's

---

[58] Hill, "Second Life and Sacraments," 7.

[59] Baptist interest in a sacramental approach to baptism was renewed in the twentieth century by such writers as Robinson, *Baptist Principles*, 26–31; Clark, *Approach to the Theology of the Sacraments*, 29–35; White, *Biblical Doctrine of Initiation*, 270–317; and Beasley-Murray, *Baptism in the New Testament*, 263–305. That this twentieth-century movement only revived a longstanding strand in Baptist thinking has been shown by Fowler, *More Than a Symbol*, 10–155.

[60] Grantham, *Loyal Baptist*, Second Sermon 15: "the Sacrament of waſhing or Regeneration."

[61] I use and explain this term in Fiddes, *Tracks and Traces*, 117. Similarly, Beasley-Murray, *Baptism in the New Testament*, 305, writes of baptism as a "trysting-place" between lovers.

saving activity in a person's life, but it is the key moment in Christian "initiation" or the period of someone's life which is marked by the beginning of a life "in Christ" as a disciple.[62] As the Standard Confession of General Baptists (1660) puts it, baptism is "the new Testament-way of bringing in Members, into the Church by regeneration."[63]

With this understanding of baptism, renewal of baptismal promises can also be understood as a significant moment of deepening encounter with God within a life-long process of "being saved" (1 Cor 1.18). Baptism has its place within initiation, and cannot be repeated, but renewal of promises has continuity with this primary event. Following the logic of the way that a virtual eucharist is a means of grace, there can only be a *renewal* of baptismal vows in a virtual context. Both virtual eucharist and renewal occupy a place on a sacramental spectrum between "local church" and the whole universe as space of God's self-disclosure.

This paper has largely been a thought-experiment, rather than reflection on practices taking place on the web. but it is essential in our age to do this kind of digital theology. On the one hand, it clarifies the very nature of sacraments by asking what qualifies as "material" or created "stuff" that can be the media for God's presence, and how God uses it as an instrument of grace. On the other hand, it takes seriously our situation today, in which "virtual reality" needs to be understood theologically, rather than leaving it simply to the realms of technology and sociology. Moreover, by practicing the two sacraments—or sacramentals—of eucharist and baptismal renewal in a virtual world, we may come to experience more profoundly the created universe itself as not only eucharistic but baptismal, where created beings, by immersion into the waters of death, come to a new creation.

Bibliography

Anon. *A Brief Confession or Declaration of Faith, Set forth by many of us, who are (falsely) called Anabaptists*. London: F. Smith, 1660.

Agreed Statement on the Eucharist. Anglican–Roman Catholic International Commission, Windsor, 1971. London: SPCK/Catholic Truth Society, 1972.

Balthasar, Hans Urs von. *The Glory of the Lord: A Theological Aesthetics*. Volume 3. *Studies in Theological Style: Lay Styles*. Translated by Andrew Louth, John Saward, Martin Simon and Rowan Williams, edited by John Riches. Edinburgh: T. & T. Clark, 1986.

[62] For the idea of a "process of initiation," see Fiddes, *Tracks and Traces*, 141–52 and 217–20.

[63] *Brief Confession*, Article XI, in Lumpkin, ed., *Baptist Confessions*, 228.

Bennett, Jana Marguerite. *Aquinas on the Web? Doing Theology in an Internet Age.* London: T.&T. Clark, 2012.

———. "Key Issues in Digital Theology." Unpublished lecture, given at "The Virtual Body of Christ?" Symposium, University of Durham, 20 April 2018.

Berger, Teresa. *@Worship: Liturgical Practices in Digital Worlds.* Abingdon: Routledge, 2018.

Brown, David. *God and Enchantment of Place Reclaiming Human Experience.* Oxford: Oxford University Press, 2004.

Church of England. *Articles Agreed Upon by the Arch-Bishops and Bishops of Both Provinces, and the Whole Clergy, in the Conviction Holden at London, in the Year 1562.* London: John Bill and Christopher Barker, 1662.

———. *Canons of the Church of England.* https://www.churchofengland.org/ more/policy-and-thinking/canons-church-england.

———. *Christian Initiation: Common Worship.* London: Church House, 2006.

Clark, Neville. *An Approach to the Theology of the Sacraments.* Studies in Biblical Theology, 17. London: SCM, 1956.

Collins, Hercules, *An Orthodox Catechism: Being the Sum of Christian Religion Contained in the Law and Gospel.* London: s.n., 1680.

Colwell, John E. *Promise and Presence. An Exploration of Sacramental Theology.* Milton Keynes: Paternoster, 2005.

De Lubac, Henri. *Catholicism: Christ and the Common Destiny of Man.* Translated by Lancelot C. Sheppard and Elizabeth Englund. San Francisco: Ignatius, 1988.

Estes, Douglas. *SimChurch.* Grand Rapids: Zondervan, 2009.

Fiddes, Paul S. "Sacraments in a Virtual World," 2009. https://slangcath.wordpress. com/tag/paul-fiddes

———. *Seeing the World and Knowing God: Hebrew Wisdom and Christian Doctrine in a Late-Modern Context.* Oxford: Oxford University Press, 2013.

———. *Tracks and Traces. Baptist Identity in Church and Theology.* Studies in Baptist History and Thought, 13. Milton Keynes: Paternoster, 2003.

———. "The Virtual Body of Christ? Sacrament and Liturgy in Digital Spaces." Paper for the CODEC Research Centre for Digital Theology, Durham University, 19–20 April 2018.

Fowler, Stanley K. *More Than a Symbol: The British Baptist Recovery of Baptist Sacramentalism.* Studies in Baptist History and Thought, 2. Carlisle: Paternoster, 2002.

Gardiner, Frank. "Interview." *The Guardian,* 10 September 1975.

Goffman, Erving. *The Presentation of the Self in Everyday Life.* London: Allen Lane/Penguin 1969.

———. *Interaction Ritual: Essays on Face-to-Face Behaviour.* London: Allen Lane, 1972.

Grantham, Thomas, *Christianismus Primitivus: or, The Ancient Christian Religion.* London: Francis Smith, 1678.

————. *The Loyal Baptist or An Apology for Baptized Believers. In Two Sermons*. London: T. Grantham, 1684.

Hill, Christopher. "Second Life and Sacraments: Anglican Observations and Guidelines." 2012.https://slangcath.files.wordpress.com/2012/09/second-life-an d-sacrament-4.pdf.

Hopkins, Gerard Manley. *The Poems of Gerard Manley Hopkins*. 4th rev. and enlarged ed. Edited by W.H. Gardner and N.H. Mackenzie. London: Oxford University Press, , 1967.

Hutchings, Tim. *Creating Church Online: Ritual, Community and New Media*. London: Routledge, 2017.

Kasper, Walter. "On the Church." *The Tablet* 255 (23 June 2001) 927–30.

Keach, Benjamin, *Tropologia. A Key to Open Scripture-Metaphors*. London: Enoch Prosser, 1683.

Locke, Neal. "Virtual World Churches and the Reformed Confessions." *Princeton Seminary Review* 17 (2010) 55–66.

Lord, Kate. "Can Eucharist Be Administered in a Virtual World? Further points for consideration by the Anglican Cathedral on Epiphany Island in Second Life." https://slangcath.files.wordpress.com/2013/02/final-copy-kates-paper.pdf

Lumpkin, William L., ed. *Baptist Confessions of Faith*. Chicago: Judson, 1959.

Macquarrie, John. *Principles of Christian Theology*. Rev. ed. London: SCM, 1966.

Peters, Bosco. "Virtual Eucharist: Can Sacraments Work in a Virtual World?" *Liturgy* 28 June 2009. http://liturgy.co.nz/virtual-eucharist

Pipkin, H. Wayne, ed. *Huldrych Zwingli, Writings*. 2 vols. Allison Park, PA: Pickwick, 1984.

Robinson, H. Wheeler. *Baptist Principles*. 4th ed. London: Kingsgate Press, 1945.

Schmidt, Catherine G. "Virtual Communion: The Theology of the Internet and the Catholic Imagination." PhD diss., The College of Arts and Sciences of the University of Dayton, 2016.

Slouka, Mark. *War of the Worlds: Cyberspace and the Hi-tech Assault on Reality*. London: Abacus, 1996.

Teilhard de Chardin, Pierre. *Hymn of the Universe*. Translated by S. Bartholomew. London: Collins, 1965.

Thomas, R.S. *Collected Poems 1945–1990*. London: Dent/Orion, 1993.

Tournier, Paul. *The Meaning of Persons*. London: SCM, 1957.

White, R.E.O. *The Biblical Doctrine of Initiation*. London: Hodder and Stoughton, 1960.

CHAPTER 7

"Richly are thy children fed:"
The Lord's Supper in the Preaching of Dr John Ryland

Lon Graham

Introduction

In 1680, Hercules Collins (1646–1702), pastor of the Wapping Baptist church in London, produced a version of the *Heidelberg Catechism*, edited to conform to his Baptist convictions.[1] In his *Catechism*, Collins asks of the Lord's supper, "How are thou in the Lords Supper admonifhed and warranted that thou art Partaker of that only Sacrifice of Christ offered on the Crofs, and of all his Benefits?" His answer reveals an understanding of the supper that is rooted in the Calvinism of the *Heidelberg Catechism*: "My Soul is no lefs affuredly fed to everlafting life with his Body, which was crucified for me, and his Blood which was fhed for me, than I receive and tafte by the Mouth of my Body, the Bread and Wine, the Signs of the Body and Blood of our Lord, received at the Hand of the Minifter."[2] According to Collins, the recipient of the elements is fed spiritually thereby.[3]

---

[1] Weaver Jr, "Hercules Collins," 152–53. Weaver details the changes that Collins made to the *Heidelberg Catechism*. Despite these changes, Collins believed himself to be within the stream of Reformed orthodoxy represented by the *Heidelberg Catechism*, writing, *Orthodox Catechism*, [2] (no page numbers are given for the preface), "In what I have written you will see I concenter with the most Orthodox Divines in the Fundamental Principles and Articles of the Christian Faith, and also have industriously expressed them in the same words, which have the like occasion bin spoken, only differing in some things about Church-constitution, wherein I have taken a little pains to shew you the true form of God's House."

[2] Collins, *Orthodox Catechism*, 38–39. He follows this with another question, "What is it to eat the Body of Chrift?" He gives the following in answer, 39: "It is . . . to be united to his facred Body, that though he be in Heaven, and we on Earth, yet nevertheleſs we are Flefh of his Flefh, and Bone of his Bones."

[3] This view of the Lord's supper is also called the "Calvinistic" view. For more on John Calvin's understanding of the Lord's supper, see Baker, *Participation in Christ*; Gerrish, *Grace and Gratitude*; and Riggs, *Lord's Supper in the Reformed Tradition*.

Collins' sacramental understanding of the supper was not unique among Particular Baptists of his era. The supper as "spiritual nourishment" is found in the landmark 1677 *Confession*.[4] In the eighteenth century, the influential pastor Benjamin Beddome (1717–95) of the Baptist church at Bourton-on-the-Water, writes of both baptism and the Lord's supper as "sacraments,"[5] and says of the Lord's supper, "by faith [worthy receivers are] made partakers of his body and blood, with all his benefits to their fpiritual nourifhment and growth in grace."[6]

Something changed by the end of the nineteenth century, however. Michael Walker has shown that the memorial, or "Zwinglian,"[7] view of the Lord's supper came to dominate Baptist understandings of the ordinance.[8] The reasons for this are, no doubt, varied. Walker roots much of it in the Baptist response to the Catholic revival of the nineteenth century, "Not least of these adverse effects of the Catholic revival upon many Baptists was their apparent inability to give priority to what they did believe about the Lord's Supper over what they did not believe."[9] More recently, Michael Haykin traced the history of the period of transition, producing evidence of the Calvinistic side in Anne Dutton (1692–1765) and Joseph Stennett (1663–1713), and evidence of the Zwinglian side in Abraham Booth (1734–1806) and John Sutcliff (1752–1814).[10] Both Walker and Haykin offer neat and convincing accounts of the Particular Baptist movement away from Calvinistic language to an almost-exclusive use of memorialist language.[11]

---

[4] Anon., *Confession of Faith* [1677], 99. The *Confession* goes on to say, 102, that "worthy receivers, outwardly partaking of the vifible Elements in this Ordinance, do then alfo inwardly by faith, really and indeed, yet not carnally, and corporally, but fpiritually receive, and feed upon Chrift crucified & all the benefits of his death."

[5] Beddome, *Scriptural Exposition*, 157.

[6] Beddome, *Scriptural Exposition*, 167.

[7] The case of Zwingli is somewhat complicated, as the traditional understanding of Zwingli as representing a memorial view has been upset by the arguments of some that Zwingli's own view is closer to that of Calvin than modern memorialists. The name "Zwinglian" is still attached to this view, and will be in this essay, though with the caveat that it is possible that Zwingli himself was not a Zwinglian, see Moore-Crispin, "Real Absence," 22–34; and Riggs, *Lord's Supper in the Reformed Tradition*, 55–74.

[8] Walker, *Baptists at the Table*, 3–8.

[9] Walker, *Baptists at the Table*, 11; cf. 84–90.

[10] Haykin, "His soul-refreshing presence," 184–93.

[11] Haykin focuses exclusively on Particular Baptists, while Walker includes both Particular and General. This essay will focus on the Particular Baptists.

However, while they offer convincing accounts of this transition, the story is, perhaps, not as neat as may be supposed. Indeed, it is a somewhat complex history,[12] and this complexity is illustrated well in the thought of John Ryland Jr (1753–1825). Ryland was a contemporary and friend of the Zwinglians Abraham Booth and John Sutcliff as well as Robert Hall Jr (1764–1831), a proponent of the Calvinistic view.[13] Ryland was the pastor of two well-known and influential churches within Particular Baptist life, the church on College Lane in Northampton (1781–93) and the Broadmead church in Bristol (1793–1825). He also co-founded the Baptist Missionary Society in 1792, worked as its secretary (1815–25), and served as President of Bristol Baptist Academy (1793–1825). What one finds in Ryland is an expression of both views, indicating that, at the time, they were not necessarily mutually exclusive.

This essay will examine Ryland's understanding of the Lord's supper as found in both his published and unpublished writings. It is hoped that it will provide a more nuanced view of Baptist understandings of the Lord's supper during the period of transition from predominantly Calvinistic terminology for the supper to that which was more Zwinglian. The essay will proceed with a brief description of the memorialist passages in Ryland, then to a more detailed description of the Calvinistic passages,[14] and finally to an explanation of how Ryland comprehends both views in his theology of the Lord's supper.

---

[12] To his credit, Walker admits the complexity of the history in his account of the Baptist response to the Catholic revival. At the height of the revival, in 1857, Baptists produced a series of articles in the *Baptist Magazine* entitled "Sacramental Meditations," in which the following is said of the proper reception of the elements: "Let us each seek, as we take the bread and wine of the supper, to take and eat the flesh and drink the blood which were to freely given *for* us on the cross, and which are given *to* us to feed and strengthen our fainting souls," see Anon., "Sacramental Meditations," 286, cited in Walker, *Baptists at the Table*, 14.

[13] Though he held to the Calvinistic view of the supper, whether or not Robert Hall Jr was himself a Calvinist is open to debate. He participated in the life of the Particular Baptists, and he eventually replaced Ryland as the pastor of the Broadmead church, but, in a letter to the church dated 9 December 1790, he rejected the name Calvinist for himself and denied aspects of traditional Calvinistic theology, see Hall Jr, *Works of Robert Hall*, 3:19–20; cf. McNutt, "Ministry of Robert Hall, Jr.," 109–16.

[14] The memorialist passages are dealt with briefly because the essay will return to them in the explanation of how Ryland holds both views together.

"To remember our dearest Friend:"[15] Ryland and Remembrance in the Lord's Supper

Ryland's memorialist theology is seen in a variety of sermons.[16] Ryland preached two different sermons on 1 Corinthians 11.29 which demonstrate the memorial view. In the first, published as "Requisites for Communion"[17] and preached three times from 1780 to 1824,[18] he offers a brief definition of the supper as "an affecting memorial of the incarnation and death of Christ."[19] In the second, published as "The Unworthy Communicant"[20] and preached just once in 1821 at a Lord's supper service at Broadmead, he goes into more detail with regard to his memorialist emphasis, writing that "he must be chargeable with this crime, who comes to the Lord's table without *understanding the nature and design* of this institution."[21] He elaborates that a person's worthy communion rests on "remember[ing] the Son of God,"[22] and then he spells out that such remembrance is to be focused on his incarnation and atonement.[23] In another sermon, on Psalm 5.7, preached at the 5 July 1814 preparation meeting[24] at Broadmead,[25] Ryland writes, "At the L.S. we

---

[15] Ryland, "Sermon Notes: Exodus 12:26," n.p.

[16] Ryland did not produce a book-length work on the Lord's supper. His theology of the ordinance is found in his sermons.

[17] Ryland, "Requisites for Communion," 63–66.

[18] Ryland kept a record, which he called his "Text Book," of every sermon he ever preached, complete with date, place, and text. It is kept at the Northamptonshire Record Office. In it, he says that he preached this sermon in 1780 at College Lane, then again in 1799 and 1824 at Broadmead's Lord's supper services. The dates of these sermons are important for establishing the ubiquity of both views in Ryland's thought throughout his life. Therefore, the dates of the sermons will, where possible, be noted.

[19] Ryland, "Requisites for Communion," 63.

[20] Ryland, "Unworthy Communicant," 59–63.

[21] Ryland, "Unworthy Communicant," 60.

[22] Ryland, "Unworthy Communicant," 60.

[23] Ryland consistently highlights incarnation and atonement as the two major touchstones of remembrance during the Lord's supper. Elsewhere, he exhorts the congregation to "recognize his most memorable Affections, Actions and Sufferings. His Incarnation and Obed[ce]. unto Death," Ryland, "Sermon Notes: Exodus 12:26," n.p.

[24] The "preparation meeting" was a practice of the Broadmead church in which the church met for a service several days before the monthly Lord's supper service in order to prepare to partake of the Lord's supper the following Sunday.

comemorate [sic] the Exhibition of the most abund^t. Mercy, & moſt inflexible Justice."[26]

One reading of Ryland, then, would place him squarely in the memorialist camp, both in his terminology and emphasis upon the subjective action of the individual partaker of the elements.[27] However, such a reading is incomplete and does not display the complexity of Ryland's understanding.

"The Appointed Means of Communion:" Christ's Presence in the Supper

Ryland also places a sustained emphasis on the supper as a means of grace and locus for the presence and activity of Christ. While it was noted above that Ryland explains the Lord's supper as a commemoration of the exhibition of the death of Jesus, in another place, he says that the Lord's supper itself is a "fresh exhibition of a crucified Saviour" that should "excite to mourn afresh for sin."[28] This exhibition is, of course, not of the Roman Catholic variety.[29] Rather, it is spiritual, a "manifestation of Christ to the soul."[30] This manifestation is made "not by discovery of new truths concerning him; but by impressing the heart with a lively sense of the excellence of discoveries already made in the Sacred Scriptures, the foundation for which was laid by regenerating grace; and which inward sense of the Saviour's excellence and glory is revived, and increased from time to time, by the influence of the Holy Spirit on the soul."[31] This is key for understanding Ryland's theology of the

---

[25] Ryland also preached the same sermon at College Lane Baptist Church in Northampton on 1 May 1785, which was the week before the church held a Lord's supper service, see Ryland, "Text Book," 1 May 1785.

[26] Ryland, "Sermon Notes: Psalm 5:7," n.p. As will be shown below, it is noteworthy that Ryland makes a distinction between the exhibition of God's mercy and justice and its commemoration, where the Lord's supper is not itself an exhibition of those things but merely memorializes them.

[27] Cf. Sutcliff, "Ordinance of the Lord's Supper," 3–9, in which Ryland's colleague and friend writes repeatedly of the individual's action in receiving the elements of the supper.

[28] Ryland, "Unworthy Communicant," 61. The complexity of Ryland's understanding is seen in this quotation when compared with the earlier quotation, in which Ryland says that the Lord's supper is merely a commemoration of the exhibition of Christ's death. In this sermon, however, it is more than a commemoration; it is itself the exhibition.

[29] Ryland rejected the Roman Catholic understanding of the Lord's supper, which he denounces as a "monstrous fiction," so "Spiritual Participation of Christ," 308.

[30] Ryland, "Nature and Evidences," 334.

[31] Ryland, "Nature and Evidences," 334–35. The language that Ryland uses here is reminiscent of that found in Jonathan Edwards' *Religious Affections*, in which Edwards

supper. What happens when the supper is eaten is not the gaining of new knowledge; it is not intellectual. Rather, it affects the heart, the inward sense, and the soul. That is to say, the effects of the Lord's supper on an individual are on that individual's inner life. It is felt in the experience of the individual.

Echoing the language found in earlier Baptists, Ryland holds that the soul is nourished by means of the Lord's supper. In the 1 Corinthians 11.29 sermon mentioned above, published as "Requisites for Communion," Ryland says that the Lord's supper is "for the benefit and refreshment of the soul, when in the outward signs the believer realizes and contemplates the things they were intended to signify."[32] The signs of the supper are meant to be *contemplated*, which has to do with the remembrance aspect of the ordinance, as well as *realized*, which, for Ryland, goes beyond bare remembrance. "Realize" may mean simply "bring to mind," as in, "She realized where she left her keys." However, Ryland goes on to say in the same sermon, "That we improve the symbols used in the Lord's supper for this end, making a difference between what we eat at the Lord's table, and our ordinary food. The Lord's supper is for the support and refreshment, not of the body, but of the soul. A small piece of bread may remind us that Christ is the bread of life; a sip of wine may remind us that his blood was shed for the remission of sins."[33] While he uses the language of remembrance, it is clear that this is more than bringing to one's memory. It is an action benefiting not the memory but the soul. For this reason, as the body and blood of Christ are "realized" in the Lord's supper, the soul is refreshed and the recipient feeds upon Christ.[34] In one sermon, Ryland refers to the Lord's supper as "the gospel feast," through which "with broken hearts we may look to him whose body was broken for us."[35]

---

speaks of the joys that the saints have in heaven. Edwards writes, "If we can learn any thing of the State of Heaven from the Scripture, the Love and Joy that the Saints have there, is exceeding great and vigorous; impreſſing the Heart with the ſtrongeſt and moſt lively Senſation of inexpreſſible Sweetneſs, mightily moving, animating, and engaging them, making them like to a Flame of Fire," so *Religious Affections*, 20; cf. 19.

[32] Ryland, "Requisites for Communion," 64.

[33] Ryland, "Requisites for Communion," 65.

[34] This is seen in Ryland's poetic answer to the question "What is the Lord's ſupper?" *Serious Essays*, 126:

> The eating bread and drinking wine,
> In mem'ry of our Lord divine;
> Who broke HIS body, ſhed HIS blood;
> To feed our ſouls with living food.

[35] Ryland, "Unworthy Communicant," 63. Using the language of John 6.53–56, Ryland says that Christ is "the bread of life" and that "his flesh is meat indeed, and his

According to Ryland, a worthy partaking of the Lord's supper also effects union (or a further union) with Christ. In an intriguing line, Ryland says that the person who has discerned the body of the Lord and, thus, is worthy of receiving the elements "actually unite[s] with him [Christ], in the pursuit of these objects, seeking after answerable affections, and correspondent conduct." "These objects" refers to "the propriety of his mediation; the suitableness of this method of salvation, by the incarnate Son of God, to the support of his government; manifestation of his grace, and full display of all his glorious perfections."[36] Ryland is not clear on how or when this union takes places, but it is clear that it happens in the event of the Lord's supper. The Lord's supper, then, may be seen as a means by which the recipient receives afresh the benefits of Christ's mediation.

In addition to his sermons and sermon notes, Ryland also left behind many poems and hymns, most of which have never been published.[37] Most of Ryland's poetic output does not touch on the Lord's supper, but the places in which he does deal with it are instructive. In a hymn which he composed for the church at College Lane, to be sung for the Lord's supper service on 14 August 1785, he wrote several verses that capture well his sacramental understanding of the table. He writes,

> Father God we hope we be
> Part of thine own family
> While we sit around thy board
> Deign thy presence to afford

---

blood is drink indeed." This meal is to be preferred "to all other enjoyments" because of the spiritual renewal and vitality given through it.

[36] Ryland, "Requisites for Communion," 65. Ryland held to the primacy of God's grace in effecting this union, saying in another sermon, Ryland, "Sermon Notes: 1 Corinthians 1:30," n.p., "Meanwhile the Apostle affirms that this Union is entirely owing to divine Appointm^t., Infl^{ce}., & Operat^n." However, he believes also that the individual has a part to play. Union with Christ is not a bare display of divine power. Ryland says, "But tho it originates with X^t. and not with us, yet it cannot be known, nor pleaded, nor the benefit of it be claimed, till it becomes mutual, & then it is a cordial, voluntary, spiritual Union. X^t. dwells in ♥ by Faith, impart^g. Light, Peace, Purity & Liberty to the Soul," Ryland, "Sermon Notes: 1 Corinthians 1:30," n.p. For this reason, preparation for the Lord's supper becomes an important aspect of Ryland's theology of the Lord's supper.

[37] Much work remains to be done with regard to Ryland's poetry. In the nineteenth century, he was remembered for his hymns and poetic output, cf. Long, *Hymns and Their Authors*, 350–53; Belcher, *Historical Sketches*, 231–34; Hatfield, *Poets of the Church*, 520–24; and Julian, "John Ryland," 984. This aspect of his work has largely been overlooked since. For a recent work on Ryland's poetry, see Graham, "The dearest of Women is gone," 66–83.

Richly are thy children fed
Christ's own body is our bread
Sure the taste of blood divine
Far exceeds the noblest wine

These appointed Symbols show
What he suffer'd here below
Set before our mental Eyes
All his dreadful Agonies

May thy Spirit now impart
To each Guest a broken ♥
Broken ♥'s alone are fed
Truly with this broken bread

All of Christ we wou'd receive
All ourselves to him wou'd give
On us now impress thy seal
Past backslidings kindly heal

Having sung this hymn we part
May we still be join'd in ♥
All united may we be
To each other and to Thee.[38]

Ryland uses vivid and sacramental language to describe the supper: Christ's body is the bread, his blood the wine. These elements are meant not merely as a help to the memory but show forth his "dreadful Agonies." He prays for God to break the heart of each partaker, and then feed the broken heart with the broken bread. Christ is received in the supper, and it involves the union of the recipient with God and with other believers.

The day prior to the composition of this poem, Ryland wrote another, a meditation on Isaiah 55.1, which he was to preach in the morning service prior to the afternoon Lord's supper service at College Lane. In it, Ryland does not mention the Lord's supper by name, but, given the historical context of the poem and what was seemingly on Ryland's mind at the time, his words are revealing:

---

[38] This hymn also appears in *Hymns and Verses on Sacred Subjects*, 65–66. "Hope" in the first stanza is changed to "trust" in that publication; the date is given simply as 1785, rather than the more specific date listed above; and the drawn hearts that Ryland often drew in place of the word "heart" are replaced with the word itself.

Come drink this blessed milk & wine
And feast on real good[39]
These delicacies all divine
Are never cloying food

All without money, without price
The sacred word ensures
Proud beggar stoop to terms so low
And all is ever yours

O Lord this bargain suits poor me[40]
Nothing have I to bring
Gladly I take thy gift so free
And feast and live and sing.

Again, the language is striking: the individual is invited to a meal that is more than "cloying food" and leads to feasting, living, and singing. One finds in Ryland's poetry, then, what is found elsewhere in his prose: belief in the nourishing power of the supper; the supper as an exhibition of Christ's death; the presence and reception of Christ in the supper; and union with Christ through the supper.

With all of the foregoing in mind, Ryland's understanding of the Lord's supper may be summed up as a theology of encounter. He believed that Christ was encountered in the Lord's supper. He held that Christ is truly, though spiritually, present in the elements, that communion is had with God in them, and that the believer is spiritually nourished through this union and communion. In a sermon on Proverbs 3.17, preached at Broadmead on 22 February 1824,[41] he speaks of the "ordinances of God" as "the appointed means of communion with him"[42] and specifically refers to the elements of the supper as "pledges of the Saviour's dying love."[43] In another place, he portrays the use of the ordinances as a signification point in the Christian life, as an institute and event full of meaning and value for the soul. He begins by saying that the believer has known that God answers prayer, been rewarded openly by God, had their heart overwhelmed, and found "support, ease,

---

[39] When this poem was published in *Hymns and Verses on Sacred Subjects*, this line was changed to "Come, feast on real good," see Ryland, *Hymns and Verses*, 71.

[40] In *Hymns and Verses on Sacred Subjects*, this line is, "O Lord, these offers are for me," Ryland, *Hymns and Verses*, 72.

[41] Ryland, "Text Book," 22 February 1824.

[42] Ryland, "Pleasantness of Religion," 125.

[43] Ryland, "Pleasantness of Religion," 126.

deliverance."[44] The picture is of a faithful Christian who is already walking in joy, hope, and peace. He then turns to the ordinances, asking, "Are his ordinances vain institutions?"[45] No, he says, and speaking of the Lord's supper, he adds, "Ye have sat at his table, and he was known in breaking of bread."[46] While this reflects the language of Luke 24.35, that he would use this to show the proper use of the ordinances and their role in the faithful Christian's life shows that the supper, for Ryland, was a real encounter with the living Christ. Indeed, to think of the supper otherwise would reduce it to a "vain institution." It is the presence of Christ in the supper that makes it meaningful.

The Language of Sacrament

While earlier Baptists did not hesitate to use the word "sacrament" or to speak of the Lord's supper as a "means of grace," by the nineteenth century, Baptists tended not to use such language.[47] Because of his theology of encounter, it would be reasonable to expect Ryland to refer to the Lord's supper as a sacrament or means of grace. The case, however, is not as straightforward as one might hope. In an early work, he uses the word "sacrament" to describe baptism and the Lord's supper. In a rhyming catechetical exercise, he asks, "How many sacraments are there?"[48] He gives the following answer:

Two—in the which are Chriftians bound,
By love and duty to be found;
But none devoid of faving faith,
A right to either of them hath.[49]

In this early writing, he freely uses sacramental terminology. However, in subsequent published writings, Ryland uses "sacrament" chiefly when quoting others or in a non-approving way,[50] preferring instead to use "ordinance" or

---

[44] Ryland, "Believers God's Witnesses," 163.

[45] Ryland, "Believers God's Witnesses," 163.

[46] Ryland, "Believers God's Witnesses," 163.

[47] Fowler, *More Than a Symbol*, 53–57; cf. Freeman, "To Feed Upon by Faith," 200.

[48] Ryland, *Serious Essays*, 126.

[49] Ryland, *Serious Essays*, 126.

[50] See, e.g., Ryland, *Candid Statement*, 24, "Roman Catholics have talked of sacraments working grace by the very deed performed. Strange things are said of the efficacy of baptism."

"positive institution."[51] Ryland is more open in using the term "means of grace," but he uses it more broadly to speak of all the instruments God might use to effect good in the life of an individual, rather than strictly as one of the two sacraments.[52] One might conclude, then, that, while the early Ryland used the word, perhaps in youthful ignorance, the later Ryland came to reject such language when describing the supper. Indeed, perhaps this is evidence of the power of the transition period upon Ryland's thinking.

This would, however, be incorrect, as a study of Ryland's unpublished sermon notes demonstrates. In a sermon preached twice, once at College Lane on 20 October 1782 and another time at Broadmead on 20 March 1803, he used "sacrament."[53] He did so in a way worth noting. He speaks of "the Means of walking with God," and, among them,[54] he notes "the Use of divine Ordinances." These he delineates as scripture, prayer, meditation, preaching, conference, and sacraments. For Ryland, then, the sacraments were but two[55] of several ordinances which God had given to his people for their benefit.[56]

What leads to this aversion toward sacramental terminology in published writings? Ryland was vehemently opposed to Roman Catholicism.[57] Ryland

---

[51] "Ordinance" is used throughout his work on baptism, while "positive institution" is in Ryland, "Love of the Spirit," 41. On the use of "ordinance" vs "sacrament" among Baptists, see Fowler, *More Than a Symbol*, 53–57. For earlier uses of "positive institution," see Ryland, "Nature of a Gospel Church," 9.

[52] See Ryland, "Jesus and Jonah Compared," 235; "Unbelief Not Owing to Want of Evidence," 279; *God's Experimental Probation of Intelligent Agents*, 25.

[53] Ryland, "Sermon Notes: Genesis 5:22," n.p.

[54] The others are the mediation of Christ, the grace of the Holy Spirit, and the observation of providence.

[55] In this particular sermon, Ryland does not specify that there are two sacraments nor does he say what they are. However, his earlier work showed that he held to two sacraments, which were baptism and the Lord's supper, see Ryland, *Serious Essays*, 126.

[56] Cf. Thompson, "People of the Free God," 240 n.87; and Cross, *Recovering the Evangelical Sacrament*, 191. Ryland shows that the terms were still not settled even in the nineteenth century.

[57] In a poem, he writes, Ryland, *Poems by John Ryland Junr, Vol. 2*, 21,

> From pagan & from papal Rome
> Much has the Church sustain'd
> But her true head who ever lives
> Has still her cause maintain'd.

> The man of sin long since foretold
> Still reigns at Rome we grant
> But his existence proves the truth
> He labors to supplant.

can speak of the "Antichriftian error" of the pre-Reformation church and "the darkeft times of Popery."[58] This opposition extended to sacramental language as well, with Ryland writing, "Nor does our Lord here refer to a mere sacramental eating his flesh and drinking his blood, in the Lord's supper; which was not instituted when he spake these words, and which, though it ought not to be neglected by true believers, yet is neither essential to salvation, nor necessarily connected with it; and many will perish, who are admitted to it, even in the purest churches."[59] With such strong disagreement with Roman Catholicism and its sacramental theology, it stands to reason that Ryland would not want to be misunderstood as advocating in print Roman Catholic doctrine, so he refrains from using a word that was coming to be understood as belonging exclusively to Roman Catholicism.[60] However, when used at his own church, where he was known and there was less of a possibility of being misunderstood, Ryland seems to have felt more freedom to use sacramental terminology.

Understanding Ryland's view of the Lord's supper must take into account this anti-Roman Catholic bias, as it shows that, despite his apprehension with regard to Roman Catholic doctrine, he feels compelled still to use the language of presence and communion in his discussions of the Lord's supper, as well as, when he felt it appropriate, using more direct sacramental language.

Not Either/Or but Both/And

It has been established that, in Ryland, we find both the memorialist and spiritual presence views of the Lord's supper. It remains to answer the question of how Ryland reconciled his Calvinist and Zwinglian ideas regarding the Lord's supper, two views that are so often portrayed separately

---

He also is distrusting of Roman Catholics in the public sphere, writing to William Wilberforce that "a man cannot be a Roman Catholic, and yet be heartily disposed to allow Liberty of Conscience to others," John Ryland, "Letter to William Wilberforce," 26 March, 1821. He also denounces the Pope as "the scull [or propeller] of Antichrist," Ryland, *Serious Essays*, 159–60.

[58] Ryland, *Promised Presence of Christ*, 29; cf. "Nature and Importance of Good Works," 239.

[59] Ryland, "Spiritual Participation," 308–9. One may see here the distinction between Ryland and earlier Baptists, for Benjamin Keach made a direct connection between John 6 and the Lord's supper, delineating no less than sixteen parallels between bread and Christ and saying bluntly, "Jefus Christ is eaten fpiritually," see Keach and De Laune, *Tropologia*, 213.

[60] Walker, *Baptists at the Table*, 11. If this is the case, then Ryland would fit well into Walker's understanding of Baptist sacramental reticence.

and even at odds.[61] Of course, it may be that Ryland was simply an inconsistent thinker, and this is evidence of such inconsistency. While it is true that no thinker is perfect and inconsistencies may be found in almost anyone who wrote enough material, such a conclusion would be too hasty, as there is evidence of a consistent understanding of the supper in Ryland, shown below. Another explanation for the presence of both views in Ryland could be that he lived in a time of transition and began using the language of memorial as it gained popularity. While it is true that Ryland lived during a time of transition, two issues plague this reading of Ryland. First, he does not seem the kind of person who would be swayed by popular opinion. For example, Ryland held to an open communion view of the proper recipients of the Lord's supper, which was a minority view in his day. If he was the kind of person swayed by the majority, he would have been unlikely to hold it or defend it in print as he did.[62] Second, it is not borne out by the evidence that Ryland transitioned from one view to the other. As shown in this essay, he preached sermons that include the memorial view in the 1780s as well as the 1820s, and he preached sermons that include the spiritual presence view during the same time span. There is no evidence of a transition from one view to the other; both are present throughout his life.

A more fruitful avenue of interpretation is to understand the role of preparation in Ryland's theology of the Lord's supper. Much of Ryland's instruction with regard to the supper centers around preparation. While his preparation language often reflects that of the scriptures, he is not simply repeating biblical wording. Rather, his appeals to his hearers to prepare themselves for the supper are instructive as to his theology of the supper, as they stem from his theology of encounter outlined above.

Ryland's preparatory exhortations show that he believed that partaking of the Lord's supper was truly a momentous event in the life of a Christian. In "The Unworthy Communicant," mentioned above, he outlines ten characteristics of the person who takes the Lord's supper in an unworthy manner, including coming "to the Lord's table without *understanding the nature and design* of this institution," coming with "a *self-righteous* spirit," eating and drinking "irreverently . . . impenitently . . . [or] ungratefully," being "*destitute of love to the brethren*," and indulging in "*a censorious spirit*."[63] The outcome of eating at the Lord's table unworthily are dire. Ryland asks the question, "What may we expect to be the consequence of thus eating and drinking unworthily?"[64] He answers himself, "If we do so habitually and

---

[61] Cf. Bierma, *Theology of the Heidelberg Catechism*, 71–72; Gerrish, "Lord's Supper in the Reformed Confessions," 245–58.

[62] Ryland, *Candid Statement*, 2nd edn, viii–xii.

[63] Ryland, "Unworthy Communicant," 61–62 (emphases original).

[64] Ryland, "Unworthy Communicant," 62.

entirely, the consequences must be absolutely fatal. A mere name will be of no avail whatever: it will only aggravate our future condemnation."[65] For Ryland, the Lord's supper was no mere ritual, but it had potentially fatal consequences for those who approached the table without due examination of themselves.[66] The call to examination is one of the most dominant themes in Ryland's Lord's supper sermons. Elsewhere, he encourages his hearers to see to which class of person they belong, "the saved or the perishing," "those who feel the power of the gospel, or those that account it foolishness."[67] They should seek to know that they are "really in Christ" and "acquainted with his doctrine, interested in his merit and righteousness, influenced by his Spirit, under his government and protection."[68]

Preparation means recognizing the importance of the event in which one is participating. He writes, "All instituted Worship, under the Gospel Dispensation, is to be performed by such only as can understand its Meaning."[69] A person must, therefore, "enter into the meaning and spirit"[70] of an ordinance in order fully to realize its potential as a means of grace. In this, Ryland leans heavily on the terminology and subjective emphases of the memorial view: the individual partaker must do something. That injunction has to do with the individual's expectation with regard to the Lord's supper. A truly prepared recipient does not expect the Lord's supper to involve merely their remembrance of a past event. Rather, part of entering into "the meaning and spirit" is expecting something more to happen when one partakes of the elements. Attending to the supper in a "proper manner," according to Ryland, includes the following: hoping to "receive fresh pledges of his love, and fresh Communications of Grace fm. him," expecting to "renew our professed Acknowledgement and cordial Reception of him in all his Offices, and

---

[65] Ryland, "Unworthy Communicant," 62. In Ryland's thinking, having a "name" only is always lethal. He says, "Sermon Notes: 1 Corinthians 11:29," n.p., "If neither the Word nor Ordinances affect your ♥, nor bind you to new Obed^ce., you must be dead in sin, & only have a name to live."

[66] Echoing Paul (2 Cor. 13.5), he implores his hearers, before partaking of the Lord's supper, to examine themselves to see if they are even of the faith, Ryland, "Unworthy Communicant," 63. In his searching appeals, Ryland included himself as a hearer, saying, "Let us all examine ourselves; especially those who have made a public profession," Ryland, "Self-Suspicion Enforced," 255.

[67] Ryland, "Preaching of the Cross," 49.

[68] Ryland, "Relation of Christ to Believers," 55.

[69] Ryland, "Sermon Notes: Exodus 12:26," n.p.

[70] Ryland, "Sermon Notes: Exodus 12:26," n.p.

looking to "revive our own Affections toward our Lord, and all that is his."[71] Preparation, then, includes expectation of further activity on the soul.

While Ryland places great emphasis on the role of the individual in preparing themselves for the Lord's supper, he nevertheless ascribes even that preparatory activity to God. In a sermon on Isaiah 38.16, preached in 1786 and 1815 in Northampton and Broadmead, respectively, he outlines his understanding of how the means of grace, which includes the Lord's supper, work. The work initiates in "the Influences of the blessed Sp^t." These influences include "Directing the ♥ into the Love of God, & the patient waiting for Jesus Christ." Through this work, the Spirit "render[s] the outward Means efficacious, & excit[es] that inward Grace, of which he was the original Author, into Exercise."[72] The Spirit, then, works to make the recipient of the means of grace fit to receive them, and then renders the means effective in the heart. Far from a mere memorial of an event in the past, in this description, Ryland portrays the Lord's supper as a present work of God from beginning to end.

While this could potentially lead to an *ex opere operato* understanding of the supper, Ryland repeatedly emphasizes the role of personal faith in a worthy reception of the elements. In a sermon on Psalm 5.7, preached at College Lane on 1 May 1785 and at Broadmead on 5 July 1814,[73] Ryland presses his hearers to understand their need of faith and dependence on divine mercy: "Oh that we may come into his House, at this time and at other times, sensible of our need of abundant Mercy! relying on Mercy alone for the forgivenefs of our past sins, and fensible that we need abundt. Mercy to pardon our prest. sinfulnefs; yea the sins of our best fervices, sins in prayr, in praise, in hearing, communicating, preaching &c Oh what abundt., Mercy do we need!"[74] While Ryland holds to the supper as a means of grace and acknowledges the role of the Spirit in the event, there is still an element of personal responsibility: the worthy recipient must come in faith in Christ, whom they expect to encounter in the supper.

Conclusion

A key passage for Ryland's understanding of the supper, one in which he includes all the elements of his theology, comes in a sermon preached from

---

[71] Ryland, "Sermon Notes: Exodus 12:26," n.p.

[72] Ryland, "Sermon Notes: Isaiah 38:16," n.p.

[73] The Broadmead sermon was given at a preparation meeting, while the College Lane sermon was preached a week before a Lord's supper service, see Ryland, "Text Book," 1 May 1785, 5 July 1814.

[74] Ryland, "Sermon Notes: Psalm 5:7," n.p.

Psalm 92.13 on three separate occasions from 1791 to 1821.[75] He exhorts his congregation, "But the promis'd Blessing belongs to those, who have a <u>cordial Attachm^t</u>. to God's house & ordin^{ces}. resulting from an <u>experiment</u>. Acq^{ce}. wth. the <u>Sweetn^s</u>. & <u>holy tendency</u> of div. Truth. Such will value div. Institutions not merely from θe Infl^{ce}. of Educatⁿ. or Custom, but f^m. a regard to their Author & End. They are <u>rooted</u> & <u>grounded</u> in Love to the Truth as it is in Jesus, & are concern'd to <u>grow</u> up into his likenefs in all things. They derive their <u>life, nourishm^t</u>., <u>support</u> & <u>fruitfulnefs</u> from the fuln^s. of Grace in X^t. Jesus, wch. is communicated to θem by θe Inflce of θe H. Sp^t. thro' the Instrumentality of div. Ordin^s."[76]

All of Ryland's emphases are included here. The Lord's supper is meant for believers; it is experiential and relational; the worthy recipient has regard for (and remembrance of) the purpose of the supper; it is centered on Christ; and it is a means of grace. With these emphases, Ryland does not fit easily into either the Zwinglian or Calvinist camps with regard to the meaning of the Lord's supper. This does not mean, however, that his theology is inconsistent or evidence of a transition from one to the other. Rather, it fits together as a whole. Fundamental to his thinking is that Christ is present and is encountered in the Lord's supper. This may mean judgment for the unworthy communicant, but it means a blessing for those who are prepared to receive the elements. Proper preparation comes through remembrance of him, especially his incarnation and atonement, as well as anticipation of what he will do for the individual as they partake of the supper.

While the presence of both these viewpoints in one person may seem surprising in light of later Baptist theologies of the supper that have fallen into one or the other of those camps, such is not so foreign to Baptist theologies of the supper prior to Ryland. The 1677 *Confession* places both remembrance and spiritual presence in the same paragraph: "The Supper of the Lord Jefus, was inftituted by him, the fame night wherein he was betrayed, to be obferved in his Churches unto the end of the world, for the perpetual remembrance, and fhewing forth the facrifice of himfelf in his death confirmation of the faith of believers in all the benefits thereof, their fpiritual nourifhment, and growth in him, their further ingagement in, and to, all duties which they owe unto him;

---

[75] In his sermon notes, Ryland writes that he preached the sermon at Northampton in 1791, Broadmead in 1795, and Watchet in 1821. The "Text Book" further adds that the dates were 14 August, 5 March, and 30 September, respectively. According to the "Text Book," the date in Northampton was a day on which the church partook of the Lord's supper, and the date at Broadmead was the day of a preparation meeting. In addition, Ryland notes in the "Text Book" that he also preached the sermon on 6 December 1821 at a Broadmead preparation meeting.

[76] Ryland, "Sermon Notes: Psalm 92:13," n.p.

and to be a bond and pledge of their communion with him, and with each other."[77]

The same is found in the work of Benjamin Keach, who writes that the those who partake of the ordinance are required to confess their sins, feel sorrow over their sins, forgive those who have sinned against them, put their faith in the death of Christ, and remember Christ's death. Keach puts the most emphasis on the last of these, delineating four different kinds of remembrance that are proper to the Lord's supper: "an affectionate Remembrance," "a forrowful Remembrance," "a Sin-loathing and felf-abhorring Remembrance," and "a thankful Remembrance."[78] At the same time, Keach calls the Lord's supper a "Sacrament" and speaks of it in instrumental terms. For Keach, the Lord's supper "feals the Covenant of Grace to us, giveth us (in the right ufe of it) much affurance that Chrift is ours." Moreover, he says that "there is a myftical Conveyance or Communication of all Chrift's bleffed Merits to our Souls through Faith held forth hereby, and in a glorious manner received, in the right participation of it."[79]

While later Baptists have embraced the memorial view, and it is common to put the two views in competition with one another, one should be careful not to read such a division back into previous generations. Ryland and other Particular Baptists do not see a contradiction nor is there competition. They are complimentary. In Ryland, one may be emphasized over the other for some reason, but this does not mean that the other is denied. Rather, they are held together in concert.

This has implications for how one understands the period of transition in the nineteenth century. While it is surely true that people such as Abraham Booth and John Sutcliff rejected the Calvinistic language found in earlier Baptists, the evidence produced from the pen of their friend John Ryland Jr suggests that this transition was less a switch from one view to another and more of a dropping of one kind of terminology where once both were found.

Bibliography

Anon. *A Confession of Faith Put Forth by the Elders and Brethren of Many Congregations of Christians (Baptized Upon Profession of Their Faith) in London and the Country*. London: s.n., 1677.

Anon. "Sacramental Meditations." *Baptist Magazine* 1, New Series (May 1857) 285–86.

---

[77] Anon., *Confession of Faith* [1677], 98–99.

[78] Keach, *Troposchemalogia*, 44.

[79] Keach, *Troposchemalogia*, 45. He even says that the Lord's supper "may animate and encourage us to fuffer Martyrdom (when called to it) for his fake."

Baker, Mary Patton. *Participation in Christ and Eucharistic Formation: John Calvin and the Theodrama of the Lord's Supper.* Milton Keynes: Paternoster, 2015.

Beddome, Benjamin. *A Scriptural Exposition of the Baptism Catechism by Way of Question and Answer.* 2nd ed. Bristol: W. Pine, 1776 [1752].

Belcher, Joseph. *Historical Sketches of Hymns, Their Writers, and Their Influence.* Philadelphia: Lindsay and Blakiston, 1859.

Bierma, Lyle D. *The Theology of the Heidelberg Catechism: A Reformation Synthesis.* Louisville, KY: Westminster John Knox, 2013.

Collins, Hercules. *An Orthodox Catechism: Being the Sum of Christian Religion, Contained in the Law and Gospel.* London: s.n., 1680.

Cross, Anthony R. *Recovering the Evangelical Sacrament: Baptisma Semper Reformandum.* Eugene, OR: Pickwick, 2013.

Cross, Anthony R., and Philip E. Thompson, eds. *Baptist Sacramentalism.* Carlisle: Paternoster, 2003.

Edwards, Jonathan. *A Treatise Concerning Religious Affections.* Boston: S. Kneeland and T. Green, 1746.

Fowler, Stanley K. *More Than a Symbol: The British Baptist Recovery of Baptismal Sacramentalism.* Eugene, OR: Wipf & Stock Publishers, 2007.

Freeman, Curtis. "'To Feed Upon by Faith': Nourishment from the Lord's Table." In *Baptist Sacramentalism,* edited by Cross and Thompson, 194–210.

Gerrish, B.A. *Grace and Gratitude: The Eucharistic Theology of John Calvin.* Edinburgh: T. & T. Clark, 1993.

Gerrish, Brian A. "The Lord's Supper in the Reformed Confessions." In *Major Themes in the Reformed Tradition,* edited by Donald K. McKim, 245–58. Grand Rapids: Eerdmans, 1998.

Graham, Lon. "'The Dearest of Women Is Gone': A Historical Study of Grief in the Life of John Ryland Jr." *Journal of European Baptist Studies* 19.2 (2019) 66–83.

Hall, Robert, Jr. *The Works of the Rev. Robert Hall, A.M.: With a Memoir of His Life.* Edited by Olinthus Gregory. 3 vols. New York: Harper, 1832–33.

Hatfield, Edwin Francis. *The Poets of the Church.* New York: Anson D.F. Randolph, 1884.

Haykin, Michael A.G. "'His Soul-Refreshing Presence': The Lord's Supper in Calvinistic Baptist Thought and Experience in the 'Long' Eighteenth Century." In *Baptist Sacramentalism,* edited by Cross and Thompson, 188–93.

Julian, John. "John Ryland." In *Dictionary of Hymnology,* edited by John Julian, 984. New York: Charles Scribner's Sons, 1892.

Keach, Benjamin. *Troposchemalogia: Tropes and Figures.* London: John Darby, 1682.

Keach, Benjamin, and Thomas De Laune. *Tropologia, or, a Key to Open Scripture Metaphors.* London: John Richardson and John Darby, 1681.

Long, Edwin McKean. *Illustrated History of Hymns and Their Authors.* Philadelphia: Joseph F. Jaggers, 1875.

McNutt, Cody Heath. "The Ministry of Robert Hall, Jr.: The Preacher as Theological Exemplar and Cultural Celebrity." PhD diss., Southern Baptist Theological Seminary, 2012.

Moore-Crispin, Derek. "'The Real Absence': Ulrich Zwingli's View." In *Union and Communion 1529–1979*, 22–33. London: The Westminster Conference, 1979.

Riggs, John. *The Lord's Supper in the Reformed Tradition: An Essay on the Mystical True Presence.* Louisville, KY: Westminster John Knox, 2015.

Ryland, John. "Believers God's Witnesses." In *Pastoral Memorials*, edited by J.E. Ryland, 1:161–65.

———. *A Candid Statement of the Reasons Which Induce the Baptists to Differ in Opinion and Practice from Their Christian Brethren.* London: W. Button, 1814.

———. *A Candid Statement of the Reasons Which Induce the Baptists to Differ in Opinion and Practice from Their Christian Brethren.* 2nd ed. London: Wightman and Cramp, 1827.

———. *God's Experimental Probation of Intelligent Agents. A Sermon, Preached at a Meeting of Ministers, at Kettering, in Northamptonshire, October 3, 1780.* Northampton: Thomas Dicey, 1780.

———. *Hymns and Verses on Sacred Subjects: The Greater Part of Which Are Now Published for the First Time from the Originals.* London: Daniel Sedgwick, 1862.

———. "Jesus and Jonah Compared." In *Pastoral Memorials*, edited by J.E. Ryland, 1:233–36.

———. "Letter to William Wilberforce." 26 March 1821. William Wilberforce Papers, David M. Rubenstein Rare Book and Manuscript Library, Duke University.

———. "The Love of the Spirit." In *Pastoral Memorials*, edited by J.E. Ryland, 2:40–46.

———. "The Nature and Evidences of Divine Manifestations." In *Pastoral Memorials*, edited by J.E. Ryland, 1:332–37.

———. "The Nature and Importance of Good Works." In *Pastoral Memorials*, edited by J.E. Ryland, 2:231–40.

———. "The Pleasantness of Religion." In *Pastoral Memorials*, edited by Ryland, 1:122–32.

———. *Poems by John Ryland Junr, Vol. 2 (1783–1795).* Bristol Baptist College Archives.

———. "The Preaching of the Cross." In *Pastoral Memorials*, edited by J.E. Ryland, 2:46–50.

———. *The Promised Presence of Christ with His People a Source of Consolation under the Most Painful Bereavements: A Sermon Delivered at the Baptist*

Meeting-House, Cannon-Street, Birmingham . . . Oct. 20, 1799; Occasioned by the Death of the Rev. Samuel Pearce. 2nd ed. Clipstone: J.W. Morris, 1800.

————. "The Relation of Christ to Believers." In *Pastoral Memorials*, edited by J.E. Ryland, 2:50–55.

————. "Requisites for Communion." In *Pastoral Memorials*, edited by J.E. Ryland, 2:63–66.

————. "Self-Suspicion Enforced." In *Pastoral Memorials*, edited by J.E. Ryland, 1:252–56.

————. *Serious Essays on the Truths of the Glorious Gospel: And the Various Branches of Vital Experience. For the Use of True Christians.* London: J. Pasham, 1771.

————. "Sermon Notes: 1 Corinthians 1:30." In *Original Manuscript Sermons: Old Testament, Vol. II (c.1773–1822)*: Bristol Baptist College Archives.

————. "Sermon Notes: 1 Corinthians 11:29." In *Original Manuscript Sermons: Old Testament, Vol. II (c.1773–1822)*. Bristol Baptist College Archives.

————. "Sermon Notes: Exodus 12:26." In *Original Manuscript Sermons: Old Testament, Vol. I (c.1771–1823)*: Bristol Baptist College Archives.

————. "Sermon Notes: Genesis 5:22." In *Original Manuscript Sermons: Old Testament, Vol. I (c.1771–1823)*: Bristol Baptist College Archives.

————. "Sermon Notes: Isaiah 38:16." In *Original Manuscript Sermons: Old Testament, Vol. II (c.1773–1822)*. Bristol Baptist College Archives.

————. "Sermon Notes: Psalm 5:7." In *Discourses on the Book of Psalms (c.1771–1824)*: Bristol Baptist College Archives.

————. "Sermon Notes: Psalm 92:13." In *Discourses on the Book of Psalms (c.1771–1824)*: Bristol Baptist College Archives.

————. "The Spiritual Participation of Christ." In *Pastoral Memorials*, edited by J.E. Ryland, 1:306–10.

————. "Text Book." Northamptonshire Record Office.

————. "Unbelief Not Owing to Want of Evidence." In *Pastoral Memorials*, edited by J.E. Ryland, 1:278–82.

————. "The Unworthy Communicant." In *Pastoral Memorials*, edited by J.E. Ryland, 2:59–63.

Ryland, John Collett. "The Beauty of Social Religion; or, the Nature and Glory of the Gospel Church." Northamptonshire Baptist Association Circular Letter, 1777, 1–15.

Ryland, Jonathan Edwards, ed. *Pastoral Memorials*. 2 vols. London: B.J. Holdsworth, 1826–28.

Sutcliff, John. "The Ordinance of the Lord's Supper Considered." Northamptonshire Baptist Association Circular Letter, 1803, 3–9.

Thompson, Philip E. "People of the Free God: The Passion of Seventeenth-Century Baptists." *American Baptist Quarterly* 15.3 (1996) 223–41.

Walker, Michael J. *Baptists at the Table: The Theology of the Lord's Supper Amongst English Baptists in the Nineteenth Century.* Didcot: Baptist Historical Society, 1992.

Weaver, G. Stephen. "Hercules Collins: Orthodox, Puritan, Baptist." PhD diss, Southern Baptist Theological Seminary, 2013.

CHAPTER 8

The Sacraments—A Stumbling Block?

Faith Bowers

The Church and People with Severe Learning Disabilities

A stumbling block? That is not how Christians usually view the sacraments, but they have often presented an obstacle for people with severe learning disabilities, especially those in churches that practice believers' baptism. This paper considers why and how this stumbling block has existed and what can happen when it is removed.

Back in 1969 the second child of a Baptist couple was born with Down's Syndrome. Doctors' prognosis was bleak: their experience doubtless limited to people institutionalized with physical care but little mental stimulation. These parents faced two persistent questions. Why did God let this happen to a baby for whom there had been much prayer, even before conception? Down's Syndrome is caused by an extra chromosome emerging as the first cells divide so cannot be blamed on damage during pregnancy or birth: it feels as if creation has gone wrong. This is an aspect of the problem of suffering. Sooner or later most Christians have to come to terms with suffering in one form or another—or lose their faith.

The second question was whether their child would have any potential for spiritual life. They could hope their elder son might, like them, go to university, have a career, make a happy marriage—as indeed he has, but his brother's life would be different. The parents hoped to share their faith with their sons but would that too be beyond this second child? Their general practitioner doctor (GP) had no experience of the condition, but told them the paediatrician would answer questions.

The paediatrician told them their child would probably learn to walk, perhaps to talk, and might even dress himself, provided clothes were laid out in the right order. Thinking the paediatrician might not understand spirituality, the mother asked tentatively if they could expect *any* capacity for thought. He brushed this aside, telling the indignant GP he would not see these parents again because they asked silly questions.

My husband and I were those parents. Academic by nature, we read all we could find on what was then called mental handicap. We noted new suggestions that Down's children might achieve more if given extra stimulation from their earliest days. We followed advice on how to improve weak muscles and engage the baby's interest. The medical establishment repeatedly and depressingly dismissed any signs of progress, so we clung to having been bred in Dissent! We found nothing that bore on spiritual life. Ministers could not answer that question either.

Not a theologian, but a Baptist historian more drawn to human story than philosophy, my reflection is informed and illustrated from experience, not least our own. In those early days we half regretted being Baptists, thinking pedobaptists would give formal welcome into the church, whereas people with Down's might be doomed to remain always on the outer fringe of a Baptist church. Much later we learned that it was not unusual for other Evangelicals, both Free Church and Anglican, to decline to baptize such a baby. With their emphasis on personal faith, some saw no point in baptizing those who would never *understand*, but that was "all right" because God loved these "holy innocents," these "angels unaware." That does not speak to parents of loving welcome. Happily, not all Evangelicals presented these scruples, which never seem to have arisen with High Anglicans, Roman Catholics or Orthodox.

It was fourteen years before I found exciting affirmation that people with learning disabilities were capable of spirituality. The writer with supportive evidence was a Roman Catholic priest,[1] leading special needs work at St Joseph's Centre in the Westminster Diocese. Exploring ways to make worship more accessible, nuns there had produced special preparation material for first communion and confirmation, and an attractive mass book with color photos showing people with disabilities as part of the congregation. Priests and nuns encouraged Baptists with similar concerns. As Father David observed, "We share the same aim. We want these people to know that Jesus loves them."[2]

For our baby, the initial diagnosis was unusually tentative. The midwife suggested Down's because at birth he lacked normal arm reflexes. GP and paediatrician thought him normal. Richard does not show all the typical features: for example, his handprints are normal, but his footprints Down's (disconcerting to see newborn hands and feet pressed into police-type inkpads). Final diagnosis depended on blood tests, so there was a month for urgent prayer that he would prove "normal." It was not to be. Once diagnosis was confirmed, it felt important to offer the child's life to God.

The service of dedication when Richard was six weeks old felt very different from that of our elder child. Our thanksgiving was muted. Promises to raise Richard in the faith felt hollow. The temptation—I use the word deliberately—was to feel that raising him would require extra but futile effort. Unable to face the usual dedication hymns, we ransacked the hymnbook for something helpful, settling on "Father, hear the prayer we offer, not for ease

---

[1] Wilson, *I am with you.*

[2] From personal notes written following a lunch at Waterloo Station in 1985.

that prayer may be." We prayed that somehow Richard's life might prove useful, not just wasted effort.

In the service we became keenly aware of the church's corporate promise of support. The words were the same as for our first son: the minister, Howard Williams, used Payne and Winward,[3] but they hit us with new force. A visiting American minister told me he had never before been so moved by infant dedication: unlike the members, he did not know why the atmosphere was so charged. That corporate dedication was taken to heart by the church and has continued through half a century, despite many changes of membership, an experience of the covenanted community being greater than the sum of its parts.

We marvel at how that desperate prayer has been answered in abundance. The adult Richard is a keen Christian, always on the look-out for opportunities of service. Meanwhile our experience fed into wider work to help churches. That pioneer work, eventually known as BUild—the Baptist Union Initiative with people with Learning Disabilities—ran from 1984 to 2017. It began with questions about how to tell such people that God loved them and how to minister to those who might come to local churches as new community care policies moved many from remote long-stay hospitals into small group homes in residential areas.

An early issue for BUild was admission to the two ordinances. I write as one on the sacramental wing of Baptist life, perhaps more from experiential than theological reasons. Emerging from the "outward and visible" waters of baptism, aged thirteen, I felt deeply conscious of "inward and spiritual grace," and of identifying with Jesus in that act. That memory is always relived when witnessing another's baptism by immersion. At the communion table I have often found the resolution to some matter with which I have wrestled, with a clear sense of hearing the Holy Spirit—usually steering in a direction I would have preferred to avoid. That was never more compelling than the call, against my natural inclination, to volunteer to lead the new working group. Memorialism alone does not suggest such dynamism. For me, the sacramental ordinances have proved meeting-places with the Holy Spirit.

It is not necessary, however, to favor sacramentalism for Baptists to know that baptism and communion are important aspects of church life and to have questions about them in relation to people with severe learning disabilities. Baptists recognize that baptism and communion were both ordained by Jesus. Closely linked to them is church membership, another concept traditionally important to Baptists. Ideally they come in the order: believers' baptism as the door to the church, reception into membership, and participation in the covenant meal, communion. The first two present the bigger hurdles over how much is understood, while inclusion or exclusion is most apparent at the table.

---

[3] Payne and Winward, *Orders and Prayers.*

Believers' Baptism

Community Care presented a challenge for churches: those who had liked worship adapted to suit them in hospital chapels would find local churches rather different. How best could churches serve them? For Baptists, there were further questions posed by believers' baptism. Could they ever understand enough? How fully could they be integrated into the church if not baptized?

An early initiative of BUild's antecedent, the Working Group on Mental Handicap and the Church, was a questionnaire to garner existing experience. Audrey Saunders prepared this and sent it to all Baptist Union churches. In youth, she had been shocked at how little support her parents received from their church as they struggled to raise her sister with learning disabilities. At her baptism, Audrey had vowed that she would make churches more aware: now the time had come. Replies, usually from ministers or church secretaries, to her question on baptism included:

"It isn't that we don't want them, but they wouldn't understand about commitment."

"He wished to be baptized . . . he understood as much as he would ever be able to understand—not the same situation as a child who would wait till he understood more—so he was baptized."

"We must not exploit their susceptibility . . . Are we really helping them to know God in Christ, or are we only proselytizing in an easy mission field?"

"It seems to me that the church cannot exemplify the full humanity revealed in Christ, or achieve unity in diversity, if it continues to acquiesce in the social isolation of disabled persons and to deny them full participation in its life."

"For severely handicapped people these things have no relevance."

"They should be loved and made to feel wanted but I cannot see the point in offering membership to a person who is incapable of understanding what it is about."

"The sacraments are God's gift to us and, in certain circumstances, to give baptism and communion to those severely handicapped is to take the step of faith and say 'God loves you—you are valued and cared for by God'."

"We would in effect be saying, 'Yes, you are part of our life'. The sacraments are a way of saying what is beyond the capacity of all of us to express in words."[3]

So BUild began to probe the awkward questions.

Boldly we wrote to Area Superintendents and Association Secretaries offering speakers. The first invitation came quickly: the South-East ministers' retreat must have lost a speaker at short notice and offered two main slots.

---

[3] Bowers, *Let Love Be Genuine*, 83–84, and *Who's This Sitting in My Pew?* 90.

New to this, but with Audrey in support, I plunged in with the cheeky title, "Where ministers fear to tread."

> Can the mentally handicapped have that sense of conviction, of personal response that Baptists require for believers' baptism? How do we know how much they understand? Some will be more articulate than others, but they are unlikely to express themselves quite like other candidates. If they do, we probably have to ask whether the sentiments, as well as the vocabulary, are second-hand.
>
> To accept a young person of limited understanding for baptism because he belongs to a Christian family and enjoys coming to church would be coming uncomfortably close to accepting the parents' faith as proxy. Proxy faith is not easy for Baptists! To refuse to recognize him as fully part of the fellowship of which he feels a member may be unrealistic, and, indeed, cruel.
>
> Ministers and churches differ in their response when faced with such a question . . . [Some] demand a level of intellectual competence, which sounds reasonable yet, however stringent "election" may be, it seems unlikely to involve an intelligence test.[4]

The questions were sharp for me. Richard came willingly to church, but we still did not know whether he would be capable of seeking believer's baptism.

For fathers who were ministers these questions were particularly hard. George Neal, writing for *Let Love Be Genuine*,[5] allowed his daughter, who had Down's Syndrome, to share in communion as part of the loving church fellowship, but judged baptism inappropriate. Michael Taylor made a careful argument against baptism for his teenage daughter. He feared it meant "trying to do the right thing in the wrong way. The right thing is to affirm that Katie is part of God's family, is loved by God". He doubted that her understanding was adequate for intentional discipleship.[6] He admitted, however, to feeling ambivalent.

It is all too easy for churches to look to parents to assess such a child's faith, and not only when the father is principal of a theological college. It is also unfair. Parents want what is good for their child, but hesitate to impose upon their church's goodwill. When Taylor's move to Christian Aid took the family to a London church, Katie convinced an experienced minister that her request was valid. Michael told me of his joy at her baptism.

When Richard was sixteen he asked the minister to "take me in the water," without mentioning this to his parents beforehand. When asked why he wanted baptism, he told the minister, "Because I love Jesus." Both the ministers and church *assured us* it was appropriate. Had we been consulted, we

---

[4] Bowers, *Let Love Be Genuine*, 60–61.

[5] Neal, "With Understanding."

[6] Taylor, "Include Them Out?"

too would have felt some ambivalence, although it helped that his elder brother, unlike Taylor's sons, had already nailed his colors to Christ's mast. Keith was indignant at our doubts: sharing a room, he heard Richard's bedtime prayers, chatting about the day with his friend Jesus. Keith particularly enjoyed a prayer on 31 December, which ended, ". . . Amen. Oh, P.S. Happy New Year, Jesus!"

When BUild first challenged ministers to take seriously baptismal requests from those with learning disabilities, it was sobering to hear how several had gone back to listen more carefully. Where they had previously dismissed requests, assuming lack of understanding, they were amazed to discover real depths of faith.

We began to hear of dramatic effects from admission to the sacraments. This, like the pioneering BUild itself, was not limited to Baptists. A vicar told how he had suggested that, to her parents' surprise, a pleasant middle-aged woman with considerable disability should be confirmed because she regularly attended the eucharist with them. He arranged two simple instruction lessons, but knew many would see this as a rather casual approach. He had not anticipated the change it would make.

> After the confirmation there was a great change in her—a change which the parents couldn't get over. I am certain that Jesus is a real person to her and that a complete change came about in her through the sacraments . . . If ever there was evidence of the Holy Spirit at work in a person it was in her. She was radiant.[7]

Positive efforts for those with disabilities often prove a blessing to the whole fellowship, with admission to the sacraments providing a focus, especially when approached with thoughtful care rather than sentimental kindness. Where churches make the event special, all benefit. After baptizing a believer with learning disabilities, the Rev. Carol McCarthy observed that the service had been "a means of grace to us all," making her consider "whether we ought to be more human, more sensitive, more sensual, ministering to the whole person in our worship."[8]

Elsewhere a vicar decided to baptize a young child with severe disabilities within the harvest festival family service: "Well over a hundred people, including a lot of children, grouped around the font. There was a great sense of God's love for all his creation, especially the feeblest. The lighting of Mandy's baptismal candle seemed to demonstrate the Light of Christ in a world where much goes wrong. Many . . . remember it as an outstanding occasion in our parish life . . ."[9]

---

[7] Bowers, *Who's This Sitting in My Pew?* 74.

[8] Bowers, *Who's This Sitting in My Pew?* 77.

[9] Bowers, *Who's This Sitting in My Pew?* 73.

One early spring day I preached at the baptism of a youth with Down's and, from a front seat, saw the shock of the minister and assistant as they entered the pool and found the water had not been warmed. The young candidate did not appear to notice the cold: his mind was on higher things. The congregation included as guests his school friends and their teacher. After the service, the church celebrated his "second birth" in style, the cake topped with his photo in icing, then a novelty. Efforts to make the baptism meaningful for him made it a high day for the whole church.[10] In such ways things material, outward and visible, enhance the spiritual experience for everyone.

The importance of belonging to the church community recurs repeatedly in these contexts. The Baptist theologian, Sally Nelson, saw this as making believers' baptism possible for her daughter Flora, who clearly loved church but was unable to confess her faith verbally. In a footnote to an article on baptism Sally explained,

> My own daughter has significant and complex needs, but is actively (in the sense of regular attendance) a part of a community that wants to be "on The Way." I do not see the need for her to articulate an independent commitment in her life of faith when she is utterly dependent on others in every other area of her life. She is unavoidably committed to community for even the smallest details. When considering her baptism we decided that because she is unable to speak and affirm her conviction, we would, as a community, reaffirm our baptismal promises together at that point. Her faith story would be shared in the form of testimony by other members of our community, who had seen faith in her.[11]

There is a fine dividing line between proxy faith, dependent on the affirmation of parents or sponsors, and being held in the corporate faith and life of the local church. This is not an easy area for Baptists, but experience suggests there is something real here which could be worth exploring further.

Faith is not easy to define, it involves belief yet goes beyond that. The writer to the Hebrews captures something of its intangible quality, "the substance of things hoped for, the evidence of things not seen."[12] The problem comes, not least when attempting to assess faith in those with learning disabilities, in trying to tie the invisible and intangible down in words. Expressed verbally or not, faith is often best seen in its fruit, not least when that is observed by others.

---

[10] Bowers, ed., *When Weak, Then Strong*, 169.

[11] Nelson, *Gathering Disciples*, 123 n.36. Nelson also wrote an account of Flora's baptism in "A Reflection on a baptism."

[12] Heb. 11.1. It is a sign of my age that biblical quotations still come most readily to mind in the *King James Version*, of which so much was learned by heart in childhood.

A young woman from an unchurched background was brought to one church's special group by an evangelist whose learning disability was greater than hers. She responded warmly to the teaching and a year or two later asked for baptism. The group's leader visited her mother, expecting to encounter suspicion, but was greeted warmly. The mother said she would attend the service because "I don't know much about church but I do know this is the best thing that has ever happened to my daughter."[13]

Another church ran a youth club that welcomed young people with special needs. A lad with Down's Syndrome and no previous church experience enjoyed the club and there came to know Christ. His enthusiasm for his new-found faith soon brought his whole family into the church. Such examples prove something real is happening.[14]

Richard's Baptism

The minister Richard asked to take him "in the water" was Barbara Stanford, one of the former deaconesses recognized as ministers in 1975. Her lifetime pastoral ministry was based at the Bloomsbury Central Baptist Church, London, and she knew Richard from birth. Her pastoral care for us had included days when she played with the baby and his brother while I did some of her typing as a relaxing change. Barbara was responsible for Richard's baptismal preparation, as for all the church's young people. To include something on all the usual topics took several months, since Richard could only cope with a little at a time, but the sessions were a joy to them both. Barbara discovered ways to engage Richard with concepts that would otherwise have been too abstract, grounding them with examples within his experience. Their first class was revelatory on two counts. Richard begged her to give him "homework:" it had not previously occurred to us that his special school had deprived him of the chore to which his brother and cousins were subjected. Secondly, he saw she had noted down some Bible references and he surprised her by looking these up for himself, going to the list of contents for less familiar books. We had no idea that he knew how to do this.

They produced an illustrated folder, entitled "Friends of Jesus: A file about Jesus and the Church and being a Christian," a record to which Richard has returned again and again. His enjoyment of the lessons, which continued in Bible studies for years after the baptism, proved something of a miracle in themselves. By the end of schooling Richard had just about mastered reading but without practice would soon have lost that; he would have resisted

---

[13] From personal notes of a conversation with Betty Leech, who led the Learning Together special needs group at Morden Baptist Church.

[14] Personal notes of a Build Day Conference at Rising Brook Baptist Church, Stafford.

parental efforts to maintain it. The delight of pursuing those studies with Barbara firmly established reading and writing skills that continue to enhance his daily as well as his devotional life.

Together they looked at different kinds of prayer. Confession he found hard: "I'm not bad," he protested." "Thank you" prayers evoked more enthusiasm: Barbara chuckled over thanksgiving for "rhubarb crumble with *thick* custard." Illustrations were culled from newspapers and magazines, but, in those days, baptisms were not usually photographed, and certainly not communion. Barbara wanted pictures to take him through what would happen at both, so the church meeting gave permission for his father to photograph the preceding baptisms and a communion service, using very fast film to avoid disturbing flash. This was long before the days of versatile digital cameras.

The church celebrated Richard's baptism with cards and gifts. The cards were added to his folder, along with photos of his own baptism. In subsequent days, several neighbors asked me about our mode of baptism. Richard had told them his good news in a way that put to shame the comparative reticence of his more articulate parents and brother. He delighted in the subsequent welcome into church membership and admission to the Lord's table.

Richard's faith has been nurtured in the church that made that commitment to help rear him in the faith. It is within this church that Richard has come to know and been enabled joyfully to serve Christ as Lord. The minister of his childhood was in his last year of Bloomsbury ministry when he preached at Richard's baptism. Howard was a great Welsh preacher, but what Richard remembers is how "Dr Williams always hugged me" (pastors could in those innocent days). Richard knew that he was loved: he thrived in the church context. His development was slow, but new achievements often took place on the church premises, where over-protective parents allowed more freedom because everybody kindly watched over him. Today, with elderly parents no longer able to travel regularly to Bloomsbury, various church friends ensure that Richard is able to join in the activities and outings, including the former minister's induction at a distant church. When going somewhere unfamiliar, they gladly meet him to ensure he has no difficulties, while appreciating his willing service within the church's life.

Those not good with words often find their own ways to testify to their faith. Vicki danced with joy, Jane sang "O wonderful love" to her own triangle accompaniment, little Grant, with hearing aids and thick-lensed glasses, so short he could barely peer over the lectern at a BUild conference, asked us to sing "Let the weak say I am strong." More articulate, but still new to the world of church, Verna moved the congregation with her declaration from the pool, "Jesus is my best mate."

An older man, moved to a group home after years in a hospital's subnormality ward, came to a London Baptist church. Soon he asked for baptism. The minister did his best to prepare the man, but could not tell what was understood. On the appointed morning the minister went to the service plagued with doubts. A group of strangers appeared and told the minister they were relatives of the baptismal candidate, there because they were all amazed at the happy change in the man since going to that church. Doubts dispersed, the minister gladly took the man into the pool.

The Lord's Table

One can argue theologically that inclusion in God's love is not dependent on any rite so baptism is unnecessary for those incapable of intentional response, but that is inadequate where churches expect baptism to precede communion. Adults with learning disabilities will be conscious of exclusion if bread and wine pass them by. Tom Rogers[15] told of the shock to congregation and minister when the tranquil atmosphere around the table was broken by a "childish, discordant voice" demanding, "Give Pauline drink!" The teenager, sitting between her parents, "suddenly asserted her desire to share in Communion." On reflection Rogers concluded that the table should be open to such people, and also baptism where clearly sought.

On holiday in Scotland my teenage son, not then baptized nor normally present at communion, heard the invitation "to all who love Jesus" and exclaimed as the plate bypassed him, "But I love Jesus!" My Baptist principles protested that he was not baptized. My Lord whispered, "Let him come to me." I broke my cube of bread in two and gave Richard half, and we shared my sip of wine, but my conscience was not entirely clear. Richard must also have been made to think, because only a few weeks later he asked for baptism "because I love Jesus."

Baptism is one-off, but communion is repeated regularly. How those who partake understand the mystery varies, so it seems unfair to use understanding as a criterion for admission to the table. Those with learning disabilities will understand exclusion and appreciate inclusion. The supper may be the most accessible part of Baptist worship for them, with more to see and taste, those outward and visible signs. Those who take words literally may wonder about the cup of Jesus' blood, which probably sounds to them like something from television sci-fi. Nevertheless, the association with Jesus, the sense of solemn celebration, and the shared fellowship are easily grasped. One church told of a man with Down's who always received with a loud "Thank you very much, thank you!" which became an appreciated part of his church's liturgy.

The drama of communion can reach those who depend on physical senses rather than words. Paul Martin remembered a non-verbal child of twelve, with minimal response to stimulation, yet "When I lift the loaf and proclaim the words of institution, 'This is my body given for you,'" it is a pleasure to see Craig's whole fragile and distorted body shake with joy, and his face break

---

[15] Rogers, "Should She Be Allowed?" 51.

into a wide grin. It is as if he intuitively knows that this is the high-point of worship."[16] Surely that implies some awareness of "inward and spiritual grace"? There is something about this Jesus whose body was broken on the cross, this vulnerable God, that speaks with clarity to those who live with broken bodies and impaired minds.

In the early days of BUild, some told us we could tell the "nice" Jesus stories but should avoid the horrors of the Passion. That felt wrong. One might manage baptism without reference to the cross, forfeiting the death and resurrection analogy, but not communion. In practice, the whole story has not proved a problem, although some protest, reasonably enough, at the cruel treatment of Jesus. Many relate only too well to the taunts—they know about being called "bad names." Watching the crucifixion at Oberammergau, I could feel Richard shudder as he *felt* each hammer blow. At a Baptist Assembly I was deeply moved to watch Philip, another man with Down's, acting Jesus in the Passion story. His face, magnified on screen as the camera zoomed in, contorted in agony as the nails were "hammered through" his hands and feet. Philip recognized and conveyed how Jesus suffered. For me, that was a healing experience. Seeing Christ with Down's features lifted the pain I had felt daily for twenty-five years at my son's condition; it has never returned.

With their own experience of suffering, people like Philip and Richard do not need to be protected from the crucified Christ. As with other Christians, it is often in suffering that they are most conscious of Christ's presence. I have written elsewhere[17] of the saving grace in Jesus's cry of dereliction: this God understands and comes alongside at the worst times. Many who have learning disabilities can sense the physical horror Jesus suffered and relate to the suffering Christ, remembered at communion.

Trying to explain communion needs care. These friends can get a bit hooked on the idea of blood: they watch television, so probably think of vampires. It is perhaps wiser to shift the focus to think about kneading dough and pressing grapes as suffering for a purpose. One newly-baptized girl was helped to make the bread shared at her first communion. Theological language is not the only way to convey the spiritual and sacramental.

Faith can be evident without being reasoned out in words. These people are not children, although they often retain some childlike qualities. It cannot be wrong to echo the Lord's words, "Let them come. Of such is the Kingdom of Heaven" (Matt. 19.14). The church proclaims that all, *just as they are*, are valued by God. That is more convincing when it is clear that they are also valued by the members of Christ's church on earth.

---

[16] Martin cited by Bowers, ed., *When Weak, Then Strong*, 169–70.

[17] Bowers, "Saving Cry of Dereliction."

Healing—Another Potential Stumbling Block?

More difficult are stories of miraculous healings. The ministry of healing can be difficult for those whose disabling condition is part of who they are. Many know that prayer has failed to change their condition. Healing often comes with acceptance rather than cure. Those who learn to accept their own impairment seem able to make the distinction between that and other illnesses afflicting them or their friends. Those they take to God in fervent prayer for healing

When, as a teenager, Richard became aware of Down's and could recognize it in others, it was painful to overhear him asking God to "change his face." Happily, his increasing involvement in BUild enabled him to accept his disability as something that God could use to help others. As adults, he and his friends speak of their disabilities in a matter-of-fact way. As Richard has said, "It's not the end of the world."

He does not often speak about *what* he believes, although he says that when he has to keep still during unpleasant medical or dental procedures, he finds it helps to think about Jesus. We learn a little from his choice of hymns and, occasionally, from drawings. When he heard that his grandmother was terminally ill, he expressed his grief, some months ahead of her actual death, in a striking picture. A tombstone inscribed "VIP grandmother 1912–1992" (we liked the confusion with RIP) stood by a path leading beyond the cemetery gate to a cross. The sun was shining.

He does not assume that disabilities will vanish in the afterlife. On the death of a man in the church, who had lost both legs to diabetic complications, Richard drew him with a halo round his curly Caribbean hair and outstretched arms but no lower limbs, and captioned this "Leonard John in glory in heaven." Again, at the death of the beloved minister who baptized him, his ageing parents were encouraged to see him cope sadly, but with Christian hope.

The majority of people with disabilities are aware of their limitations, mental and physical. If they are to develop a personal faith, it has to be within that context, accepting and being accepted as the people they are. That is not always easy. In itself, this gives a certain maturity to their faith.

Being the Body of Christ

Those with learning disabilities cannot deal with abstract concepts, but use physical senses to grasp realities of here and now. Richard is relatively articulate, but words on their own flow over him; they need to be set in context and backed up with things that speak to his physical senses. To know Christ, people like him need to experience God's love through God's people becoming, in the hymn's words, "as Christ to them." Often skilled at reading body language, they know whether welcome is genuine or forced. If they feel part of the church community, it is because members enable that sense of

belonging. A man with autism, often a misfit socially, told me he loved going
to his church home group although he rarely spoke, because "I feel I belong."
Liking to belong does not only apply to those with disabilities: "People are
almost always converted by meeting Christ in the members of his body, who
become means of grace to one another."[18]

There is something incarnational in this: the Word became flesh to express
God's love for humanity and the church as the body of Christ has ongoing
responsibility to flesh out the gospel. Sometimes we seem to wrap the gospel
up in more and more words, but it needs to be lived as well as preached.
Seeing people who cannot deal in words brought to a joyful, life-changing
knowledge of Christ through their experience of Christ's people sheds fresh
light on this. It relates to the sacramental mystery at the heart of communion:
there is a reality here that goes beyond memorialism.

Looking back over a Baptist lifetime, I have not found this a dominant
aspect of communion services. As Evangelicals, we have focused more on an
individual relationship with God than on the community made one in Christ,
which is clearer in Anglican eucharistic liturgy. It is rather strange since the
covenanted, godly community came before believers' baptism in our
denomination's development. Baptist forefathers emphasized the holy nature
of a church made up of intentional disciples, "visible saints," rather than
everybody in the parish. Poor practice, where the mystic drifted towards the
superstitious, made them wary of sacramentalism, a wariness strengthened in
reaction to the Oxford Movement in the nineteenth century. Obliged to
practice the Lord's supper as an ordinance of Christ, "a token of the New
Covenant,"[19] they preferred to focus on remembering Christ's death and
eschatological promise.

This downgrading of communion sadly resulted in its appearances in
Baptist history mainly as a means of discipline and an area of argument over
permitted participation, whether "closed" or "open." In my youth in the 1950s,
communion was usually a separate add-on after the main service, with a gap to
allow non-members to leave. Access to the table was felt as a privilege, yet the
service could be tedious, with long, extempore yet predictable prayers from
deacons over bread and "wine," and members' tickets added to the offering
plate to prove attendance. Baptist practice has improved, but we could still be
more aware of being the body of Christ, not in some mystical way, but in
conscious recognition that the behavior and actions of members have power to
convey God's love.

Observing how Richard, Katie, Craig, Flora, and many others with severe
learning disabilities have been held in the love of their church communities

---

[18] Pinnock, "Physical Side of Being Spiritual," 13.

[19] Thus described in an account, 1643, of the Jacob-Lathrop-Jessey church in
London, in McBeth, *Sourcebook*, 28.

gives fresh awareness of the church community made one in Christ as we share bread and wine. Belonging to the worshipping community is a dominant feature of their faith. That this is so speaks volumes about churches that "get it right." Sadly, parents tell us this is still not universal experience. Nevertheless, many churches rise well to the challenge to make people with learning disabilities feel they belong and are valued. That is cause for thanksgiving.

Incarnating the Word

Religious teaching that avoids "abstract" concepts is quite a challenge, yet that was surely what incarnation was about. As a post-baptismal discipleship course for Richard, Barbara Stanford devised a series of Bible studies on the fruit of the Spirit. All those abstract virtues presented a challenge, but she had learned how to ground "abstracts" for him. She explained each "fruit" with examples of people exhibiting the virtue and ask Richard to find further illustrations. Thus, gentleness was seen in someone cradling a baby and a child stroking a pet animal. A Baptist Missionary Society magazine provided patience with a woman sewing and a medical worker peering down a microscope. A newspaper offered a striking photo for joy: the snooker champion brandishing his cue in both hands over his head in sheer delight. One lesson Richard declared, "I get it, Barbara! Patience is what I need when people make me say things over and over again!"—we all felt reproved for having thought *we* needed it to understand his speech. The whole exercise proved effective teaching. At a BUild conference, a Religious Education advisor dealing with special schools studied the file Richard had compiled with Barbara and declared it was the best example she had seen of what was possible. The teaching was done by grounding–incarnating–the abstract virtues in examples from human life.

Richard greatly enjoyed those studies and the fruit of the Spirit remains one of the few Bible verses he knows by heart. Even so, he does not find it easy to distinguish between sacred and secular, often a rather endearing trait among such Christians. When his school teacher wanted her class to list items found at a fruiterers, she was surprised to read, "Oranges, apples, love, joy, peace, bananas, goodness, plums . . ." She told us she was glad that, being a Christian herself, she knew he was not just being silly.

How Can They Learn Unless Taught?

It used to be assumed that formal teaching was beyond those with severe learning disabilities. The 1970 Education Act considerably extended English school provision for those with "special educational needs." Richard, born in 1969, was among the early beneficiaries. Previously it was widely assumed that children with Down's could not learn to read or write. We were rebuked by a child psychologist for having taught our five-year-old to read some thirty words on flashcards. "You middle-class parents who think reading matters! Can't you understand that he cannot learn to read? He may say the words parrot-fashion to please you but they will have no meaning for him."

His schoolteachers, mostly new to special needs, happily had no such assumptions. Slowly Richard and many like him learned to read and even to write. That was useful when it came to Richard's studies with Barbara, as well as for life generally. His present level of independence would be impossible if he could not read station names and the destination of buses. When people like Richard learn to read, they want to use this skill. Alas, because "normal" people with low literacy levels avoid books, there is limited easy-reading material. The potential market is too small to attract religious publishing houses (Collins had thought of following the *St Joseph's Mass Book* with something similar on the Lord's Prayer, which would have been useful across other churches, but were too disappointed in the first book's sales). Richard still enjoys much excellent non-fiction for older children, but religion there is mostly comparative.

Bible stories are readily available, from toddler level up, but there is little to bridge the gap between those and the church today. Richard acquired several picture Bibles, the favorite a Ladybird edition with colorful pictures, where no story exceeded a single page-spread. With concentration span more limiting than reading vocabulary, that was an encouragement. When his reading improved, Richard used a *Good News Bible*. We were once surprised to be told this was no longer any good: the Psalms had fallen out of the middle due to much use.

As BUild challenged churches to think about baptismal preparation, this lack of material was apparent, so an early initiative produced some. Three lay women, two teachers and me (for experience in homespun publishing), were charged with this. We decided on four booklets with simple text and line drawings, coaxing artist friends to provide these unpaid. *Knowing Jesus* was about God and prayer, *The Church* was seen as a family in which all have a part to play, *Joining the Church* looked at baptism and communion, and *Following Jesus* was on discipleship. When we reported we would begin with the Trinity, ministers on the Working Group fell around laughing: "They say they want something simple and then begin with the most profound mystery!" We reasoned that "Father, Son and Holy Spirit" would often be heard so needed something, however inadequate, to ground the words: God the Creator, Jesus known from Bible stories, the Spirit as enabler of prayer. Those booklets, produced on a shoestring budget, have been widely used.[20]

---

[20] See Bowers, *Knowing Jesus*; Bowers, Robertson, and Wright, *The Church*; Robertson, *Following Jesus*; Wright, *Joining the Church*.

"Pray that I may have the grace to let you be my servant too"

This hymn line has added poignancy in the face of disability. Learning disabilities are not necessarily a hindrance to intentional discipleship. The BUild booklets showed how many different roles contribute to church life, with something for almost everyone. Many with disabilities are potential contributors, provided people have the grace to allow them to serve. Loving churches find many ways to enable them to give as well as to receive. Some undertake practical tasks, many prove faithful in prayer. The nature of the work matters less than whether it is valued as a contribution to the whole.

As a child, Richard used to sing in the bath, "I like church. I do like church"—that was in part because he was encouraged to work for Jesus. His active service began almost as soon as he could walk. The former minister's widow, when on coffee duty, used to take him to load empty cups on the second deck of the trolley, too low for her arthritic legs. I watched in awe the grace that saw this little child as a helper, saving her extra journeys to the kitchen. As he grew, others encouraged him. The "sums" he resisted at school became interesting in the kitchen as he divided cakes into an agreed number of slices or was helped to count out change. He joined other children in searches for Barbara's lost keys, getting wise to places she might have put them down. He was included in most youth activities. When missing his brother, away at university, two young men filled the gap on Sunday afternoons, Gary playing snooker and Mark taking him for interesting walks. Richard joined the stewarding and catering rotas, helped deal with rubbish and recycling, and ran errands around the multi-level building. These practical tasks, being "a useful church member," are effectively part of his worship, part of his offering to the Lord, climaxing when he takes the offering forward with visibly solemn pride in this priestly act on behalf of the people. Richard's joy in serving the church is echoed by many others around the country. Those aware of their limitations—and the low opinion many have of them—are delighted to find themselves valued at church. Many accounts bear witness to this.

It is particularly telling when people beyond the church notice the improvement in happiness or self-confidence. Richard has for twenty years enjoyed adult education classes at a local college with a big special-needs department. One of their early students, in the second year he was enrolled for six classes instead of the usual three. The departmental head explained that tutors welcomed his presence because he had the rare self-confidence to speak up, which helped others to join in. What struck me was that they attributed this to his church, saying other students had supportive homes, but they realized Richard was valued in a wider community, and he left them in no doubt that this must be the church about which he spoke so often. Again, he is not alone in such Christian witness by people whose minds cannot cope with drawing lines between the sacred and secular.

A Sacramental Story Through and Through

Brian Haymes suggested[17] that I might contribute to these studies something of a "pastoral theological nature . . . mainly narrative in style," because he has been "struck by how securely baptism features in Richard's self-identity." Brian had little direct experience of learning disability before coming to the Bloomsbury ministry in 2000. Richard has a great respect for those he refers to as "Reverends," and expects to love his ministers. He and Brian soon developed a warm friendship, largely based on their shared delight in worship and church. Brian understood that Richard "came for baptism uncoerced save by the call of Christ," and that his church and family took his request seriously, "in the flesh which is where Richard made his response, i.e. not is some spiritualized sphere alone.[21]

About four years after Richard was baptized, I was asked to get from him a contribution on what he liked about church for a meeting at Westminster Cathedral to promote Church Action on Disability, an ecumenical pressure group. To my surprise, Richard dictated an account of his baptism.

> Bloomsbury Central Baptist Church is a very nice place. I was baptized there four years ago, when I became like a Christian. My family all came to the worship of the church. Howard Williams and Barbara and Maurice Johns [church secretary] were there. I wore special clothes—white shirt and cream trousers and just feet. Maurice Johns led Barbara into the water—it was open. Then he took me to the baptismal water. I go down the steps. Barbara was preaching. My hands together on my tummy. Barbara said: "Father, Son and Holy Spirit take me" and I was baptized. Barbara tip me over under the water. My brother came in the water and helped me, wrapped me up to keep me warm. I changed my clothes. Afterwards all my family in the porch in the front of the church—my father took photographs. Then we come back downstairs and everyone helped celebrate of me—with nice cards and presents. I am a member of the church. I like the communion service. I wear a little cross to show I am a Christian.[22]

Strangely, Richard's down-to-earth account was the only contemporary description of believer's baptism in this country that Roger Hayden had been able to find. I remember taking the phone call from the editor, Professor Paul Fiddes, seeking Richard's copyright permission. Paul appreciated Richard's clarity on the trinitarian nature of baptism.

A decade later Richard was moved to write another piece showing his understanding of the sacrament.

---

[21] Email to the author from the Rev. Dr Brian Haymes, 22 March 2018.

[22] Hayden, "Believers Baptized," 17.

Sometimes there is a Baptismal Service. people are baptized to show they love Jesus. first the men have to get the pool ready. they take away the big table and chairs and then lift up the floor. underneath there is a big pool with steps. It has to be filled with water. the people who want to be baptized go into the water one by one. The minister helps them. the river Jordan the baptism.

The minister tells all the people that this person loves Jesus and want to be [baptized]. then the minister says: I baptize you in the name of the father and of the son and of the holy spirit. Amen.

Then the minister dips the person under the water. the Church baptizes People because Jesus told us to.[23]

Richard always celebrates the anniversary of his baptism. Each new family diary is heavily inscribed on 23 March to ensure we mark the occasion. He usually persuades the minister to make reference to it in church, often including his chosen baptismal hymn, "Low in the grave he lay, Jesus my Saviour." He enjoys the contrast between the sad verses and the triumphant chorus, "Up from the grave he arose!"

Abstract spiritual language has little meaning for him, but baptism, communion and church membership are physical realities. Being a useful church member is important to him. He may doze through some church meeting business, yet picks up pastoral news as matter for prayer and requests for practical help within his capability. He had not long been a church member when the man who ran the bookstall and dealt with the *Baptist Times* asked for a successor as he was leaving London. Richard promptly offered to become the *Baptist Times* agent: he knew he could cope with that, but not the book stall. He looked after the *Baptist Times*, recording payments in a notebook, for the rest of its life as a printed paper.

At home he devotes much time to private devotions, using his large collection of recorded hymns and prayer anthologies, alongside his own free prayer. This might indeed be described as his favorite "hobby." He loves to suggest hymns for particular themes. It is hard to know *what* he understands, but faith brightens his life. Occasionally his insights take people by surprise, as when a minister asked him what he thought Christmas was about, expecting the nativity or even Father Christmas. The reply was immediate, "It's about Emmanuel—'God with us'."

As Richard's mother, I hesitate to claim too much, so quote from Brian Haymes' letter explaining his suggestion that I should contribute to *Baptist Sacramentalism*. He wrote of "a sacramental story through and through. God uses flesh and blood to engage with us as we are," and of Richard's

understanding of incorporation into Christ evident by his serious church membership and service. Richard takes this "embodiment" very seriously,

---

[23] Letter to Barbara Stanford, written by Richard on the fourteenth anniversary of his baptism, 23 March 2000.

something he has learned from observing his parents and other church members. All this brought to light in his surprising pastoral instincts . . . The church lives the story of God by participating in a developing memory. That this has happened in Richard is gloriously obvious. Now in his own flesh and blood he shares the life in Christ and receives by trust a faith that has already seen him through hard time[s] and will bring him to God's promised end with all the saints . . . It is a gospel story.[24]

It is right for the church to take the sacraments seriously, but that should not mean that those outward and visible signs, the water, bread and wine, should be permanently withheld from those who cannot voice what, if anything, they understand of their spiritual meaning. They will sense whether or not they are truly included in Christ's church.

Richard, the fellow Christian who shares our daily life, is one example among many with learning disabilities who have been enabled, thanks to their churches, to know that God loves them just as they are, to savor the life-changing joy of knowing Jesus as friend and of being valued members of the church. For them, the sacraments have not proved a stumbling block, but the door to more abundant life.

Bibliography

Bowers, Faith. *Knowing Jesus*. Didcot: BUild/Baptist Union of Great Britain, 1991.

———, ed. *Let Love Be Genuine*. London: The Baptist Union, 1985.

———. "The Saving Cry of Dereliction." *Baptist Ministers' Journal* 255 (July 1996), 19–20.

———, ed. *When Weak, Then Strong: Disability in the Life of the Church*. London: Bloomsbury Central Baptist Church on behalf of BUild, 2008.

———. *Who's This Sitting in My Pew?*, *Mentally Handicapped People in the Church*. London: Triangle/SPCK, 1988.

Bowers, Faith, Ena Robertson, and Susan Wright. *The Church*. Didcot: BUild/Baptist Union of Great Britain, 1991.

Cross, Anthony R., and Philip E. Thompson, eds. *Baptist Sacramentalism*. Studies in Baptist History and Thought, 5. Carlisle: Paternoster, 2003.

Fiddes, Paul S., ed. *Reflections on the Water: Understanding God and the World through the Baptism of Believers*. Regent's Study Guide, 4. Macon, GA: Smyth & Helwys, 1996.

Haydon, Roger. "Believers Baptized: An Anthology." In *Reflections on the Water*, edited by Fiddes, 9–21.

McBeth, H. Leon, *A Sourcebook for Baptist Heritage*. Nashville, TN: Broadman Press, 1990.

---

[24] Email from Brian Haymes to the author.

Neal, George. "With Understanding." In *Let Love Be Genuine*, edited by Bowers, 53–54.

Nelson, Sally, "A Reflection on a Baptism." *Baptist Ministers' Journal* 340 (October 2018), 28–29.

Nelson, Sally. "'The Water Buries Like a Tomb': Baptists and Baptism." In *Gathering Disciples: Essays in Honor of Christopher J. Ellis*, edited by Myra Blyth and Andy Goodliff, 112–27. Eugene, OR: Pickwick, 2017.

Payne, Ernest A., and Winward, Stephen F. *Orders and Prayers for Church Worship: A Manual for Ministers*. London: Kingsgate, 1960.

Pinnock, Clark H., "The Physical Side of Being Spiritual: God's Sacramental Presence." In *Baptist Sacramentalism*, edited by Cross and Thompson, 8–20.

Robertson, Ena. *Following Jesus*. Didcot: Build/Baptist Union of Great Britain, 1991.

Rogers, Tom. "Should She Be Allowed?" In *Let Love Be Genuine*, edited by Bowers, 51–53.

Taylor, Michael. "Include Them Out?" In *Let Love Be Genuine*, edited by Bowers, 46–50.

Wilson, David D., *I Am with You: An Introduction to the Religious Instruction of the Mentally Handicapped*. Slough: St Paul, 1975.

Wright, Susan. *Joining the Church*. Didcot: Build/Baptist Union of Great Britain, 1991.

Practices

CHAPTER 9

The Sacramental Practices of the Believing Community

Linda Aadne

"Wherever the Spirit of God is, there is the church, and all grace."[1]

Introduction

A recent gathering of church leaders took place at an annual church planting conference in Oslo, Norway. There were representatives from church denominations throughout Scandinavia in attendance, and they were encouraged to share what they felt was most important in the ongoing life and ministry of the church. Several themes emerged in the conversation, but it was interesting to note that "discipleship" was the most important concern for the vast majority of the participants. The group was unified in their desire not simply to "win" new believers, or merely to gather a group of believers to plant churches, but to be faithful in working to facilitate means of faith formation and spiritual growth in their members. Sustainability for the churches and their continued growth through the missional task of the church were seen to be directly related to the spiritual maturity and commitment of their members. While there was a recognition of the differences represented in each of the denominational traditions, there were areas of complete consensus and concern. The conversation centered largely on facilitation of the traditional practices of various disciplines of the Christian faith, such as personal Bible study and prayer, and participation in worship. What was largely absent from the conversation was a strong consciousness of the role of the entire church community in faith formation.

In this chapter I aim to explore the role of the church community in faith formation. In doing so, I will argue that the life and practices of the local church are sacramental in nature, as they are derived from the church's life in covenant fellowship with the triune God. I will explore how practices of the local church are the embodiment of the participation of the church in the life of the triune God and are instrumental in the *missio Dei* as the church lives and serves within the world. In describing the practices of the church as sacramental, I aim to expand a perspective of the sacramental practices of the

---

[1] Irenaeus, *Against Heresies*, 3.24.1.

church to include the practices of life in Christian community that involve the dynamic engagement of its members who serve in the diversity of their spiritual gifts. These come to expression within the realm of human relationships and acts performed that manifest the salvific grace of God and are channels of his healing and restoration. Consequently, Christian practices are viewed as intrinsically sacramental in nature because they become the means of conveying grace and communicating the gospel. This perspective includes the embodiment of Christian faith within a multiplicity of practices born out of life in Christian community and its mission in the world. These include baptism, communion, preaching and teaching of the word of God, prayer, and communal discernment, but can and should also include the ministries of various prophetic gifts, hospitality, healing, and social engagement as well. Clark H. Pinnock provides us with an expansive vision of the sacramental nature of human existence:

> Sacraments exist simply because we are bodily creatures inhabiting a material world. There is in theory no limit to the number of them. Created reality is richly imbued with sacramental possibilities. The world reflects God's glory; therefore, anything can mediate the sacred, where there are eyes to see and ears to hear. Since the Spirit pervades the universe, any event or experience can bring God to mind and mediate his presence.[2]

This expansive vision resonates with Acts 17.28 where it states, "For in Him we live and move and have our being." It encompasses the richness of life in the Spirit of God both in Christian community and within the material world. It can be considered as an acknowledgment of God's free sovereignty in his continual self-disclosure within his church and within creation. The triune God is not limited by human constraints.[3]

Dykstra and Bass provide us with a distinctive understanding of Christian practices which they define as

> . . . the constituent elements in a way of life that become incarnate when human beings live in the light of and in response to God's gift of life abundant. Thus, when we refer to Christian practices, we have something normative and theological in mind. Each element in our approach presumes that Christian practices are set in a world created and sustained by a just and merciful God, who is now in the midst of reconciling this world through Christ.[4]

---

[2] Pinnock, *Flame of Love*, 120.

[3] The freedom and sovereignty of God is presented as a core conviction of early Baptists by Thompson, "People of the Free God," 226–27.

[4] Dykstra and Bass, "Theological Understanding of Christian Practices," 21, who acknowledge their indebtedness to MacIntyre's concept of "social practices" in *After Virtue*, 187–88.

With this definition in mind, sacramental practices can be viewed as embodied expressions of life in Christian community, which can be instrumental both in worship, evangelism, faith formation, the ministry of reconciliation of the church (2 Cor. 5.19), and the *missio Dei*. When Christian practices are infused with the life of the Spirit, believers participate in the triune God and are thereby inspired and empowered to express and embody God's love in their relationships to others. It is in the realm of these participatory practices that the presence of the triune God becomes incarnate in the lives of believers.

A Focus on Christian Formation

Philip E. Thompson describes a resurgence of interest in issues concerning spiritual formation among Baptists. While lauding this development, he expresses concern that there is a lack of consciousness of the richness of resources found within the Baptist tradition for this purpose, and that there has been an undue individualistic focus. Thompson draws upon early Baptist theologians in presenting a theology of formation that emphasizes the role of the ritual acts of worship when practiced in the realm of the believing community. Here Thompson does not only include the ritual acts that normally constitute a worship service, but rather the composite of communal acts that characterize the service and life of a believing community on a daily basis and within the liturgical calendar. For early Baptists, the role of the believing community was vital to spiritual formation. This perspective was fundamentally different from that witnessed in contemporary individualistic approaches to fostering Christian practices in that they were fully communal in character. Thompson notes that the seventeenth-century General Baptist, Thomas Grantham, affirmed that the church is the locus of God's presence. Indeed, Christ indwells the church by the Holy Spirit, and through the Spirit the church is the habitation of God.[5]

The determinative element of early Baptist theological convictions concerning faith formation lay in their belief in the freedom of God. Thompson states, "Baptists spoke two words concerning God's freedom. First, God is free *from* any sort of control by creation in God's work of redemption. Second, God also is free *for* using creation in the same work of redemption."[6] He states further,

---

[5] Thompson, "Practicing the Freedom of God," 123. His underlying purpose in writing his essay is to focus on the early Baptist belief in the freedom of God, which emphasizes the clear distinction between the Creator and the creature, and the humble acknowledgement of the sovereignty of God in his self-disclosure and in the spiritual formation worked within the church community and its practices.

[6] Thompson, "Practicing the Freedom of God," 120–21 (italics original).

The Church was thus the principle locus of God's freedom for using the things of creation as means of grace . . . While early Baptists believed God to be free from the Church, human beings were not seen as likewise free, precisely because of God's freedom *for* the Church in the work of redemption. So, they could say in the "Orthodox Creed" that it is to the Church "and not elsewhere, all persons that seek for eternal life, should gladly join themselves."[7]

Early Baptists sought to guard against human presumption and vanity in their knowledge of God. Because of this, the revelation of God was believed to be mediated primarily within the realm of the communal practices of worship. Benjamin Keach emphasized that while personal and family worship was to be encouraged it was in the realm of the corporate worship of the gathered community that the spiritual edification of its members was effectuated through the power of the Holy Spirit in their midst.[8] The faith formation and edification of the members of the church was also seen to be instrumental in their corporate ministry to the surrounding community as well. This was accomplished through the corporate habits of virtue, which were infused with the grace of the Spirit and effectuated the spiritual transformation of members in the image of the love of Christ.[9]

James K.A. Smith

While keeping this traditional Baptist approach to discipleship in mind, it is interesting to compare it to more contemporary approaches to accomplishing this task. In exploring means of contributing to spiritual formation, James K.A. Smith has written a three-volume work called *Cultural Liturgies*. In the first volume, *Desiring the Kingdom*, Smith questions the purpose of Christian education, and suggests that the prime objective should perhaps be "the formation of hearts and desires" and "the shaping of hopes and passions" rather than absorption of ideas and information.[10] In recognizing the formative power of cultural practices (liturgies), Smith calls his readers to examine their environment and their habits (a so-called "liturgical audit")[11] with the purpose of "the formation of radical disciples who desire the kingdom of God."[12]

---

[7] Thompson, "Practicing the Freedom of God," 124–25 (italics original).

[8] Thompson, "Practicing the Freedom of God," 126.

[9] Thompson, "Practicing the Freedom of God," 132–33.

[10] Smith, *Desiring the Kingdom*, 1:18. See also 1:27–28.

[11] Smith, *You Are What You Love*, 53.

[12] Smith, *Desiring the Kingdom*, 1:19.

Homo Liturgicus—We Are What We Love

Smith claims that human beings are ultimately creatures of desire that are motivated and shaped by the objects of their affections. Taking inspiration from Augustine, he claims that "we are what we love." He presents a philosophical anthropology that describes human beings as "*homo liturgicus*," stating that

> humans are those animals that are religious animals not primarily because we are believing animals, but because we are liturgical animals—embodied, practicing creatures whose love/desire is aimed at something ultimate.[13]

Human affections come to expression in formative practices that are lived not only within the context of life within the church, but often even more profoundly within the realm of culture. In considering how we should live as Christians within contemporary cultures, he challenges us to ask, "What would the church's practices have to look like if they're going to form us as the kind of people who desire something entirely different—who desire the kingdom? What would be the shape of an alternative pedagogy of desire?"[14] While Smith addresses the ultimate purpose of Christian education, he does not confine it to schools, but also sees the necessity of applying these questions to life within families as well. His perspectives are borne by a central axiom, "that behind every pedagogy is a philosophical anthropology, in other words, behind every constellation of educational practices is a set of assumptions about the nature of human persons—about the kind of creatures we are."[15] As a result, he challenges the imbalanced focus upon the formation of the intellect within most pedagogical philosophies, and strives to emphasize the formative role of ritual and habits in creating an alternative vision of the "good life," or a "social imaginary" that is "precognitive and pre-reflective."[16] This refocusing should serve to counteract what he considers a dualistic human view by encouraging practices that emphasize a "more holistic (and less dualistic) understanding of human persons as essentially embodied."[17] Readers are challenged to consider two very different understandings of education: the informative, and the formative.[18] In emphasizing formative education he presents the worship practices that involve the physical embodiment of worship in the tangible, sensory and symbolic elements within the Christian

---

[13] Smith, *Desiring the Kingdom*, 1:40.

[14] Smith, *Desiring the Kingdom*, 1:25.

[15] Smith, *Desiring the Kingdom*, 1:27–28.

[16] Smith, *Desiring the Kingdom*, 1:29 and 133.

[17] Smith, *Desiring the Kingdom*, 1:57.

[18] Smith, *Desiring the Kingdom*, 1:31.

liturgy, and sees within their practices an affirmation of the created material world. Smith hereby emphasizes the aesthetic nature of worship which is instrumental in capturing our imaginations through the material, physical nature of liturgical worship.[19] The liturgical sacramental practices of the church are considered to be

> sites of a special presence of the Spirit that is both revelatory and formative in a unique way. While the whole world is a sacrament, we might say that *the* sacraments and the liturgy are unique "hot spots" where God's formative, illuminating presence is particularly "intense."[20]

Recognizing the material and embodied and the spiritual nature of the sacraments, Smith states that "Christian worship is nothing less than an invitation to participate in the life of the triune God."[21]

Churches today struggle with contemporary issues that work powerfully against the realization of the vision for "the formation of radical disciples who desire the kingdom of God." Faithful and consistent participation in worship and fellowship has become an increasing challenge for believers in the face of individualistic and materialistic cultural values that are generally construed to be representative of the "good life." The current "cultural liturgies" dominating Western societies exercise enormous power in the formation of values and practices within society that require Christians to be conscious of how to counteract these influences by making counter-cultural choices in their daily lives in order to facilitate spiritual formation. Smith's engagement with pedagogical and social theory is fascinating. The wealth of his imagination and the richness of his creativity are thought provoking.[22] For instance, he describes the local shopping mall as "one of the most important religious sites in our metropolitan area,"[23] and uses the marketing of "Victoria's Secret" as an example of how advertisers intentionally exploit the erotic and religious nature of consumers in contrast with the typically cranial and intellectual worship style and practices of evangelical churches.[24] His work includes insights that are valuable because they are rooted within a broader comprehension of both human nature and current social settings.

---

[19] Smith, *Desiring the Kingdom*, 1:146.

[20] Smith, *Desiring the Kingdom*, 1:148 (italics original).

[21] Smith, *Desiring the Kingdom*, 1:149–50.

[22] The ideas presented in *Desiring the Kingdom* are explored at length in his other works as well. The most relevant in this discussion is Smith's *You Are What You Love*.

[23] Smith, *Desiring the Kingdom*, 1:19–25.

[24] Smith, *Desiring the Kingdom*, 1:75–79.

Smith draws upon the elements found within a liturgical worship service to illustrate the wealth of formative potential to be discovered within the historical practices of the church. In considering Smith's emphasis on the necessity for the creative and sensory within worship, we can look to basic pedagogical theory concerning "multi-sensory" learning. Human beings learn and are engaged through the composite impulses and stimulation provided through their senses. Individuals respond differently to different types of stimuli. When creating a worship space with the intention of spiritual formation, we should necessarily engage a congregation creatively through a variety of elements combined together to speak and resonate effectively within the hearts of a diversity of worshippers. Liturgical practices in worship are multi-sensory in character and provide a wealth of impulses that can communicate, and, in fact, be a means of grace as they contribute to the awakening and renewal of faith. As creatures created in the image of our Creator, we carry both the potential for creative engagement with the material world, at the same time as we are profoundly affected by the sensory environment that surrounds us. It is significant that symbolic elements that represent and comprise the very stuff of daily life are the means by which we gather to celebrate our common life in the triune God. The cleansing and renewing waters of re-birth and life, the bread broken together in reverence as nourishment for our souls, the oil of anointing, the wine poured out and shared for the cleansing of our sin and shared with the promise of redemption, and joy in life everlasting are all elements that speak to depths within us as we worship together.

As a former musician and music pedagogue, I appreciate the emphasis upon the importance of continual practice, repetition, and habituation. We all know the well-known phrase "practice makes perfect." Any pastor would also support measures that contribute to the regular practice of central disciplines of the faith for the purposes of spiritual formation. At the same time, most of us recognize the struggles encountered when we seek to effectuate fundamental ontological transformation simply through changing our habits. What often fails is the actual consistent practice of the things that can effectuate change. Some of the greatest frustrations many people encounter in striving for both sanctification and maturity as believers lie within the limitations and inconsistency of human nature. One need only to think of the many well-intentioned resolutions made by most people every New Year's Day which seldom result in significant change, as they are not sustained by individuals in the long run. It is here that the formative aspect of life in Christian community is essential.

While being fascinated by Smith's focus on spiritual formation through liturgical practices, I am nevertheless left questioning the role that the Christian community plays in spiritual formation in this picture. Where can we situate the agency of spiritual formation? Is it to found within the liturgical worship practices themselves? Of course, liturgical practices do not occur in a vacuum. There is an assumption of the presence of a body of worshippers performing these liturgical practices together, and, as mentioned above, there is the affirmation of God's presence within the realm of creation that is expressed in the liturgy. However, coming from a country with a Lutheran state church tradition, it is often painfully clear that the regular encounters that people have with the church through the liturgical celebrations of key rites of passage in their lives have little effect on their personal faith formation. These include infant baptisms, confirmations, weddings, and funerals. The familial and cultural obligations within Norwegian society necessitate participation in a variety of these services on a regular basis for most Norwegians. Unfortunately, for most people these services do little to affect faith formation in the attendees because they are often not recognized as being more than traditional cultural practices, and those in attendance have little contact with the local church otherwise. Smith himself recognizes the dangers of reducing these practices to something similar to baseball batting practice, because of his emphasis on the formative value of the repetition of practices.[25] He counters these concerns by emphasizing that the spiritual nature of worship practices elevates them above the normal mundane activities of life, and situates them in the realm of actual participation in the life of the Trinity.[26] That being said, he does place a very strong emphasis on liturgical practices and insists that worship is something that we *do*, and that "the practices of Christian worship do this work nonetheless because of the kind of creatures we are. The practices carry their own understanding that is implicit within them."[27] In a footnote he counters anticipated objections to this claim stating,

> I understand that some might be uncomfortable with this claim, since it seems to suggest that there is some kind of virtue in "going through the motions". On this point I'm afraid that I have to confess that I do indeed think this is true. While it is not ideal, I do think that there can be some sort of implanting of the gospel that happens simply by virtue of participating in liturgical practices (this is the ballpark of the principle of *ex opere operato*).[28]

My unease with Smith's emphasis on liturgical practices also lies in the fundamental ecclesiological differences that exist between the Reformed tradition and the Believers Church tradition that has its roots in the churches of the radical reformation. In *The Household of God*, Lesslie Newbigin addresses the question, "By what is the Church constituted?" His answer is

---

[25] Smith, *Desiring the Kingdom*, 1:149.

[26] Smith, *Desiring the Kingdom*, 1:150

[27] Smith, *Desiring the Kingdom*, 1:166–67.

[28] Smith, *Desiring the Kingdom*, 1:167.

expressed in the presentation of three main categories of churches: the Protestant, the Catholic, and the Pentecostal. Newbigin's "types" are somewhat caricatured descriptions, but they do serve to illustrate the prime focus of each ecclesial model, in spite of being painted with very broad strokes. Baptists fall under the category of the "Pentecostal" type. He carefully maps out how each group has beliefs and practices that are biblical, but that they cannot be considered to constitute the fullness of the church alone. Accordingly, they must be considered together as overlapping or complementary expressions of the church within the world, and only together are capable of constituting the fulness of the church universal. All of the traditions emphasize the primacy of people's faith response to the triune God as fundamental to the constitution of the church. Roman Catholics further emphasize the apostolic succession and the incorporation of Christians into the mystical body of Christ through the sacraments.[29] Lutherans and Reformed Christians alike emphasize the primacy of the right preaching of the word and the right administration of the sacraments.[30] James W. McClendon describes this view of the church as "not an institution, but an event—a repetitive event, as Sunday by Sunday acts of preaching and of sacramental ministry constitute the church anew."[31] According to Newbigin, the main contribution of the Pentecostal "type" is the experienced power and presence of the Spirit of God within the church today. In asking the question, "Where is the church," he says, we must also ask, "Where is the Holy Spirit recognizably present with power?"[32] In his description of this type, Newbigin states that "The church is, in the most exact sense, *a Koinonia*, a common sharing in the Holy Spirit."[33] McClendon applies Newbigin's Pentecostal typology to the Baptist vision of the church, and describes it as comprised of "a regenerate church membership," where "new birth, life delivered by the nurturing divine Spirit, is a necessary condition of membership." He continues, observing that "not all have seen what Newbigin saw, that the Spirit in individuals may come to nothing apart from the Spirit in the community."[34] The practices of the community draw their sacramental effectiveness because they flow from the life of the triune God. When considering what constitutes a Baptist approach to faith formation through the sacramental practices of the church, the starting point must always be the triune God himself. It is the triune God, Father, Son, and Holy Spirit, who

---

[29] Newbigin, *Household of God*, 61.

[30] Newbigin, *Household of God*, 47–48.

[31] McClendon, *Doctrine*, 335.

[32] Newbigin, *Household of God*, 95.

[33] Newbigin, Household of God, 97

[34] McClendon, *Doctrine*, 343.

graciously calls a people to himself and includes them in the outworking of his redemptive plan for all of creation.

Trinitarian Ecclesiology

The last decades have witnessed a remarkable interest in trinitarian theology. Not only are Baptist theologians among them, non-Baptist theologians as well draw from early Baptists. Their work is helpful in considering the role of Christian community in effecting spiritual formation. Let us briefly examine the thought of Miroslav Volf, whose background is Croatian Pentecostalism, and the English Baptist, Paul S. Fiddes in considering the role of Christian community in effecting spiritual formation.

Miroslav Volf

Miroslav Volf has sought to define a trinitarian Free Church ecclesiology in dialogue and contrast with the Roman Catholic and Orthodox traditions for the purpose of counteracting individualism within the church.[35] He draws on the work of John Smyth (1554–1612) (the Anglican, Puritan, then Separatist, Baptist, and finally aspiring Mennonite) to define early Free Church ecclesiology. Volf quotes Smyth as stating,

> We say the Church or two or three faithful people Separated from the world & joyned together in a true covenant, have both Christ, the covenant, & promises, & the ministerial powre of Christ given to them . . .[36]

Smyth based this statement on his understanding of Matthew 18.20. Volf summarizes this by saying, "It is the 'faithful people' who have Christ and his power; it is they who have the covenant and the promises."[37] He explains that this understanding of Matthew 18.20 already had "pre-eminent importance quite early in church history," but that it was Free Church theologians who applied it systematically in their definition of the church. The passion for biblical faithfulness was the driving motivating force for early Baptists and other Separatist groups in their attempts to define their ecclesiology.[38] While still a Separatist, Smyth stated that "Gods word doth absolutely describe vnto

---

[35] Volf, *After Our Likeness*, 191.

[36] Volf, *After Our Likeness*, 132, referring to Whitley, ed., *Works of John Smyth*, 2:403, which is quoting from Smyth's *Paralleles, Censvres, Observations*, 47. This was written in 1607 and printed in 1609, once Smyth had become a Baptist.

[37] Volf, *After Our Likeness*, 10.

[38] Weaver, *In Search*, 9.

vs the only true shape of a true visible church."[39] He held that the local church, when comprised of believers in covenant with one another in the triune God, had everything that they needed to be defined as a true church. Christ's authority was afforded to the gathered community when they sought the mind of Christ in fellowship with one another. The government of the church was to be held by the entire congregation in its submission to the Lordship of Christ. It was on the basis of his understanding of this scriptural passage that Smyth defined the church:

> A visible communion of Saincts is of two, three, or more Saincts joyned together by covenant with God & themselves, freely to vse al the holy things of God, according to the word, for their mutual edification, & Gods glory ... This visible communion of Saincts is a visible Church.[40]

Unfortunately, Volf ultimately claims that Smyth's description of the church is flawed, because, in his opinion, Smyth's fundamental approach was christological and not trinitarian. He goes so far as to state that Smyth's ecclesiology was primarily shaped by modalism.[41] Whether he is correct in his judgment or not is beyond the scope of this essay. For our purposes, let it suffice to observe that he does so in order to construe the church as an analogy to trinitarian perichoresis.

Even today, Baptists base their ecclesiological beliefs on their interpretation of Matthew 18.20. The collaborative work, *On Being the Church*, states that

> Baptists have historically looked to the promise in Matthew 18.20 as foundational to the calling and the being of the church. Where people gather in the name of the Lord, then and there the Lord has promised to be present. This presence of the triune God is the *esse* of the church.[42]

What should also be recognized however, are the theological developments that occurred in the life of John Smyth, and his close relationship with Thomas Helwys. Smyth was restlessly driven in his efforts to define and find a church that was faithful to what he considered to be the New Testament church order. His transition from Anglican to Puritan to Separatist to Baptist and finally his application for reception as member of the Mennonite church in Amsterdam occurred over a remarkably short period of time (1606–10) and

---

[39] Smyth, *Principles and Inferences Concerning the Visible Church* (1607), 4, in Whitley, ed., *Works of John Smyth*, 1:252. From 1607–9 Smyth was a Separatist, not a Baptist.

[40] Volf, *After Our Likeness*, 135, Whitley, ed., *Works of John Smyth*, 1:252, being Smyth's *Principles and Inferences*, 4.

[41] Volf, *After Our Likeness*, 194.

[42] Haymes, Gouldbourne and Cross, *On Being*, 197 (italics original).

testifies to this. He was continually in dialogue with, but also in opposition to, other Separatist leaders. His writings reflect the evolution of his views.[43] His close friendship with Thomas Helwys and their co-leadership of the church in Gainsborough led them to seek refuge in Amsterdam, where they arrived at their convictions concerning believers' baptism as being constitutive for the church. This is reflected in Smyth's treatise entitled *The Character of the Beast*.[44] This resulted in his own self-baptism and his baptism of Thomas Helwys, and, with Helwys, the other members of their congregation. Within a short time, however, Smyth experienced great regrets concerning his self-baptism, and he encouraged the congregation to seek membership with the Waterlander Mennonites. His *Short Confession* from 1610 defines his theology and ecclesiology and is considered to be part of this application for membership, though it was not published at that time.[45] Because he considered his baptism to be valid, and also his disagreement with Smyth on other theological issues, Helwys parted ways with Smyth and his congregation.[46] Consequently, it was primarily Helwys who continued to lead the small congregation, and further worked to define core Baptist convictions which are common to most Baptists even today. They were united, however, in their trinitarian grounding of ecclesiology.[47]

---

[43] Cross, "Adoption of Believer's Baptism," presents the emergence and development of the theology and practice of believer's baptism among early Baptists under the leadership and influence of both John Smyth and Thomas Helwys. He charts Smyth's development and convictions which were shared and further developed by Helwys after they parted ways in Amsterdam. See also Lee, *Theology of John Smyth*.

[44] Smyth, *Character of the Beast or the False Constitvtion of the Chvrch*.

[45] Lumpkin, ed., *Baptist Confessions*, 99.

[46] Yarnell, "Foreword" to Jones, *Beginning of Baptist Ecclesiology*, xi, emphasizes this stating, "It was not Smyth's advocacy but Helwys's rejection—his refutation *inter alia* of the need for baptismal successionism, of the exclusion of Christian magistrates from the church, and of the celestial flesh doctrine of early Dutch Anabaptism—that carried the day among later Baptists" (italics original).

[47] In his *Short Confession of Faith in XX Articles by John Smyth*, Smyth starts with this trinitarian statement, "WE BELIEVE WITH THE HEART AND WITH THE MOUTH CONFESS: (1.) That there is one God, the best the highest, and most glorious Creator and Preserver of all; who is Father, Son, and Holy Spirit," in Lumpkin, ed., *Baptist Confessions*, 100. Thomas Helwys begins his *A Declaration of Faith of English People Remaining at Amsterdam in Holland* from 1611 stating, "WEE BELEEVE AND CONFESSE I. That there are THREE which beare record in heaven, the FATHER, the WORD, and the SPIRIT; and these three are one GOD, in all equalitie, 1 Jn.o. 7.7; Phil.2.5, 6. By whome all thinges are created and preserved, in Heaven and in Earth. Gen. 1 Chap.," in Lumpkin, ed., *Baptist Confessions*, 117.

John Smyth and Thomas Helwys were preoccupied not only with defining a true biblical ecclesiology in opposition to the Church of England, but also in their relationship to other dissenting groups. They both rejected the practice of infant baptism practiced among other Separatists and concluded that the practice of believers' baptism was an essential identifying feature of a true New Testament church.[48] This was based on their understanding of a radical contrast between the old and the new covenants, where the circumcision of the flesh was understood by them to be a "carnal sign," whereas the sign of the new covenant was the seal of the Holy Spirit. In rejecting the validity of infant baptism based upon an understanding of its practice as justified by its correlation to Old Testament circumcision, Smyth wrote,

> There are two seales: Circumcision a seale of the carnal covenant vppon the carnal children: Gen. 17.11. & the Holy Spirit of promise a seale of the Spirituall covenant vppon the Spirituall seed . . . Gen. 17.10, 11.12. this place proveth that circumcision was a seale of the carnall covenant made with the carnall seed, & not a seale of the Spirituall covenant made with the Faithful: For the Spirit is the seale thereof, who is therefor called the Spirit of promise, & the seale.[49]

Helwys employed the same reasoning in his rejection of the practice of infant baptism in presenting his understanding of the relationship between a person's conscious faith and the sealing of the Holy Spirit which was necessarily manifested in the visible sign of the seal in believers' baptism. He wrote,

> If you will examine the New Testament throughout, you shall find no seal, nor none sealed, but they that believe, "who are sealed with the Holy Spirit of Promise." . . . The Seal of the covenant must needs be answerable to that holy covenant, a seal of life and salvation only to them that believe and are baptized. (Ephesians 1:13–14; Revelation 2:17–18) The apostle here to the Ephesians does show that "after they believed they were sealed with the Holy Spirit of promise."[50]

The earliest Baptists envisioned a church that was not constituted through the administration of the sacraments through an episcopal office, but rather through the conscious response of the faith of individuals who freely chose to enter into Christ through believers' baptism. Believers' baptism marked an entrance into the "new creation" in Christ (2 Cor. 5.17). Consequently, life in

---

[48] Jones, *Beginning of Baptist Ecclesiology*, 127–28.

[49] Jones, *Beginning of Baptist Ecclesiology*, 127–28, citing Smyth's *Character of the Beast*, in Whitley, ed., *Works of John Smyth*, 2:580–81.

[50] Jones, *Beginning of Baptist Ecclesiology*, 131, citing Helwys' *Mystery of Iniquity*, 127–28.

regenerate Christian community was to be gathered and centered in their corporate covenant relationship to the triune God and to one another (John 17.21). The shared life in the triune God was not only the object of their eschatological hope, but a vital, and powerful present reality for the church (1 John 1.1–4). Their ecclesiology was thoroughly communal in nature and came to expression in the practices of Baptist believers.

The core convictions of both John Smyth and Thomas Helwys were instrumental in defining a distinct vision of the local church that emphasized that life in Christian community is constituted through the power and presence of the triune God at work within its members. This comes powerfully to expression in the Great Commission (Matt. 28.19–20), where the church's task of baptizing disciples of Christ is performed in the name of the Father, Son, and Holy Spirit. It is the sealing of the Holy Spirit that coincides with the faith response of believer's baptism, that simultaneously draws believers into both the vertical and the horizontal covenantal relationship to both the triune God and the body of Christ. The Great Commission provides the church with the assurance of both the authority of his name, and also the promise of his constant presence in their midst ("For behold, I am with you until the end of the age") and as they engage missionally with the world at large.

Paul Fiddes

Paul Fiddes also emphasizes the historical central influence of covenantal theology when describing key features of early Baptist ecclesiology and identity.[51] Covenantal theology has its roots in the Separatist heritage preceding the emergence of the Baptists and became a central defining feature of both the first General and Particular Baptist churches. Although this faded as a central aspect of Baptist ecclesiology throughout the course of the seventeenth century (seemingly because of the centrality of believers' baptism), covenantal theology has enjoyed a recent resurgence of interest among Baptists.[52] Its relevance for this work is that covenant theology grounds the life of the gathered community in its corporate relationship to the triune God. The mutual covenant within a local congregation is at once both horizontal and vertical, and founded upon the gracious inclusion of the gathered community within the triune relationship of the Godhead. Fiddes states,

> as God the Father makes covenant of love eternally with the Son in the fellowship of the Spirit, so simultaneously God makes covenant in history with

---

[51] Fiddes, *Tracks and Traces*, 21–47.

[52] Fiddes, *Tracks and Traces*, 24.

human beings. In one movement of utter self-giving God elects both the divine Son and human children as covenant partners.[53]

I would like to suggest that it is this adjustment in perspective concerning the situation of the agency of spiritual power associated with formative practices which needs to occur. It is within the regenerate community of the faithful, in the power of the Spirit in their participation in the life and activity of the triune God in its corporate life, that sacramental practices come to life and expression. This shift in focus moves the effectiveness of sacramental acts from the acts themselves to the Holy Spirit working within the regenerate believing community enacting these practices. The common life of the Spirit in the community is that which makes sacramental acts constitutive of the church's life and existence, where new members are incorporated into the fellowship through believers' baptism, and are sustained and strengthened in their faith in the sharing of the Lord's supper. At the same time, other practices can indeed be classified as profound sacramental means of grace, such as the preaching and teaching of scripture, or the gathering of the church to seek direction under the lordship of Christ in their practice of common discernment within the church meeting. Hospitality, which involves the breaking of bread with "the other," involves table fellowship which serves to break down the walls of separation between people and invites participation in the life of Christ who is present and residing at the table.

Indeed, Fiddes presents a trinitarian model that emphasizes *participation* in the life of the Trinity that is based on the concept of perichoresis. However, what distinguishes his understanding from that of Volf is that he understands the perichoretic "dance" to be "movements of relationship" within the Trinity, where one perceives this in terms of the patterns of the dance itself, "an interweaving of ecstatic movements."[54] He dismisses any attempts to found a trinitarian theology through drawing an analogy between human and divine "persons," claiming that "the closest analogy between the triune God and human existence created in the image of this God is not in persons, but in the *personal relationships* themselves." Consequently, he insists that we not merely encourage an imitation of the life of the Trinity, but rather conceive of life in the Christian community as participation in the "places opened out within the interweaving relationships of God."[55] The participation of the church in the relational flow of the triune God is founded in the covenantal relationship that God has made with his people. This is based upon the professed faith of each of its members. He states, "God the Father makes a covenant of love eternally with the Son in the fellowship of the Spirit, so simultaneously God makes

---

[53] Fiddes, *Tracks and Traces*, 36.

[54] Fiddes, *Participating in God*, 72.

[55] Fiddes, *Participating in God*, 49–50 (italics original.)

covenant in history with human beings."[56] Fiddes insists that a local church is then never comprised of an incidental gathering of individuals, but rather a gathered community under the direct rule of Christ, living its life in covenantal relationship in a balance of independence and interdependence with other churches under the same rule of Christ. This has always been the hallmark of Baptist ecclesiology.[57]

This relationship of the disciples to the triune God is clearly manifested in the sending of the disciples by Jesus in John 20.21–22, where they are also entrusted with the authority inherent to that relationship. The sending of the disciples is the natural extension of the reciprocal sending within the Trinity itself. The movement within the relationships of the Trinity is always a movement of sending and is the impetus and source for his mission in the world through his church. Far from being mere imitation, participation in the movement of sending involves the actual representation of Jesus in their acts.[58] As such, the church community is essential to the mission of God in the world, and its communal practices are vital to the formation of disciples that are commissioned by the triune God to do his will. It is precisely within this interweaving of relationships that we can situate the true source of effective power which infuses sacramental practices with salvific grace. If we take Jesus at his word (that "where two or three come together in my name, there am I with them," Matt. 18.20), it is within the realm of this common life in fellowship with the triune God that the practices of the church emerge and can be described as sacramental.

Let us imagine for a moment that the final tones of a ballet orchestra are drawn to a close by the conductor, and that for a brief moment in time performers and audience alike are suspended together in a reverent, pregnant silence. Then, suddenly, as though awakening from a dream, the hall erupts into glorious shouts of "Bravo! Bravo! Bravissimo!" The theater thunders with ecstatic and tumultuous applause as people stand together in fervent acclaim at the completion of a ballet performance. For a brief period of time the audience has been swept into the drama, grace, and exquisite beauty of dancers carried on the wings of orchestral music over a stage flooded by lights within the world created on the stage. They have been enraptured and drawn into the dance for this brief period of time as a story has enfolded where individual soloists, couples, clusters, and company alike have complemented one another in their movements in response to the music. The dancers and the audience are transported in time and place by the orchestral music, and the force of the story they are a part of and are telling. Each individual has a vital role to play,

---

[56] Fiddes, *Tracks and Traces*, 36.

[57] Fiddes, *Participating in God*, 86–88. See also his "Baptist Concepts of the Church and Their Antecedents."

[58] Fiddes, *Participating in God*, 51.

but they are also mutually dependent upon one another in the greater context of the entire performance. What is often not as apparent to the audience, however, is that the performances are the cumulative expression and result of intense commitment to practice, coordination, and discipline, sensitivity to the movements of others and to the music led by the skill of the conductor. In many ways this experience can be compared to the life and the ministry of the church before the watching world, as it participates in the eternal perichoretic dance of the triune God as the story of the people of God unfolds in time.

I imagine that perhaps while you can still faintly hear the strains of an oboe and harp in your inner mind, that you may be protesting, along with Volf, that this idealized portrait of the church is far removed from the present brokenness and imperfection witnessed within Christian communities of faith. We are by no means the "Bolshoi Ballet." In fact, if the truth be told, we frequently bear greater resemblance to a primary school class performing their annual Christmas pageant. However, one of the mysteries of the faith is that the power of God is manifested in our weakness and sinful human frailty. This is an ongoing theme in Paul's apostleship as his ministry and calling were lived in the consciousness of his own human limitations and weakness (2 Cor. 12.7–10). Paul was painfully conscious of his own human limitations, but he firmly believed that his weakness ultimately served as an avenue for the glorification of God. Paul's own ministry as an apostle was based on his participation in the life of the risen Christ. In his confrontational letter to the Corinthians he writes, "On my return I will not spare those who sinned earlier or any of the others, since you are demanding proof that Christ is speaking through me. He is not weak in dealing with you but is powerful among you. For to be sure, he was crucified in weakness, yet he lives by God's power. Likewise, we are weak in him, yet by God's power we will live with him in our dealing with you. Examine yourselves to see whether you are in the faith; test yourselves. Do you not realize that Christ Jesus is in you—unless, of course, you fail the test?" (2 Cor. 12.3–5). Here it is also clear that he viewed the church in its sinfulness and imperfect state as indwelt by Christ. Paul was ever conscious of his life being lived "in Christ," claiming that "I have been crucified with Christ, and I no longer live, but Christ lives in me" (Gal. 2.20). His faith in the resurrected and glorified Christ was not merely fashioned in imitation of Christ, but in his participation in his death and resurrection. In line with Paul, we have the treasure of "the light of the gospel of the glory of Christ" in jars of clay (2 Cor. 4.1–12). The jars of clay that the denuded army of Gideon carried into battle in the night were shattered in the darkness to reveal the light within (Judg. 7.19–21). It is patently clear from Paul's correspondence with the Corinthians that the church was not in an elevated state of perfection, but that he still considered them to be in their human state to be "in Christ" and included in his redemptive plan for the world.

The Practice of the Sacrament of Believers' Baptism

Believers' baptism and the Lord's supper are what Stanley J. Grenz characterizes as "community acts of commitment."[59] He explains that

> In the context of its worship, the community employs a variety of symbolic acts that carry great significance. Because certain of these practices symbolize the gospel itself, they serve as vehicles by means of which we confirm our participation in the grace God offers us through Christ and consequently in the fellowship of the covenant people. These practices are community acts of commitment.[60]

In providing this description of believers' baptism and the Lord's supper, Grenz thereby illustrates the challenges associated with choosing adequate terminology for their theological significance and function. Most Baptists today would still refrain from using sacramental terminology for what they consider to be the two "ordinances" of the church. Grenz explores the historical background for the discarding of sacramental terminology among many Baptists, and explains this development as a Radical Protestant reaction against both sacramentalism and sacerdotalism which was also further affected by the rationalistic age in which Baptists emerged as a movement.[61] While recognizing that Baptists and other radical branches of the church were justified in rejecting the abuses associated with sacramentalism and sacerdotalism, he would insist that there is an equal danger in a reductionist view of the sacraments as well. This has unfortunately resulted in a devaluation of their significance for the life of the church, where they are merely attributed symbolic significance, or, as with believers' baptism, viewed as acts of obedience required for church membership. Grenz seeks to counteract this tendency by exploring key terminology frequently used to describe the two sacraments which he hopes will serve to enrich our understanding of their theological significance and function. The term "ordinance" has been traditionally employed to emphasize the faithful commitment and obedience involved in the practices. While both sacraments are visible enactments of our identification with Christ, they do not have merely symbolic significance. Grenz states,

> Through our participation we not only declare the truth of the gospel, however, we also bear testimony to our reception of the grace symbolized . . . The acts of commitment become enactments of our appropriation of God's action in Christ.

---

[59] Grenz, *Theology for the Community of God*, 665.

[60] Grenz, *Theology for the Community of God*, 666.

[61] Grenz, *Theology for the Community of God*, 670.

As we affirm our faith in this vivid symbolic manner, the Holy Spirit uses these rites to facilitate our participation in the reality the acts symbolize.[62]

A sacramental view of believers' baptism does not diminish its function as a sign or symbol of the believer's entrance into the death and resurrection of Christ and their eschatological hope. Every aspect of its embodied practice illustrates the mystery of the believer's cleansing from sin, and deliverance from death into life as they identify with the death and resurrection of Christ. It becomes an embodied proclamation of the gospel as it communicates through the material means of the waters of redemption. A sign always points to a greater reality than the sign itself.

Others have also sought to define a Baptist perspective of sacramentalism. While appreciating the lengths that Grenz goes to attribute the "ordinances" with sacramental, symbolic and theological significance, it is also helpful for the purposes of this chapter to use the definition provided by Anthony R. Cross, who defines sacraments as "the Word of God in action which must be responded to in the act of participating. Sacraments are, quite simply, means of grace."[63]

The scope of this chapter does not allow for an extensive discussion of the sacrament of believers' baptism. However, it is essential to emphasize that it is fundamental to all of the other sacraments of the church because it is constitutive for its life and practices. John E. Colwell states this emphatically in the Foreword to Cross' *Recovering the Evangelical Sacrament*:

> The only gospel appeal we find within the New Testament is the appeal to believe the gospel, to repent, and to be baptised, this baptism linked to the promise of the Spirit. A man or a woman is "in Christ" by virtue of being baptised into Christ. The Church is the body of Christ by virtue of its members being baptised into Christ . . . It is baptism that is defining of the Christian. It is baptism that is defining of the Church.[64]

W.M.S. West presents the natural relationship between the individual believer, the church community, and the triune God within the realm of both the initiatory preparation of baptismal candidates and their baptism as believers. He links this naturally to all other aspects of Christian life and states that

> The full experience of being a Christian requires that the person is linked for worship, witness, teaching, fellowship etc. with the company of the saved,

---

[62] Grenz, *Theology for the Community of God*, 672.

[63] Cross, *Recovering the Evangelical Sacrament*, 189.

[64] Colwell, "Foreword," in Cross, *Recovering the Evangelical Sacrament*, xiii.

namely the Church. The New Testament makes it abundantly clear that entry into the Church is through baptism.[65]

Cross describes New Testament baptism as "faith baptism," and the "sacrament of faith."[66] What distinguishes a sacramental view of believers' baptism is that its effectiveness is derived from the faith-response of the individual to the gracious self-disclosure of God within the community of the faithful. He argues this convincingly through both a thorough examination of New Testament passages referring to water baptism by stating that "It is clear, therefore, that God's gift to faith and baptism is one, namely salvation in Christ. This is what Peter says in 1 Peter 3:21, 'baptism . . . now saves you.'"[67] The essential link between the conscious faith response of believers to the gospel of Christ, and baptism into the body of Christ is also directly related to the promise of the Holy Spirit to those who believe. In entering the baptismal waters in faith, believers are incorporated into Christ and the regenerate community of faith—his body. Herein lies the wellspring of the life and ministry of the church.

Practicing the Sharing of the Lord's Supper

Every week students and staff gather together at our theological faculty chapel to celebrate communion together. Men and women of different ages, ethnic origins and church denominations gather at the Lord's table to share this simple meal of bread and wine. We form a circle which emphasizes both unity and equality among the participants, and in reverence break the bread and share the cup which passes from one person to the next as we together "proclaim the Lord's death until he comes" (1 Cor. 11.26). The covenantal unity between believers and the triune God comes to powerful expression in the celebration of the Lord's supper. Jesus invites believers to participate in this meal as a commemoration of his death and his sacrifice for our sin. At the same time, believers gather in unity at the table in humble acknowledgement of their common need for his grace and forgiveness. The meal shared is also a shared proclamation of the eschatological hope of the people of God. We celebrate communion in the consciousness of his presence at the table through his Spirit.

---

[65] West, "Baptist Church Life Today," 39.

[66] Cross, *Recovering the Evangelical Sacrament*, 51.

[67] Cross, *Recovering the Evangelical Sacrament*, 60.

Practicing Hospitality

The fellowship that we share at the communion table should naturally be seen as a means of grace in that our participation motivates and enables the inclusion and participation of others. There are few of our practices that embody the Spirit of Christ more than our hospitality, not merely for one another, but even more expansively to include the stranger. In a time of history that is characterized by religious and ethnic strife, where millions of people are driven and displaced from their homes, it has been evident among most European Baptist churches that measures must be taken to attempt to address their needs in a multitude of ways. Churches have received refugees and worked for their integration not only within churches, but within society as well. They have mobilized efforts to provide clothing, food, and shelter. They have worked to advocate for the rights of victims of war and terror, and have thereby embodied the justice and mercy of the triune God in their efforts. Dental and medical care have been provided as well as schooling for children of displaced families and their parents. Language instruction has been provided for the facilitation of employment of those making their way in a new country. Private hospitality has been extended and new friends have been made as Christians have responded to the needs of those alone in their new cultural setting. The church becomes a new family. Communities of faith have experienced that these practices have resulted in the inclusion of new members as they have responded both to the call of the gospel, and to the love manifested in the life of Christian communities of faith. These intentional hospitable practices are remarkably counter-cultural in an age that is tragically witnessing a resurgence of nationalistic sympathies which foster the xenophobic rejection of "the other." The love of Christ is manifested when believers extend hospitality which has the power to break down barriers of hostility. This is also manifested in the willingness to receive hospitality from those who have come to be socially isolated and recipients of refugee aid. Receiving hospitality is also instrumental in restoring a sense of personal dignity to people who have experienced a profound loss of identity in their attempts to establish themselves in their new cultural settings.

Hospitality can be practiced more intentionally within families, where in continuity with Jewish tradition, gathering at the sabbath table in the home is a central worship practice and place of faith formation. Worship practices are manifested in daily prayer, the lighting of sabbath candles, the breaking of bread, and in the sharing of food and fellowship. Christian families gather at table with the consciousness of the presence of Christ through his Spirit as we gather in his name. Here intentional choices must be made to establish a rhythm of life that enables family meals that secure not only the physical health, but perhaps just as importantly the spiritual health of families growing together. Getting home from work in rush hour traffic and preparing for a host of extra-curricular activities for children often means that meals lose their central place in families. It can also mean that hospitality is rarely extended to others. However, an intentional approach to the centrality of sharing meals together and with others can be instrumental, and indeed fundamental, to faith fostering in families and communities of faith. For many, the prospect of a lifestyle of hospitality is challenging because they imagine that it means white linens, polished silver, crystal and china, and culinary expertise surpassing their abilities. Consequently, visits from guests are preceded by extensive housecleaning, meal planning, shopping, and preparation. This can make the prospect of having guests daunting to say the least. but if we envisage hospitality as the "warp and woof" of family life it can open doors for spontaneous celebrations of the ordinary. There is a great deal of love exhibited in the preparation of a simple meal and a place within the circle of a table. Sharing life in authentic forms has the capacity to knit hearts and lives together. Here we rather enter the realm of bare tables with highchairs, the clamour of children and spilled milk and simple meals. What is of the essence is that the gracious love inherent to these practices both manifests and reveals the hospitality and inclusion of the triune God in our midst.

Hospitality can also manifest itself through programs initiated by churches that are geared to extend needed support to families and children. Many parents can feel remarkably isolated and struggle with coping with the stresses of everyday life because they are separated from their extended families. Single parent families are becoming more the norm today than the traditional family unit. This means that parents and children alike can feel as though they are cut adrift and forced to cope alone with issues they had never imagined having to bear and are ill equipped to meet. Young boys are particularly vulnerable in single parent families because they lack godly male role models that can contribute in a positive way to their development into manhood. Church fellowships can take intentional measures to build relationships between families in their midst. Ideally, this can provide a network of significant relationships between children and other adults that can be formative in contributing to their growth as disciples of Christ. However, this can only be borne out of a common vision for what the triune God can work within the realm of hospitable sharing. Many Christian families also recognize a calling to provide loving homes for children through adoption and foster care. Responding to God's calling in this area of ministry can be crucial for the protection and care of children who are in critically vulnerable circumstances but can also prove to be an infinite source of blessing for the families welcoming them into their homes. Care for "widows and the fatherless" is a fundamental expression of the love of our heavenly Father, but it is manifested and embodied in the intentional practices of those who respond to his calling. This is an area of need in society today, which goes deeper than the measures taken by the welfare state. It reaches into the realm of the fundamental spiritual needs that can be met through intentional measures taken to provide hospitality and loving support for children and parents by communities of faith.

Of course, consideration must be taken to the needs of other groups of people as well. The measures taken for hospitable inclusion must be extended to people of all ages. Examples of this include both single adults and the elderly. A growing percentage of the elderly often experience isolation and increasing marginalization, both because of growing mobility in society at large which often separates them from their immediate families, but also because of the phenomena of ageism, which serves to rob many of their sense of inclusion, purpose, and dignity. Churches should strive to facilitate inclusion within the many areas of ministry that would benefit from the insight and wisdom of those who have years of life experience as disciples of Christ. At the same time, ministries of mercy and care are means of manifesting the love of Christ in visitation, prayer, and practical assistance for those beyond their years of active ministry.

The Practice of Sojourning in Community

Luke provides us with a glimpse of life in the community of disciples after the resurrection. He shares the story of two disciples who decide to leave Jerusalem after the crucifixion and resurrection of Christ and proceed to travel together on the road to Emmaus (Luke 24.13–35). As they walk together, they express their grief, disillusionment, and confusion about what they have witnessed. As they walk together, a stranger joins them on their journey, and proceeds to explain to them how the death and resurrection of Jesus was in fulfilment of scripture. The stranger's identity is hidden from them until they share a meal together after reaching their destination. It is first during the breaking of the bread, and in the giving of thanks, that Jesus finally reveals himself to them, only once again to disappear from their sight. They then ask one another, "'Were not our hearts burning within us while he talked with us on the road and opened the Scriptures to us?'" (Luke 24.32).

This story of two disciples walking on a road away from Jerusalem is in continuance of one of the running themes throughout Luke–Acts. In Luke 9.51, Jesus turns his face *towards* Jerusalem and walks on the journey together with his disciples to fulfill that for which he was sent. The ultimate destination is Jerusalem from where the mission of the church would proceed after Pentecost, from Jerusalem, to Judea, Samaria, and to the ends of the earth after the sending of Spirit at Pentecost (Acts 1.8). These two disciples are ultimately re-directed from their path away from Jerusalem in order to return to the other disciples in Jerusalem to testify to that which they have experienced on the way. The presence of the risen Christ on their way together serves to draw them back onto the right way through his illumination of scripture. The post resurrection mission is soon to be carried through the common journey of disciples on "the way." They never walk alone, for in their fellowship and through the promise of the constant presence of Christ, they would be encouraged, led, and empowered. The role of scripture on the way is significant in that it serves to provide clarity in confusion, and renewed purpose and direction on their journey. If we understand this story in relationship to the current life of the Christian community, we see the necessity of sojourning together in mutual support while turning to the scriptures to find the same clarity and direction for our common life in mission together on the way. The practice of the communal reading of scripture and discernment is a hallmark of the Baptist tradition. These practices emerge from the conviction that the triune God is present within his body when they gather to discern the will of God through prayer and the study of scripture. These practices can be coupled with Spirit-led encouragement within the prophetic gifts of words of wisdom and knowledge within the mutual edification of the body of Christ, and are avenues for the self-disclosure of the Lord through the ministry of one another.

Conclusion

In raising questions concerning discipleship and faith formation, it is clear that the Baptist historical tradition has a unique communal emphasis which emerges from their vision for the church. The church is the body of Christ, comprised of the diversity and complexity of its individual members, both constituted, gathered, and empowered by the presence of the Holy Spirit in her midst. The sacramental practices that are formative for discipleship in Christian community derive their effective power through the common participation of the community of faith in the relational life of the triune God. It is the presence of the Holy Spirit within the community of the faithful that infuses sacramental practices with salvific grace. This happens through the baptism of believers who respond to God's divine self-disclosure in his Son. The church community lives, moves, and has its being in the realm of covenantal relationships, both within the body itself, and in its corporate relationship to her head. She is called to embody the life of the Trinity while participating in the unfolding of the eternal eschatological drama that seeks continually and gracefully to include others in the perichoretic dance of the triune God. This is embodied in the sacramental practices of the believing community.

The earliest Baptist pioneers provide us with insight into their belief in the transformational power of the Holy Spirit at work within the regenerate community of faith. In doing so, they also provide us with a foundation for both evaluating and shaping Christian community through the practices that embody and infuse our common life in Christ with his life and presence. When considering liturgical practices, they necessarily include the practices most commonly considered to be sacraments, whereas other elements of worship practice can certainly be deemed as sacramental in character.

As Christians we are called to live our lives in the unity of the faith in local fellowship, at the same time as we retain a consciousness of our place within the grander universal church which includes all Christians throughout the course of the unfolding of human history, and which will ultimately lead to the fulfilment of our eschatological hope in Christ at the end of time.

Bibliography

Cross, Anthony R. "The Adoption of Believer's Baptism and Baptist Beginnings." In *Exploring Baptist Origins*, edited by Anthony R. Cross and Nicholas J. Wood, 1–32. Centre for Baptist History and Heritage Studies, 1. Oxford: Regent's Park College, 2010.

———. *Recovering the Evangelical Sacrament: Baptisma Semper Reforandum.* Eugene, OR: Pickwick, 2013.

Dykstra, Craig, and Dorothy C. Bass. "A Theological Understanding of Christian Practices." In *Practicing Theology*, edited by Volf and Bass, 13–32.

Fiddes, Paul S. "Baptism and Creation." In *Reflections on the Water: Understanding God and the World through the Baptism of Believers*, edited by Paul S. Fiddes, 47–67. Regent's Study Guides, 4. Macon, GA: Smyth & Helwys, 1996.

———. "Baptist Concepts of the Church and Their Antecedents." *The Oxford Handbook of Ecclesiology*, 2018. https://doi.org/10.1093/oxfordhb/97801996458 31.013.2

———. *Participating in God: A Pastoral Doctrine of the Trinity.* London: Darton Longman & Todd, 2000.

———. *Tracks and Traces: Baptist Identity in Church and Theology.* Carlisle: Paternoster, 2003.

Grenz, Stanley J. *Theology for the Community of God* Nashville, TN: Broadman & Holman, 1994.

Haymes, Brian, Ruth Gouldbourne, and Anthony R. Cross. *On Being the Church: Revisioning Baptist Identity.* Studies in Baptist History and Thought, 21. Milton Keynes: Paternoster, 2008.

Helwys, Thomas. *A Short Declaration of the Mystery of Iniquity.* Edited by Richard Groves. Classics of Religious Liberty, 1. Macon, GA: Mercer University Press, 1998.

Jones, Marvin. *The Beginning of Baptist Ecclesiology: The Foundational Contributions of Thomas Helwys.* Monographs in Baptist History, 6. Eugene, OR: Pickwick, 2017.

Lee, Jason K. *The Theology of John Smyth: Puritan, Separatist, Baptist, Mennonite.* Macon, GA: Mercer University Press, 2003.

Lumpkin, William L. *Baptist Confessions of Faith.* Philadelphia: Judson, 1959.

MacIntyre, Alasdair. *After Virtue: A Study in Moral Theory.* 2nd ed. Notre Dame, IN: University of Notre Dame Press, 1984.

McClendon, James William. *Systematic Theology:* Volume 2. *Doctrine.* Nashville, TN: Abingdon, 1986.

Newbigin, Lesslie. *The Household of God: Lectures on the Nature of the Church.* New York: Friendship, 1954.

Pinnock, Clark H. *Flame of Love: A Theology of The Holy Spirit.* Downers Grove IL: InterVarsity Press, 1996.

Smith, James K.A. *Desiring the Kingdom: Worship, Worldview, and Cultural Formation.* Volume 2. Cultural Liturgies. 3 vols. Grand Rapids: Baker Academic, 2009.

———. *You Are What You Love: The Spiritual Power of Habit.* Grand Rapids: Brazos Press, 2016. http://ebookcentral.proquest.com/lib/dtl/detail.action?docI D=4633427

Smyth, Iohn. *The Character of the Beast or the False Constitvtion of the Chvrch. Discovered in certayne passages betwixt Mr. R. Clifton & Iohn Smyth, concerning true Christian baptisme of New Creatures, or New borne Babes in Christ: and false Baptisme of Infants borne after the Flesh.* s.l.: s.n., 1609. In *Works of John Smyth,* edited by Whitley, 2:563–680.

Thompson, Philip E., "People of the Free God: The Passion of Seventeenth-Century Baptists." *American Baptist Quarterly* 15.3 (1996) 223–41.

———. "Practicing the Freedom of God: Formation in Early Baptist Life." In *Theology and Lived Christianity,* edited by David M. Hammond, 119–38. The Annual Publication of the College Theology Society, 45. Mystic, CT: Twenty-Third Publications, 2000.

Volf, Miroslav. *After Our Likeness: The Church as the Image of the Trinity.* Sacra Doctrina. Grand Rapids: Eerdmans, 1998.

Volf, Miroslav, and Dorothy C. Bass, eds. *Practicing Theology: Beliefs and Practices in Christian Life.* Grand Rapids: Eerdmans, 2002.

Weaver, C. Douglas. *In Search of the New Testament Church: The Baptist Story.* Macon, GA: Mercer University Press, 2008.

West, W.M.S. "Baptist Church Life Today." In *The Pattern of the Church: A Baptist View,* edited by A. Gilmore, 13–53. London: Lutterworth, 1963.

Whitley, W.T., ed. *The Works of John Smyth, Fellow of Christ's College, 1594–8.* 2 vols. Cambridge: Cambridge University Press, 1915.

CHAPTER 10

The Priesthood of All the People:
Theological Imperatives for a Church Beyond Religion

Frank Rees

A generation ago, when a tide of political and cultural change was sweeping the Western world, as youth culture challenged moral and social norms, and theological upheavals confronted the traditions of many Christian churches, Findley Edge, a Southern Baptist leader wrote these challenging words:

> It is imperative that we become a people who understand who we are, who God is, what God is about in the world and what God is calling us to be about in the world.[1]

The contention of this paper is that the same imperative continues to apply for us in a vastly changed situation today. Whereas Edge's call to the churches to participate in the mission of God was expressed in terms of the development of local churches as mini theological seminaries, the context of local church life has now vastly changed. In response to these changes, my contention is that the focus of church life and mission needs to move from the activities of the church when gathered to what may be called the "dispersed" life, the lives of people when not gathered in church buildings or for church meetings and programs. The primary context and focus of faith will be in the everyday life and activities of Christian people. This life, I shall argue, is the fundamental meaning of the doctrine of the priesthood of all believers and may be understood as the primary sacrament of the church. It is in the lives of the people of faith that we make up a collective offering of thanks and praise, "a living sacrifice, holy and acceptable to God, which is [our] reasonable worship" (Rom. 12.1).

We begin, then, with seven affirmations which I propose as theological imperatives for the church today. These affirmations draw specifically upon Baptist heritage and ecclesiology, but in such a way as to provide a shift in emphasis towards a possible response to the changed circumstances of the churches in contemporary society. It is the contention of this paper that the aspects of Baptist ecclesiology to be emphasized here provide a particular

---

[1] Edge, *Greening of the Church*, 37.

opportunity for Baptist churches to embrace the current context with creativity and spiritual vigor.

1. The church must be understood fundamentally as the people, the people called to faith, hope and love, through the gospel of Jesus Christ.
2. By implication, this means that the life of the church is not to be identified primarily with the ministry of those identified as clergy or ministers and their specific activities.
3. Rather, the life of the church is essentially the lives of the people when they are not gathered together, the life and activities of the church "dispersed" in the world.
4. The mission of the church is to participate in the mission of the Spirit in the world, in all the aspects of home, social and economic life.
5. The church, then, is a priesthood, the sacramental life of all the people.
6. The gathered life of the church, in congregations and other forms and activities, reflects and enables this dispersed life.
7. The church worships God in all its life, the offering of its service and praise, in dispersed and gathered life.

Collectively, these affirmations lead to the assertion that the priesthood of all the believers is a collective concept and has its primary focus in the lives of the people. On this basis, this paper offers the following theological imperative for Baptist church life today:

It is imperative that we become a people who understand who we are as a priestly people, called to offer all of our lives as a collective priesthood, participating in the salvific mission of God in the world.

This vision of the church and its mission stands in sharp contrast to the perception of the church as a religious institution. To reclaim the differentiation of Baptist church life from such religious institutions should resonate with our historic origins as a marginalized and dissenting people. Nonetheless, it is no easy thing to consider moving beyond our focus upon things we can measure, our buildings, budgets and baptism statistics, thought to be indicators of who we are and what our ministry essentially is. Nonetheless, the theological imperative moves us towards something more profoundly challenging and hopeful, the possibility of a life centered upon the people as living witnesses to and participants in the mission of God in the world, working with the Spirit of God in bringing light and healing, hope and community.

To engage with this possibility, then, it is first necessary to recognize the radically changed and often challenging context of our witness today, which I shall describe with the phrase "beyond religion."

Beyond Religion

The situation of the church in Western societies at least, though increasingly also in the majority world, can best be characterized in terms of a rejection of religion in its traditional institutional forms. The most obvious element of this rejection is the decline is church attendances. At the time of writing, the most recent Pew Research Report is titled "Decline of Christianity continues at rapid pace."[2] Even those who do attend church regularly do not, in many instances, go every week. Numerous studies have documented the decline in church attendances.[3] Australian Christian researcher Philip Hughes has observed that an increasing number see themselves as Christian but do not want to identify themselves with a specific denomination or church.[4] An additional factor, however, is the increasing proportion of people who identify in surveys and on the census as having "no religion."[5]

These phenomena have given rise to profound reflection on the character and meaning of secularity. Whereas on a simplistic interpretation the growth in the "No religion" response might indicate the absence of or even opposition to faith and spiritual practice, in many respects this is evidently not the case. Diverse forms of spiritual practice, ranging from personal prayer, meditation, and forms of reflection, are affirmed amongst a substantial proportion of the population self-described as "Spiritual but not religious."[6]

The "decline" in religious affiliation, however, should not be simplistically interpreted as meaning that Western societies are as secular as might appear, if

---

[2] Pew Research Centre Report, *In U.S., Decline of Christianity Continues at Rapid Pace.*

[3] A helpful summary of recent surveys relating to the United Kingdom is found at Wikipedia. "Religion in the United Kingdom." It should be noted that the *British Social Attitudes* surveys do not include Northern Ireland. In the United States, a summary of several studies can be found in Butler Bass, *Christianity Beyond Religion*, particularly chapter 2, 39–64.

[4] Bond and Hughes, "'No Religion' in Australia"; and Hughes, "Australia's Changing Religious and Social Profile."

[5] E.g., a recent study by the Olive Tree Media found that 31% of respondents identified themselves as having no religion or spiritual belief, see Anon., *Australian Communities Report*, 5.

[6] Australian social psychologist Hugh Mackay has traced this movement in his book *Beyond Belief.* Mackay has a chapter on SBNR—the common description people give of themselves as "spiritual but not religious," see chapter 4, 95–123.

by secularity we mean that religion has little influence or part to play in the public and political life of these societies. A recent collection of essays has examined the role played by religion in communal responses to the influx of large numbers of refugees into northern and central Europe, particularly in 2015. Religion was found to be a significant marker of difference between communal groups and a consideration when people assessed the suitability of refugees for acceptance into existing social orders. These phenomena suggest that Western Europe is perhaps not as "secular" as it might have imagined itself to be. An underlying concept of religion and its part in social cohesion played its part in the response to this crisis.[7]

Thus when we use the expression "beyond religion" to describe the wider context of contemporary church life, it is with the recognition of a complex of factors: a strong decline in church attendance and religious affiliation, mixed with an increasing number of people who describe themselves as having "no religion," whilst many of these do identify as "spiritual" persons. Though many people in these contexts claim no specific religious affiliation, there appears yet to be a broad social identification with one religious tradition (some form of Christianity) in contrast to the cultural and religious traditions of immigrant or refugee communities. The concept of secularity thus has led not so much to the disappearance of religion as such, but to the loss of a clear and dominant religious hegemony, and a wide range of responses to various spiritual and religious traditions.

A further critical consideration here is the concept of "religion" itself. Valuable work has been done in recent times on the history of this concept, leading to the conclusion that what has been meant by this term is essentially a modern conception or indeed invention. Whereas Dietrich Bonhoeffer famously proposed a "non-religious interpretation of Christian concepts" and a "religionless Christianity," he did not provide a detailed analysis of what he was denying or seeking to avoid.[8] His biographer Eberhard Bethge did later offer a broad description of factors that were involved. In this expression, religion was largely individualistic and "partial," having carved out an area of life as its own domain. It exercised a "tutelage" over society, professing a position of moral superiority and responsibility, expressed in monarchical and patriarchal values. It was inherently conservative of the established order. In theological terms, its focus is metaphysical, a God who is "beyond" and yet functions as a source for "answers" or solutions. Bonhoeffer likened such religion to a chemist shop dispensing remedies. All this led to the

---

[7] The response to the "refugee crisis" in Europe in 2015 has been the subject of a number of studies. One such study, which explores various contexts and religious traditions, is Schmiedel and Smith, eds, *Religion in the European Refugee Crisis.*

[8] See Bonhoeffer's letter to Eberhard Bethge, 30 April 1944, in Bonhoeffer, *Letters and Papers from Prison*, 361–65.

characteristic of "dispensability:" actually, people could do very well without this religion.[9]

Two specific interests have driven contemporary scholars to consider the history of the concept: the desire to separate religion and politics, and thus to articulate the notion of a secular society, and the attempt to clarify the distinct areas and claims of religion and science.

Australian philosopher Peter Harrison's book, *The Territories of Science and Religion*, helpfully traces the second of these concerns, while in the United States William Cavanaugh addresses the former issue in *The Myth of Religious Violence: Secular Ideology and the Roots of Modern Conflict*.[10] Both of these works build upon the argument of Wilfred Cantwell Smith, who contended that the term "religion" as we know it is essentially an invention of the modern West.[11] No such idea existed in the ancient cultures of Greece or Egypt, nor have the movements we call religions seen themselves as "religions" (if they do now) until well into the modern era. It is on this basis that Cavanaugh speaks of the "invention" of religion.

Here I will briefly outline the basic elements of Harrison's study of the history of the concept "religion." The Latin term *religio* does have a long history, but its primary meaning was to identify an "inner disposition," more like what we might call a habit of piety or even integrity. Harrison begins with the work of Thomas Aquinas (1225–74), for whom *religio* was one of the virtues, but interestingly not one of the theological virtues. It is a moral virtue: Harrison explains that "in its primary sense *religio* refers to the interior acts of devotion and prayer, and that this interior dimension is more important than any outward expressions of this virtue."[12] So while there may be behavioral expressions of the virtue, such as prayers and good deeds, these are secondary. Most crucially then, Harrison adds, "There is no sense in which *religio* refers to systems of propositional beliefs, and no sense of different religions (plural)." A shift can be identified specifically in the move from Latin language (which does not have either the indefinite or definite articles) into languages with these facilities.

For his part, Cavanaugh has traced the way the term religion, annexed with definite articles, became associated with various forms of conflicting or competing claims: by the seventeenth century books appeared with titles relating not only to "the Christian Religion" but also "the Protestant Religion" and so forth, and thus the idea of religions in the plural.[13] Over the succeeding

---

[9] Bethge, *Dietrich Bonhoeffer*, 757–95.

[10] Harrison, *Territories of Science and Religion*; and Cavanaugh, *Myth of Religious Violence*.

[11] Smith, *Meaning and the End of Religion*.

[12] Harrison, *Territories of Science and Religion*, 7.

[13] Cavanaugh, *Myth of Religious Violence*, 74.

centuries, the studies of religion addressed matters of comparison as well as an interest in the foundations of religion in human nature, with what aspects of mind or personality this religion was based, and whether it was rational or even supra-rational.

As a result of these shifts in meaning, in the last century we have seen increasing conflicts in the respective claims about the "territories" of religion and science, on the one hand, and the role of religious beliefs and values in relation to politics and civil society at large. Conflicts between people groups are often portrayed as "religious," leading to the concern addressed in Cavanaugh's study, the claim that religion is a major cause of violence in the world.

Bonhoeffer scholar Barry Harvey concludes from these studies that "the domains of 'religion' and the 'secular' are complementary artefacts that operate in concert to help weave the various threads of creation into the technological fabric of modern society."[14] In Bonhoeffer's time, religion functioned within society as a whole to "help provide social capital, a stock of relations and shared values" and to legitimate the various sub-sections of society, defining each in its place and the appropriate expectations from each.[15] In his Christology lectures (1931–32), Bonhoeffer had identified what Harvey calls "the partiality of religion that illegitimately restricts God to one area of life, God as a possession of human beings, and religion tied to the concept of culture." By contrast, as Harvey summarizes the emphasis in Bonhoeffer's *Ethics,* "The church's concern is not religion, but the form of Christ and its taking form among a band of people."[16] For Bonhoeffer, discipleship means always living in one sphere only and that sphere is the world at large.[17]

In light of the growing rejection of "religion," there is then the opportunity for Christian theology to engage with a different vision of discipleship and community. This kind of thinking has already been indicated in the quotations from Bonhoeffer cited by Barry Harvey: the life of the people, taking form as the body of Christ. It is this life which forms the church, the priesthood of all the believers. Our contention is that this, too, is a fundamentally Baptist conception of the church, a sacramental offering of everyday life in discipleship and faith.

---

[14] Harvey, *Taking Hold of the Real,* 151–52.

[15] Harvey, *Taking Hold of the Real,* 152.

[16] Harvey, *Taking Hold of the Real,* 132–33.

[17] This aspect of Bonhoeffer's thought is particularly well explained by British Baptist scholar, Keith Clements, *SPCK Introduction to Bonhoeffer,* 39–43.

The Church: A Priesthood of All the People

Baptist identity is fundamentally concerned with the nature of the church. Brian Haymes, Ruth Gouldbourne and Anthony R. Cross say in their introduction to *On Being the Church: Revisioning Baptist Identity*, "When Baptists have written about their convictions and principles, in explanation of themselves to other Christians or to each other, they have usually started straight in with their doctrine of the church."[18] Similarly, in his study of Particular Baptists, Ian Birch helpfully sets out the vision of this movement for "a true visible church of Christ." His contention is that Christology was the guiding principle of this ecclesiology: the rule of Christ.[19] The idea was that Christians are called to follow Christ wherever his purposes may lead and thus to become a visible gathering of believers. Thus, the "true visible church" will be a believers' church, consisting of those "gathered out of the World by the preaching of the Gospel, by the powerful ministry of the Spirit."[20] but whereas there is an emphasis here on the "gathering" of the church "out of the world," this does not mean that the life of the church is somehow apart from the world. On the contrary, it is in the world at large, in everyday life and not only when attending a "church" service or meeting, that the followers of Christ are the church. The church is the people, those called to faith in Christ, in a community of discipleship that affects all aspects of their lives.

In order to advance this argument, it is necessary first to reconsider briefly the idea of priesthood in the Bible and to consider how it applies to the church. We shall then proceed to the argument that the context of this Christian priesthood is primarily the everyday lives of people when not gathered as "the church."

It is significant that the only passage in the New Testament which uses the imagery of priesthood in relation to Christians refers to the collective life of the people:

> But you are a chosen race, a royal priesthood, a holy nation, God's own people, in order that you may proclaim the mighty acts of him who called you out of darkness into his marvelous light. Once you were not a people, but now you are God's people; once you had not received mercy, but now you have received mercy (1 Pet. 2.9–10).

To understand the import of this passage it is necessary to consider aspects of priesthood in the Hebrew Bible and its traditions.[21]

---

[18] Haymes, Gouldbourne and Cross, *On Being the Church*, 3.

[19] Birch, *To Follow the Lambe*, 48.

[20] Birch, *To Follow the Lambe*, 37.

[21] What follows here draws in summary, with some replication, from the argument of Rees, "Worship of All Believers."

Priesthood in the Bible is generally associated with several elements or activities. Whereas priesthood may predate the temple, it is most clearly associated with the temple. Priests were people called by God, albeit that this calling was mediated through familial and tribal means. The orders of priests (Aaron and Melchizedek) were seen as instituted by God. Priests, then, are closely associated with God: they are to know God and to represent God to the people. but they are also called to know the people. Moses, as the archetype of such priesthood, is familiar with the people and their "murmurings," loss of purpose and hope, and outright disobedience to God's way. Through this dual representation, of God and people, the priests were commissioned to make sacrifices and blood offerings on behalf of the people, which meant that the activity of priests was intimately associated with the gift of God's salvation. Priestly service enabled the people to receive and enter in the grace and favor freely offered by their God and thus, too, to fulfil their calling as witnesses to this God.

Priesthood in the Old Testament generally involved familial office and status, as Numbers 3.1–5 indicates. With this priestly office, at least at times, went much power to gather and shape the life of the people, or indeed to control and oppress. For this reason, it is important to notice one crucial text which functions to undercut any suggestion of the priestly office as *above* the nation, namely Exodus 19.5–6a:

> Now therefore, if you obey my voice and keep my covenant, you shall be my treasured possession out of all the peoples. Indeed, the whole earth is mine, but you shall be for me a priestly kingdom and a holy nation.

Scholarly discussion of this verse has included consideration of whether it indicates three separate designations of attributes, three tasks or even three groups, within the nation—a treasured possession, a priestly kingdom or group of priestly kings, and the nation itself called to be holy. The exegetical consensus is that all three elements are interlocking: Israel is set apart from other peoples as God's own people, dedicated to serving God in the way that the priests are dedicated within a nation. Thus, the three phrases "treasured possession," "priestly kingdom," and "holy nation" all refer to the whole nation.[22] As God's covenant people, Israel is "committed to the extension throughout the world of the ministry of Yahweh's presence." The role of priests in the formation and life of the nation is explained by John Durham: Israel is not to be a kingdom run by politicians working by strength and connivance, but "by priests dependent on faith in Yahweh."[23] It is crucial then to note the implication that priestly ministry as exercised by the castes of priests serves and represents the macro priesthood of the whole nation.

---

[22] So argues Childs, *Exodus*, 367.

[23] Durham, *Exodus*, 263.

Given this historical and cultural background, it is perhaps startling to observe that not once is the word "priest" used in the New Testament to describe a person who holds a position or "office" in the church. The Roman Catholic theologian Hans Küng, working for the ongoing renewal of ministry following the Second Vatican Council, made this point most trenchantly.[24] His argument is that in the wider society there were numerous words which reflected ideas of power, hierarchy, office and dominion, and all of these are studiously avoided when discussing the leadership of the churches. Instead the word that is consistently and deliberately chosen is the term "minister," *diakonos*.

There *are* priests in the New Testament, however. First, there is the Christians' one High Priest, Jesus Christ. His priestly office and offering are unique, unsurpassed and not to be repeated. The Letter to the Hebrews is an extended reflection on this theme. There it is clear that all the elements suggested above as involved in the biblical ideas of priesthood are true of Christ.

There is another priesthood in the New Testament, as well. This is the priesthood of the whole community of believers, the church—which leads us back to the central text, in 1 Peter.[25] Here the temple imagery is transferred from what is implied as a static situation into what is now dynamic, a lively people, a new people of God. This people of God may include the "old" people, Israel, though the text clearly stresses the new people, those who once were not a people and who did not know God at all. So, the metaphors of a building for priestly service are mixed with those of a living body, an active community set aside for service to God. The most important factor here is the resonances with Exodus 19: a *collective* priesthood. Here we have the priesthood not of each believer, but the priesthood of all the believers, the church. This is a collective, communal priesthood.

Stephen Winward wrote of the corporate priesthood of the church as "*representing* the world to God and God to the world."[26] This priesthood is to take the form not only of worship but also service: not only *leitourgia* but also *diakonia*. Winward adds, "For the 'spiritual sacrifices' include not only praises and prayers, but also sharing and loving deeds, gifts of money, evangelistic

---

[24] Küng developed his ideas about priesthood and the priesthood of all believers in several works, see *Why Priests?* chapter 2, 25–36, and *The Church*, especially Section E, chapter 1, "The Priesthood of all believers," 363–87.

[25] Rev. 6.10 also envisions the fulfilment of the church's mission to be a kingdom of priests.

[26] Winward, "Church in the New Testament," 62, and his discussion of "The Media of the Ministry of Jesus Christ," 63–74. A similar New Testament argument for the priesthood of all believers as corporate in nature is found in Robinson, *Essays on Being the Church in the World*, chapter 4, 72–82.

endeavor, and holy living. Priesthood is expressed not only in worship, but in diakonia and mission."[27]

These suggestions lead us then to consider two critical questions concerning this idea of the collective priesthood of all the believers: *where* and *how* is this priesthood exercised? Consideration of these questions will significantly assist us in understanding what the historical concept of the priesthood of all believers actually means for the church today.[28]

The Priesthood of All the People and the Sacrament of Everyday Life

The foundational document of contemporary ecumenical dialogue, Faith and Order Paper 111 *Baptism, Eucharist and Ministry*, known as the Lima Document, offers a very helpful affirmation of the ministry of the whole people of the church. Two very helpful elements are identified in this affirmation. First, since the life of the church is based on Christ's victory over the powers of evil and death, all people are called to share the fellowship of forgiveness, new life, freedom, and a life oriented towards the coming of God's reign. It is not only some who are to enter into this quality of life. New life in Christ is for all the baptized, without distinction. Secondly, the church is called to proclaim and prefigure the kingdom of God: both by announcing the gospel and by its life as the body of Christ.[29] Specific aspects of this life as signs of God's reign are also mentioned in the following paragraphs: identifying with the joys and sufferings of all people and seeking to care for them; struggling with the oppressed for their freedom and dignity; this is seen to require political, social and cultural involvement and will require relevant forms of witness and service.[30]

Clearly these involvements are not possible if ministry is restricted to the activities of a small number of "ministers," nor if ministry or priesthood is limited to things that happen when the church is gathered. What is envisaged here has to do with the life of the faithful believers in all aspects of society and not merely through organized "church" programs and activities. The context of the priestly ministry of all the people is all of life, not only "church life." This calls us to recognize that "church life" must be redefined to include the church "dispersed" as well as the church when gathered. The historic

---

[27] Winward, "Church in the New Testament," 62.

[28] In this discussion, I have not engaged with some other Baptist arguments concerning the priesthood of all believers and the congregational life, particularly in the context of the Southern Baptist Convention. For a consideration of these arguments, see Muthiah, *Priesthood of All Believers*; and Tie, *Restore Unity, Recover Identity, and Refine Orthopraxy*.

[29] Anon., *Baptism, Eucharist and Ministry*, "Ministry," I.2, and I.4, 2.

[30] Anon., *Baptism, Eucharist and Ministry*, "Ministry," I.4, 2.

understanding of the church as a gathered people should not primarily focus upon the literal gathering or congregating. The significance of that term is in the calling of God to people out of the world who lack an identity as God's people into relationship with God. The church then is a people gathered *to* God and God's purposes, and this may refer not only to when the people gather together but also to when they are dispersed in the many activities and structures of contemporary life. Whether at a worship service or at the supermarket, at work or at play, the people of God are gathered to God and called into ministry as the "royal priesthood" of God.

It is, therefore, essential that the concept of the priesthood of all is not limited to participation in activities "at church." Indeed, this is perhaps one of the many misunderstandings which have limited its significance and transformative power in the contemporary forms of Baptist church life. The priesthood of all believers is not primarily about who can do what, a kind of "division of labor," or of authority within the worship service or church life in general. It is not primarily about office, nor even about function. Though it does challenge the idea that only some people may pray or preach, allowing that the gifts of God for these public activities may extend to people other than those ordained as pastors, and it strongly affirms the idea of all believers having access to God without the mediation of others, these again are not the fundamental basis of this priesthood.

The priesthood of all believers is first of all an idea of the church, a church which is not centered in certain people or certain functions, but an idea of the church as the people, people of and with God: the whole life of the whole people of God. The church is a community of faith, a spiritual community. It is spiritual life together, that is a life in and of the Spirit of God, a life with God. Only within this life is there any priesthood, any ministry, and the idea here is that each and all, together, are priests, a collective priesthood of all of life offered in service and praise to God.

Simon Carey Holt has written extensively of this priesthood through the notion of the spirituality of everyday life, and we shall draw upon his works to explore specific implications of this concept of the priestly dimensions of everyday life. Holt is a pastor and theologian who is passionate about the practices of faith in the contemporary world, drawing upon historic spirituality, but engaging with the realities of everyday life. His book, *Heaven All Around Us*, is thus sub-titled *Discovering God in Everyday Life*. In the opening chapters, he describes God as "the all-present force" transforming all of life. He argues that we need to acknowledge the broadness of the Holy Spirit's presence, which can never be the exclusive possession of individuals nor of the church. Although the Spirit is with the church, Holt affirms John Taylor's assertion that the go-between Spirit is present "through the whole fabric of the world," mediating "between Christ and culture; between the church and the world; between the Christian and her neighborhood."[31]

The central part of this book, "Looking for God in different places," has chapters addressing many areas of everyday life: God at Home; God at the Table; God in the Neighborhood; God on the Sports Field; God at the Supermarket; God among Friends; God in the Workplace; and God on the Weekend. Our purpose here is to draw upon just a few of these aspects to indicate what it might mean to see everyday life as the context and forms of "spiritual sacrifices," the sacrament of all the priestly people. It is perhaps also important to add that while Holt is suggesting "looking for God" in these places, his purpose is at least as much to say that we may be *found by* God as to find God in these contexts and activities. The spirituality envisaged here is one of seeking and being found as much as seeking and finding.

When discussing the spirituality of home life, Simon Holt identifies *laundry* as a spiritual practice. This reflection is set within a broader theme about the home as a place of "now and not yet." There are two elements involved in homemaking, Holt suggests, following the ideas of Wendy Wright. First, there is the desire for "being at home," which includes stability and caring. but "home" also has to do with a sense of meaning and ultimacy, which is always more than how things are or what we have to do right now. At home we may at one moment be submerged in things that need to be done, such as cleaning and meal preparation, but in the next we may contemplate or reach out for something new, unrealized possibilities and hopes. Both elements belong to the spirituality of the home.[32] It is here that we are aware of our difficult failings, precisely in the context of love and intimacy. Together, these longings for home and belonging, livelihood and rest are occasions for seeing the grace of God.

These ideas are then applied to the "spiritual practice" of laundry. It is a menial task, a term which is explained as meaning "of the household". Holt says that the routine nature of laundry is its greatest gift. In this it is like worship, which is also repetitive and mundane.[33] Doing the laundry has three key aspects: it is a formative act; a sacramental act; and a prayerful act. As a formative act, laundry consistently affirms relationships and service. Attending to each other's underwear is one of the things that makes a household. When suggesting that laundry is a sacramental and prayerful act, Holt leads us to think of God's immediate presence in the things of the world. Sacraments are the means of God's gracious presence: "In acts large and small, we have opportunity to *sign* grace for others. Laundry can be one of these."[34] The vital

---

[31] Holt, *Heaven All Around Us*, 28. The reference is to Taylor, *Go-Between God*.

[32] Holt, *Heaven All Around Us*, 59–60. Wendy Wright, *Sacred Dwelling*, 1989, 21.

[33] Holt, *Heaven All Around Us*, 61.

[34] Holt, *Heaven All Around Us*, 62.

aspect here is the offering of this menial act as a means of grace to others and, in so doing, also to find that grace with ourselves. To this end, Holt suggests a prayer which might express the spirituality of the laundry:

> Lord God,
> I offer you the work of my hands,
> And the soiled garments of our lives.
> May those who receive them washed clean
> Know the cleansing of your grace.
> Amen.[35]

Like every sacrament, the things themselves are mundane, thoroughly ordinary, and yet may also become the means of grace. Only one attentive to that grace in one's own life could pray this prayer and thus, too, be blessed by the sacrament of laundry. Although this prayerful openness does not make the laundry into a sacrament, it is a component in receiving or seeing what is given by God amidst the soiled water of our lives.

Before becoming a Baptist pastor, Simon Holt was a chef and has continued his passion for and theology of food. His chapter on "God at the Table" is thus focused on the meal table and links the tables of our everyday lives, at home and at work, with the gathering of Christians at the Lord's table. In an earlier book, *Eating Heaven: Spirituality at the Table,*" Holt provides the foundations to the method and directions of this chapter. *Eating Heaven* is indeed "about eating and the tables of daily life" which "play host to so much more than biological necessity," inviting us to places of intimacy and familiarity, identity, conversation, reconciliation and belonging.[36] Holt considers a number of tables which make up our daily lives: the kitchen table, the café table, the five-star restaurant table, the work table (where food is prepared), the festive table, the multicultural table, and finally the communion table.[37]

While it is impossible to recount the wonders of this book, there are several key elements which merit specific attention and which also resonate with the argument of Holt's later work. First, in regard to the "festive table," Holt notes the necessity of gathering. As affirmed by one of the parables of Jesus, and any number of parents calling their children, it is necessary to come to the table: "the gathering makes the feast, and the more the merrier."[38] The sharing

---

[35] Holt, *Heaven All Around Us*, 62.

[36] Holt, *Eating Heaven*, 2–3.

[37] One delightful feature of this book is Holt's provision of recipes with each of these chapters, as a means of inviting his readers to participate in the delights of eating heaven.

[38] Holt, *Eating Heaven*, 98–100.

of food and drink mark the rhythms and relationships of life, events great and small. "We feast to welcome, to farewell, to celebrate, to boast, to remember, to bond and to encourage. We even feast to mourn." Here we share identity, history, and belonging.

These practices are also evident in the ministry of Jesus. Holt notes, along with many other scholars, that "All through the gospel story, from the very earliest days of his public ministry to the last, Jesus is eating and drinking, so much so his detractors label him 'a glutton and a drunkard'."[39] Jesus' final meal is deeply related to his consistent and intentional practice of eating and celebrating with those not welcome in the homes of respectable and "religious" people. His table is always a table of grace, a sacrament of the coming reign of God. On this basis, Holt also notes how the gathering at the communion table links with every other table where believers may gather to eat. Here, too, is the sacrament of everyday life, the priesthood of all of life and all the people, where again the surprising grace of God may be seen and known.

While the meal table may distinctively be a place of conversation, Holt devotes a specific section of his *Heaven All Around Us* to the spirituality of conversation. This is set within the chapter, "God among Friends." While it is a commonplace that "talk is cheap," this same phenomenon may also be a means of grace, "a tool in the deepening and transforming of our spirits."[40] Here he notes three vital elements: attending or listening; then investing, which involves a willingness to engage, persist, allowing some things to grow; and, finally, the practice of confronting, which means a willingness to consider different aspects of what we assume we know, an openness not only to someone else's ideas, but to change one's own. The spirituality of conversation can also be a spirituality of conversion, perhaps slowly, and a deepening of relationship, all of this even without recognition. Here, too, Holt draws many parallels with experiences of prayer.[41]

Finally, I note the discussion of a spirituality of the weekends. Drawing a rich contrast with the weekends of his childhood, when Saturday was a time spent at home and Sundays a very predictable round of church activities and formal family meals, Holt observes now that the weekend is as busy a time as any other part of the week. There is, as he puts it bluntly, "no *off*." The substance of his reflection, seeking God in the weekend, is specifically focused on the activity of sleep. Sleep, he argues, is an act of faith, an offering of oneself into the hands of God. It may also be a space into which God may speak, perhaps through dream, but also through the simple reality that things may look different in the morning. In light of both of these, Holt describes

---

[39] Holt, *Eating Heaven*, 134.

[40] Holt, *Heaven All Around Us*, 146.

[41] Holt, *Heaven All Around Us*, 149–50.

sleep as a form of sabbath rest, an affirmation of what is good and a willingness to let things be.[42]

In another place, I have explored the possibility of seeing the weekend as it is now experienced as a form of sabbath.[43] Whereas the majority of people do not go to church, a large number of people do engage in life-affirming and celebratory forms of activity. Many undertake some form of sporting or recreational activity. Family gatherings or meeting up with friends and neighbors, perhaps for "brunch," are another prevailing feature. Other activities include home maintenance as well as tasks preparatory for the week ahead. Altogether these activities are life-affirming and have many of the features Holt describes as indicators of "heaven all around." Here, in the thoroughly ordinary fabric of everyday life is the reality of sabbath, an affirmation of what is good, what has been given and achieved, and what may yet need to be done or developed. This is entirely in keeping with the divine sabbath recounted in Genesis 1. To see and value our weekends in this way is again to find and participate in the priesthood of all the people and in all life.

It has been helpful to consider in some detail the arguments from Holt's work. Now, however, we turn to considering the implications of these ideas for the collective priesthood of the church and, more specifically, for the gathered life of the church.

The Gathered Church: Learning to See

There are a number of stories in the Gospels where Jesus asks his disciples what they see or even what they expected to see. Frequently he urges them to use their eyes and ears, to see and hear what God is doing around them. This seems to me the most fundamental purpose of the gathered community of faith: to learn to hear and to see God's presence and thus to celebrate in worship. This seeing, hearing and celebrating is also essential to the collective priesthood we have been proposing.

In Mark 8.22–26 there is a short story of Jesus healing a man who is blind; but in this episode Jesus' first attempt does not lead to the man's sight being fully restored. The story follows an interchange between Jesus and his followers, who have no bread. He asks them, "Do you still not perceive or understand? . . . Do you have eyes, and fail to see?" (verses 17–18). The episode with the blind man exemplifies the life of the community, in which it may take time, and perhaps more than one attempt, to perceive and to understand the reality of God's presence with them.

---

[42] Holt, *Heaven All Around Us*, 179–84.

[43] Rees, "New Directions in Australian Spirituality." Holt makes reference to this work in his own discussion of the weekend as sabbath, *Heaven All Around Us*, 174.

In another context, Luke tells of Jesus sending seventy disciples into towns and places ahead of him and their return to him with astonished stories of what they had seen of God's kingdom among them (Luke 10.1–20). Jesus later declares how blessed they are to have seen what they see (verse 23).

These stories lead us back to the theological imperative of a church discerning and participating in the salvific mission of God in the world. Here it is helpful to consider the essential disciplines of spiritual discernment, which are *seeing, judging, testing, praying, and acting*. Angela Reed has helpfully explored the role of congregational life as a source of spiritual guidance. She notes the growing trend amongst many congregations for individuals to seek spiritual guidance or direction, but argues that this should not remain an individual concern or focus. Christians may and should participate in such guidance together as a community of Christians. Within some groups who were experiencing such spiritual renewal, Reed found "an emphasis on *experiences of God* rather than *ideas of God*."[44] Nonetheless, in explaining what this means for local churches, she also emphasizes the importance of a theology of the Spirit: "it is necessary to develop a theology of the Spirit that can foster spiritual guidance," which will include recognizing that God's presence is characterized by life and energy.[45] Crucially, this presence is to be known in all aspects of life. Similar to Holt's work, Reed asserts that it is essential to the ministry of spiritual guidance to see God's presence and vitality "in the world." There are two vital aspects here: an explicitly Christian spirituality "finds God both in the incarnation of the Son and the indwelling of the Spirit in creation." In common with Holt, Reed asserts that "one of the most important reasons to practice spiritual guidance in our culture is to become aware of God's presence in everyday life."[46] An "improvising church," as Reed calls it, will encourage people to see and enjoy the "rains of God's presence" in all aspects of life and to share the stories of these blessings.[47]

Here, then, are the first three aspects of spiritual discernment inter-woven in the life of the church: seeing, judging and testing. These elements are akin to the man in Mark 8 telling Jesus what he is seeing. Vital to this activity is the honesty to declare that he does not fully see: he discerns people, but they look like trees walking around. In a community of discernment and mutual spiritual guidance, no one claims full insight or declares with unquestionable authority. Rather, testimony is an offering and an invitation to the community, which then engages in testing: is this really the presence and activity of the Spirit we are seeing? Here the two aspects of Christian

---

[44] Reed, *Quest for Spiritual Community*, 75.

[45] Reed, *Quest for Spiritual Community*, 119.

[46] Reed, *Quest for Spiritual Community*, 126.

[47] Reed, *Quest for Spiritual Community*, 127.

spirituality named by Reed above come together, for the presence of the Spirit is tested in the light of what we know of God's mission and purposes in Jesus Christ. There is a crucial interdependence here, for the Spirit enables us to know Christ and he enables us to discern the Spirit's action. The community thus prays and judges, and in knowing the presence and call of God—in what Baptists classically have called "the mind of Christ"—proceeds then to action. The action may be some collective project, but much more likely it will be the task of just some, even an individual, in the context of "everyday life," at work or home or other situations. This missional activity is the means of the church's participation in God's presence and purposes in the world.

These processes and activities are essential to the gathered life of the church as a priestly community. They will require regular attention to the stories of Jesus and his life within the mission of God through Israel, the revelation of God's nature as creator, redeemer and sanctifier. The church can only be a community of discernment as it hears and discovers the stories of God, not merely as ancient stories, but as continually happening, as contemporaneous.

Thus, the gathered life of the church is the context in which such discernment may take place, though it is not the focus of that discernment. Rather, the purpose of the community as a priestly people is to participate in the mission of God in the world. Evoking a vision of and for that mission is part of the discernment: learning to see and to understand.

As a result of this seeing and understanding, the gathered life of the church will involve celebration and worship. Here too the sacrament of all the life of all the people will be evident, as stories are told of the "rains" of God's presence. There must be room for such story-telling. In times past it was called "testimony." At the same time, there will be prayer for those engaged in all manner of activities reaching out for God's reign, caring for those in need, working for justice, nurturing, home-making, teaching and in a myriad of ways participating in the spiritual presence in everyday life.

The sacrament of everyday life thus involves the ebb and flow of church life, from gathered to dispersed, from dispersed to gathered, and in every way seeking to know and participate in the salvific mission of God. This is the priestly sacrament of all the people.

Bibliography

Anon. *Australian Communities Report: Research into Key Belief Blockers and Questions about Faith, Christianity and God Held by Australians Today.* Sutherland, NSW: Olive Tree Media, 2011.

Anon. *Baptism, Eucharist and Ministry.* Faith and Order Paper, 111. Geneva: World Council of Churches, 1982.

Anon. *Religion in the United Kingdom, en.m.wikipedia.org/Religion in the United Kingdom,* accessed 14 May 2019.

Bethge, Eberhard. *Dietrich Bonhoeffer: Theologian, Christian, Contemporary*. Translated by Eric Mosbacher, Peter and Betty Ross, Frank Clarke and William Glen-Doepel. New York: Collins, 1970.

Birch, Ian. *To Follow the Lambe Wheresoever He Goeth: The Ecclesial Polity of the English Calvinistic Baptists 1640–1660*. Monographs in Baptist History, 5. Eugene, OR: Pickwick, 2017.

Bond, Sharon, and Philip Hughes. "'No Religion' in Australia." *Pointers: Bulletin of the Christian Research Association* 13.3 (2003) 1–5.

Bonhoeffer, Dietrich. *Letters and Papers from Prison: Dietrich Bonhoeffer Works*. Volume 8. Edited by John de Gruchy. Minneapolis, MN: Fortress, 2009.

Butler Bass, Diana. *Christianity Beyond Religion: The End of Church and the Birth of a New Spiritual Awakening*. New York: HarperCollins, 2012.

Cavanaugh, William T. *The Myth of Religious Violence: Secular Ideology and the Roots of Modern Conflict*. Oxford: Oxford University Press, 2009.

Childs, Brevard. *Exodus: A Commentary*. London: SCM, 1974.

Clements, Keith W. *The SPCK Introduction to Bonhoeffer*. London: SPCK, 2010.

Durham, John. *Exodus*. Word Biblical Commentary. Waco, TX: Word, 1987.

Edge, Findley B. *The Greening of the Church*. Waco, TX: Word Books, 1971.

Gilmore, Alec, ed. *The Pattern of the Church: A Baptist View*. London: Lutterworth, 1963.

Harrison, Peter. *The Territories of Science and Religion*. Chicago: University of Chicago Press, 2015.

Harvey, Barry. *Taking Hold of the Real: Dietrich Bonhoeffer and the Profound Worldliness of Christianity*, Eugene, OR: Cascade, 2015.

Holt, Simon Carey *Eating Heaven: Spirituality at the Table*. Brunswick East: Acorn, 2013.

———. *Heaven All Around Us: Discovering God in Everyday Life*. Eugene, OR: Cascade, 2018.

Hughes, Philip. "Australia's Changing Religious and Social Profile." *Pointers: Bulletin of the Christian Research Association* 30.1 (2020) 1–6.

Küng, Hans. *The Church*. Translated by Ray and Rosaleen Ockenden. Tunbridge Wells: Search, 1968.

———. *Why Priests?* Translated by John Cumming. London: Collins, 1972.

Mackay, Hugh. *Beyond Belief: How We Find Meaning, with or without Religion*. Sydney: Pan Macmillan Australia, 2016.

Muthiah, Robert. *The Priesthood of All Believers in the Twenty-First Century*. Eugene, OR: Pickwick, 2009.

Pew Research Centre Report. *In U.S., Decline of Christianity Continues at Rapid Pace*, 17 October 2019. https://www.pewforum.org/wp-content/uploads/sites/7/20   19/10/Trends-in-Religious-Identity-and-Attendance-FOR-WEB.pdf, accessed 21 October 2019.

Reed, Angela H. *Quest for Spiritual Community: Reclaiming Spiritual Guidance for Contemporary Congregations*. London: T. & T. Clark, 2011.

Rees, Frank D. "New Directions in Australian Spirituality: Sabbath beyond the Church." *Colloquium* 47.1 (2015) 75–88.

———. "The Worship of All Believers." *Baptist Quarterly* 41.3 (2005) 175–89.

Robinson, John A.T. *Essays on Being the Church in the World.* London: SCM, 1960.

Schmiedel, Ulrich, and Graeme Smith, eds. *Religion in the European Refugee Crisis.* London: Palgrave Macmillan, 2018.

Smith, Wilfred Cantwell. *The Meaning and the End of Religion.* Rev. ed. Minneapolis, MN: Fortress, 1991. [1st ed., 1962]

Taylor, John V. *The Go-Between God: The Holy Spirit and the Christian Mission.* London: SCM, 1972.

Tie, Peter L, *Restore Unity, Recover Identity, and Refine Orthopraxy: The Believers' Priesthood in the Ecclesiology of James Leo Garrett.* Eugene, OR: Wipf & Stock, 2012.

Winward, Winward, Stephen. "The Church in the New Testament." In *Pattern of the Church,* edited by Gilmore, 54–78.

Wright, Wendy. *Sacred Dwelling: A Spirituality of Family Life.* New York: Crossroad, 1989.

CHAPTER 11

The "Laying on of Hands" Controversy: Convictional Analysis of Performative Practice

Joseph C. Delahunt

I

About the English General Baptists in the second half of the seventeenth century, early nineteenth-century Baptist historian Adam Taylor observed, "Though the baptists were heavily oppressed by outward trials, yet they were too ready to devour one another." He was referring to their disputes over the practice of the laying on, or imposition, of hands with prayer for receiving the Holy Spirit, soon or even immediately after a convert was baptized.[1] This essay seeks to discover some of the roots of that readiness, by looking at the practice,[2] and the controversy among early Baptists through the lens of the more developed statements by two Baptist leaders, the General Baptist, Thomas Grantham,[3] and the Particular Baptist, Henry Danvers.[4]

---

[1] Taylor, *History*, 1:206. Ward, *Pure Worship*, 71, observes that the controversy was "explosively disruptive" and "disintegrative to the early Baptists." See also White, *English Baptists*, 42, who says the laying on of hands caused much dissension among General Baptists. Descriptions of the practice among Baptists and the course of the disputes can be found in Bass, *Thomas Grantham*, 104–36; Payne, "Baptists and the Laying on of Hands," 208–15 and "Baptists and Christian Initiation," 150–52.

[2] While English Baptists in the seventeenth century practiced the laying on of hands for a variety of purposes, including ordination and healing, throughout this essay I will be referring to laying hands upon a baptized person, with prayer, for the receiving of the Holy Spirit, unless otherwise indicated.

[3] Two recent books on Grantham are Bass, *Thomas Grantham*; and Essick, *Thomas Grantham*. See also W.L. Johnson Jr and R.L. Greaves' entry on Grantham in Greaves and Zaller, ed., *Biographical Dictionary of British Radicals in the Seventeenth Century*, 2:23–24.

[4] There are no book length studies about Danvers. The most in depth treatment is a substantial pamphlet by Lane, *Henry Danvers*, while Greaves gives a helpful outline of his life in, "The tangled careers of two Stuart radicals." See also the entry on Danvers by R.L. Greaves in Greaves and Zaller, ed., *Biographical Dictionary of British Radicals in the Seventeenth Century*, 1:210–12. An analysis of Danvers' major treatise on

In order to clarify the often bitter roots of this controversy it will be necessary to lay bare the deeply held convictions that are involved. A number of concepts developed by modern writers influenced by analytic philosophical methods, namely, the concepts of "convictions," "performative acts," and "practices," are particularly helpful. These debates involve a clash of strongly held beliefs, centering on the significance of the act of the laying on of hands, which profoundly affected the practices of initiation, discipline and inter-church relationships of a significant number of early English Baptist churches.

Willem Zuurdeeg pioneered[5] the use of the term "conviction" as a tool of philosophical analysis.[6] Much of the following study looks back to his work. The same question will be asked of this early Baptist controversy as that which Zuurdeeg himself asks about conflicting views of objectivity, "What convictions lie behind the conflict?"[7]

Zuurdeeg uses "convictions" to identify a kind of discourse that is not strictly "indicative" on the one hand (scientific language being a strong example), nor strictly "emotive" (affectional, expressive of preference, directive) on the other. "Convictional" language expresses deeply held beliefs that guide one's actions. Such expressions are not "objective" in the way science or any dispassionate or disinterested statements of the "facts" are. "We will not say that a scientist *is convinced* that a hypothesis is true, but that he takes it to be true."[8] but neither are convictions "subjective" in the way matters of taste and preference are. Rather, convictions express views of the world, society, divinity, ethics, etc., that are held with enough certainty and passion that they determine how one lives. The scope of reality that is embraced by convictions and the level of certainty they entail make it impossible for them to be scientifically objective, and yet they claim their own kind of objectivity. They are far from disinterested and involve the passions, but they also claim to be saying something true about the way things are. In fact, "a person who speaks convictional language has reality in mind, but in his case, it is the totality of reality as he sees it in the light of his specific convictions."[9]

---

baptism can be found in Renihan, "Henry Danvers' A Treatise of Baptism." There is some confusion about whether Danvers was a General or Particular Baptist due to the fact that he started as a General and became a Particular, on which see Dunan-Page, *Grace Overwhelming*, 50–51 n.10. More specifically, it seems that he became a Particular Baptist in 1651, see Haykin and Jones, *Drawn into Controversie*, 290.

[5] McClendon and Smith, *Convictions*, 99. See also McMillan, "Willem Zuurdeeg and the Concept of Convictional Theology," 72–80.

[6] Zuurdeeg, *Analytical Philosophy of Religion*, 23–68.

[7] Zuurdeeg, *Analytical Philosophy of Religion*, 49.

[8] Zuurdeeg, *Analytical Philosophy of Religion*, 26 (italics original).

[9] Zuurdeeg, *Analytical Philosophy of Religion*, 46.

Convictions shape the life and consciousness of a true religious believer, a loyal Nazi or a dedicated Communist.[10] This could also be said of a devoted secular humanist. In fact, "Nobody can live totally without convictions."[11] Some beliefs about the way things are will always be engaged in how a person lives life. Zuurdeeg goes so far as to say, "we are our convictions."[12]

Three other aspects of Zuurdeeg's understanding of convictions are important for what follows. The first is that they are inculcated, maintained, and modified in communities.[13] The second is that these communities are bound together by narratives.[14] While Zuurdeeg does not use the language of "practice," it is clear that he sees the ordered practices of convictional communities and the narratives they enact are what hold and nurture convictions.

The third aspect of "convictions" according to Zuurdeeg is that convictions are plural.[15] To use Zuurdeeg's terminology, a conviction is a being grasped or overcome by some good, value, or vision of reality which impresses its truth upon us. This he calls a "convictor."[16] Normally a person has more than one convictor that guides life. Some are explicit, while others may not be. Furthermore, one will have a hierarchy of these convictors, some being more important than others. A major part of life is negotiating the shifting of the relative importance of various convictors. We will observe this at work in the convictions expressed by Grantham and Danvers.

While Zuurdeeg initiated numerous trains of thought in his analysis, much remained sketchy, as he himself admitted. Some things are more fully discussed later in his book,[17] but there remained a great deal that could be developed. Much of McClendon and Smith's book *Convictions* does just that. Of particular interest for this essay is the use they make of J.L. Austin's analysis of what McClendon and Smith call "speech acts."[18] Theirs is a

---

[10] Zuurdeeg, *Analytical Philosophy of Religion*, 26.

[11] Zuurdeeg, *Analytical Philosophy of Religion*, 31. See also 38, "everybody possesses convictions, whether he is aware of the fact or not. If a person does not present his convictions in the form of religious or moral persuasions, we should do well to look for his convictions elsewhere. They can hide in his politics, his poetry, or his philosophy."

[12] Zuurdeeg, *Analytical Philosophy of Religion*, 57.

[13] He calls them "confessional groups," following Hendrik de Graaf, Dutch philosopher of religion. Zuurdeeg, *Analytical Philosophy of Religion*, 32–35.

[14] Zuurdeeg, *Analytical Philosophy of Religion*, 55.

[15] Zuurdeeg, *Analytical Philosophy of Religion*, 40–44.

[16] Zuurdeeg, *Analytical Philosophy of Religion*, 27–28.

[17] Zuurdeeg, *Analytical Philosophy of Religion*, 61.

[18] What Austin calls "illocutionary utterances," *How to Do Things with Words*, 98.

detailed argument which I cannot follow here.[19] but I do draw from the discussion the insight that, like some forms of speech, ritual actions do things. By their very nature baptism or the laying on of hands carry more freight than that of a "mere" symbol. Even relatively "non-sacramental" views understand baptism, for instance, to do things. Baptism reminds and instructs the one baptized and the congregation that they are part of a continuing story shaped by the death and resurrection of Jesus. Moreover, it is like an oath or promise, that binds the one baptized in obedience to the Lord as covenant partner. I will argue that the disputes about the laying on of hands are rooted in the reality that other things are also being "done" in baptism than memorializing. Much earlier, McClendon wrote an essay applying the notion of "performative sign"[20] to discussions about the nature of baptism among Baptists. Stanley Grenz also wrote in a similar vein about baptism as a "community action."[21] These reflections about baptism will be useful for discussing the convictions around the laying on of hands as well.

One well-known analysis of "practice" is found in Alasdair McIntyre's most famous book, *After Virtue*,[22] and his later books as well. MacIntyre develops some themes we have already seen with Zuurdeeg. Speaking of virtues, rather than convictions specifically,[23] he stresses their being situated in communities of practice that are bound together by narratives. McClendon develops this concept of "practice" in his *Systematic Theology*.[24]

This essay will conclude with some reflections on the laying of hands as a potentially significant part of baptismal practice among Baptists. This will draw on the analysis of the controversy, particularly of Grantham's position, and will interact with H. Wheeler Robinson's thinking about the Holy Spirit and baptism.[25]

---

[19] McClendon and Smith, *Convictions*, ch. 3, "A Speech-Act Theory of Religious Language," 47–79.

[20] Developing Austin's notion of "performative utterance." Austin discarded this concept and replaced it with "illocutionary utterance," *How to Do Things with Words*, 91 and 98. This is what McClendon and Smith come to call a "speech-act," *Convictions*, 52.

[21] Grenz, "Baptism and the Lord's Supper as Community Acts."

[22] MacIntyre, *After Virtue*, especially 186–203.

[23] Since convictions involve moral discourse and action, they are manifested in the practice of virtue. MacIntyre, *After Virtue*, 185–95.

[24] See McClendon, *Ethics*, especially 162–77, and *Doctrine*, especially 28–41.

[25] Robinson, *Baptist Principles*. See also, Cross, "Pneumatological Key to H. Wheeler Robinson's Baptismal Sacramentalism."

II

Thomas Grantham published his major work defending the laying on of hands, *A Sigh for Peace*, in 1671, in reaction to an anonymous publication (which no longer exists) attacking the practice, *A Search for Schism*. As the title suggests, in *A Search for Schism* the advocates of the laying on of hands are accused of dividing the churches. Then, in opposition to views like Grantham's, Henry Danvers published, *A Treatise of Laying on of Hands*, in 1674. There, Danvers refers to Grantham as a supporter of the practice[26] and seems to refer directly to *A Sigh for Peace*.[27] Grantham in turn responded to Danvers with *The Fourth Principle of Christs Doctrine Vindicated*, also in 1674.

The beginnings of the practice of the laying on of hands among English Baptists go back to the mid-1640s. Henry Danvers thought it was in 1646 specifically at the church then meeting, as he says, "*in the* Spittle *Bishopsgate Street, Lond.*" This church, he says, was influenced in this regard by the preaching of Francis Cornwell, a General Baptist minister from Kent.[28] Stephen Wright argues convincingly that it was actually Edward Barber's church which was the first Baptist congregation in London to practice the laying on of hands in 1645.[29] It seems likely, however, that the laying on of hands was practiced somewhat earlier in Kent, where the practice was associated with the ministries of William Jeffrey, Francis Cornwell, and Christopher Blackwood.[30] Benjamin Keach also challenges Danvers' account on the basis of reports from people he deems were in a position to know: "there was more than one Church before that time in the practice of it."[31]

The issue of the laying on of hands was of enough concern among seventeenth-century English Baptists that a significant number of their leaders wrote treatises to address the topic. Three seventeenth-century General Baptist confessions call for its practice. According to Article XII of *The True Gospel-Faith Declared According to the Scriptures* (1654), "God gives his Spirit

---

[26] He identifies four advocates of the practice, S(amuel) Fisher, Jo(hn) Griffith, W(illiam) Rider and T(homas) Grantham. Danvers, *Laying on of Hands*, 28. He mentions Griffith a second time, 41.

[27] Danvers says in *Laying on of Hands*, 41, that Grantham affirms Hebrews 6.1–2 to be "the great *Charter* of the *Church* for this point of Faith and Practice," which Grantham does in *Sigh*, 27.

[28] Danvers, *Treatise of Laying on of Hands*, 58.

[29] Wright, *Early English Baptists*, 100.

[30] Bass, *Thomas Grantham*, 104.

[31] Keach, *Darkness Vanquished*, 102.

to believers dipped through the prayer of faith and the laying on of hands."[32] *A Brief Confession or Declaration of Faith* (1660), states,

> XII. That it is the duty of all such who are believers Baptized, to draw nigh unto God in submission to that principle of Christ's Doctrine, to wit, Prayer and Laying on of Hands, that they may receive the promise of the holy Spirit, Heb. 6. 1. 2. Acts 8. 12, 15, 17. Acts 19. 6. 2 Tim. 1. 6. whereby they may mortifie the deeds of the body, Rom. 8. 13. and live in all things answerable to their professed intentions, and desires, even to the honour of him, who hath called them out of darkness into his marvellous light.[33]

The *Orthodox Creed* (1679) declares,

> XXXII. Article. Of Prayer, with Laying on of Hands. Prayer, with Imposition of Hands by the Bishop, or Elder, on Baptized Believers (as such), for the reception of the Holy, Promised Spirit of Christ, we believe is a Principle of Christ's Doctrine, and ought to be practised and submitted to by every Baptized Believer, in order to receive the Promised Spirit of the Father, and Son.[34]

None of these statements link the laying on of hands directly with the act of baptism, only that it is performed on baptized (or "dipped") believers. However, in both *The True Gospel-Faith* and the *Brief Confession* this article immediately follows the one that deals with baptism. Stanley K. Fowler, in commenting on this article in the *Brief Confession*, says that

> It is not clear what the temporal relationship would be between baptism and the imposition of hands, i.e., whether they are two parts of one event (much like the Eastern conjunction of baptism and confirmation) or two isolated events (much like the Western separation between baptism and confirmation).[35]

If Danvers and Grantham represent the common understanding of the practice, then it normally took place immediately after baptism but before the Lord's supper which followed.[36] All three statements relate the practice to the

---

[32] Written by Thomas Lover, and adopted by General Baptist churches in London represented by John Foxwell, John Griffith, Thomas Parrat, and Francis Smith. See Lumpkin and Leonard, eds, *Baptist Confessions*, 172–79. The text is from a facsimile copy of the document found in the British Museum. The only other copy is in The Angus Library, Regent's Park College, Oxford.

[33] Anon., *Brief Confession or Declaration of Faith*, 7 (otherwise known as *The Standard Confession*).

[34] Anon., *Orthodox Creed*, 44.

[35] Fowler, *More than a Symbol*, 16.

[36] Danvers, *Laying on of Hands*, 29. He says of those churches practicing the rite, "amongst whom respecting this Practice, we *observe* . . . 5. The *Time* or Order in

receiving of the promised Spirit. The *Brief Confession* suggests that this reception of the Spirit is what enables a life that honors God. This connection of the Holy Spirit to the power of moral transformation is important for Grantham, as we shall see.

This important controversy was about two related issues. The first was, should Baptist congregations practice the laying on of hands? This question generated a great deal of biblical exegesis and argument. Of particular interest to advocates of the practice was Hebrews 6.1–2 (to which both the *Brief Confession* and the *Orthodox Creed* refer).[37] Ward aptly underlines the importance of this passage in these controversies, "The six principles of Hebrews 6 . . . deserve special note as an intersection of biblical interpretation, worship and division."[38] Here is the rendition of the Authorized Version,[39]

> [6.1] Therefore leaving the principles of the doctrine of Christ, let us go on unto perfection; not laying again the foundation of **repentance from dead works**[(1)], and of **faith toward God**[(2)],
> [2] Of the **doctrine of baptisms**[(3)], and of **laying on of hands**[(4)], and of **resurrection of the dead**[(5)], and of **eternal judgment**[(6)].[40]

All seventeenth-century English Baptists affirmed five of the six items they understood to be listed here; repentance, faith, baptism, the resurrection of the dead, and eternal judgment. The controversy was about the fourth, the laying on of hands, hence the title of at least two publications defending the practice, *The Fourth Principle*,[41] the main point being that this practice is one of the "foundational principles" of the doctrine of Christ. As such, from their point of view, it is on a par with the other principles.

Two other scripture passages figure prominently in all these arguments because the advocates identify what those passages describe with the fourth principle of Hebrews 6.2. They are both from the Acts of the Apostles, one being chapter 8, particularly verses 14–17, which says according to the Authorized Version,

> [8.14] Now when the apostles which were at Jerusalem heard that Samaria had received the word of God, they sent unto them Peter and John: [15] Who, when

---

which this is administered; betwixt *Baptism* and the *Supper*, or presently after *Baptism*." Grantham, *Fourth Principle*, 10, quotes Danvers' observation without any correction.

[37] Anon., *Brief Confession*, 7; and Anon., *Orthodox Creed*, 44.

[38] Ward, *Pure Worship*, 70.

[39] One of the available English translations in seventeenth-century England, used by both Danvers and Grantham, as can be seen by comparing the texts.

[40] The principles are in bold and numbered.

[41] Grantham, *Fourth Principle*; and Tillam, *Fourth Principle*.

they were come down, prayed for them, that they might receive the Holy Ghost:
[16] (For as yet he was fallen upon none of them: only they were baptized in the
name of the Lord Jesus.) [17] Then laid they their hands on them, and they
received the Holy Ghost.

The other passage is Acts 19.1–7 (Authorized Version):

[19.1] While Apollos was in Corinth, Paul passed through the inland regions and
came to Ephesus, where he found some disciples. [2] He said to them, "Did you
receive the Holy Spirit when you became believers?" They replied, "No, we have
not even heard that there is a Holy Spirit." [3] Then he said, "Into what then were
you baptized?" They answered, "Into John's baptism." [4] Paul said, "John baptized
with the baptism of repentance, telling the people to believe in the one who was
to come after him, that is, in Jesus." [5] On hearing this, they were baptized in the
name of the Lord Jesus. [6] When Paul had laid his hands on them, the Holy
Spirit came upon them, and they spoke in tongues and prophesied—[7] altogether
there were about twelve of them.[42]

One of the basic interpretive questions that arises again and again is, are these
passages to be taken as prescriptive or descriptive? Are the experiences related
in Acts 8 and 19 meant to be models of what Christians in every age should
do and experience, or are they unique descriptions of what happened to
particular people in a certain time and place? Similarly, is Hebrews 6.1–2 a
template laying out the structure of Christian belief and action for all times, or
does it describe the unique transition of apostolic times? Grantham and the
others advocating the laying on of hands answer the first part of both
questions in the affirmative, while denying the second option in both
questions. Their opponents, like Danvers, tended to affirm the latter[43] part of
both.

These particular passages are repeatedly argued about in many treatises.
The same basic arguments consistently appear. Those by Grantham and
Danvers are no exception. One feels as if the opposing parties have argued
themselves to a standstill. At that point they might do one of two things:
expand the field of scripture passages used to support one's argument, as
Grantham does quite effectively; or move to different ground. This second
option seems to be what happens with the extensive appeals to tradition that
we find in Danvers and Grantham, as well as others.[44] On a first reading of

---

[42] Regarding the use of these two passages, see Danvers, *Laying on of Hands*, 45–49;
Grantham, *Fourth Principle*, 10, 13, 19–21, and *Sigh*, 6–8, 12–23, 36–43; Griffith,
God's Oracle, 38–58; Keach, *Darkness Vanquished*, 6–16; and Tillam, *Fourth Principle*, 3,
17–23.

[43] Danvers, *Laying on of Hands*, 41–50.

[44] Danvers, *Laying on of Hands*, 6–39. Grantham, *Fourth Principle*, 2–9. Keach,
Darkness Vanquished, 17–39.

these treatises, it comes as a bit of a shock to read these basically biblicist writers discoursing expansively on the treatment of baptism and the laying on of hands in the Christian tradition, particularly in the earliest three centuries, and in contemporary non-baptistic churches.[45] but in the end, there is the sense that while one or the other of these writers may have the better arguments, and the better grasp of the Bible, neither is fully convincing. Each, however, provides a great deal of food for thought particularly in regard to principles of interpretation, as well as the history of the practice and thought about Christian initiation.

But what are the convictions that lie behind the conflict? After all these opponents have many shared convictions about an authoritative Bible, the nature of the free church constituted of converted saints, who are baptized upon their confession of faith. They share with all Baptists of that time a certain primitivism[46] involving a desire to establish a pure form of worship.[47] With so much in common, why do they differ here?

What has been mostly overlooked are the expressed commitments and feelings that each writer has, which explain core motivations, and show where they have failed to understand one another at a deep level. We shall begin with Danvers. What are his fundamental concerns? In his introduction he tells us that his method is to first give an account of the rite of the laying on of hands,[48] by which he means a scriptural account.[49] Then he will look at the tradition of the church in the early centuries.[50] Thirdly, he describes the teaching practice of Roman Catholicism,[51] followed by that of the Church of England.[52] The fifth point of his method is to examine the teaching and practice of Independents and Presbyterians.[53] Then, finally, he examines the various English Baptists, where his deepest interests lie.[54] This is where his critique of his opposition is expounded. This sixth part continues to the

---

[45] I rely here on Bass' excellent but succinct discussion of this feature in the writing of both Danvers and Grantham on the laying on of hands, *Thomas Grantham*, 116–18.

[46] Underwood, *Primitivism*.

[47] Ward, *Pure Worship*.

[48] Danvers, *Laying on of Hands*, 4.

[49] Danvers, *Laying on of Hands*, 4–5.

[50] Danvers, *Laying on of Hands*, 6–15.

[51] Danvers, *Laying on of Hands*, 15–16.

[52] Danvers, *Laying on of Hands*, 17–24.

[53] Danvers, *Laying on of Hands*, 24–28.

[54] Danvers, *Laying on of Hands*, 28–55.

conclusion,[55] in which he summarizes his arguments and then explains how the laying on of hands came to be practiced in England.[56]

At this point the deeper concerns that drive his whole argument come to the surface. He addresses the second basic question involved in the controversy, what is the status of the baptized people who have not received or refuse to receive the laying on of hands?[57] Here we learn that from his point of view, the church that formerly met *"in the* Spittle *Bishopgate Street, Lon."* was disrupted by the group advocating for the laying on of hands. Contrary to their promise of maintaining a peaceable manner, they pressed their views to the point where they said that those without the laying on of hands[58] were not babes in Christ and did not have communion with God, and so could not receive the Lord's supper. Furthermore, one of the chief advocates of the laying on of hands, John Griffith, published a book, *Gods Oracle & Christs Doctrine*,[59] that tore up the church and urged separation from the group that will not participate in the laying on of hands. This sort of behavior, Danvers says, has now spread throughout England; namely, not recognizing other Baptists as brethren, not esteeming them or having fellowship with them as the true church because they are defective in one of the foundational principles (the fourth). Here we see Matthew Ward's description of the result of the pursuit of pure worship on full display. Here is "the intersection of biblical interpretation, worship and division." The pursuit of biblical purity requires the exclusion of or separation from those who differ (see above). Danvers is outraged by this treatment of himself and others.[60] His conclusion is that the practice and advocacy of the laying on of hands must be corrupt and vicious,[61] and so obviously a mistaken principle. After all, a corrupt tree produces evil fruit.[62]

For Grantham's part, his title, *A Sigh for Peace*, says it all. You can feel his weariness with the dispute, his frustration with his opponents, and his longing for peace in the church. Apparently, the tone of *A Search for Schism* was at least as accusatory as Danvers' was. While John Griffiths may have held the extreme views Danvers inveighs against, the General (Baptist) Assembly in

---

[55] Danvers, *Laying on of Hands*, 56–60.

[56] Danvers, *Laying on of Hands*, 58–59.

[57] The first question was, should Baptist congregations practice the laying on of hands? See above.

[58] Danvers, *Laying on of Hands*, 58.

[59] Danvers, *Laying on of Hands*, 40, 58; and Griffith, *God's Oracle*, 87–89.

[60] Danvers, *Laying on of Hands*, 59.

[61] Danvers, *Laying on of Hands*, 60.

[62] Danvers, *Laying on of Hands*, 61.

London, which advocated the laying on of hands, and certainly Grantham himself, held to more moderate ideas. In defense of the General Assembly, he scoffs at the idea, held it seems, by the authors of the *A Search for Schism* (the "Searchers" he calls them), that the Assembly unchurches all churches that disagree with it. In fact, there would be no point in reproving the opponents of the laying on of hands if they didn't represent a real church.[63] The question isn't about the legitimacy of a church, but the level of fellowship that can be maintained between churches that differ on a foundational principle.

Having dedicated his book to the General Assembly in London, Grantham now addresses the Searchers directly. They may be outraged like Danvers, but so is he at the slanders he thinks they have flung at the General Assembly. He thinks they accuse the advocates of consigning their opponents to hell. but he wants to resist giving as good as he gets. He refrains from returning "railing for railing."[64]

Grantham begins his book proper by indicating he will deal with three issues, the proper practices of churches, the issue of withholding communion, and the purpose of the laying on of hands itself. He puts the last first,[65] because it expresses his deepest concern. The most important thing is the promise of the Holy Spirit. The point of the laying on of hands is that it is the God-given way for Christians to wait for receiving that promise.[66] And the promise is essential to the Christian life. To receive the Holy Spirit is to have the Spirit manifesting and operating in us.[67] Grantham is concerned that the church lacks power and experiences more weakness than it should, because it does not take advantage of God's ordinary way of pouring out the Spirit. In making his argument, Grantham expands the scriptures used in this sort of argument. He includes passages that speak of the promise of the Spirit like Acts 1.4–5 and 2.38.[68]

A Sigh for Peace is a long pamphlet, 165 pages in all. What is most important for our purposes is Grantham's focus on the promise of the Holy Spirit, in line with *The True Gospel-Faith*, the *Brief Confession* and the *Orthodox Creed*. The *Fourth Principle* is a much shorter and condensed presentation. Nevertheless, Grantham's major concerns are in the forefront. Over and over again he refers to the promise of the Spirit and its significance.

---

[63] Grantham, *Sigh*, "The Epistle Dedicatory."

[64] Grantham, *Sigh*, "Letter to the authors of *A Search for Schism*."

[65] Grantham, *Sigh*, 3–80. For the second part on the constitution of the church, see 81–106. For the third part, on the question of who can receive communion, see 106–37. The treatise ends with an appendix about the ministry of messengers, 138–65.

[66] Grantham, *Sigh*, 3.

[67] Grantham, *Sigh*, 5.

[68] Grantham, *Sigh*, 6. Acts 8 and 19 are discussed later in *Sigh*, see above.

And once again, he is concerned that he and his associates are being slandered.[69] In the process of addressing Danvers' objections point by point, he presents his own assessment of the historical tradition of the church and continues to expand his scriptural base. He argues, for instance, for a parallel between Jesus' experience of baptism and ours. Just as, after his baptism, Jesus prayed (in Luke's Gospel) and then received the Spirit, so should we wait for the promise through the laying on of hands with the invocation of the Spirit.[70]

On reading Danvers' *Treatise* alongside Grantham, the reader is struck by how devoid it is of serious discussion of the Holy Spirit, beyond the question of the Spirit's relation or lack thereof to the laying on of hands. He misses entirely what is foundational for Grantham in the entire discussion. This would confirm Grantham's fear that the opponents of the laying on of hands fail to recognize the Spirit's essential role in God's plan for the church. At the same time, while Grantham is horrified by the thought that his allies would regard baptized believers who have not received the laying on of hands as having no communion with God, he remains somewhat tone deaf when it comes to the pain and the outrage an opponent like Danvers feels about the exclusion practiced toward him and the churches he serves.

Grantham wants to "seriously consider" the "pinch" or pain expressed in the Seekers' demands.[71] These revolve around the desire that their congregations be recognized as true churches. Grantham acknowledges their concerns, reassuring them at length that he and the General Assembly do indeed regard them as true churches, though in a sense disabled by their neglect of the fourth principle.[72] It may be that some have had this very negative judgement about these churches, but not his group, the General Assembly.[73] Indeed, he speaks of one of his opponents as a "very worthy Brother."[74] Grantham makes an effort to meet his opponents half-way, but his arguments nevertheless have a certain sense of condescension, which would hardly help. Furthermore, he often gives with one hand while taking away with the other. After expressing a conciliatory attitude, he then rigidly insists that he is right and does not seem to understand the legitimate questions his opponents have. This happens in his encounter with the "very worthy Brother" mentioned above, where he refuses to engage the man's different interpretation of Hebrews 6.[75] He

---

[69] Grantham, *Fourth Principle*, 2.

[70] Grantham, *Fourth Principle*, 13.

[71] Grantham, *Sigh*, 89.

[72] Grantham, *Sigh*, 89–93.

[73] Grantham, *Sigh*, 117–18.

[74] Grantham, *Sigh*, 53.

[75] Grantham, *Sigh*, 53–57.

regularly fails to understand how his opponents think the ambiguity of the texts ought to mitigate his certainty that the laying on of hands is a fundamental principle on which he cannot compromise. While being stung by his opponents, Grantham still cannot see the pain his approach causes.

In addition to their common convictions mentioned earlier, these men have others that lead to conflict. They appear to have different convictions about the Bible, or at least about how to read it. Like other defenders of the laying on of hands, Grantham takes Hebrews 6.1–2 a certain way, reading it as one of the most important, and clear statements of Christian teaching. "The great Charter of the Church, for this point of faith,"[76] he calls it. As such, the failure to practice its fourth principle seems to him like willful disobedience. Danvers, like other opponents, is more attuned to the difficulties in the passage.[77] There are, they insist, different ways to read this passage, given the interpretive difficulties it presents. Similar problems are involved in interpreting the texts from Acts 8 and 19. It is little wonder that advocates of the practice, given their orientation toward Hebrews 6.1–2, have such strong convictions on the matter. People like Danvers, on the other hand, given the way they read the disputed texts, say in effect, can't we live together with our different interpretations?

Perhaps there is another unexpressed conviction operative as well. Both men are keenly sensitive to others' opinions, particularly those of other Baptists. Perhaps this is because of the difficult circumstances in which they found themselves politically. The early 1670s were the days of the restoration of the monarchy, with the attendant difficulties and even persecution that meant for Dissenters. For a relatively despised minority, attacks from co-religionists, instead of affirming a needed solidarity, would be particularly stinging and unsettling.

And yet for both men there is interesting potential for a shift in their convictions. There are hints in both Danvers and Grantham indicating that they could relax their rhetoric and exclusionary practices if only the other side would meet them half-way. If only the advocates of the laying on of hands could acknowledge the good faith of their opponents and the good gifts they offer the church, then, Danvers suggests, he could live with that.[78] And if only the opponents would not be so violent in their opposition and disagree respectfully, having a listening heart to hear the concern that the work of the Spirit might flourish unhindered in the church, Grantham can also conceive of fellowship with them.[79] There appears to be an emerging conviction that

---

[76] Grantham, *Sigh*, 27.

[77] Danvers, *Laying on of Hands*, 42–44.

[78] Danvers, *Laying on of Hands*, 51.

[79] Grantham, *Sigh*, 93–95.

perhaps unity is a goal toward which to strive. This outlook is characteristic of the course this controversy takes among the Particular Baptists for whom, not only do the arguments fade, but the practice also, during the first half of the eighteenth century. The General Baptists continued to argue among themselves, but in the course of the eighteenth century the laying on of hands became widely practiced among them. Unity was achieved for both bodies, but not between them, each pursuing a different path.[80]

But the question of Grantham's deep conviction about the importance of the Holy Spirit remains. For Grantham, the laying on of hands seems to function as a performative sign,[81] which expresses his fundamental conviction about how believers are to engage the promise of the Spirit. Whatever Danvers may say elsewhere, in what he writes about the laying on of hands, the Spirit does not appear to be a deep part of the pattern of his convictions.

Perhaps his passion for baptized believers to receive the fullness of what they are promised is important for today's church as well. Is it possible that the inclusion of the laying on of hands in our practice of Christian initiation would create an expectation to receive more from the Spirit? Perhaps a renewal of the practice of the laying on of hands would strengthen us as Grantham believed. Would we not benefit from a new focus and understanding of the intended place and power of the Holy Spirit in our lives? It is to these thoughts that our final section turns.

III

The converted man, as has been said, is the convinced man, and to be convinced means literally to be conquered. The man thus conquered by the Spirit of God becomes, to the measure of his conviction, a lever by which human life is lifted. Convictions are the key to history . . . At each cross-road, someone has arisen, having for his chief equipment not birth nor wealth, not intellect nor influence, but a conviction. Convictions lie at the back of life, and down among its roots.[82]

For H. Wheeler Robinson only one conviction matters—or should we say "convictor"?—God who conquers by the Spirit. His *Baptist Principles* is pervaded by the association of the Holy Spirit with baptism. The New Testament convinced him of that association. It is a bond so strong that he is able to say, "Baptism, in its New Testament context, is always a baptism of the

---

[80] Payne, "Baptists and the Laying on of Hands," 212–14, and "Baptists and Christian Initiation," 152; and Bass, *Thomas Grantham*, 134–36.

[81] Borrowing a phrase from McClendon's analysis of baptism, see, e.g., McClendon, "Baptism as a Performative Sign," and the discussion throughout this essay.

[82] Robinson, *Baptist Principles*, 18.

Spirit."[83] Like so many British Baptists in the last century and today, he was reaching for more in baptism, and in the Lord's supper.[84] The "more" was found in the Spirit that meets the faith of the believer and the believing community in baptism and the Lord's supper.

Some Baptists have put the themes discussed earlier, which were inspired by analytic philosophical approaches, to good use in approaching an understanding of sacraments. Examples already mentioned are McClendon in his article, "Baptism as a Performative Sign," and Grenz's "Baptism and the Lord's Supper as Community Acts." McClendon's use of Austin developed a great deal after this article, which can be seen in chapter three of his and Smith's *Convictions*, "A Speech-Act Theory of Religious Language."[85] Nevertheless, in his article published nearly three decades earlier, he brings to bear upon baptism the notion put forward by Austin of "performatives utterances."[86] No doubt, as co-author of *Convictions*, he would have developed this in a different way. but the article gets across strongly an extension of the idea of "performative acts," which, like a liturgical act, accompanied by a shared narrative and faith, accomplishes something, both from the human side and the divine. He quotes with approval from R.E.O. White,

> The sacrament consists not in the thing done, but in the doing of that which gives expression to faith in appointed ways. On the one side, the faith of the person doing the appointed things invests the rite at that moment, for himself, with sacramental meaning; on the other side, God, accepting this response, in fulfillment of His promise in the gospel invests the rite at that moment, for the convert, with sacramental power.[87]

McClendon himself goes beyond this emphasis on the individual person. Necessarily so, because performatives depend on conventions, which exist only in communities.[88] Furthermore, he recognizes the leap he makes between human use of performatives and divine action in them. For this reason, I think, he speaks of "the analogy of the performative." This illuminates his

---

[83] Robinson, *Baptist Principles*, 72. Speaking of Baptist writing in 1996, McClendon, "Baptism," 406, asserts, "Our authors would insist that there are not two Christian baptisms to be contrasted, water-baptism and Holy Spirit-baptism, but one baptism, which is in water and in the Holy Spirit."

[84] Amply documented by Cross, "Pneumatological Key."

[85] A good example, noted above, n.20, is how McClendon and Smith follow Austin's shift away from the concept of "performative utterance" to that of "illocutionary utterance" which they call a "speech-act."

[86] McClendon, "Baptism," 408–9.

[87] McClendon, "Baptism," 406, quoting White, *Biblical Doctrine of Initiation*, 308.

[88] McClendon, "Baptism," 409.

sacramental understanding of baptism, "Here is an act of God. Here heaven touches earth afresh. Here is the holy one in holy action."[89]

Stanley Grenz relies more on sociology than philosophy, though he is aware of philosophical work as well (Alasdair McIntyre and Josiah Royce in particular).[90] Nevertheless, he hits some similar notes in speaking of "Baptism and the Lord's Supper as Community Acts." He also develops in his own way the picture of the convictional community bound together by communal practices linked to the narratives that provide meaning and identity. Baptism and the Lord's supper function as community acts connected to the main events of the biblical story, focused on the life, death and resurrection of Jesus, "together with the sending of the Spirit."[91] Again, the goal toward which baptism points is "accomplished by the renewing work of the indwelling Holy Spirit."[92]

My question is, how does baptism point to this work of the Spirit? How can it symbolize the sending and receiving of the Spirit? How is this sacramentally signified or "enacted?" How can Robinson's Spirit-soaked understanding of baptism be represented? Thomas Grantham might suggest, by including in the act of initiation the laying on of hands with prayer for receiving the Holy Spirit.

For McClendon, seeing baptism as a performative sign makes sense of the fact that in the New Testament baptism is the conventional place marking a believer's initiation into the faith. This is reflected in what Paul says in Galatians 3.27, "As many of you as were baptized into Christ have put on Christ."[93] It is important to see the context of this statement. Galatians 3 contains what are perhaps Paul's earliest reflections on Christian initiation. The reality put forward at the beginning of his argument is the Galatian Christians' experience of the power of the Spirit. "Did you receive the Spirit by doing works of the law or by believing what you heard? Are you so foolish? Having started with the Spirit, are you now ending with the flesh? Did you experience so much for nothing? . . . does God supply you with the Spirit and work miracles among you by your doing the works of the law, or by your believing what you heard?" (Gal. 3.2–5, NRSV). This is Paul's first line of argument. Further on he makes an argument involving baptism: "As many of you as were baptized into Christ have clothed yourselves with Christ" (Gal. 3.27, NRSV). This comment is prefaced by another, "In Christ Jesus you are all children of God through faith" (Gal. 3.26, NRSV). Here he clearly

---

[89] McClendon, "Baptism," 411.

[90] Grenz, "Baptism and the Lord's Supper as Community Acts," 86–87.

[91] Grenz, "Baptism and the Lord's Supper as Community Acts," 91.

[92] Grenz, "Baptism and the Lord's Supper as Community Acts," 93.

[93] McClendon, "Baptism," 411.

attributes entry into God's family to faith, yet can refer to the process as happening with baptism. What he does not have in mind is an initiation process that takes place without the faith of the initiate. Nor does he seem to envisage Christian initiation without water-baptism. There appear to be for Paul three facets of initiation into Christ: the power of the Spirit; believing the message; and baptism. There are three implied actors here: God who gives the Spirit; the community that baptizes; and the initiate who believes.

We also see this pattern in the Acts of the Apostles. After Peter's Pentecost sermon, he says to the crowd, "Repent and be baptized every one of you in the name of Jesus Christ so that your sins may be forgiven; and you will receive the gift of the Holy Spirit" (Acts 2.38, NRSV). Again, at the outset of the Christian life three actors are engaged: the individual who repents; the community which baptizes; and God who forgives sin and gives the Spirit. Peter's conviction is that the human dimension of baptism (the performative act) accompanied by repentance will be met by the divine action of forgiveness and giving the Spirit who can be seen acting so powerfully throughout Acts.

Accepting the pattern of these passages from Galatians and Acts as representative of the New Testament, we can say that there are three parties involved in Christian initiation: God; the believer; and the believing community (the agent of baptism). In becoming a believer, God is the primary actor giving the Spirit. Grantham was right to emphasize the vital importance of the promised Spirit to the gospel. This is given in response to the believer's embrace of the gospel of the crucified Lord. Baptism is the act of the believing community (including the new believer), which enacts God's saving grace in a ritual that identifies the believer with the death and resurrection of Jesus and displays the cleansing from sin so achieved. It receives the believer into the community of believers and marks him or her off from the "world." Christian initiation holds all three elements tightly together; God who forgives and gives the Spirit, the believing individual, and the baptizing community.

The practice of believers' or conversion-baptism rightly seeks to embody in a clear and dramatic way the vital importance of personal faith in the process of Christian initiation. but is it not equally true that this initiation also involves the divine action of giving the Spirit? To repeat Robinson's dictum, "Baptism, in its New Testament context, is always a baptism of the Spirit." What performative act in Christian initiation can give expression to and support such a conviction? We have available in the history of the church going back to the earliest centuries, as part of Christian initiation, the laying on of hands to signify, even enact, the gift of the promised Holy Spirit. It has the additional benefit of links to the early English Baptists as well. Should we take advantage of this resource in our practice today?[94]

---

[94] Ellis and Blythe, *Gathering for Worship*, 74–76, provide patterns and prayers to this end.

Bibliography

Anon. *A Brief Confession or Declaration of Faith. Set Forth by Many of Us, Who Are (Falsely) Called Ana-Baptists.* London: Printed for F. Smith, 1660.

Anon. *An Orthodox Creed or a Protestant Confession of Faith, Being an Essay to Unite and Confirm All Protestants In the Fundamental Articles of the Christian Religion, Against the Errors and Heresies of Rome* (London: s.n., 1679.

Austin J.L. *How to Do Things with Words.* Edited by J.O. Urmson and Marina Sbisa. The William James Lectures Delivered at Harvard University in 1955. 2nd ed. Cambridge, MA: Harvard University Press, 2009.

Bass, Clint C. *Thomas Grantham (1633–1692) and General Baptist Theology.* Centre for Baptist History and Heritage Studies, 10; Oxford: Regent's Park College, 2013.

Cross, Anthony R. "The Pneumatological Key to H. Wheeler Robinson's Baptismal Sacramentalism." In *Baptist Sacramentalism*, edited by Cross and Thompson, 151–76.

Cross, Anthony R., and Philip E. Thompson, eds. *Baptist Sacramentalism.* Studies in Baptist History and Thought, 5; Eugene, OR: Wipf & Stock, 2006.

Danvers, Henry. *A Treatise of Laying on of Hands: With the History Thereof, Both from the Scripture and Antiquity: Wherein an Account Is given How It Hath Been Practised in All Ages since Christ, the Mistakes about It Rectified and the Sence of Heb. 6.2. Cleared.* London: Printed for Francis Smith, 1674.

Dunan-Page, Anne. *Grace Overwhelming: John Bunyan, the Pilgrim's Progress and the Extremes of the Baptist Mind.* New York: Lang, 2006.

Ellis, Christopher J., and Myra Blyth. *Gathering for Worship: Patterns and Prayers for the Community of Disciples.* Norwich: Canterbury, 2005.

Essick, John Inscore. *Thomas Grantham: God's Messenger from Linconshire.* Macon, GA: Mercer University Press, 2013.

Fowler, Stanley K. *More than a Symbol: The British Baptist Recovery of Baptismal Sacramentalism.* Studies in Baptist History and Thought, 2; Carlisle: Paternoster, 2002.

Grantham, Thomas. *A Sigh for Peace, Or, The Cause of Division Discovered: Wherein the Great Gospel Promise of the Holy Ghost, and the Doctrine of Prayer with Imposition of Hands, as the Way Ordained of God to Seek for It, Is Asserted and Vindicated, as the Interest and Duty of Christs Disciples in General: In Answer to a Book Intituled A Search for Schism.* London: s.n., 1671.

———. *The Fourth Principle of Christs Doctrine Vindicated: Being a Brief Answer to Mr. H. Danvers Book, Intituled, A Treatise of Laying on of Hands, Plainly Evincing the True Antiquity and Perpetuity of That Despised Ministration of Prayer with Imposition of Hands for the Promise of the Spirit.* London: s.n., 1674.

Greaves, Richard L. "The Tangled Careers of Two Stuart Radicals: Henry and Robert Danvers." *Baptist Quarterly* 29.1 (1981) 32–43.

Greaves, Richard L., and Robert Zaller, eds. *Biographical Dictionary of British Radicals in the Seventeenth Century.* 3 vols. Brighton: Harvester, 1982.

Grenz, Stanley J. "Baptism and the Lord's Supper as Community Acts: Toward a Sacramental Understanding of the Ordinances." In *Baptist Sacramentalism,* edited by Cross and Thompson, 76–95.

Griffith, John. *Gods Oracle & Christs Doctrine, or, the Six Principles of Christian Religion ... Opened and Cleared: With an Answer to Eight Questions ... about Laying on of Hands ...* London: R. Moon, 1655.

Haykin, Michael A.G., and Mark Jones. *Drawn into Controversie: Reformed Theological Diversity and Debates within Seventeenth-Century British Puritanism.* Göttingen: Vandenhoeck & Ruprecht, 2011.

Keach, Benjamin. *Darkness Vanquished: Or, Truth in Its Primitive Purity: Being an Answer to a Late Book of Mr. Henry Danvers, Intituled A Treatise of Laying on of Hands. BY B.K.* London: s.n., 1675.

Lane, G. Eric. *Henry Danvers: Contender for Religious Liberty.* Dunstable: Fauconberg, 1972.

Lover, Thomas. *The True Gospel-Faith.* s.l.: s.n., 1654.

Lumpkin, William L., and Bill Leonard, eds. *Baptist Confessions of Faith.* 2nd ed. Valley Forge, PA: Judson, 2011.

MacIntyre, Alasdair C. *After Virtue: A Study in Moral Theory.* Notre Dame, IN: University of Notre Dame Press, 1984.

McClendon, James William. "Baptism as a Performative Sign." *Theology Today* 23.3 (1966) 403–16.

———. *Systematic Theology:* Volume 1. *Ethics.* Nashville, TN: Abingdon, 1986.

———. *Systematic Theology:* Volume 2. *Doctrine.* Nashville, TN: Abingdon Press, 1994.

McClendon, James William, and James M. Smith. *Convictions: Defusing Religious Relativism.* Valley Forge, PA: Trinity, 1994.

McMillan, David. "Willem Zuurdeeg and the Concept of Convictional Theology." *Baptistic Theologies* 6.1 (2014) 72–80.

Payne, Ernest A. "Baptists and Christian Initiation." *BQ* 26.4 (1975) 147–57.

———. "Baptists and the Laying on of Hands." *BQ* 15.5 (1954) 203–15.

Robinson, H. Wheeler, *Baptist Principles.* London: Kingsgate, 1925.

Renihan, James M. "Henry Danvers' A Treatise of Baptism: A Study in Seventeenth-Century Historiography." *Baptist Review of Theology* 7.1–2 (1997) 27–47.

Taylor, Adam. *The History of the English General Baptists: In Two Parts.* London: Printed for the Author, 1818.

Tillam, Thomas. *The Fourth Principle of Christian Religion: Or, the Foundation Doctrine of Laying on of Hands.* London: Printed for Henry Eversden, 1655.

Underwood, T. L. *Primitivism, Radicalism, and the Lamb's War: The Baptist–Quaker Conflict in Seventeenth-Century England.* New York: Oxford University Press, 1997.

Ward, Matthew. *Pure Worship: The Early English Baptist Distinctive.* Eugene. OR: Pickwick, 2014.

White, Barrington Raymond. *The English Baptists of the Seventeenth Century.* A History of the English Baptists, 1; London: Baptist Historical Society, 1983.

White, R.E.O. *The Biblical Doctrine of Initiation.* London: Hodder and Stoughton, 1960.

Wright, Stephen. *The Early English Baptists, 1603–1649.* Rochester, NY: Boydell, 2006.

Zuurdeeg, Willem Frederick. *An Analytical Philosophy of Religion.* New York: Abingdon, 1956.

CHAPTER 12

A Holistic Approach to Water-Baptism:
An Eastern European Perspective

Sergiy Sannikov

Introduction

The Eastern European Baptist movement presents a unique and, as Albert
Wardin[1] has shown, rather original phenomenon. In the vast Russian Empire
Baptist-minded groups appeared in the eighteenth century and long before
the first church associations which called themselves Baptists, came into
existence, some so-called sects held Baptist principles and views. Among them
Stundists and Malyovantsi in Ukraine, Molokan groups in the Caucases, and
other "sectarian" congregations strongly emphasized their loyalty to the *sola
scriptura* principle, insisted on the absolute independence and autonomy of the
local church, rejected ritualism and ceremonialism, and accentuated the
importance of the all-believers' priesthood.

From 1867 in Russia these groups which acknowledged the necessity of the
visible, material baptism became known as Baptists (the first church was
started in Tiflis—modern Tbilisi), and from 1869 in Ukraine (the first
churches were started in the villages of Karlovka and Lyubomirka in the
Ekaterinoslav Province). Adult baptism became the sign which singled out
this religious group in the Orthodox environment not only in a mental but
also in a visible, material way, allowing it to identify itself with a part of the
world Baptist movement. In other words, it was baptism that became a
Rubicon which made this group stand out as a real church association in the
general religious free thought movement widespread in the nineteenth
century. Since then the Eastern European Baptist movement has always
emphasized the importance of water-baptism during the debates with
Molokans and so-called "dry" Baptists, who recognized baptism as a purely
spiritual experience, in that they insisted on "regeneration without baptism."
On the other hand, Baptists have constantly defended their views while
debating with the Orthodox who baptize babies and affirm "regeneration
through baptism."

---

[1] Wardin, "How Indigenous," 29–37.

Because of these controversies, the theology of baptism developed mainly in its apologetic aspect, emphasizing primarily the procedural aspects such as the state of faith of the person baptized, the symbolism of the baptismal actions (the importance of full immersion) or actively criticizing the views of other denominations. At the same time almost no attempt at indigenous theological reflection on baptism was made. A similar situation can be observed in the world Baptist movement. As one of the earliest twentieth-century Baptists exploring the theology of baptism, H. Wheeler Robinson noted almost a hundred years ago, "A common fault of many addresses on baptism by Baptists is that they are too negative, that they are often more concerned with showing what New Testament baptism is not, rather than what it is."[2]

Symbolical and Sacramental Approaches to Baptism

In the Eastern European tradition there were no real debates on the doctrine of water-baptism until the 1990s. However, from the very beginning of the Baptist movement in that part of the world there have been two theological groups which can be called the Westerners and the Nativists. Regarding water-baptism, the Westerners repeated the formulas of the British Baptists of the Victorian era, who said that baptism is only a symbol of an already accomplished salvation, while the Nativists treated this rite with more reverence.

The development of the symbolical doctrine of water-baptism was greatly influenced by Vasiliy Pavlov[3] (1854–1924), who was educated at the Hamburg Baptist Seminary under the supervision of a well-known Baptist leader Johann Gerhard Oncken (1800–83), and who translated into Russian and published the famous sermon of Charles Spurgeon on *Baptismal Regeneration*. That work refuted the thought that baptism plays any part in the process of salvation.

Another group, the Nativists, deliberately left the Molokan context, deeply reflected on the necessity of water-baptism and its meaning. For example, Vasiliy Ivanov-Klyshnikov, a famous leader of the Caucasian Baptist movement, describes in his memoirs[4] how he had to take a stand for the meaningfulness of the act of baptism in discussion with the Molokan elders, who were known to reject this ritual. On the other hand, he had to emphasize its secondary nature while debating with the Orthodox missionaries, stating that only those who believe should be baptized. A more sacramental

---

[2] Robinson, "Place of Baptism," 209.

[3] Vasiliy Pavlov also came from a Molokan background, but he accepted Baptist beliefs when he was young and was not rooted in Molokan traditions, but was guided mostly by German Baptists.

[4] Ivanov-Klyshnikov, *Selected Articles*, 11–23.

understanding of baptism and a more symbolic one did not differ from each other in principle and coexisted almost until the end of the twentieth century.

Serious debates as to the meaning of water-baptism began in the 1990s when in the Eastern European churches there appeared many brochures and books which contained the popular explanation of the foundations of Baptist teaching. The latter represented mostly American tradition which leaned towards fundamentalism. At the same time there appeared quite a few seminary and college graduates who knew English well. They could study the literature which reflected both the views of Baptist sacramentalists and the beliefs of their opponents. Thus, the young Eastern European scholars got access to books including those by Baptist theologians such as George R. Beasley-Murray, *Baptism in the New Testament*, Neville Clark's *An Approach to the Theology of the Sacraments*, *Christian Baptism* edited by Alec Gilmore, and R.E.O. White's *The Biblical Doctrine of Initiation*. These thinkers began to restore the traditional Baptist understanding of water-baptism as an intrinsic part of one broad process of salvation and, thus, they became the forerunners of Baptist sacramentalism.

By the end of the twentieth century and at the beginning of the twenty-first century one can note a strong interest in the theology of water-baptism which for a while was prominent in Eastern Europe as well. At that time, there appeared thorough and serious researches on the topic. Such famous and influential British scholars as Paul S. Fiddes, John E. Colwell, Brian Haymes, Christopher J. Ellis, and Anthony R. Cross facilitated the restoration of the interest and a deeper and more stable development of the theology of baptism. One should especially acknowledge the works of Anthony R. Cross on this topic. He not only published many articles and books about baptism, but also co-edited the series of collected works under the title *Baptist Sacramentalism*.[5] Also the books and articles of Paul Fiddes should be noted.[6] At the same time, in North America there appeared many enthusiasts who developed a deeper understanding of water-baptism. Among them were Stanley K. Fowler with his book *More Than a Symbol*, Mikael Broadway, Curtis W. Freeman, Barry Harvey, Elizabeth Newman, Philip E. Thompson, and James Wm. McClendon, Jr., in "Re-Envisioning Baptist Identity,"[7] and Brandon Jones who represented the reformation wing of the Baptists in the United States. Also, it is appropriate to mention such famous American Baptist theologians as Clark H. Pinnock, Stanley J. Grenz, Steven R. Harmon, and Curtis W.

---

[5] See, e.g., Cross, *Baptism and the Baptists*, and *Recovering the Evangelical Sacrament*, and Cross and Thompson, ed., *Baptist Sacramentalism*, and *Baptist Sacramentalism 2*.

[6] See, e.g., Fiddes, ed., *Reflections on the Water*, *Tracks and Traces*, and "Baptism and the Process of Christian Initiation."

[7] See the appendix in Freeman, "Can Baptist Theology be Revisioned?" 303–10.

Freeman, all of whom argue for the sacramentalist position in the Baptist theology of baptism.

At the same time, many works defending the Zwinglian understanding of baptism appeared in Eastern European churches. These were mostly translations by North American and British theologians advocating an anti-sacramentalist understanding.[8] A particularly strong influence in this region came from the missionaries who mainly adhered to the official view of the Southern Baptist Convention. John S. Hammett comments on the Southern Baptist understanding of baptism in the following terms: "Baptists have historically insisted that baptism is not salvific, that it is not essential to salvation. It does not accomplish identification with Christ, but symbolizes the identification that happens when one places faith in Christ."[9] Lloyd Harsch, a Professor of New Orleans Baptist Theological Seminary, analyzed the Baptist confessions of faith of the last four centuries and came to the opposite conclusion to Stanley Fowler from Toronto, who also studied the same confessions carefully. Harsch states the following: "It seems clear that from their infancy, Baptists have been non-sacramental in their understanding of baptism. Their confessions of faith intentionally distance themselves from the prevailing sacramental view. Early doctrinal writings are consistent with this stance."[10] At the same time, Stanley Fowler, whose study of the history of Baptist sacramentalism claims that the early confessions of faith formulated before the Victorian era in Great Britain, the cradle of Baptists, clearly point to a continuous tradition advocating a sacramental understanding of baptism.[11]

The Sacramental vs Anti-Sacramental Debate in Eastern Europe

The debate between the sacramental and anti-sacramental understanding of baptism also touched Eastern Europe. As a case study which shows the different approaches to the understanding of the essence of water-baptism in the Eastern European context, one can cite the discussion which started because of the article on baptism published in the *Theological Reflections* journal.[12] In 2006, the editors of the journal received the article "On Several Peculiarities of the Understanding of Baptism in the Russian Baptist Church"

---

[8] E.g., see Gay, *Baptist Sacramentalism*, which is a harsh critique of the sacramental concept of baptism.

[9] Blount and Wooddell, *The Baptist Faith and Message 2000*, 73.

[10] Harsch, "Were the First Baptists Sacramentalists?" 40.

[11] Fowler, *More Than a Symbol*.

[12] This is the only academic journal of Evangelical theology in Eastern Europe, published by the Euro-Asian Accrediting Association.

by Constantine Prokhorov. It clearly showed that the sacramental understanding of baptism exists among Slavic Evangelical Christian Baptists and cites the various interpretations given by the influential leaders of this movement over the preceding fifteen to twenty years. The article analyzes the ontological meaning of water-baptism from the biblical perspective. In his conclusions, Prokhorov points out that "the fullness of salvation is found in repentance and baptism, not in repentance only (and not in baptism only)."[13] In light of a study of the practice of water-baptism, hymnography, and oral tradition on this religious act, the author offered the conclusion that those who receive this ritual perceive it in practice as "a sacrament and the one doubtlessly connected with salvation and the gift of eternal life."[14] He argued that the close connection of water-baptism and baptism by the Holy Spirit is a widespread view among Slavic Baptists.

The article was sent anonymously to a contest and was rated #4, so it was published in issue 7 of the journal. However, one of the members of the journal's supervisory board vetoed it arguing that it was not in line with the Euro-Asian Accrediting Association (EAAA) confession of faith adopted by the editors of the journal. In order to confirm or revoke the veto, two meetings of the EAAA Council took place on 27 October 2006, and on 27 June 2007. It was decided that the article would be published in the theological discussions section and accompanied by the material which offered the theological foundation of the anti-sacramental view of baptism. That material was written by Mark Saucy, a Russian-speaking missionary living in Ukraine. Both articles were published in *Theological Reflections* 8 in 2007.

In his article, Saucy treated water-baptism in the broader context of the development of national theology, pointing out the merit and possible errors of that process. He commenced his analysis of the phenomenon of water-baptism within the Baptist context with the statement that "Baptism even in the presence of faith does not mark the moment of salvation, regeneration, or reception of the Holy Spirit."[15] He then provided an exegetical study of the biblical passages on the salvific role of baptism showing the priority of faith before baptism. He agrees that baptism is not an empty symbol, but at the same time rejects the connection of the material acts (rituality) with the spiritual processes to which the former point. He contends that "baptism cannot by this be reduced to an empty symbol, but neither is it appropriate to make it bear the weight of marking the effective point of salvation."[16] It is interesting to note that in the last part of his work, Saucy offers conclusions

---

[13] Prokhorov, "On Several Peculiarities," 75.

[14] Prokhorov, "On Several Peculiarities," 81.

[15] *Saucy*, "Baptism as a Test Case," 140.

[16] *Saucy*, "Baptism as a Test Case," 150.

which are very close to Prokhorov's sacramentalist approach. He maintains that the apostolic church did not "separate baptism from the moment of belief" and that "In the early church baptism was truly an initiatory rite."[17] The later tradition, he argues, artificially broke this process into several parts. Prokhorov also insists on the holistic approach to baptism in his article.

This journal discussion, and the passionate debates on this topic among the leaders of theological education, clearly showed the presence of the two rather steady trends in Eastern European Baptist theology—one sacramental, and the other anti-sacramental in nature. Analyzing traditional Baptist sources, especially ones written at a popular level and looking at water-baptism from different perspectives, one can easily see that the majority of authors who write on the subject are mostly concerned to show that baptism does not save. In his book *Basic Baptist Beliefs*, translated into Russian and popular among Eastern European Baptist churches, Harold Rawlings insists that "baptism is an outer *manifestation* or a *symbol* of salvation; it neither saves nor even conduces salvation (1 Pet 3.21; 1 Cor 1.17)."[18] It is interesting to note that the author argues on the basis of 1 Peter 3.21, according to which baptism "saves by the resurrection of Jesus Christ," he concludes the opposite to the text. This is an example of looking at the New Testament text through one's denominational glasses.

The same thought, though in less categorical terms, is expressed in many official documents by Slavic Baptists. For example, *The Concise Catechism of the Russian Baptist Union* states, "3.9.2 Does water baptism give salvation?— Person receives salvation at the moment of repentance and water baptism testifies to the salvation already accomplished."[19] Similar statements are clearly directed against the advocates of infant baptism. They defend the idea of believer's baptism in the discussion which tries to find an answer to the question whether baptism saves. but the problem with these discussions is that the question itself is not formulated correctly. This is why the answers of both the pedobaptists and credobaptists sound narrow and unconvincing. Both strive to find the arguments in the holy scriptures or tradition in order to prove the salvific power of baptism or, vice versa, to reduce or reject its role in salvation. Both sides get their implacability from the same source, but in the heat of discussion they do not ask themselves whether this question needs to be answered at all.

---

[17] *Saucy*, "Baptism as a Test Case," 156.

[18] Rawlings, *Basic Baptist Beliefs*, 244 (italics original).

[19] Ivanov, *We believe*, 96.

Holistic Understanding of Baptism

The question whether baptism saves or not is incorrect because it singles out baptism and separates it from the other components of salvation. It would be the same to ask whether faith saves or whether repentance saves. The Bible and the church declare that only Christ saves. He is the Savior and the rest are mere instruments which he uses. Ripping out one of the elements from the living fabric of salvation that he accomplishes makes the picture of salvation defective. It destroys the integrity and dooms theology to endless and futile discussions. The right questions should be formulated differently: does water-baptism take part in the process of salvation? Is it a component of salvation and the mission of the church? What does this component mean in the whole picture of the advancement of the church and the kingdom of God? Is baptism one of the integral elements of the spiritual journey of a Christian or can it be left out under certain circumstances? If the questions are formulated like this, it will be possible to find objective biblical and theological answers to them without getting into polemics and yet analyzing various discourses and conflicting points of view.

Thus, in order to evaluate the phenomenon of water-baptism properly one needs to use a holistic approach which takes into account various perspectives and understandings of this religious act in the broad context of the formation of a Christian. Because of the traditional Baptist principle of a hermeneutic of freedom in the Eastern European churches there are various approaches and interpretations of water-baptism. Different congregations treat the theology of baptism differently, but in truth their views supplement each other creating a wonderfully holistic picture of this phenomenon. We will try to describe the seven aspects of water-baptism keeping in mind that each of its following images is in a sense correct and biblically based. Each reflects the understanding of this phenomenon which a concrete Baptist group formed in a certain historical period. Therefore, the task of holistic perception is not to study critically each image and choose the only right and the best one, but to put them together in a holistic picture.

Convention or Reality?": Baptism as a Symbol

The interpretation of water-baptism as a symbol is obviously the most popular feature which helps identify Baptist theology of baptism in Eastern Europe. This view is confirmed by many Baptist authors. Presenting the Baptist understanding of baptism at the *Understanding Four Views on Baptism* symposium, Tom Nettles insisted on perceiving baptism as no more than a symbol which testifies in a purely metaphorical manner to the act of the salvation already accomplished. He wrote, "No saving efficacy inheres in either the form or the matter itself. The person baptized has no scriptural warrant to believe that in baptism Christ's saving activity is initiated, augmented, or completed."[20] The modern confession of faith of the Ukrainian Baptist Council also speaks of baptism in a traditionally symbolic spirit, but in a more reserved manner: "Baptists insist that baptism is a mere symbol of our union with Christ and our participation by faith in His death, burial and resurrection."[21] However, the early Baptists, while rejecting *ex opere operato*, still clearly pointed out the real connection of baptism with entering Christ, uniting with his death and resurrection, and even with the forgiveness of sins.

The insistence on emphasizing the metaphorical and symbolic meaning of baptism was not characteristic of the first-generation Baptists in the early seventeenth century. As Stanley Fowler (and other authors) have shown, the first Baptist, John Smyth and his followers talked about baptism using the language of a factual presence of Christ and true unity with him.[22] For example, the *Second London Confession* of 1677–79 says in chapter XXIX that "Baptism is an Ordinance of the New Testament, ordained by Jesus Christ, to be unto the party Baptized, a sign of his fellowship with him, in his death, and resurrection; of his being engrafted into him; of remission of sins."[23] Only later, under the influence of many historical circumstances, water-baptism separate from spiritual. John Smyth writes about baptism openly calling it a sacrament: "Therefore, the baptism of water leadeth us to Christ, to his holy office in glory and majesty."[24] This statement clearly shows the instrumental power of baptism. It really does something—it leads the person being baptized into the presence of Christ. The *Baptist Catechism* of 1689 explains that baptism, along with the word, the Lord's Supper, and prayer passes to the believers "the benefits of Redemption."[25]

If baptism is only a symbol, then what does it signify? What does the sign of baptism point to? It is usually believed that it is a testimony to faith and obedience, a sign of death to sin and resurrection to the new life of holiness. In his *Teaching on Faith of Evangelical Christians* (1910), the famous leader of the Evangelical Christians Ivan Prokhanov writes that "baptism by water is an

---

[20] Nettles, "Baptism as a Symbol," 25.

[21] Educational Council of All-Ukrainian Council of Evangelical Baptist Churches, *Confession of Faith*, 25.

[22] Fowler, *More Than a Symbol*, 31–32.

[23] Lumpkin, ed., *Baptist Confessions*, 290–91

[24] *Short Confession of Faith* (1610), Article 30, signed by John Smyth and forty-three members of his group, in Lumpkin, *Baptist Confessions,* 110.

[25] Keach, *Baptist Catechism* (also known as *Keach's Cathecism*), 23, Question 95 and the answer to it, written for the *Second London Confession of Faith* at the end of the seventeenth century, states that "The outward and ordinary means whereby Christ communicates to us the benefits of redemption are His ordinances, especially the Word, Baptism, the Lord's Supper and Prayer."

outer sign of baptism by the Holy Spirit or the death for the sin and the
resurrection to the righteousness which took place earlier in the soul of a
person."[26] He separates the moment of baptism by the Holy Spirit which,
according to him, accompanies regeneration and the act of water-baptism
without explaining why these actions should be separated in time. This led to
the fact that in Prokhanov's movement (the Evangelical Christians) the role of
water-baptism (as of the other church rituals) was significantly reduced. For
that group, adult water-baptism was not considered obligatory, and this led
during the early years of the movement to tensions in its relationship with
Caucasian Baptist churches.

The Russian Baptists, who were under the influence of the *Hamburg
Confession* of 1847, tended to a more sacramental and realistic understanding
of water-baptism. They accepted the *Confession of Faith of Christian Baptists*
(1906), which states that baptism "is a solemn announcement, confession of a
sinner . . . that he commits his body and soul to Christ and puts Him on as
His righteousness and strength, that he puts his old self to death with Him
and wants to walk with Him in a renewed life."[27] Such phrasing proved to be
acceptable for the leaders of Transcaucasian Baptists, most of whom were
former Molokans, in their conflict with the theology of spiritual Christians,
who denied water-baptism altogether. Baptists who debated with them
constantly had to defend the necessity and deep sacramental meaning of
baptism.

Emphasizing that the outward act of baptism is completely meaningless
without the required inner state, Baptist authors do not break the connection
of faith with baptism, but instead point out the unity of the outward act and
inner state. Thus, Nikolay Khrapov, one of the most influential Baptist
ministers of the Soviet period, says of water-baptism that "Although the only
instrument of the salvation of sinners is the blood of Christ which cleanses us
from sin, our salvation is established and realized through baptism into the
death of the Lord. The resurrected life of Jesus is realized in us only by means
of baptism into His death."[28] Alexey Kolomiytsev, a famous modern preacher,
writes that "baptism is not a rite or a religious establishment. It points out the
deep inner process which Paul compares with death and burial . . . The true
baptism is a set of inner processes expressed by the outward act of immersing
oneself into water."[29]

The strong side of the symbolic approach to baptism is doubtlessly its
emphasis on conscious faith and personal decision which leads to the personal

---

[26] Quoted by Sannikov, *History of Baptism*, 451.

[27] See Sannikov, *History of Baptism*, 426.

[28] Khrapov, *House of God and Ministry*, §5.

[29] Kolomiytsev, "Purpose and Meaning," line 196.

responsibility and also the affirmation of the commitment to the classical principles of the Reformation—*sola fides* and *sola gratia*. The symbolism of baptism also demonstrates a more spiritual and democratic way of thinking. Fixed church membership in this case becomes non-obligatory, the control of a congregation weakens and that leads to the lessening of legalism and sectarianism. The absence of the stable connection of baptism with salvation allows the inclusion among the latter (and by this in salvation as well) of a broader circle of people whose baptism is not certainly known or whose Christian faith is proved only by their ethical behavior.

In the symbolic approach there is considerably less danger of idolatry. In the insistence on emphasizing baptism as a symbol one can hear the pathos of Old Testament prophets who spoke against idolatry and demanded spiritual worship without visible rituals. This understanding seems to be a continuation of the tradition of Hezekiah who destroyed the bronze snake Nehushtan (2 Kgs. 18.4). This snake was made by the order of God himself, but because of human sinful nature it became an idolatrous object of worship. Symbolism is in fact an attempt to distance oneself as far as possible from the dangerous border that separates us from idolatry which replaces the unfathomable God with his visible sign, an idol of God. In its extreme expression it becomes a program of demythologization of all churchliness in order to obtain "the pure Spirit."[30]

According to many critics of the symbolic model of baptism, the main weakness of this approach is its lack of biblical support. The adherents of the symbolic understanding have to make many exegetical efforts in order to reinterpret about a dozen clear scriptural passages which point at the direct connection of baptism with salvation. The symbolists always seem to have a problem with so-called difficult texts which do not fit an accepted dogmatic system, while the clear instructions of Christ, the practice of the Book of Acts, and the testimony of Ante-Nicene Christianity speak against their view.

Another weak point of the symbolic discourse of baptism is an excessive spiritualization when all the processes connected with the activity of God in the New Testament are considered to be of a purely spiritual nature. The words of Christ about the worship in Spirit and truth and the struggle of Paul against the ritualism and legalism of the Pharisees of the Second Temple period are understood by symbolists as a complete separation of the material world from the spiritual one. Such understanding breaks the oneness of the world and practically makes God the Lord and Master only of the spiritual realm. Thus, the symbolic understanding of baptism is dualistic, and it does not take into account the integratedness of human nature which needs to communicate with the help of material signs and rituals.

---

[30] The ideal example of such an approach which rejects all institutions and corporate aspects of the church reducing the faith to an individual responsibility and personal convictions is the book by Nesterenko, *Institutional Captivity*.

Besides, the symbolic model has some practical weaknesses. It leads to desacralization of the worship service and the decline of churchliness as a cultural phenomenon, reducing it to an ordinary secular performance. Rationalization and de-ritualization inevitably produce a decrease in the meaningfulness of baptism as well as of its authority and importance. In practice it is seen in the growing number of people who are not ready to be baptized, yet they consider themselves practicing Christians. That is reflected in the decreasing number of the adult "credobaptisms."

Door to the Church: Baptism as Initiation

The concept of initiation as acceptance of a new convert into the church allows us to see joining the congregation as a process and an event; to analyze the objects and subjects of becoming part of the church, and to evaluate the role of each participant.

Christian baptism as a completing act or a final point of conversion includes a wide complex of preliminary assimilation of theology, behavior, and church culture of a certain group. In other words, a newcomer must master "the mother tongue of the church" and to testify to it through a certain ritual act. The result is a new identification of the newcomer and the confirmation on the part of the society that it is ready to accept this new member. Thus, starting from a certain moment, the existential status of a baptized neophyte radically changes. Not only his baptism leads them into a new association of the elect and the initiated, it also separates them from the whole surrounding world of the uninitiated.

Gerard Kelly, who is guided by the works of Louis-Marie Chauvet, divides initiation into three basic elements.[31] The first one includes hearing and assimilating the stories about the new association. These are the stories of its origin and relations. It is a description of cultural characteristics, traditions, models of behavior, appearance and other subcultural elements, and also an understanding, perspective, and evaluation of the society which exists outside this subculture. Usually this phase implies the intentional didactic impact in the form of special training, courses, and the like, and also non-verbal pedagogical methods that are normally much more effective than verbal ones. At this stage neophytes often subconsciously accept the models of behavior, approved standard vocabulary, specific language, and stories which are not comprehensive but are, in a sense, enigmatic and secret in the eyes of the uninitiated.

The second phase of practically all the initiation procedures is a certain trial, examination, or test to check the readiness of the one being initiated to enter the new association. In traditional or primitive cultures, it is often

---

[31] Kelly, "Baptism in the Roman Catholic Church," 35. We present three basic elements of initiation which Kelly shows in a different order.

connected with mutilating oneself and showing the ability of a neophyte to bear the mutilation and live according to the norms of the new association. The third element of initiation is the ritual itself which takes place as an event in the presence of the whole community and its most authoritative members. It is arranged in a solemn manner and can be accompanied by some material signs or proofs.

Not all the researchers agree with such an interpretation of the concept of initiation. For example, James Dunn says, "I describe the event of becoming a Christian by the inelegant title 'conversion-initiation.'"[32] He believes that the initialization is the rite of baptism itself. Thus, he tries to separate the spiritual processes which he calls "conversion to Christianity" from the rite of baptism itself in which he does not see any spiritual component. However, one can hardly agree with Dunn since the idea of initiation has a broader meaning than simply the event of water-baptism, and it is quite suitable for describing the concept of "joining the church."

Baptism as the door or the gateway to the church is one of the favorite and widespread images used to explain this religious rite. Early Baptist confessions of faith already emphasized this aspect of baptism. For example, *The Faith and Practise of Thirty Congregations* (1651) says in paragraph 50, "That those which received the word of God preached by the Ministrie of the Gospel, and were Baptized according to the Counsel of God, at the same time or day they were of the visible Church of God, Acts 2.41."[33] The same statement can be found in many other early Baptist documents, for example, in Article XI of the so-called *The Standard Confession* of 1660.[34]

From the very beginning, Slavic Baptists also clearly articulated the meaning of water-baptism as the instrument for joining the church. *The Rules of Confession of Faith for a New Convert of the Russian Brotherhood*, signed by Mikhail Ratushny and about 100 Ukrainian Stundists and presented to the Tsar in 1871, point out in paragraph 5 that "By means of baptism we are accepted into the visible Church of Christ on earth."[35] *The Confession of Faith* of Odessa Theological Seminary states that "A person joins a local church through water baptism which is the first fruit of faith, love, and obedience to Christ, a visible sign of the entrance into His Universal Church."[36] The same is stated in *The Confession of Faith of Evangelical Christian Baptists* of 1985[37] and other doctrinal documents. In his abstract that was read at the forty-first

---

[32] Dunn, *Baptism in the Holy Spirit*, 5.

[33] Lumpkin, ed., *Baptist Confessions*, 182.

[34] Lumpkin, ed., *Baptist Confessions*, 228.

[35] Zhabotinskiy, "Petition of Ivan Ryaboshapka," 143.

[36] In Sannikov, *History of Baptism*, 479.

[37] See Sannikov, *History of Baptism*, 405.

Congress of All-Russian Union of Evangelical Christian Baptists, Michael Zhidkov points out that baptism "is the door for joining a local church where all those who love the Lord Jesus Christ are united into 'one body' of holy fellowship."[38]

The idea of baptism as initiation inevitably leads to several important practical conclusions. First of all, the idea of joining a local church implies the *presence of the church*. This is why baptism is usually performed in the presence of the community or a significant part of it. As a rule, it is a celebration and the people who have just been baptized are given commemorative signs or certificates. From the theological point of view, it is explained that during baptism the community demonstrates its acceptance of new members which is testified by the laying of hands on those who have been baptized. This is why Baptist ministers are reluctant to allow private, secret baptisms, and they do it only when forced by certain adverse circumstances.

Another important practical outcome of understanding baptism as initiation is the practice of preparing for baptism and arranging a test before the actual baptism. This practice is a surprising exception in the traditional Baptist approach which base all aspects of baptism on the biblical texts. It is difficult to find any biblical warrant or New Testament examples affirming a long period of catechetical instruction before baptism. After a serious exegetical study, even the so-called Great Commission (Matt. 28.19), which is sometimes used to justify educating new converts before they get baptized, cannot explain such a practice.

One of the strongest sides of this understanding of baptism is its general acceptance not only in various Baptist circles but also by practically all Christian denominations. The integral element of such an understanding is its emphasis on the collective instead of individualistic aspect of this act. Initiation points to the participation of the church community and joining this community. The absence of notions of the collective, ecclesiological component of baptism, as well as the tendency to treat it as personal relationship between people and God, breaks the holistic fabric of baptism and virtually destroys it.

Baptism as the gateway to the church community allows us to prepare neophytes for this moment and in this way to form the church as a fellowship of the single-minded not only in the area of orthodoxy but also in the area of orthopraxy. There appears not only the opportunity, but also the requirement, for serious catechetical preparation which includes various elements of testing—the candidate's testimony and those surrounding him, oral interviews, and the like.

Such an understanding allows us to make an easy division between the church and non-church, to draw a clear, visible line between different communities, to build a stable, institutionalized form of the church, to provide

---

[38] Zhidkov, "Water Baptism," 57.

it with the coating of organization without which the spiritual organism cannot live long in the material world. Thanks to such obvious signs, a stable local church is created, and becomes a community of the faithful with a fixed membership.

Initiation leads to moral obligations of a special holy life in Christ, in the fellowship of saints, the church. This is why Beasley-Murray points out that "baptism in the Apostolic Church is a moral-religious act,"[39] that is, it imposes certain moral and religious requirements.

Of course, this understanding of baptism has its weak point as well. Considering water-baptism as system-forming sign of churchliness one can easily make a mistake and create an appearance of the church while losing its most important ontological attributes such as, for example, spiritual otherness. Looking on water-baptism as a sign of belonging to the church, provides the possibility (and the actuality) of the cases of hypocrisy and even self-deception when a person who has been baptized never really experiences regeneration. Preparatory conversations and test periods are rather unreliable filters which often let through undeserving candidates.

The understanding of baptism as initiation is exclusive rather than inclusive. According to Fiddes, it does not include into the church those who are still on their way to faith, or those who have been leading a righteous Christian life without being baptized, or those who were baptized in the other denominations. Therefore, it excludes from the church a large group of Christians who have both faith and the fruit of faith. Although many consider this understanding as a strong side of baptism, Paul Fiddes, following Jürgen Moltmann, recognizes the church as a group which is able to accept something she finds unpleasant, and be able to remove the limitations.[40] This is why these researchers see exclusivity as a weakness.

Seal of the Testament: Baptism as Promise

For the majority of Slavic Baptists baptism is understood as a pledge of a good conscience toward God and a making of a covenant with him. In "On the Life of the Local Churches" section of the *Bratskiy Vestnik* (*Brotherly Herald*) journal there was often published the reports of water-baptisms along the following lines: "The city of Poti. The converted souls have made a covenant with the Lord and joined the church through water baptism of faith. The act of baptism was performed by brother I.D. Varavin, the presbyter of the church,"[41] or "Recently in South Sakhalin church a solemn worship service took place at which the souls who had turned to the Lord made a covenant

---

[39] Beasley-Murray, *Baptism in the New Testament*, 284.

[40] Fiddes, *Tracks and Traces*, 14.

[41] Anon., "On the Life of the Local Churches, 1978," 60.

with Him through holy water baptism. It was performed by brother Y.A. Maksimchuk."[42] Such descriptions can be found in most of the information entries about baptism.

Nikolay Kolesnikov, a famous Baptist minister, asserts that in "receiving water baptism we make a covenant with God. Thus, we get the right to participate in the beneficial sacrament of remembering the death of Christ— Lord's Supper—and to be called 'children of God.'"[43] Brian C. Brewer points out that on the basis of the works written in the seventeenth and eighteenth centuries "many Baptist groups and leaders held that the rites of baptism and the Supper were effective covenantal signs which encompassed both human and divine action during their enactment."[44]

It would seem that proclaiming baptism to be a sign of the covenant between God and people is the obvious truth in the Baptist theology of baptism. However, an attempt to find a direct reference to baptism as a covenant in the Baptist confessions of faith is doomed to failure. All the early English confessions, as well as the descriptions of the doctrines of Slavic Baptists, do not make a strong connection between the concepts of baptism and covenant. One rare exception is in *The Orthodox Creed*, composed by General Baptists in England in 1678 in response to *The First London Confession* of the Particular Baptists written in 1677. It states that baptism is established by Jesus Christ as "a sign of our entrance into the covenant of grace, and ingrafting into Christ, and in the body of Christ, which is his Church."[45]

In the confession written by J.G. Oncken (both in the original version and in the Russian translation by Pavlov) there is a hint of the covenant relationship when the responsibility of the person being baptized and the response of God are described. Thus, while avoiding an explicit reference to baptism as a covenant, this confession still uses covenantal language. In the Confession of Faith of St Petersburg Evangelical Christians (written by Kargel) there is nothing identifying baptism with covenant.[46] There appears, therefore, to be a paradox when on the level of church consciousness, as well as in the liturgical texts and other generally accepted Baptist documents, the act of baptism is clearly articulated as the moment at which the covenant is made, while in the official dogmatic texts written by both English and Slavic Baptists such phrasing is carefully avoided.

---

[42] Anon., "On the Life of the Local Churches, 1988," 86.

[43] Kolesnikov, "Let's Press On to Perfection," 35.

[44] Brewer, "Signs of the Covenant," 419.

[45] Lumpkin, ed., *Baptist Confessions*, 317.

[46] See Kargel, *Short Exposition*.

Probably one of the reasons for this is that the early Baptist creeds were composed in opposition to the theology of Pedobaptists. The understanding of baptism as a sign of the covenant based on Colossians 2.11–12 is the main theological argument of this theology. If baptism is a sign of the covenant which replaces Old Testament circumcision, the sign of the covenant between God and Abraham and his descendants, it means that baptism is, first of all, interpreted as a reference to joining the people of God. In this case, it possesses a corporate instead of individualistic nature, and by the Old Testament analogy it can be performed on children, not on the basis of faith, but rather on the basis of the covenant. This is probably why Baptist ministers carefully avoid making a direct connection between baptism and covenant despite the fact that there is a biblical basis for it.

The image of Christian baptism as a sign of the covenant actually points to its being an official encounter between God and people. It is a meeting territory richly decorated and filled with symbolism, a visible place and ceremony of signing an eternal and unbreakable agreement between free but completely unequal partners in the presence of many witnesses both on the side of people (the community) and on the side of God (numerous spiritual powers). The stipulations of the covenant were proclaimed by Christ during his incarnation and preaching in Palestine, and the covenant itself was made on Calvary through the shedding of his blood. but the personal acceptance of the covenant by a new convert is realized in the act of baptism. This is why it has also God's side, since it is God who sets out the stipulations, promises cleansing from sin, eternal life, blessings, and am imperishable inheritance— all this can be received only in Christ. The human part includes the acceptance of these stipulations by faith and the confirmation of one's agreement by baptism, which demonstrates that a neophyte enters Christ. Using modern terminology, baptism is a territory of co-working where God and human beings together publicly declare their reconciliation and establishment of eternal union.

The analogy of the covenantal signs (circumcision and baptism) effectively demonstrates the similarity and distinctions between the two covenants. Just like Old Testament circumcision pointed to the faith that Abraham had before he was circumcised, New Testament baptism is meaningless without prior faith. Circumcision demonstrated the ethical affiliation to the children of Abraham according to the flesh, while baptism demonstrates the affiliation to the children of God according to the Spirit. Yet, just as when not all the Israelites who had the sign of circumcision were the true people of God (Rom. 9.6), not all those who have accepted the sign of water-baptism will belong to the New Testament church. In other words, both circumcision and baptism are, so to speak, the initial signs of their covenants which are actualized by further confirmation. but despite many similarities, the deepest distinction between these signs lies in their spiritual contrast—the first was earthly and fleshly, and the second one is heavenly and spiritual.

Schreiner puts it like this: "Paul does not establish a connection between physical circumcision and baptism, but *spiritual circumcision and baptism.*"[47] Stephen Wellum provides a comprehensive study of the relation between the covenants[48] and comes to the conclusion that circumcision marks people and nations only physically, therefore, its similarity with spiritual circumcision cannot be complete. It cannot be transferred to the material actions at baptism, such as type, time, and circumstances. Thus, the conclusion that the analogy between baptism and circumcision allows the baptism of babies on the eighth (or any other) day is theologically illegitimate because of the principal difference between the Old and New Covenants.

Among the strengths of such an understanding is the demonstration of the intrinsic unity of God's actions in all times, the inviolability of his principles, and the coherence of his approaches during the various dispensations of the advancement of God's kingdom. Another advantage is its emphasizing the responsibility of the one being baptized as they enter the covenant. For this covenant to take effect, a person must not only participate in the ritual, but also make a promise to obey the stipulations of the covenant, in particular, to pledge a good conscience toward God. For Slavic Baptists this component of baptism is very important. The sense of duty is an integral element of social consciousness in this part of the world. From the pastoral perspective, it seems that knowing one's obligation to God, remembering one's duties and great responsibility, and the cost of the covenant can keep a church member in line and help them go through the difficult periods of spiritual weakness.

Such an interpretation of baptism gives an opportunity to present it nowadays as a meeting, an encounter, a place where God and people can work together. This, in its turn, provides the ground for a fruitful dialogue in which various opinions and traditions are expressed.

The weakness of a covenantal understanding of baptism is its allowance for false correlations on the basis of the analogy between the signs of the covenant. Although Colossians 2.11 speaks of the connection of circumcision, which is done not by the hands of men but by Christ, with water-baptism, many theologians still see in this text an interrelation between the actual circumcision and actual baptism, and they draw the conclusion that there is room for pedobaptism on the basis of belonging to the family. Such an understanding is not supported either by the hermeneutics of the passage or by its general theological context.

Another weakness lies in the ambiguity of one of the main passages used by this approach, namely, 1 Peter 3.21, and in the difficulties connected with the interpretation of the word *epirotema*. The pledge of a good conscience at baptism is often understood as a promise to lead a sinless, holy life, which is

---

[47] Schreiner, "Baptism in the Epistles," 78.

[48] Wellum, "Baptism and the Relationship," 97–161.

impossible for an honest Christian. This interpretation is hinted upon even in *The Guide for the Preparation for Water Baptism* edited by Mikhail Ivanov: "Baptism is the pledge of a good (i.e., pure, blameless) conscience toward God. Our conscience is pure only when it is not burdened by sins which torture and torment a man. Baptism is a promise to God to avoid sin and live a holy and righteous life (1 Pet. 3:21)."[49] Similar statements, though more carefully phrased, still perplex perfectionists who don't understand the impossibility of avoiding sin completely, and so do not wish to take upon themselves such a responsibility while making a baptismal covenant.

This probably explains the ardent desire of the younger generation of Slavic Baptist theologians to interpret the word *epirotema* in the sense of a plea or a prayer and not in the covenantal sense of agreeing with the stipulations of the covenant. Their active fight is quite understandable, but it is directed rather against an incorrect interpretation of the phrase "the pledge of a good conscience" which is perceived as a promise of sinlessness. But, in fact, the pledge to have a good conscience is a promise to be sensitive to sin, to understand it, to react against it, and to recognize its manifestations. Using modern terminology, it is a promise to have an instrument which easily recognizes sin, but not a promise never to sin. Therefore, the reaction to the distortion of an understanding of baptism often leads to the opposite reaction, that of a complete rejection of a covenantal idea and sometimes of baptism itself.

Death and Resurrection: Baptism as the Unity with Christ

Despite the fact that on the theological level most Baptists reject all the elements of sacramentalism in water-baptism, almost all of them understand baptism as the unification with Christ in his death and resurrection, and describe the nature of baptism in terms of the unity with Christ. This can be seen already in the earliest confession of faith by John Smyth, written in 1609. Article 14 of his *Short Confession of Faith* states "That baptism is the external sign of the remission of sins of dying and of being made alive, and therefore does not belong to infants."[50] A similar statement can be found in Article 14 of Thomas Helwys' *A Declaration of Faith* (1611).[51] The claim that from the perspective of the one being baptized baptism is a sign of the unification with the death and resurrection of Christ is repeated in chapter XXVIII of the General Baptists' *Orthodox Creed* written in 1678,[52] and other widely accepted

---

[49] Ivanov, *Guide for the Preparation*, 35–36.

[50] Lumpkin, ed., *Baptist Confessions*, 101.

[51] Lumpkin, ed., *Baptist Confessions*, 120.

[52] Lumpkin, ed., *Baptist Confessions*, 317.

early confessions. The Particular Baptists' *Second London Confession* of 1677 and 1688 states in chapter XXIX that baptism is "a sign of his fellowship with him (Christ), in his death and resurrection."[53]

The earliest Slavic Baptist confessions of faith clearly state the same. For example, in the description of baptism in the petition to the Emperor written by Ivan Ryaboshapka and Mikhail Ratusnhy in 1871 it is declared that "baptism is a symbol of laying Christ in the tomb and of His resurrection which the Apostle Paul clearly proves. Rom. Ch.6, vv.4.5.8."[54] The doctrinal teaching of Ivan Kargel composed in 1913 for the second St Petersburg congregation, states that baptism is "a sign of burial and resurrection with Christ (Rom.6,2–4)."[55] The same thought is repeated almost word for word in *The Confession of Evangelical Christians* written by Ivan Prokhanov in 1910 (ch. 14), *The Confession of Baptists* of 1906 (ch. 8), and in *The Doctrinal Teaching of the ECB Union of 1985* (ch. 8). All of them refer to the words of the Apostle Paul in Romans 6.2–4, and should, as such, be considered as the main texts that explain the phenomenon of baptism.

The idea of baptism as unity with Christ raises several important theological issues. The first one is connected with the question of the meaning of the unity with Christ through his death and resurrection. In what sense should one understand the expression "in Christ" which is used so often? It is a physical reality? A metaphor? A synecdoche? A metonymy? Some other trope? Also, by what means can entering and abiding in Christ be accomplished?

The expressions "in Christ" and "with Christ" and their derivatives are frequently found in the New Testament (about eighty times), especially in the writings of Paul. Unity with Christ is a key topic for the Apostle, primarily in the area of soteriology. Jack Cottrell underlines that this idea is not only repeated many times in the Epistles of Paul but it also definitely states, for example, that "in Christ" alone people receive redemption and forgiveness of sins (Eph. 1.7; Col. 1.14), obtain the eternal life (Rom. 6.23; 1 John 5.11), get enriched "in all utterance and in all knowledge" (1 Cor. 1.5), become heirs of eternal riches (Eph. 1.11).[56] It is impossible to interpret these statements literally as a physical immersion of one personality into another. Clearly, they are stylistic figures of speech which reflect reality, yet it is difficult to determine to which class of utterances this expression belongs.

---

[53] Lumpkin, ed., *Baptist Confessions*, 291.

[54] Zhabotinskiy, "Petition of Ivan Ryaboshapka," 134–36.

[55] Kargel, *Short Exposition*, 8.

[56] Cottrell, *Baptism*, 80.

James Dunn believes that the expressions like "immersion into Christ, into his death, and resurrection" are nothing more than metaphors.[57] Usually metaphor is understood to be a word or a phrase which transfers the meaning from one concept to another on the basis of well-established similarity existing between them. Biblical language is filled with metaphors with the help of which the attempt is made to explain the spiritual phenomena on the basis of their similarity with material ones. For example, Christ said, "You are the salt of the earth" implying that his disciples should have certain qualities of salt: just like salt prevents the rotting process, the disciples of Jesus need to restrain evil in the society where they live. Many researchers have analyzed the New Testament language from the perspective of its use of figures of speech.[58] Studying the parables of Jesus, Stephen Wright has shown how many various rhetorical figures and tropes are used in the biblical text.[59] He points to metonymy, synecdoche, irony, among many others, which often cross and overlap. Therefore, a final conclusion about the metaphorical nature of the expression "in Christ" seems to be an oversimplification.

Most exegetes criticize Dunn's understanding of the metaphorical nature of the expression "in Christ."[60] For example, Anthony R. Cross analyzed his arguments carefully and in great detail and showed their groundlessness.[61] He pointed out that in fact the descriptions and arguments used by Dunn in his explanation of the phrase "baptized into the death and resurrection of Christ" do not prove the metaphorical nature of the expression "in Christ," but instead they show it to be a *synecdoche*. This is the kind of trope used by a speaker when he sometimes consciously, but more often subconsciously, names a part while implying the whole, so the listener, in his turn, replaces the part taking it for the whole. For example, Christ proposes to pray for "daily bread" meaning not just bread as such but food in general. Another example of a synecdoche would be talking about the whole as about a part like in the phrase "the whole Judean countryside" went out to him. It is clear that not each and every inhabitant of Judea went out, but this synecdoche emotionally and expressively presents the idea of a multitude.

Unlike metaphor, synecdoche as a particular case of metonymy is based on the substitution of words by contiguity (the word "cup" is used instead of "wine", that is, its contents), while metaphor is based on the substitution of

---

[57] Dunn, *Baptism in the Holy Spirit*, 112.

[58] E.g., see Naboka, "On the Role of Tropes," 99–106.

[59] Wright, *Voice of Jesus*.

[60] Lars Hartman writes that "Dunn . . . is virtually alone in regarding 'baptise' as a metaphor here." Hartman, *"Into the Name of the Lord Jesus,"* 55 n.7. A similar statement is made by McDonnell and Montague, *Christian Initiation*, 42.

[61] Cross, *Recovering the Evangelical Sacrament*, 136–53.

words by formal similarity (face of a man and face of the earth). Thus, synecdoche differs from metaphor because the former is characterized by a greater reality of the substituted words. It is based on the transfer of a quality from one object to another on the grounds of its real logical connection. Cross argues that New Testament descriptions of baptism in its connection with the immersion into Christ has all the characteristics of synecdoche and not metaphor. He points out that in this case the whole—to become a Christian, to unite with Christ—is substituted with a part, that is, baptism.[62] If baptism is a synecdoche, and not a metaphor that points at the process of uniting with Christ, it requires the establishment of a much stronger connection between the designated phenomena than a metaphor would. This is contiguity by objective connection between the named phenomena and not by their external similarity. This leads to the conclusion that baptism in Christ is connected with water-baptism based on reality and not on external similarity.

The concept of being united with Christ and living with him usually implies two aspects: a pure personality aspect, as a mystical unity of two personalities, and a corporate one, as joining the body of Christ, the church.

In all Christian mystical traditions the personality aspect of abiding in Christ can be expressed differently, but its essence lies in special technologies which allow us to identify and find ourselves in the Supreme Being. In order to receive that, a Christian is usually offered to realize himself in one of the four areas: *asceticism*—through various methods of prayer, spiritual meditation, contemplation, and the like; *imitation*—when one is required to have the same feelings, desires, incentives, and motives that Jesus has; *morality*—to lead a life based on the same ethical system of values that Jesus led (such as peacemaking, all-forgiveness, meekness); *behavior*—to act like he did according to the Golden Rule and the commandment to love God and neighbor.

The second aspect of unity with Christ is a corporate one. It implies joining his body, the church. To enter Christ means not only to achieve unity with him personally (I and the Lord), but also corporately (I with others and the Lord). To unite with Christ means to enter his body, to become a member of his organism, to be nourished by his Spirit, to interact with other members of this organism. In 1 Corinthians 15.18–22, the Apostle Paul contrasts the life in Adam and the life in Christ. This is a typical double synecdoche: while saying "in Adam" (a concrete personality, a part of the whole humankind) the Apostle points at existence in a regular human society (the whole). A human being can become a member of this society at his first birth. In this case, each member of this society has not only a metaphorical connection by similarity with the first human being—Adam—but also a genetic one by origin, since the whole of humanity at some point was in the "loins of Adam" as the holy

---

[62] Cross, *Recovering the Evangelical Sacrament*, 76. The same thought is expressed in Schreiner, "Baptism in the Epistles," 75 n.26.

scriptures say. According to the Apostle, it is in the same way that the unity "in Christ" is formed: the concrete personality of Jesus, a teacher from Nazareth, stands for the whole phenomenon of the God–man with the head and the body which consists of many members, that is, concrete Christians connected by "every supporting ligament" (Eph. 4.16) with each other and with the head, Christ. In this case the connection is established not only by similarity, but more organically—by the blood shed by the Son of God.

Yakov Vins, a well-known teacher and missionary in the Slavic Baptist Brotherhood, explained Baptist principles to the young people in these terms: "Baptism is also an outward expression of an inner spiritual experience of a believer. The immersion of a believer into the water shows that he has died spiritually and now he is being buried for the world and sin just like Jesus Christ died and was buried. His coming out of the water indicates his renewed life which he now lives by the power of resurrection of the Lord Jesus Christ (Col. 2.12–13)."[63] This reasoning raises an important question: does somebody enter Christ through baptism, or is baptism a reflection of the process of uniting with Christ which happens earlier, or is baptism the concluding part of this process (which is also possible)?

The question of the correlation in time of spiritual processes and visible ritual actions are evidently secondary, the most important, and most controversial one in the Eastern European Baptist theology of baptism, is usually formulated in terms of what is the interrelation between water-baptism and baptism by Spirit? There are many different answers to this question. As many authors have noted, the connection between two kinds of baptism became the topic of passionate debates, although the tradition of early English Baptists clearly and unequivocally connects these two baptisms giving the reason to perceive baptism holistically. Article 30 of *The Short Catechism* of 1610, written by the first Baptist congregation in Amsterdam, states

> The whole dealing in the outward visible baptism of water, setteth before the eyes, witnesseth and signifieth, the Lord Jesus doth inwardly baptize the repentant, faithful man, in the laver of regeneration and renewing of the Holy Ghost, washing the soul from all pollution and sin, by the virtue and merit of his bloodshed; and by the power and working of the Holy Ghost, the true, heavenly, spiritual, living Water, cleanseth the inward evil of the soul, and maketh it heavenly, spiritual, and living, in true righteousness or goodness.[64]

These differences in understanding the expression "baptism by the Holy Spirit" (βαπτίζειν ἐν πνεύματι ἁγίω) becomes the biblical and theological foundation for separating or connecting water-baptism and spiritual-baptism. This expression is used seven times in the New Testament (Matt. 3.11; Mark

---

[63] Vins, *Our Baptist Principles*, 27–28.

[64] Lumpkin, ed., *Baptist Confessions*, 110.

1.8; Luke 3.16; John 1.33; Acts 1.5; 11.16; and 1 Cor. 12.13) and it is interpreted differently by different Evangelical groups. Its detailed analysis in the Slavic context can be found in our article included in the *Slavic Bible Commentary*, where it states

> The meaning of the expression largely depends on how the Greek preposition "en" is understood, and the meaning of the preposition varies due to the context. Some read this phrase as "baptism into the Holy Spirit", i.e., the Spirit is the One into whom people are baptized (get immersed) . . . Another understanding of this phrase had been proposed in the Synodal translation long before the discussion on the topic started in the Evangelical circles: "baptism by the Holy Spirit", i.e., by Him and not into the Holy Spirit (into Him).[65]

The most heated debates in the post-Soviet territory have been about the words of the Apostle Paul which supplement the statement by John the Baptist, "we were all baptized by one Spirit into one body" (1 Cor. 12.13). The understanding which presumes that one should read not "by the Spirit" (instrumental case) but "into the Spirit" is advocated by a well-known Pentecostal theologian, Thomas Wespetal,[66] while the instrumental understanding of the preposition έν in the sense of "by the Spirit" (instrumental case) is characteristic of the Baptist theology which keeps the Synodal interpretation of all the baptismal texts presenting baptism as performed by the Holy Spirit into the body of Christ (1 Cor. 12.13).[67] It implies the unity of the personal, spiritual conversion and corporate aspect of joining the universal church through water-baptism.

Analyzing the views of the leading theologians on the connection between water-baptism and spiritual-baptism, Anthony R. Cross shows the arguments of George R. Beasley-Murray, the most ardent advocate of this connection, and the ones of James Dunn and Gordon Fee who reject this connection. He then concludes,

> It is difficult to accept that 1 Cor. 12.13, which refers to Christian initiation in which water-baptism is an essential component (cf. Acts 2.38), excludes any reference to water-baptism. While it is not necessary to reject the metaphorical (in the broadest sense) application of the reference to baptism, recognition that

---

[65] Sannikov, "Baptism by the Holy Spirit," 1390–91.

[66] Wespetal, *Word on God*, 1423–33.

[67] The discussion on the baptism by the Holy Spirit as the holistic or second experience is not only characteristic of Slavic theology, but is very common in the Evangelical world. Thus, the two of the most famous British theologians of twentieth century, John Stott and Martyn Lloyd-Jones, held opposing views on the subject. See the analysis of their theological stands in the article O'Donnell, "Two Opposing Views on Baptism," 311–36.

"baptism" is here an example of synecdoche (which is the more precise term than metonymy) is strongly suggestive that the referent is to both Spirit- and water-baptism and the rest of the conversion-initiation process.[68]

An important element in this discussion is an attempt to understand correctly Luke's narrative which describe the cases of water-baptism in the Book of Acts. These descriptions irrefutably confirm that there are examples of both water-baptism taking place before the spiritual one (the story of the Samaritans in Acts 8.5–17) and of it taking place after the spiritual one (the story of Cornelius in Acts 10). There are also numerous examples of water-baptism taking place at the same time as the spiritual one—the conversion of 3,000 people on the Day of Pentecost (Acts 2.37–41); baptism of the Ethiopian eunuch (Acts 8.28–39); the believers in Ephesus (Acts 19.1–5).

Thus, although the evidence from the apostolic period suggests that it is statistically more plausible that water-baptism and spiritual-baptism should happen at the same time, we cannot see a univocal interrelation between these two phenomena. God is not bound by theological reasoning and he acts freely depending on historical and cultural circumstances, the state of faith of the people being baptized, and many other factors.[69] Paul Fiddes warns that we should be careful when we try to connect unequivocally the spiritual-baptism and the "completion of initiation" in water-baptism. He refers to Karl Barth who, when speaking about baptism, emphasizes that the Spirit has many various methods to commence and finish his work in people. Fiddes continues, "We may say that there are different comings of the Spirit appropriate to various stages of the process of initiation, as well as to the whole life-long journey of Christian growth."[70]

Therefore, with the right course of all the spiritual processes water-baptism must reflect and focus spiritual-baptism although in reality many different variations are possible.

The strength of this understanding is its deep rooting in New Testament imagery, and especially in the theology of the Apostle Paul. The literal and direct interpretation of such biblical texts as "baptized in Christ," "clothed with Christ," and many phrases with the words "in Christ" or "in him," more naturally suggests the unity of spiritual and physical baptism than their fundamental separation. The narratives of the Book of Acts in most cases demonstrate that spiritual-baptism, regardless of attributes which Luke ascribes to it (joy, tongues of fire, new tongues) takes place simultaneously with water-baptism, although, of course, Christ who baptizes with the Spirit

---

[68] Cross, "Spirit-and Water-Baptism," 147–48.

[69] See more about the reasons for this divergence of water-baptism and spiritual-baptism in Sannikov, *Baptism by the Spirit*, 13–14.

[70] Fiddes, *Tracks and Traces*, 149.

does so based on the faith of the recipient and not on the external ritual. Therefore, it can take place before water-baptism or after it, and sometimes it does not happen at all, if faith is absent, but is there only when there is the desire to become a Christian.

It is also important to note that connecting water-baptism with joining the body of Christ, the scriptures point at the broad ecclesiological perspective. At that moment a recipient joins not only a concrete local church and the invisible body of Christ, but also the whole Christian community. In other words, when a Christian becomes a member of the local community, they become a member of all Christ's family in the sense that he understands it. Objectively a baptized person becomes a member of the pilgrim church of those who still remain on earth, and also of the triumphant church, which consists of those who have already gone over to eternity. Yet subjectively a baptized person unites with his own congregation and with the other ones, and in a more real sense—with concrete people from different geographically distant churches which he perceives as his brothers and sisters, the same members of the body of Christ as he is. This helps him get confidence and support on a broader scale.

Regarding water-baptism as the concluding stage of the process of conversion, which is completed with immersion into Christ and resurrection to new life, Christians obtain the external sign confirming the spiritual process. It reduces the risk of focusing on the signs, miracles, emotional experiences, and helps concentrate on Christ and growth in sanctification. It means less danger of getting lost and making a mistake in search for an additional experience which often happens to those who look for signs and miracles to affirm their life in Christ and in the Holy Spirit, because this kind of searching can find an emotionalism which replaces spirituality. At the same time, the tendency of connecting water-baptism and the spiritual one has many weaknesses. Stating that the spiritual-baptism is confirmed by the water one should always remind us that the opposite cannot be maintained. In other words, water-baptism does not necessarily confirm the spiritual one. As has already been pointed out, the connection between the two depends on the faith of the recipient. Therefore, in this case, the inverse rule is not equivalent to the direct one. However, in practice many people tend to comfort themselves with the thought that they have received water-baptism and so have got immersed into Christ. Moreover, during the baptism ceremony the choir usually sings that "Those who baptize in the name of Christ, clothe themselves with Christ," and the preachers give sermons on Romans 6. This often leads to formalism in the church life as well as to ritual satisfaction and absence of the fullness and joy of the spiritual life.

The combination of spiritual and emotional experiences of union with Christ and the act of water-baptism gives joy and an emotional climax, but this is a one-time splash which is often followed by a prolonged period of complacency. When renewal and freshness in one's personal relationship with

Christ, which testify to abiding in him, are absent, it makes the life in Christ defective and forces us to look for an emotional support instead of a spiritual one. This is another weakness of such an understanding.

Sign of Grace: Baptism as a Means of Grace

A classical Baptist doctrine points at water-baptism as one of the means of grace. The confession of faith of Christian Baptists of 1906, written by V.G. Pavlov, dedicates the whole unit (VI) to the means of grace and their ordering, stating that these are not common human institutions, but God's establishments and their order is unchangeable. The first of these means of salvation is the word of God and the second one baptism.[71] The same point is made in the concise doctrinal teaching of Evangelical Christians composed by M.P. Friesen and mentioned in the court case of E. Grositskaya in Kiev in 1903. Heavily dependent on Oncken's confession of faith, this teaching being was proposed by Prokhanov at the Odessa Congress of Evangelical Christians in 1908, and then published in 1909 by the Sevastopol congregation. It shows that this understanding clearly satisfied not only Baptists but Evangelical Christians as well despite the fact that neither in Prokhanov's confession nor in the confession by Kargel, which is similar, says anything about the gracious effect of baptism.

The Concise Doctrinal Teaching states that

> means of grace established by the Holy Scriptures through which the Holy Spirit acts in conversion and sanctification because of the redeeming sacrifice of Christ are the following: the Word of God (preaching) at conversion; the Word of God, holy baptism, and holy Lord's Supper for the believers in the fellowship of the Christ's Church. The prayer is inextricably connected with all these means of grace and with all the manifestations of the spiritual life of a Christian and the Church.[72]

In this text we can clearly see the division of the means of grace into two categories: 1) the means of saving grace—the word of God in the sense of preaching, which affects the heart of an unbelieving sinner; and 2) the means of sustaining grace for the members of the church, among which the first one is baptism.

The notion of baptism as a means of grace must appear rather strange to Slavic Evangelicals considering there anti-sacramentalism. Usually this group reject the understanding of Pedobaptists who believe that during the act (or ritual) of baptism grace is transmitted or performed. However, if we look more closely it becomes clear that, in fact, they reject an "automatic," or

---

[71] Sannikov, *History of Baptism*, 425.

[72] Anon., *Concise Doctrinal Teaching*, 4.

passive transmission of grace and not the grace itself, which functions
according to the faith of the person getting baptized.

Why is baptism called a means of grace? Does this definition contain the
connotation with a classic Augustinian notion of a sacrament as a visible act of
invisible grace? What does the 'graciousness' of baptism really imply?

These questions make us think of the understanding a phenomenon called
'grace.' Usually the idea of grace and graciousness is connected with the notion
of gift. This is a gracious, wonderful, undeserved, and unusual gift which
transcends all understanding and comes from above (2 Cor. 9.15). The word
χάρις has many nuances of meaning, and is one of the most frequently
encountered concepts in the New Testament. There are many ways to
describe grace, and most often it is defined by the instrumental language as a
general and special grace through which God acts in our world. It means that
general grace encompasses all the people and gives them mercies, while special
grace acts only to provide salvation.[73] In either case, it is some kind of means
existing apart from God.

Such a narrow instrumental understanding of grace, which is used to
systematize theological knowledge, can mislead us rather than clarify its
nature. Grace, even by the semantic meaning of the word, *is a gift, not a
givenness*. This gift is holistic because through it the Giver grants himself to
the world in the Persons of Jesus Christ and the Holy Spirit without any
reason, only by his love. When we talk about general grace for all people
which nurtures and warms everybody, restrains hatred, and prevents the Earth
from collapsing because of the all-devouring evil, we do not talk about it in a
greater or lesser degree than when we discuss the grace which saves a people,
brings them to Christ, and then leads them through life. This is the same
grace and the same God who, through Jesus Christ, disperses the grace among
all including (although in a different way) the saved ones.

It is incorrect to perceive grace only as an instrument or a given, that is,
something created by God but existing apart from him although being under
his control. In such a narrow sense grace is a given, simply a static reality
which becomes a fact at a certain moment. The real grace is of another nature.
It is a gift, not a givenness. It is connected with the living act of God as the
transcendent reality. God does not just act in the world through his grace—he
is in it. Grace and God himself are inseparable and indivisible. God presents
himself in his gift. He is both a gift and a Giver.

If one tries to present grace as a separate phenomenon existing apart from
God, it will turn into something different, which is of a lower order and is not
God. It runs a risk to turn into his likeness, into an idol. But, in fact, grace is
causa sui, that is, its own cause. No-one and nothing can make God give a gift
of grace, but he gives himself because it is his inner nature. In grace God is
present everywhere, but not as an object, and this is why it is invisible because

---

[73] See Hughes, "Grace," 479–82.

of its obviousness. Grace is not noticed and it is neglected, but without it life, space, time, and mere existence disappear.

Since grace always exists in the "presence–absence" dichotomy, it cannot be possessed or won, it cannot be owned as a thing or grasped as some phenomenon. It possesses a person, it grasps and wins him, it owns him. Therefore, no rites and rituals, even the most correct ones, are not able to hold grace. At the same time, it promises itself in some physical actions without being bound by them, but freely consenting to be present through them. In this sense baptism is a certain sign of grace, its mark, its feature, its token or, better to say, following the Platonic understanding, an imprint of a signet ring in wax. In fact, baptism as an imprint is a sign left by grace, which is in itself elusive.

Baptism as an imprint focused in time and space, or as a mark of invisible grace, gives the right place to the role of the church as a mediator which can only withhold the gift intended for a baptized person or fail to convey it to him, but it is not able to generate or produce this gift. In other words, the church's ministers who administer the rite of baptism can only be visibly present—and not always precisely—what grace is doing in the heart of the person being baptized. but that does not imply the low value of the mark of grace. Without a materialized imprint, grace, though obvious in its "presence-absence" dichotomy, does not become complete in a person. Since God uses the material world as an imprint or a mark of his creative, gracious power, he desires to see a person as a holistic creature who is fully sanctified, that is, when his spirit, soul, and body all have the stamp of the work of grace until "the coming of our Lord Jesus Christ" (1 Thess. 5.23).

Baptism as a gift in which in real time a baptized person receives the Giver and gives himself to the latter, is, in this sense, an encounter of God with a person. This is a mutual process of giving and receiving. This is not just a meeting of two business partners or negotiating sides, but rather a lovers' date. This is why Beasley-Murray called baptism a "trysting-place"[74] of the sinner with his Savior. But such a tryst happens only when both lovers have trust and love. God has loved each one from the beginning of the world, and he has given his only begotten Son to prove this love. but not everybody loves him in return. Since God gives himself completely to people and becomes open to them, he expects the same surrender and openness from them. Because of this we need to reflect theologically on the cases when during an act of baptism the person did not have a true love and faith in his heart, and so could not give her/himself up to God completely. Although the external ritual of baptism could have been performed correctly and by a rightfully appointed minister, a tryst has not taken place if the inner nature of a person was closed to grace. What is it, then, that baptism becomes a sign of if a person has not accepted the infinite Gift?

---

[74] Beasley-Murray, *Baptism in the New Testament*, 305.

John Stott studied baptism from three perspectives. 1) *Ex opere operato*—the approach which presupposes that grace is inevitably and implicitly conveyed by the power of the sacrament itself or of God's promise defining this sacrament. He shows that from the perspective of the nature of the church and the nature of grace described above, this view is completely unacceptable. 2) *The bare token*—the approach which implies that grace is in no way connected with baptism. Stott rejects this with the simple statement that, if baptism does not convey anything to the recipients, the Apostles would never have ascribed any effect to it. However, they did say, for example, "repent and be baptized, every one of you, in the name of Jesus Christ for the forgiveness of your sins" (e.g., Acts 2.38), that is, pointing out that baptism presupposes certain results. Thus, this view also does not reflect the biblical truth that, 3) *the sign of grace*—the understanding which Stott calls evangelical explaining its action the following way: "The third and evangelical view is that the sign not only signifies the gift, but seals or pledges it, and pledges it in such a way as to convey not indeed the gift itself, but a title to the gift—the baptized person receiving the gift (thus pledged to him) by faith, which may be before, during or after the administration of the sacrament."[75] In other words, from Stott's perspective, baptism conveys grace "in a way" yet it does not do it mechanically, but it entrusts a person with the so-called "title to the gift" and then, when a baptized person really acquires faith, he truly inherits blessings from the act of baptism.

Stott explains that, since at baptism people receive primarily the right to the gift and the ritual itself is only a sign, an imprint, or, in some way, a document (a certificate) confirming this right, then the reception of the gift and the reception of the right to it are not necessarily connected in time. If the person being baptized has a sincere faith at the moment of baptism and is capable of functioning in the eyes of the law (and so is able to be responsible for their actions), then in the act of baptism they receive the right and gift of grace—Jesus Christ himself. If they do not have the fullness of faith at the moment of baptism, but come to believe fully after the ritual and open their heart to all-penetrating grace, they do not get rebaptized but in a way they actually take possession of their right. In other words, the right to possess the gift they have received becomes real only at the moment of faith and surrender to the Giver. Similar arguments can be proposed in the case of faith that comes before baptism. If a person has a real encounter with the Giver before water-baptism and they have already surrendered to the grace of God, they have become a true possessor of the gift before they receive a legal document giving them the right to own this treasure. Thus, they receive later the title to the gift which they have acquired earlier and, in this way, the holistic process is completed.

---

[75] Stott, "Evangelical Doctrine of Baptism," 51

Such an understanding of baptism as a material sign or an imprint of grace that captures the legislative meaning and legally confirms the relationships of the Giver with the receiver explains the idea of one and non-repeated baptism even in the situation when a person insults grace by their sinful behavior and turn away from the Giver of mercy in their words and deeds. Unity with Christ confirmed by water-baptism is unbreakable. This is why the mainstream of early Christian congregations accepted back even the apostates who had been guilty of idolatry and then repented without rebaptizing them although it led to schisms and discussions that lasted for years.

The image of baptism as a legal, juridical act signifying some spiritual event was often used by Slavic Baptists during the Soviet era. Thus, Nikolay Khrapov wrote,

> The legal power of the New Testament comes into effect only when we add our seal, i.e., baptism, to this document. The bride and the groom have fallen in love with each other. Their friends and families have prepared all they need in their life—the house and everything in it. They have officially registered their marriage at the appropriate place, but their life together starts only after the wedding ceremony when God and the Church confirm their vows. Baptism is a kind of wedding ceremony at which a Christian joins the Body of Christ, the Church.[76]

Alexander Dudnik in a way continued this, "What gives a person the right to call Christ his 'groom'? It is known that a young man can love a girl with all his heart and be loved in return and yet he cannot call her his bride until he officially proposes and she accepts. We call this act an engagement ... At baptism the Church and each of her members becomes engaged to Christ as their Heavenly Groom."[77]

Regarding baptism as a sign of grace allows to focus on two key concepts connected with this act—grace and imprint.

Since the main baptismal texts speak of the unity with the church—the body of Christ—and Christ himself, pointing at grace helps see Christ himself in this gift. All the mercies and blessings for the earthly and eternal life are only the results of union with Christ because both life and blessings are found in him alone and there is no life apart from him. Thus, the Giver of this gift reveals himself in the very gift, that is, in Christ. This is undoubtedly a very strong side—to see the gift and the Giver in the unity of the Son of God who unites with a believer and the latter unites with him as if doubling and strengthening this unity.

The idea of an imprint of grace helps understand and explain the time gap between faith and the act of baptism. If we see baptism as legalization of the

---

[76] Khrapov, *House of God*, §5.

[77] Dudnik, *Elementary Truths*, 32–33.

reception of the gift, that is, as obtaining a certain deed to the gift (title), then there comes an opportunity to explain theologically one unrepeatable baptism of which the Apostle Paul writes in Ephesians 4.5. Baptism gives the right to own the gift, but one can only take actual possession of it if they fulfill all the conditions, and most importantly, if they have faith and inward consent to the stipulations for unity with Christ.

The explanation of water-baptism with the help of the sign or imprint of grace also has certain weaknesses. The main one is the possibility of the illusory possession of grace on the basis of the existing sign. In other words, there is a danger that we can mistakenly think that the process of union with Christ is complete because the act of water-baptism took place. It creates the foundation for the idea of *ex opere operato*.

Another weakness of understanding grace in baptism as a sign is a purely instrumental perception of grace as of some acting power which is only an instrument in God's hands. Such an understanding makes the key event of baptism—encounter with Christ—fade into the background and become overlooked. Then it seems that at baptism people simply receive something from God instead of experiencing a mysterious encounter with him.

Proclamation of the Word: Baptism as a Confession of Faith

In his famous sermon on *Baptismal Regeneration*, preached on 5 June 1864 in London, Charles Haddon Spurgeon harshly criticized the sacramentalization of baptism and its separation from faith, saying, "baptism is the avowal of faith; the man was Christ's soldier, but now in baptism he puts on his regimentals ... It is the avowal of his faith."[78] *The First London Baptist Confession* of 1644 states in Article XXXIX "That Baptism is an Ordinance of the new Testament, given by Christ, to be dispensed onely upon persons professing faith, or that are Disciples, or taught, who upon a profession of faith, ought to be baptized."[79]

Confession of faith, open recognition—these attributes of baptism are practically standard in Baptist theology. In 1924, Yakov Yakovlevich Vins, a well-known Baptist missionary, published a brochure, *Our Baptist Principles*, which is still popular among Eastern European Baptists. In it he writes, "In one word, baptism means publicly confessing the Lord Jesus Christ as one's personal Savior and willingly devoting oneself to serving God. It is impossible to express these spiritual experiences of a believer through a religious act or rite but only through a careful performance of baptism according to the New Testament teaching and example."[80]

---

[78] Spurgeon, *Baptismal Regeneration*, 40.

[79] Lumpkin, ed., *Baptist Confessions*, 167.

[80] Vins, *Our Baptist Principles*, 28.

These and similar statements are doubtlessly some kind of a carryover from the Anabaptist tradition, which emphasized primarily the public confession aspect of baptism. Balthasar Hubmaier, one of the most influential Anabaptist theologians, writes, "Water baptism . . . is an external and public testimony of the inward baptism of the Spirit, set forth by receiving water. By this not only are sins confessed, but also faith in their pardon, by the death and resurrection of our Lord Jesus Christ, is declared before all men."[81] The idea that at baptism a person's sin is publicly admitted and their faith is confessed is very important for the Baptist interpretation of the New Testament because it is based on Paul's statement, "If you declare with your mouth, 'Jesus is Lord,' and believe in your heart that God raised him from the dead, you will be saved" (Rom. 10.9).

First of all, a confession of faith should be personal. Also, from the perspective of Baptist teaching, faith should be expressed in external actions—both words and deeds. It cannot be a corporate action or simply a conviction, a mental process or a paradigm. The faith which is not expressed in the outer material world is not faith at all, with the exception of some extreme situations. However, one should keep in mind that faith is primarily an inward and not an outward phenomenon. In other words, faith originates in the spiritual side of a person, but it cannot remain in it exclusively. Eastern European Baptists flatly reject Luther's understanding that external rites can give birth to faith,[82] although they admit that external confession, works of faith, and church establishments strengthen and enrich faith making it more steadfast and confident. Thus, despite the Zwinglian influence which separates the internal and external worlds, at baptism these two realities become closely connected with each other. Faith and its confession must coexist in harmony and become personalized for each baptized person.

A confession of faith should be public. It is believed that baptism needs to be a testimony before the society and the spiritual world. Alexander Dudnik, a well-known Baptist preacher, recollects his baptism:

On the day of my baptism there were multitudes of people at the banks of the river. The choir was singing, "All of you who got baptized into Christ, clothed yourselves with Christ!" The sun was shining brightly as if it too was happy because of my engagement with the Savior. And it seems that in the cloudless

---

[81] Vedder, *Balthasar Hubmaier,* 202.

[82] There are still many discussions among the Baptists as to how faith comes to life. The Particular Baptists usually emphasize that faith is the gift of God, and the General Baptists primarily point out that "faith comes from hearing the message, and the message is heard through the word about Christ" (Rom. 10.17).

sky He was standing Himself with the myriads of His holy angels and He was looking tenderly at me while accepting my sacred vow."[83]

The idea that baptism is a confession not only before the people but also before the spiritual world is also often found in the descriptions of water-baptism written by various authors from the former Soviet Union.

What does a person confess at baptism? The so-called *Standard Confession*, Article XI, explains that the candidates for baptism can be "such only of them, as profess *repentance towards God, and faith towards our Lord Jesus Christ.*"[84] In other words, baptism as a testimony is connected with repentance and pointing at Jesus Christ. Anthony R. Cross states that from the beginning of the twentieth century there has been a "significant move within the denomination to see baptism not only as an 'acted parable', but as an 'acted creed'."[85] He quotes Gilbert Laws, "'When a man goes down into the solemn waters to be buried with Christ by baptism, and thence is raised in the power of a new life, what a tremendous creed he has professed!'"[86] In other words, the confession of faith includes not only the words of the baptized and the baptizing person, but the act of baptism itself, although the oral confession of faith is considered the primary and obligatory one. This is why it is more appropriate to speak not of baptism "based on faith" but of baptism *based on a confession of faith*.

The expression "baptism based on faith" is rather inclusive and theoretically it includes almost all the advocates of infant baptism. On the theological level the Lutherans, Reformed, Catholics, and Orthodox would not deny the term "baptism based on faith." They differ from Baptists in the definition of the time and phenomenon of faith itself, but not in the concept of baptism based on faith. The uniqueness of the Baptist understanding lies in the term *credobaptism*, that is, baptism based on a confession of faith that takes place at baptism itself. This is something that no advocate of pedobaptism can accept.

An important aspect of understanding credobaptism is the performative nature of speech acts used during the rite. It means that the words employed in the context of the solemn ceremony of baptism themselves produce an action without the help of other instruments. In the old confessions of faith we can often find a concept of the "visible word" or "visible speech." For example, in Article 74 of *The Propositions and Conclusions about the True Christian Religion*, published in 1612–14, it says that "the sacraments have the same use that the word hath; that they are a visible word, and that they teach

---

[83] Dudnik, *Elementary Truths*, 34.

[84] Lumpkin, ed., *Baptist Confessions*, 228 (italics original).

[85] Cross, *Baptism and the Baptists*, 31.

[86] Cross, *Baptism and the Baptists*, 32.

to the eye of them that understand as the word teacheth the ears of them that have ears to hear."[87]

Baptists believe that the words pronounced at the rite of baptism have the same effect as the words of vows, official ceremonies of engagement, weddings, or legal declarations. It is significant that Tertullian, using the word "sacrament," meant a military vow or an oath.[88] When a baptized person accepts the words of a baptizer by faith, and affirms them with a loud "Amen," they are introduced into a new spiritual reality of the one who is now legally bound to Christ or, according to Spurgeon, has become an official warrior of Christ. It is important to note that the words pronounced must be heard. This is why an argument against pedobaptism in the old confession of 1612–14 states that "the word teacheth the ears of them that have ears to hear," and if infants are not able to hear the word, it will not have an effect on them.

Can we really regard the baptismal formula, "I baptize you in the name of the Father, and the Son, and the Holy Spirit," as anything other than performative? The words of the baptismal formula which a minister utters, echo the words of Christ: "'Go and make disciples of all nations, baptizing them in the name of the Father and of the Son and of the Holy Spirit . . . And surely I am with you always, to the very end of the age'" (Matt. 28.19–20). He remains with his people just as he has promised in each act of baptism. Outwardly the immersion into water takes place, but, in fact, baptism is realized through the performative speech of a baptizer which acts by its being pronounced, if, of course, the context and the circumstances are right. In this case, there is no mediator between the word and the act, no mediating function is present. The words make an effect directly and not indirectly through some instruments.

The strong side of such an understanding is, first of all, that it presupposes repentance as confession of a sinful lifestyle and the rejection of this lifestyle. In this case a person ready to be baptized realizes that they have to leave behind the former way of life, old habits, behaviors, and words. Baptism becomes a visible sign of turning from sin to holiness.

Metanoia begins with repentance and finishes with baptism. This accounts for the radicalism of baptism and understanding the irrevocability of the change. Before a person is baptized, even if they have repented and confessed their sins, they can still keep some of their old habits and elements of their old lifestyle. but they approach baptism with the realization of the irrevocability of their decision. They must firmly believe that there is no going back. It is probable that such an understanding was present in Ante-Nicene Christianity, and it was this understanding that made the candidates for baptism postpone

---

[87] Lumpkin, ed., *Baptist Confessions*, 138.

[88] Tertullian, *Ad martyras*, 3.

this important step indefinitely, sometimes until the time of death, the classic example of which is the Emperor Constantine.

The congregations themselves also were not in a hurry to baptize neophytes, testing the firmness of their decision sometimes for many years. Thus, the act of baptism became a boundary which divided the old from the new, and this understanding tested the resoluteness of the neophytes. It is well-known that a church only recognized conversion to Christianity after a person was baptized. It is especially evident in the Islamic context. It is after baptism, and not after repentance, that persecution becomes relentless. And if a candidate for baptism understands the consequences of their action, they must make a final and courageous decision to be baptized.

A clear, courageous, and public declaration of the decision to join the church and Christ unquestionably has a missionary aspect in it. To the people closest to a neophyte it becomes a kind of witness of their radical break with the past, and of the beginning of a new life. It also serves as a certain example for those who are interested in Christianity.

Another very strong side of understanding baptism as a confession is the emphasis of a confessional creed on Christ and the fundamental truths of Christianity. It makes faith more focused, defining faith's rightful object. It also teaches someone to formulate their faith and become ready to explain it to society, that is, "to give the reason for the hope that you have" (1 Pet. 3.15).

A weakness of understanding baptism as a confession of faith lies in the danger of substituting faith itself with its confession. Indeed, a confession of faith is an outward action which can be performed (intentionally or unintentionally) without sufficient spiritual grounds. Thus, both a society and a church community can be misled, and this sometimes happens in practice. However, such dangers and potential mistakes should not minimize the meaningfulness of faith at the act of baptism.

Sometimes a weak faith is not ready for open confession, and a neophyte needs to have a period of spiritual growth. In such a case a hasty or premature confession of faith at the act of baptism can lead to trials which a newly baptized person is not able to bear. This is why baptism should take place under serious supervision.

Humble Acceptance: Baptism as an Act of Obedience

Most Baptist descriptions of baptism begin with the declaration "Baptism is an Ordinance of the new Testament, given by Christ."[89] The confession of 1651, which is called *The Faith and Practise of Thirty Congregations*, calls baptism "Action of obedience" in Article 49 and states: that "for men to refuse

---

[89] See *The First London Confession* (1644), Article XXXIX; *Second London Confession* (1677), Article XXIX; *The Orthodox Creed* (1679), Article XXVIII; and others. See Lumpkin, ed., *Baptist Confessions, passim*.

it, they are said to reject the counsel of God against themselves."[90] In Eastern European churches one can often hear that "We receive baptism because Jesus has commanded it." This is the simplest explanation of baptism on the church level and often it is a quite satisfactory answer to the question about the meaning and necessity of baptism. The confession of faith of the Ukrainian Council of Evangelical Christian Baptists which was accepted in 2006 begins the chapter entitled "Baptism by Faith" with the statement, "We believe that baptism is a commandment of our Lord Jesus Christ."[91] The corresponding chapter of *The Doctrinal Teaching of Evangelical Christian Baptists* of 1985 begins with the same words.[92]

The description of baptism as the fulfilment of the Lord's commandment explains why the Baptists use the neutral term "ordinance" instead of "sacrament," which has an obvious connotation of understanding baptism in Catholicism, Orthodoxy, and the Magisterial Reformation. The explanation of baptism as an act of obedience is, first of all, connected with a general Baptist conception of the necessity strictly to obey the letter of the New Testament and, secondly, with the imitation of the actions of Christ himself. Jesus obediently received baptism from John although it was not necessary for him to repent. John was trying to stop him but the phrase "'it is proper for us to fulfill all righteousness'" (Matt. 3.15) is a key one for inducing us to imitate this act in all ages. In other words, the example of Jesus who participated in the ritual without explaining its purpose, is an important foundation of Baptist practice. Although, according to many Baptist ministers, baptism is not the most important commandment of the ones that Jesus has left for us, it should be fulfilled literally because he gave a clear instruction about it (Matt. 28.19).

It is well-known that the discussion on the necessity of the literal fulfilment of this commandment was a heated one for Transcaucasian Baptists who primarily came from Molokan congregations. N. Lopukhin spoke about the Molokans emotionally in the journal, *Baptist*, in 1909:

> It seems exceedingly strange that those who call themselves believers fight against baptism so openly and fiercely. To prove that they are right they use all kinds of arguments, including uselessness of baptism, its revocation together with circumcision, the suggestion that it is not revealed to them yet, and such other nonsense . . . The Holy Spirit induces believers and prompts them to fulfil the entire will of God, all the commandments of Christ of which the first one is baptism.[93]

---

[90] Lumpkin, ed., *Baptist Confessions*, 182.

[91] AUEBC, *Confession of Faith of Evangelical Christian Baptists*, 16.

[92] Sannikov, *History of Baptism*, 467.

[93] Lopukhin, "Why Shouldn't I Be Baptized?" 8.

The main argument in this discussion has almost always been the necessity to be baptized because it is a commandment of the Lord. A humble obedience shown in the willingness to fulfil a commandment of Christ seems very attractive, and it may satisfy a Christian at the very beginning of their spiritual life, but modern people do not always perceive it as a sufficient reason. If it was crucial to prove in the Baptist–Molokan discussion that baptism is a commandment instituted by Christ together with the other New Testament commandments, and so the disciples of Jesus cannot avoid fulfilling it, it is not enough in the new cultural and historical circumstances. The essence of this commandment needs to be explained. In fact, the statement that baptism is a commandment of God explains nothing, although it does answer the question of why one should be baptized. If such a statement does not have an informative continuation, it is not perceived as a proper response by the generation which has learned to ask questions instead of merely accepting ready-made answers. Therefore, as a rule, all the Baptist confessions of faith include the explanation of the essence of baptism following the statement that it is an institution of Christ.

Anthony R. Cross points out that "because baptism is an act of obedience, it is also an act of consecration, and has also been described as a badge or mark of Christian discipleship."[94] Referring to the opinion of many influential theologians he reminds us that one of the most significant inputs of the Baptist movement into the world treasury of Christianity is an insistence on putting into practice the idea of discipleship. A disciple is known obediently to fulfil what their teacher commands them to do even if the explanation is not given why it should be done. It is believed that in the times of the early church a follower of Jesus was most often called a "disciple" (*mathetes*). In any case this term and its derivatives are found more than 262 times in the New Testament. Discipleship presupposes the teacher–disciple relationship and, as Peter Penner has convincingly shown, the concept of "teaching" or "making a disciple" not only implies the giving and assimilation of information but also includes teaching right living and to practice this teaching.[95]

Baptism as a part of the call to discipleship is clearly expressed in the very commandment to baptize. Matthew wrote down the instruction of Jesus, "'Go and make disciples of all nations, baptizing them in the name of the Father and of the Son and of the Holy Spirit, and teaching them to obey everything I have commanded you'" (Matt. 28.19). These words remind us that Jesus is the only Teacher (cf. Matt. 23.9–10), and his followers are disciples in the strict sense of this word. They are supposed to know his teaching and keep it literally. Discipleship *per se* in the Judean and early Christian context primarily meant the fulfilment of everything that the teacher commanded, and not the

---

[94] Cross, *Baptism and the Baptists*, 39.

[95] Penner, *Teach All Nations*, 45–46.

study of his texts. It should be remembered that unlike the modern Guttenberg civilization, the ancient world not only relied heavily on oral tradition and the personal relationship between the teacher and their disciple, but also disdained the written tradition.[96] To follow the instructions of a teacher was the sacred responsibility of a disciple. According to Matthew's text, baptism is a part of the process of following Christ and getting the status of a disciple.

The Matthew 28.19 passage is not an easy one for an exegetical reconstruction and it allows for various interpretations which lead to differences in understanding the sequence of discipleship and baptism. When Daniel Wallace analyzes the adverbial participle in his advanced grammar course, he uses the text of the Great Commission as a controversial case of the use of such a participle. He points out that the first part of the phrase "'Go and make disciples'" is a common one for Matthew (cf. 2.8; 9.13; 11.4; 17.27; 26.6, etc.), and that "every time a participle of the verb *poreuomai* in aorist followed by the main verb in aorist (in the indicative or imperative mood) clearly expresses the concomitant adverbial."[97] According to him, it does not allow us to ascribe to this participle only the meaning of the tense, but it points at the concomitant action—to go and by this to make disciples of people.

The second difficult exegetical problem lies in the syntax of two other participles—*baptizing* and *teaching*—which are connected with the main verb "teach" (μαθητεύσατε—make disciples). Are these participles indirect ones which describe the method or mode of disciple-formation or do they coordinate the imperatives "baptizing and teaching" as those following in time the action "make disciples"? Wallace claims that both participles—βαπτίζοντες (baptizing) and διδάσκοντες (teaching)—"should not be considered the ones describing the concomitant adverbials. First of all, they do not have the structure which is common for such participles (they are in the present tense and they follow the main verb). Secondly, they obviously have the quite legitimate meaning as the participles of means, i.e., the means by which the disciples should produce disciples is baptism and then teaching."[98] In other words, from the syntactical perspective, as understood by Wallace, the means by which a person is made a disciple is, first of all, baptism and then teaching that helps him know the remaining commandments of Jesus.

---

[96] It is sufficient to remember the second part of *The Phaedrus* (*Dialogue*) of Plato in which Socrates demonstrates the limitations of any written text in comparison to the oral word.

[97] Wallace, *Greek Grammar beyond the Basics*, 645 (translated from the Russian version).

[98] Wallace, *Greek Grammar beyond the Basics*, 645.

Beasley-Murray supports this opinion from the theological perspective. He asks the question of how the process of disciple-making takes place and reasons that

> It might be considered as self-evident that disciples are made by the preaching of the gospel; that such as have become disciples are then baptized, and the baptized proceed to instruction; the two participles baptizing . . . teaching . . . successively follow the action of the main verb. Objection has been taken to this interpretation, however, for since the New Testament Epistles do not appear to reckon with the phenomenon of an unbaptized disciple, how can one become a disciple and then be baptized? Accordingly it is proposed that the participles describe the manner in which a disciple is made: the Church is commissioned to make disciples *by* baptizing men and putting them under instruction.[99]

The standard Baptist practice in our time is different: it starts with: 1) "go," that is, go on a mission instead of sitting around; then 2) the "make disciples" process follows through preaching Jesus and accepting Christ's sacrifice by faith; then 3) "teaching" through special courses and programs; then 4) "baptizing" by water-baptism; and 5) "teaching them to obey" all the commandments, constitutions, and rules of the New Testament. Everett Ferguson does not think that such an interpretation of the Great Commission is based on the style and text of Matthew, and neither does it correspond with the grammar. He writes, "while all the participles derive an imperatival force from the main verb, the initial participle is coordinate with the main verb ("go and make disciples") and the two participles subsequent to the verb are circumstantial, describing the means of making disciples, with the "teaching" accompanying the "baptizing.'"[100] In other words, Ferguson includes teaching and baptism in the process of the formation (making) of the disciples. However, there is no uniform exegetical and theological interpretation of this commandment, sometimes called the Great Commission. This is why it is also impossible to construct a unequivocal interpretation of the sequence of the actions which are to be performed so that people can become the disciples of Christ. Only one thing is sure—baptism is an integral component of this process regardless of interpretation.

The strongest side of such an understanding is an obedient, resigned, and literal acceptance of the words of Christ that testifies to the humility of mind and heart of the person to be baptized. In Christianity, meekness and humility have always been seen as the highest virtues which help accept by faith those regulations or norms the meaning of which is only partially or completely hidden.

---

[99] Beasley-Murray, *Baptism in the New Testament*, 88–89 (italics original).

[100] Ferguson, *Baptism in the Early Church*, 137.

Another strength of this understanding is the emphasis on the link between baptism and discipleship. This idea is very clearly expressed in the words of Christ in Matthew 28.19 regardless of whether teaching follows baptism or vice versa. A Christian cannot help being a disciple, and a disciple is one who is constantly learning while he remains a disciple. When they stop learning from the great Teacher, a Christian loses their high title of the follower of Christ. Becoming a disciple, a Christian establishes a personal contact with Jesus, the Teacher, and they have to find a coach who can help them understand and learn the lessons. Thus, perceiving baptism as a stage or a phase of discipleship leads to the correct understanding of the following commandments and develops a skill to fulfil them with humility.

Such an approach also has a certain weakness as the mindless fulfilment of a commandment deprives a person of initiative and, in fact, stunts the spiritual growth. Discipleship can easily deteriorate into dogmatism and quotation-mongering which lies in a thoughtless repetition of rubber stamps and patterns as some kind of incantation. Bible study can become a mechanical memorization of texts according to the method suggested by a mentor and, as a result, a person is able to recite all the necessary biblical passages, but is incapable of applying them to real-life situations. Thus, for such people the Bible remains an historical and not a real-life book while Christ is perceived simply as an historical personality and not as a living Teacher acting in their lives. Modern liberated people want to feel the life of Christ and understand him. They want to hear not only what they have to do, but also why they have to do it. And the people have the right to ask such questions because Christ does not need silent robots. Instead he wants thinking and feeling individuals who have an experience of spiritual life, and who are ready to act consciously and freely not because it is ordered from above, but because of their own inner desire motivated by love.

Another weakness of such an understanding is the absence of celebration and sublime emotional experience which is remembered forever. If baptism is simply an obligatory fulfilment of a commandment because the Lord says so and the New Testament teaches it, then, instead of a tremendous realization of the transition from death to life, instead of a spiritual and emotional transformation and union with Christ, baptism becomes just the first of many acts of discipleship. The dramatic sensation passes away, the perception of baptism as something truly connected with salvation disappears, and baptism is reduced to an act of pure obedience. A real drama is associated exclusively with repentance.

Such understanding diminishes the value of baptism pushing it to the periphery of the conversion process and makes a person forget the price that the first baptized Christians paid for this seemingly simple act of immersion in water. Probably one should recollect the blood and ashes of the fires, thousands of deaths and executions of brothers and sisters who gave their lives for accepting credo-water-baptism. The executioners of the sixteenth century put people to death not for the repentance and inner spiritual experience connected with their conversion to Christ, but for this visible and voluntary water-baptism. We are reminded of the drama of baptism by an emotional exclamation of Hubmaier who advocated water-baptism in a letter to Oecolampadius in January 1525, in which he asserts that "The inner work of the Spirit must, must, must be accompanied by visible ablution."[101]

Summary: Encounter as a Holistic Integrality

The different images described above are separate yet at the same time intersect, intensifying one another and setting one another off, without fusion meeting together at the encounter appointed by God and accepted by the person who has freely and consciously heard a divine call.

Baptism as a symbol and initiation, as promise and union with the death and resurrection of Christ, as a means of grace and confession of faith, and as obedience, is an event that has a temporal aspect. It is not a fact, although it is factual, rather it is an occurrence. It happens, it takes place, and, thus, it has a temporal component. It is a meeting that can be presented as a fact only when looked at from the future into the past and the words, feelings, and experiences of what happened are remembered. Therefore, the integrality of baptism includes all the images, "sewing" them together in such a way that it is impossible to find the seams and margins of each image, considering it from both a modal or temporal, dynamic perspective.

This integrated picture of baptism does not imply finiteness of the number of its parts. Employing other contexts and applying new lenses one can see not only the seven discussed above, but many other aspects of baptism. They can be divided and multiplied, but this will not injure their integrality because it becomes apparent in the event of the encounter of the spiritual and the material, and the images representing this encounter are simply gleams and facets of the mysterious and, in some way, incomprehensible fact and event. All of them become interconnected in the encounter and at the same time each of them, in its own way, reflects the organic integrality which appears as a re-ontologization of baptism when the purposefulness and life, that is, existential essence, are ascribed to it as to a system of various images. And this happens only when through a prism of each image the central event of baptism becomes visible—the encounter of God and a person in the presence of the church as a community of the faithful.

This encounter enlivens all the images of baptism and becomes their center. It provides baptism with an ontological form of existence and fits into the event the integrality of other church life phenomena, becoming a special landmark on the way of a Christian to the kingdom of God. Encounter is a point in space and time at which God and a person meet, and it turns baptism

---

[101] As cited in Rainbow, "Confessor Baptism," 205–6

into a life-changing event. Baptism as an encounter helps us "grasp" its components in a holistic way and describe them using correct, scholastically precise but, as it sometimes seems, excessively rational symbols. As the summary document of Baptist–Catholic dialogue states, "The sacraments/ ordinances are experiences of encounter with Christ that transform the lives of those who enter into these moments of worship by the presence and power of the Holy Spirit."[102] In other words, the sacrament of baptism is a teleologically organized whole which in all its parts presupposes the pursuit of the main goal—to change the life of the recipient during their encounter with God in the context of a congregation.

As we consider the integrality of baptism which consists of seven (or more) fractal parts/images, it is important to see baptism in a holistic picture of a higher level, that is, the place of baptism in the whole drama of salvation. As it has been pointed out above, discussions about baptism are most often based not on the understanding of its nature or its components, but on its place in a broader process of conversion to Christianity or in the formation of a Christian. Theological debates on what sequence the elements of the salvation process should follow start because people approach salvation systematically instead of doing it holistically. A systematic approach to salvation presupposes a strict order and hierarchical co-subordination of individual elements, while the holistic one does not concentrate on the order and implies a certain flexibility as it treats salvation phenomenologically.

Nowadays many Baptist theologians speak about the unity and phenomenological integrality of the process of conversion to Christianity. Thus, Robert Stein insists, in an expressive and image-bearing way, that "In the New Testament, conversion involves five integrally related components or aspects, all of which took place at the same time, usually on the same day. These five components are repentance, faith, and confession by the individual, regeneration, or the giving of the Holy Spirit by God, and baptism by representatives of the Christian community."[103] He demonstrates how in the New Testament these five different components led to one and the same result—salvation and justification. To the people of the first century they most often represented various ways of describing the same process of accepting Christianity.

The same integrality in understanding baptism is demonstrated by one of the first Caucasian Baptists, a prominent leader of the Baptist Union at the end of the nineteenth and beginning of the twentieth century, Vasily Vasilievich Ivanov-Klyshnikov. In 1911 he wrote,

---

[102] Commission on Doctrine and Unity of the Baptist World Alliance, "The Word of God in the Life of the Church," §85.

[103] Stein, "Baptism and Becoming a Christian," 6.

Now we are going to see the conditions for obtaining salvation and all the God's blessings through Christ the Savior. "Whoever believes and is baptized will be saved, but whoever does not believe will be condemned" (Mark 16:16). "Repent and be baptized, every one of you, in the name of Jesus Christ for the forgiveness of your sins. And you will receive the gift of the Holy Spirit" (Acts 2:38). Who wouldn't see in these passages the three necessary conditions—faith, repentance, and baptism—which are established by the Lord and without which it is unthinkable to obtain salvation, forgiveness of sin, and reception of the Holy Spirit?[104]

Vasily Ivanov-Klyshnikov emphasizes the three conditions for salvation—faith, repentance, and baptism. Stein points out five components, one which is water-baptism and the rest are repentance, faith, confession of sins, and gift of the Holy Spirit. Strictly speaking the number of the components of the holistic phenomenon of salvation can vary. It depends on the rational and subjective approach of the researcher. The way of emphasizing certain characteristics of a studied subject is brought into the research by the scholars themselves and it depends on the presuppositions, ideological settings, and denominational preferences of the latter.

Cross emphasizes the modern tendency (at least in the British Baptist Union) to change the language of the description of Christian life. Instead of discreet rational-subjectivist characteristics describing not the Christian life phenomenon itself but the facts interpreted by the authors of individual narratives (justification, faith, adoption) today's theologians try to present a more holistic perception of broad theological categories.[105] Such a holistic perception is probably the most accurate reflection of the New Testament descriptions although in real life the holistic process of conversion is always broken into individual temporal phases/states. Still, it has to be remembered that salvation has a double nature being both a state and a process. Therefore, the process of the formation of a true Christian should be considered, first of all, phenomenologically and not onto-theologically.

Salvation is a holistic phenomenon in which one can discern individual parts and components. Yet it is not possible to determine the only way to collocate them temporally. All the systematic theology textbooks try to put the components of salvation in a certain order and they fiercely advocate this order. Some say that Christianity starts with repentance which is followed by faith and baptism, the others put God's mysterious decree first and faith and repentance second. In the Orthodox and Catholic Churches, the first place is given to baptism followed by faith and obedience. but the main thought of modern Baptist sacramentology is that one should not try to determine the order of the components of salvation but take the latter as a whole.

---

[104] Ivanov-Klyshnikov, "On Baptism," 7.

[105] Cross, "One Baptism," 174–75.

Of course, in practice there is always an order of events, but it is not fixed. Some are like the Samaritans who were baptized and this was followed by the coming of the Spirit. The others have the experience of Cornelius—the Spirit comes first and then they get baptized. Still the others have only faith without any baptism like the thief crucified next to Christ. From the human perspective, salvation lies in experiencing all the main components of this drama, and the integrality is not destroyed if one of the parts is missing for some reason. The important thing is the encounter.

Bibliography

Anon. *Bratskiy Vestnik* (*Brotherly Herald*) 1 (1988) 73–95. [Из Жизни Поместных Церквей, *Братский Вестник* 1 (1988) 73–95.]

Anon. *Concise Doctrinal Teaching of Evangelical Christians Who Receive Water Baptism by Faith (sometimes called Baptists)*. Sevastopol: P.A. Kovalev, 1909. [*Краткое вероучение христиан евангельского исповедания, приемлющих водное крещение по вере, (именуемых иногда баптистами)*. Севастополь: П.А. Ковалев, 1909.]

Anon. "On the Life of the Local Churches." *Bratskiy Vestnik* (*Brotherly Herald*) 6 (1978) 60–68. [Из Жизни Поместных Церквей, *Братский Вестник* 6 (1978) 60–68.]

Beasley-Murray, George R. *Baptism in the New Testament*. Grand Rapids: Eerdmans, 1973.

Brewer, Brian C. "'Signs of the Covenant': The Development of Sacramental Thought in Baptist Circles." *Perspectives in Religious Studies* 36 (2009) 407–20.

Clark, Neville. *An Approach to the Theology of the Sacraments*. Naperville, IL: Alec R. Allenson, 1956.

Commission on Doctrine and Christian Unity Baptist World Alliance. "The Word of God in the Life of the Church. A Report of International Conversations between The Catholic Church and the Baptist World Alliance 2006–2010." Baptist World Alliance, 2013. http://bwanet.org/images/pdf/baptist-catholic-dialogue.pdf.

Colwell, John E. *Promise and Presence: An Exploration of Sacramental Theology*. Milton Keynes: Paternoster, 2005.

Cottrell, Jack. *Baptism: A Biblical Study*. Joplin, MO: College, 1989.

Cross, Anthony R. *Baptism and the Baptists: Theology and Practice in Twentieth-Century Britain*. Carlisle: Paternoster, 2000.

———. "'One Baptism' (Ephesians 4.5): A Challenge to the Church." In *Baptism, the New Testament and the Church: Historical and Contemporary Studies in Honour of R.E.O. White*, 173–209. Sheffield: Sheffield Academic, 1999.

———. *Recovering the Evangelical Sacrament: Baptisma Semper Reformandum*. Eugene, OR: Pickwick, 2012.

————. "Spirit-and Water-Baptism in 1 Corinthians 12.13." *Dimensions of Baptism: Biblical and Theological Studies*, 120–48. Sheffield: Sheffield Academic, 2002.

Cross, Anthony R., and Philip E Thompson, eds. *Baptist Sacramentalism.* Eugene, OR: Wipf and Stock, 2006.

————. *Baptist Sacramentalism 2.* Eugene, OR: Wipf and Stock, 2009.

Dudnik, Alexander. *The Elementary Truths of Christ's Teaching.* Volume 2. Makeevka: Svet Voskreseniya, 1997. [Александр Дудник, *Начатки учения Христа*, т. 2, Макеевка: Свет Воскресения, 1997.]

Dunn, James D.G. *Baptism in the Holy Spirit: A Re-Examination of the New Testament Teaching on the Gift of the Spirit in Relation to Pentecostalism Today.* Philadelphia: Westminster John Knox, 1970.

Educational Council of All-Ukrainian Council of Evangelical Baptist Churches. *Confession of Faith of Evangelical Christian Baptists and Practice of Christian Life and Ministry.* Kyiv: АСЕВС, 2000. [Учбова Рада ВСОЄХБ, *Визнання віри євангельських християн-баптистів та практіка християнського жіття і служіння*, Київ: ВСОЄХБ, 2000.]

Ferguson, Everett. *Baptism in the Early Church: History, Theology, and Liturgy in the First Five Centuries.* Grand Rapids: Eerdmans, 2009.

Fiddes, Paul S. "Baptism and the Process of Christian Initiation." *The Ecumenical Review* 54 (2002) 48–65.

————, ed. *Reflections on the Water: Understanding God and the World through the Baptism of Believers.* Macon, GA: Smyth & Helwys, 1996.

————. *Tracks and Traces: Baptist Identity in Church and Theology.* Eugene, OR: Wipf and Stock, 2007.

Fowler, Stanley K. *More Than a Symbol: The British Baptist Recovery of Baptismal Sacramentalism.* Vol. 2. Eugene, Or: Wipf and Stock, 2007.

————. *Rethinking Baptism: Some Baptist Reflections.* Eugene, OR: Wipf and Stock, 2015.

Freeman, Curtis W. "Can Baptist Theology be Revisioned?" *Perspectives in Religious Studies* 24.3 (1997) 273–310.

Gay, David H.J. *Baptist Sacramentalism. A Warning to Baptists.* Biggleswade: Brachus, 2011.

Gilmore, Alec, ed. *Christian Baptism: A Fresh Attempt to Understand the Rite in Terms of Scripture, History, and Theology.* Cambridge: Lutterworth, 1959.

Hammett, John S. "Baptism and the Lord's Supper." In *The Baptist Faith and Message 2000: Critical Issues in America's Largest Protestant Denomination*, edited by Douglas K. Blount and Joseph D. Wooddell, 71–81. Lanham, MD: Rowman & Littlefield, 2007.

Harsch, Lloyd. "Were the First Baptists Sacramentalists?" *Journal for Baptist Theology and Ministry* 6 (2009) 25–44.

Hartman, Lars. *"Into the Name of the Lord Jesus": Baptism in the Early Church*. London: A&C Black, 1997.

Hughes, Philip Edgcumbe. "Grace." In *Evangelical Dictionary of Theology*, edited by Walter Elwell. Grand Rapids: Baker Academic, 2001.

Ivanov-Klyshnikov, Vasily. "On Baptism." *Baptist* 45 (1911) 6–7. [Иванов-Клышников, Василий. "О покаянии." *Баптист* 45 (1911) 6–7.]

————. *Selected Articles and Sermons*, Sacramento, CA: Grace, 2017. [Иванов-Клышников, Василий. *Избранные статьи и проповеди*, Сакраменто: Grace, 2017.]

Ivanov, Mikhail. *The Guide for the Preparation for Baptism*. Moscow: Theology and Catechism Department of the RU ECB, 2005. [Иванов, Михаил. Ред. *Пособие Для Подготовки к Водному Крещению*. М.: Отдел богословия и катехизации РСЕХБ, 2005.]

————, ed. *We Believe. Catechism for the Churches of Evangelical Christian Baptists*. Moscow: Theology and Catechism Department of the RU ECB, 2010. [Иванов, Михаил. Ред. *Веруем. Катехизис для церквей евангельских христиан-баптистов*. М.: Отдел богословия и катехизации РС ЕХБ, 2010.]

Jones, Brandon C. *Waters of Promise: Finding Meaning in Believer Baptism*. Eugene, OR: Pickwick, 2012.

Kargel, Ivan. *Short Exposition of Doctrinal Teaching of Evangelical Christians*. St. Petersburg: Second St. Petersburg Congregation of Evangelical Christians, 1913. [Каргель, Иван. *Краткое изложение вероучения евангельских христиан* (СПб: 2-я С-Петербургская община евангельскихъ христіанъ, 1913.]

Keach, Benjamin. *The Baptist Catechism*. Philadelphia: B. Franklin and D. Hall, 1748.

Kelly, Gerard. "Baptism in the Roman Catholic Church." In *Baptism: Historical, Theological, and Pastoral Perspectives*, edited by Gordon L. Heath and James D. Dvorak, 26–52. Eugene, OR: Pickwick, 2011.

Khrapov, Nikolay. *House of God and Ministry in It*. Council of Evangelical Christians–Baptists, 1972. http://www.blagovestnik.org /books/00280. htm#5. [Храпов, Николай. *Дом Божий и Служение в Нем*. Союз Церквей евангельских христиан-баптистов, 1972. http://www.blagovestnik.org/books/00280.htm#5.]

Kolesnikov, Nikolay. "Let's Press On to Perfection." *Bratskiy Vestnik (Brotherly Herald)* 2 (1979) 34–41. [Николай Колесников, 'Поспешим к Совершенству', *Братский Вестник* 2 (1979) 34–41.]

Kolomiytsev, Alexei. "Purpose and Meaning of Water Baptism." https://www.slovo. org/ru/resursyi/blog/tsel-i-znachenie-vodnogo-kreshchenia. [Коломийцев, Алексей. "Цель и значение водного крещения," https://www.slovo.org /ru/resursyi/blog/tsel-i-znachenie-vodnogo-kreshchenia].

Lopukhin, N.A., "Why Shouldn't I Be Baptized?" *Baptist* 13 (1909) 8–9. [Лопухин. Н.А., "Что препятствует мне креститься?" *Баптист* 13 (1909) 8–9]

Lumpkin, William, ed. *Baptist Confessions of Faith*. Valley Forge, PA: Judson, 1959.

McDonnell, Kilian, and George T. Montague. *Christian Initiation and Baptism in the Holy Spirit: Evidence from the First Eight Centuries*. Collegeville, MN: Liturgical, 1991.

Naboka, Elena. "On the Role of Tropes in the Phraseologization of Gospel Utterances (based on the text of Gospel according to Matthew)." *Writings in Romance-German Philology* 18 (2007) 99–106. [Набока, Елена. "О роли тропов во фразеологизации евангельских речений (на материале Евангелия от Матфея)." *Записки з романо-германської філології* 18 (2007) 99–106.]

Nesterenko, Maksim. *Institutional Captivity of the Church*. Kharkov: Impress, 2017. [Нестеренко, Максим. *Институциональное Пленение Церкви*. Харьков: Импресс, 2017.]

Nettles, Thomas. "Baptism as a Symbol of Christ's Saving Work." In *Understanding Four Views on Baptism*, by Thomas J. Nettles, Richard L. Pratt Jr, Robert Kolb, and John D. Castelein. Grand Rapids: Zondervan, 2009, 25–41.

O'Donnell, Matthew Brook. "Two Opposing Views on Baptism with/by the Holy Spirit and of 1 Corinthians 12.13: Can Grammatical Investigation Bring Clarity?" In *Baptism, the New Testament and the Church: Historical and Contemporary Studies in Honour of R.E.O. White*, edited by Stanley E. Porter and Anthony R. Cross, 311–36. *Journal for the Study of the New Testament* Supplement Series, 171. Sheffield: Sheffield Academic Press, 1999.

Penner, Peter. *Teach All Nations. Mission of Theological Education*. St. Petersburg: Bible for Everybody, 1999. [Пеннер Петр, *Научите все народы. Миссия богословского образования*. СПб: Библия для всех, 1999.]

Prokhorov, Constantine. "On Several Peculiarities of the Understanding of Baptism in the Russian Baptist Church." *Theological Reflections: Euro-Asian Journal of Theology* 8 (2007) 89–105. [Прохоров, Константин. "О некоторых особенностях понимания крещения в русском баптизме", *Богословские Размышления: Евро-Азиатский Журнал Богословия* 8 (2007) 89–105.]

Rainbow, Jonathan H. "Confessor Baptism: The Baptismal Doctrine of the Early Anabaptists." *American Baptist Quarterly* 8 (1989) 276–90.

Rawlings, Harold. *Basic Baptist Beliefs: An Exposition of Key Biblical Doctrines*. Springfield, MO: 21st Century, 2005.

Robinson, H. Wheeler. "The Place of Baptism in Baptist Churches of To-Day." *Baptist Quarterly* 1 (1923) 209–18.

Sannikov, Sergey. *Крещение Духом и дары духовные*. М.: Библейская лига, 2013.

————. "Baptism by the Holy Spirit." In *Slavic Bible Commentary*, Kiev: EAAA Knigonosha, 2016, 1390–91. [Санников, Сергей. "Крещение Духом Святым." В *Славянский библейский комментарий*, Киев: ЕААА Книгоноша, 2016.]

————. *Baptism by the Spirit and Spiritual Gifts.* Moscow: Bibleiskaya Liga, 2013. [Санников, Сергей. *Крещение Духом и дары духовные*. М.: Библейская лига, 2013.]

Sannikov, Sergey, ed. *History of Baptism*. Volume 1. Odessa: Bogomyslie, 1996. [Санников, Сергей. ed. *История Баптизма*, т. 1, Одесса: Богомыслие, 1996.]

Saucy, Mark. "Baptism as a Test Case for the Nature and Limits of National Theology." *Theological Reflaction* 8 (2007) 135–59.

Schreiner, Thomas R. "Baptism in the Epistles: An Initiation Rite for Believers." In *Believer's Baptism*, edited by Schreiner and Wright, 67–96.

Schreiner, Thomas R., and Shawn D. Wright, eds. *Believer's Baptism: Sign of the New Covenant in Christ*. Nashville, TN: B&H Academic, 2006.

Spurgeon, Charles H. *Baptismal Regeneration*. Minneapolis, MN: Curiosmith, 2014.

Stein, Robert H. "Baptism and Becoming a Christian in the New Testament." *Southern Baptist Journal of Theology* 2 (1998) 6–17.

Stott, John R W. "The Evangelical Doctrine of Baptism." *Churchman* 1 (1998) 47–59.

Thompson, Philip E. "Re-Envisioning Baptist Identity: Historical, Theological, and Liturgical Analysis." *Perspectives in Religious Studies* 3 (2000) 287–302.

Vedder, Henry Clay. *Balthasar Hübmaier, the Leader of the Anabaptists*. New York: Putnam's Sons, 1905.

Vins, Yakov. *Our Baptist Principles*. Kharbin: L.M. Abramovich, 1924. [Винс, Яков. *Наши баптистские принципы*. Харбин: Л.М. Абрамович, 1924.]

Wallace, Daniel B. *Greek Grammar beyond the Basics: An Exegetical Syntax of the New Testament*. Grand Rapids: Zondervan, 1996.

Wardin, Albert. "How Indigenous Was the Baptist Movement in the Russian Empire?" *Journal of European Baptist Studies* 2 (2009) 29–37.

Wellum, Stephen J. "Baptism and the Relationship between the Covenants." In *Believer's Baptism*, edited by Schreiner and Wright, 97–161.

Wespetal, Thomas. *The Word on God: Evangelical Theology for Eastern Christians. God's Plan*. Moscow: MTI, 2013. [Веспетал. Томас, *Слово о Боге: Евангельское богословие для восточных христиан. План Бога*, М. МТИ, 2013.]

White, Reginald Ernest Oscar. *The Biblical Doctrine of Initiation*. Grand Rapids: Eerdmans, 1960.

Wright, Stephen I. *The Voice of Jesus: Studies in the Interpretation of Six Gospel Parables*. Eugene, OR: Wipf and Stock, 2007.

Zhabotinskiy, Evgeniy. "Petition of Ivan Ryaboshapka." *Bogomyslie* 19 (2016) 125–43. [Жаботинский, Евгений. "Прошение Ивана Рябошапки," *Богомыслие* 19 (2016) 125–43.]

Zhidkov, Mikhail. "Water Baptism and Lord's Supper." *Bratskiy Vestnik* (*Brotherly Herald*) 2 (1975) 54–60. [Михаил Жидков, «Водное крещение и вечеря Господня», *Братский вестник,* 2 (1975) 54–60.]

CHAPTER 13

Powerful Practices:
Celebrating God's Farewell to the Powers That Be

Henk Bakker

Introduction

In James McClendon's theology we find the rare combination of two empirical observations, namely powerful practices and rhetorical catachresis, which become vital for his perspective on how B/baptist (Free Church) theology actually works.[1] McClendon signals that primary theology embedded in Free Church tradition basically operates by means of its storied, and for that matter porous, identity. First, I want to explain how the phenomenon works, then I set out to dig deeper into the question of how the re-enactment of this storied identity develops into an awareness of the presence of Christ in the gathered church, and, finally, how this together emerges into a sacramental view of celebrating the communal farewell to the powers that be.

Powerful Practices

The first observation pertains to the cultivation of powerful practices, which are disposed to construe communal self-understanding and to bring about shared narratives telling the story of the community. Together these narratives construct the identity-narratives as they originate from the church's full engagement with the gospel-story. For McClendon all ecclesial practices are powerful practices, because in them the life of the Spirit is channeled in such a way that they somehow structure the body-life of the community and endow it with durability, continuity, and expectation.[2] Hence, practices catalyze the orientation of the community, as they reflect much of its moral space and

---

[1] "Baptist" indicates the (denominative) name, whereas "baptist(ic)," also professing faith baptism, does not.

[2] McClendon, *Doctrine*, 28, "Social practices, like games, strive for some end beyond themselves . . ., require intentional participation on the part of practitioners, employ determinate means, and proceed according to rules." A practice "is a complex series of human actions involving definite practitioners who by these means and in accordance with these rules together seek the intended end."

intentionality. They embody communal interests and actualize shared concerns, such as looking after each other, worship, witness, discernment, preaching, penance, and education.

According to McClendon, Baptists generally failed to produce theology because they "failed to see in their own heritage, their own way of using Scripture, their own communal practices, their own guiding vision."[3] They disregarded their practices as a resource for doing theology, simply because orthopraxis was not considered theology. Good praxis was the result of good theory, and hence good theology. but more recently this perspective has changed thoroughly. After all, more often than not communal practices become habitual (and even common) before words and doctrine can be found to articulate what people are actually doing. First there is the experience, which is the act of immediacy, then there is reflection as a means of understanding, and finally theology comes in, as the legitimization of how all of this is "our way of believing." As such, practices not only produce or reflect theology, they also most certainly comprise theology, because of their close attention to immediacy, the reality of the here and now.

Practices tell the story of a specific community, any societal entity, and in doing that spell out its virtues, whether good or bad.[4] This is how they become powerful practices, for they always connect to basic moral drives (intentions) embraced and empowered by the in-group. So, if a Christian group is convinced of the validity and moral obligation of forgiveness because God offers, and requires, the possibility of atonement, then a community may be urged, by a sense of experiential immediacy, to have this conviction evolve into an outright politics of forgiveness that consists of an overall strategy for everyone to approve.[5] Even though every practice is considered a social practice, in terms of Christian tradition ecclesial practices should be denoted as "Spirit-gifted community practices."[6] Without a doubt, they mirror, and gracefully work to accomplish, nothing less than a powerful corporate orientation of the redeemed.

Proper functioning of practices is central to human flourishing, because this is how people become "engaged with a world that enters them as identity-constituting in the most profound way imaginable." People's practices determine their identity, but can also become destructive if they are subservient to "powers and principalities," the dark side of reality.[7] Therefore,

---

[3] McClendon, *Ethics*, 26.

[4] McClendon, *Ethics*, 167–82.

[5] McClendon, *Ethics*, 185 and 213–41.

[6] McClendon, *Doctrine*, 367.

[7] Newson, *Inhabiting the World*, 41–42. Cf. Bakker, "James Wm. McClendon," 114–31.

Christians need powerful practices to hold on to their identity and convictions, and to find language to express these.

Catachrestic Sense-Making

McClendon's second observation, the rhetoric of catachresis, becomes apparent. Indeed, powerful practices, identity and convictions cluster together and critically hinge on the power of language. Here, McClendon benefits from the pioneering analysis of John Austin, the merits of whose work began to be more clearly appreciated in the second half of the twentieth century. It needs a so-called "community of meaning" to meet certain conditions for understanding the language of a group with its own storied identity (Austin, and Wittgenstein).[8] For example, people need a narrative context to explain what words mean within the settings of their specific social reality. Communities of meaning deliver stories for participants to live by in which the meaning of words, the idiosyncrasy of its vernacular, is illuminated and confirmed, and by means of which its convictions are reposited in the individual. Convictions order our beliefs and construct our identity, our basic "self"; in other words, we are our convictions.[9] With the help of convictions we map our identity and community of meaning, and *vice versa*, with the help of our community we map personal stories and convictions. Therefore, nobody really owns his or her private story or identity, because people need others to confirm (or falsify) their narrative. Identity has shared ownership. Man is not wholly "in his own acts," he is never in full possession of himself, Hauerwas propounds. Others make us aware of ourselves, because by engaging others, we come to understand ourselves.[10]

This does not make McClendon a blatant relativist, maybe, rather, a soft perspectivist, because he does not give up on the epistemology of communication. Yet it takes much effort to understand the fabric of communication.[11] Texts constitute social relations, and hence they are multilayered and highly complex. Inasmuch as meaning is encoded in words, phrases and sentences, it is the task of those who decipher to decode well.[12] Now, from its very beginning onward the gospel story has brought change; yet, in order to remain attuned and susceptible to the gospel of change—in

---

[8] Newson, *Inhabiting the World*, 33.

[9] Newson, *Inhabiting the World*, 35. See in particular McClendon and Smith, *Convictions*.

[10] Hauerwas, *Work of Theology*, 71 and 88.

[11] Newson, *Inhabiting the World*, 37.

[12] Volf, *Captive to the Word of God*, 28–32.

any case *ecclesia reformata semper reformanda*—the church, so to speak, has to embark on the adventure of catachrestic theory in order to pass on the flame.[13]

Catachresis refers to inexactness or the insufficiency of words, and for that matter to the "abuse" of words (*katachrèsis*).[14] By catachresis people introduce current terminology for that which has as yet no actual wording (*non habentibus nomen suum*).[15] It takes language to go where no one has gone before for the purpose of explanation. Technically, old words may capture new meanings by proximity (*quod in proximo est*),[16] because with proximity of words comes porosity and creativity. Of themselves words are open to new contexts, which make them cross their iconic frames. Indeed, verbal proximity may induce new meaning and modify current definitions. However, according to Aristotle the borrowing of an existent word for a non-existent one should never be far-fetched (*ou porrōthen*), and should rather be taken from things related (*ek tōn suggenōn*).[17]

Hence, catachresis is about the creative molding of language in order to express what has no definite wording yet. In bridging worlds, cultures and subcultures, catachrestic inexactness may be unavoidable, even crucial, for the sake of sensemaking. Although words are not inexhaustible, they may change from the inside out by proxy, as so-called "Übersetzungslehnworte."[18] As time

---

[13] Newson, *Inhabiting the World*, 38.

[14] Quintilian, *Institutio Oratoria* 8.2.6. Cf. *Rhetorica ad Herennium* 4.33 (*abusio* or *inopia*).

[15] Catachresis is "a conventional word used wrongly to indicate something for which there is no conventional word," and "one of several solutions when an author is looking for a word to describe something for which there is no conventional term." Catachresis "thus lies on the border between barbarism and the effective use of a trope," Anderson, *Glossary of Greek Rhetorical Terms*, 66. Hence, catachresis is all about the creative molding of language in order to express what has no definite wording yet. This brings us to the basic idea of dynamic equivalence, which likewise is a rhetorical device. Rhetorically put, dynamic equivalence is primarily about translation of effects. It seeks to move a given target reader as deeply as the source text once did the source reader.

[16] Quintilian, *Institutio Oratoria* 8.6.34. Cicero differentiates between metaphor and catachresis, which he denotes as "borrowed" words. "Borrowed" implies that a proper word is substituted for another, "with the same meaning drawn from some other suitable sphere" (Cicero, *Orator* 27.92–94). However, according to Aristotle a proper name is lacking, not substituted, Aristotle, *Technè rhetorikè* 3.2.10–13 [1405a.b].

[17] Aristotle, *Technè rhetorikè* 3.2.11 [1405a]. See in particular Kennedy, *Aristotle: On Rhetoric*, 224.

[18] Lausberg, *Handbuch der literarischen Rhetorik*, par. 577. Cf. Leeman and Braet, *Klassieke retorica*, 106.

goes by, fresh terminology minted to express the new faith actually grow old and have to be replaced "to afford glimpses of the one new state of affairs they share, thanks to Jesus Christ," McClendon states.[19] This is how the deep impact of salvation as revolution, by experience and by collective memory, may be preserved for future generations.[20] In the face of the hybridity of western secularism and the post-secular resurgence of religion, churches have to find new ways of voicing the gospel of hope to the un-churched.

In carefully employing catachrestic renewal, Baptists not only seek full engagement with the surrounding culture, but also revive the so-called "Baptist vision," the naive and almost mystical blending of "this is that" and "then is now" in scripture. When Baptists read scripture, the horizons of Bible times and modern times seem to merge in such a way that their own situation is taken up in the biblical narrative, and the vibrant young church more or less becomes their own church. In the immediacy of the hearing of God's word, grace happens, and as Baptists say, "this, what I experience now," is "that, which the Bible narrates," and "the community of the faithful of Biblical times, the end-times, is our community."[21] Somehow, by the power of God, times and places are turned upside down, and Bible stories and Baptist stories meld together. When grace like this happens, it is also constitutive of catachrestic innovation, leading churches to review their powerful practices, and to render certain that they still embody the newness of Christ today.

With regard to hermeneutical sense-making, catachrestic theory may be integrated as a general theory of understanding.[22] Baptists, too, have the tendency to prolong themselves by proposition, by passing on timeless truth. but in the immediacy of things, in the thick of things, sheer propositions may just not be enough to make any sense. Convictions come about by language not restricted or prescribed by authority, but conditioned by experience and persuasion. Of course, being the church is such an experiment of personal persuasion, as the church lives by conviction by its practices.[23]

---

[19] McClendon, "Toward a Conversionist Spirituality," 23.

[20] McClendon, *Doctrine*, 105–22. Cf. Smit, "Das Neue," 375–84.

[21] See McClendon, "Baptist Vision," 23–35. Cf. the significantly revised and expanded version of this text, "Mennonite and Baptist Vision," 211–24 and 258–60. Cf. *Ethics*, 26–34, and *Doctrine*, 44–46, 105 and 464–68. Cf. also *Ethics*, 26–34, and *Doctrine*, 34–46, especially 45.

[22] Derrida introduces catachresis as a general theory of understanding in his *Margins of Philosophy*, 255–56. Not what we read, but what we do not read in the text is decisive for understanding, says Derrida. There is no exactness of language whatsoever, because meaning is not confined by word and matter, but by sheer absence.

[23] Cf. McMillan, "Convictions, Conflict and Moral Reasoning," 30–50.

Christ's Sacramental Presence

I now set out to explore how powerful practices and catachrestic celebration together highlight the storied identity of the community, and in doing so foster the shared awareness of the presence of Christ. Practices tell and (again and again) retell the story of the gospel and the church, and as they catch up new meaning and relevance—yes, in the immediacy of things, and in the thick of things—communal celebration may have sacramental effect. The very presence of Christ, mediated by corporate embodiment of practice, gracefully permeates the cold confinement of every day's reality. What seems impermeable unexpectedly becomes open to newness of thought, heart, and senses. Christ's promise to be present where disciples gather in his name proves true, because, all of a sudden, those who sing and celebrate seem to "know" that heaven and earth fuse (Matt. 18.18–19). The happy realization that God's eyes are upon this world, looking through the barricades of human life into the fragility and the tenuous nature of being, is actually redemptive. but how so?

According to McClendon the church is the historic community where the followers of God treasure the identity narratives, the Bible, even more so the gospel. The gathered church remembers and relives the gospel story as their own story. These narratives bind and weave together, as they become part of a divine, perichoretic dance in which the triune God and his people transcend their own faculties. This is where new practices start and reform comes in. In living the gospel story Christians feel compelled (and blessed) to assemble, to pray, to preach and teach, and to expect God to respond to that. Practices are more or less performances, re-enactments, in which the gathered church waits for God to come.[24] This explains the dictum "in Christ" perfectly well. "It has passed from denoting physical location to declaring—in quasi-physical, or better, ontological, realism—the presence of Christ with those for whom the new has come."[25] Quite interestingly so, the presence of Christ for the Christian community has ontological, quasi-physical, significance.

The presence of Christ, as a presence that is ontologically warranted, is of the utmost importance for lived theology germinating from the church's preoccupation with the gospel. Nevertheless, this presence is not to be seen as a static condition locked up in itself. Christ's presence is to be explained as the Spirit coming to, imparting himself to and from, the church. Being "in Christ" does not stand for eternal freeze, but for dynamic movement, including worship, work, and witness. Knowing Christ by "quasi-physical realism" happens because he himself participates in these practices by the

---

[24] Immink, *Het heilige gebeurt*, 42–46.

[25] McClendon, *Doctrine*, 113–17 ("The presence of Christ"), at 114.

Spirit.[26] The first verses of the first letter of John profess the lasting correspondence between the Christ in the flesh, the risen Christ, and the tangible fellowship of the Christian community:

> [That] which we have heard, which we have seen with our eyes, which we have looked at and our hands have touched—this we proclaim . . . We proclaim to you what we have seen and heard, so that you also may have fellowship with us. And our fellowship is with the Father and with his Son, Jesus Christ. (1 Jn 1.1–4; NIV.)

Moreover, if the presence of Christ is to be defined as dynamic coming (*parousia*), as much as sending (*missio*), the result can only be that sacramentalism should be spoken of in terms of "becoming" (*fieri*) and not in terms of "being" (*esse*). Sacramentalism is all about the processes by which being comes about, and is accordingly concerned with the presence and hiddenness of Christ, the revelation and the mystery of Christ, the sacredness and commonness of Christ's embodiment in the church. If this is the case, that sacramentality is not static after all, and pertains to a vivid picture of powerful practices coping and dealing with concealment and mystery, the idea of Christ's presence definitely should be attuned to the frame of covenantal thinking.

Baptists, surely by their rooting, are acquainted with the practice of covenant making. As Paul Fiddes points out, historically Baptists looked at God's eternal covenant with the world as an eternal model to be copied and applied to the community of the faithful on earth here and now.[27] So in 1606 or 1607, following the impulse of their hearts, the English separatists of Gainsborough solemnly declared to enter into a covenant with God and with one another. The gathered Dissenters literally covenanted, and founded a new church, as they promised both to "give themselves up to God" and to "give themselves up to each other"; to "walk in the ways of the Lord" and "to walk together"; to obey the "rules of Christ" and to "watch over each other." The vertical dimension (God, Lord, Christ) and the horizontal dimensions (each other, together, each other) together stand well-grounded in one covenantal perspective.[28] If there is any sacramentality in Baptist's earliest awareness (slightly pre-Baptist), it is here: grace happens, binding and bonding Christians in unison together, and moving them to be a new church, with altogether new and reviving practices.

---

[26] McClendon, *Doctrine*, 240–44 ("The present Christ"), at 240, and 477–82 ("three other forms of Christ's presence"), at 478.

[27] Fiddes, "Covenanting Communities."

[28] See Bradford, *History of Plymouth Plantation*, 1:20–22.

God's coming to the world unfolds by means of covenant, more precisely, by means of covenantal sacrament. After all, the sacrament is the people, who unite, who covenant with God and with one another, metaphorically sealed with "promise," even if no words were spoken, by mere spontaneity of character. The redeemed form a new social brand, called to represent a new human species, a kingdom people who are about to enter the new creation when Jesus returns to the world. This new kind of humanity, certainly, manifests itself as an eschatological people, but nevertheless appears on the scene as the signal, and the symbol, that penultimate times have arrived ("das Vorletzte"). Belonging to Christ implies/entails being part of the new people of God, and *vice versa*. In other words: there is no sacrament without covenant; there is no immediacy without history.

Salvation history is not about encountering God by escaping fallen creation, by fleeing from the disappointments and depressions of life. In order to be close to God evasion is not an option, for notions of God beyond life as it is are mere abstractions, lofty ideas, almost phantasms. The God of Israel can never be encountered apart from his dealings with the world. Without any exception whatsoever, God's revelation comes with awe, wonder, and clear instruction. Engagements with God always lead to agreements as to how the relationship is structured, deepened, and secured. It almost goes without saying that "coming equals covenanting." These words, *in nuce*, briefly epitomize God's mission to the world. When God visits Adam, before and after sinning, his presence comes with reflection on the agreement they have. When he chooses Noah, and Abraham, instructions follow immediately. In the story of Moses and the salvation of the Jewish people, right after the liberation from Egypt, the ten commandments are given. No dealings with God without appointments and stipulations to regulate the reciprocity. Even the new covenant heralded by Isaiah, Jeremiah, and Ezekiel, sets out conditions for the new order to live by. When Jesus is introduced in the Gospel of Matthew, his first lecture is on the commandments of God and his way of understanding, applying, and fulfilling them.

Scripture testifies that divine coming goes hand in hand with covenanting, that the experience of encountering God not only brings release, jubilation, and the ecstatic, but also shock, silence, trembling, and containment. Both the *mysterium tremendum* and the *mysterium fascinosum* are caught up in a divine bipolar symbiosis. The late A.W. Tozer, in his 1961 address to the pastors of the Associated Gospel Churches of Canada (recorded and edited), passionately argues for the worship of God in "awesome wonder and overpowering love," "in the presence of that ancient Mystery, that unspeakable Majesty, which the philosophers call the Mysterium Tremendum, but which we call our Father which art in heaven."[29] In his campaign against evangelical rationalism, Tozer pushes the right buttons, but sixty years later, the

---

[29] Tozer, *Worship*, 9–10.

pendulum has very much swung the other way. Evangelical churches, among which most Baptist churches would count themselves, certainly have cultivated an atmosphere of worship and overpowering love, but almost at the loss of reason, trembling, and moral imperatives. Tozer anticipates this deficiency as well, and marks it as a religious experience that is too familiar with God, is without Jesus Christ, and without moral commitment.[30]

Thus, the presence of Christ in the church should be envisaged as a dynamic coming of God to covenant with us, and with one another. The sacramentality is in the reviving realization of the *mysteria* of salvation, which the practice should undergo again and again. Christ finds his way to the community, and imbues its moral space with freshness of love and dedication, with readiness to listen to God and, if necessary, to renew covenant. He manages to enter into every situation as "life-giving Spirit," as the "Spirit of Jesus," or the "Spirit of Christ," and make interventions (1 Cor. 15.45; Acts 16.7; Rom. 8.9). Here, he also overrides the contingencies and necessities of life that by and large determine the course of history. Christians, too, seem to think that determinants and coincidence somehow dictate things as they are. but this is not the case. God's coming to the world rules, for the Spirit makes his way to covenant. Most of this is concealed from our hearts and eyes, and some of it is sacramentally in the open, when the Spirit reorganizes the steely harness of coincidence and determinants so as to make space for Jesus.

Quite understandably, Baptists have to explore their own sources and traditions—since this is what they have failed to do[31]—to discern how their vision fits into a sacramental view of Christ's covenantal coming. Nonetheless, from a Baptist viewpoint, critical questions should be raised with regard to the sacramentality of the church. Can grace be institutionalized after all, and can Baptists go along with theorizing about taking the mysteries of God into our own hands? According to Paul Fiddes, rituals like baptism and ordination do have sacramental implications. God has always performed his work by mediation of worldly realities, such as objects and human action, which he turns into signs ("icons") of the world under his command. Indeed, he uses the world as a means to draw humanity into the realm of the transcendent. Therefore, a rejection of the possibility of the mediation of grace *ex opere operato* may be liable to a rejection of God's freedom to act as he wishes.[32]

Consequently, God does not diverge from his original plan to consecrate the world as he covenants with man, and builds creation into a people he gives his instructions to and to whom he sends his words and Word. This people he calls, and he sends back into the world, throughout the ages and throughout the world; and assuredly, this people transcends their determinations and

---

[30] Tozer, *Worship*, 21, 23 and 25.

[31] See above n.3.

[32] Fiddes, "*Ex Opere Operato*." Cf. Bakker, "Roaring Side of the Ministry."

restrictions, because he unites them and lets them share in his divine activity as sacrament.[33] Somehow, the church of all ages, which is the church of all covenants (Old and New Testament), serves as a mediating symbol in the world in accord with God.[34] The community of God enacts his presence, embodies his presence as a covenanting humanity, and hereby effectually communicates grace to the world. Covenanting relations, by the grace of Christ, become the operative means to God's implicit ends. Relations, in the hands of God, are redemptive.

However, the church is not to be regarded as an extension of the incarnation of Christ.[35] The Spirit makes community, builds it into a covenanting "body," replete with newness and powerful practices, but it obviously does not coincide with God. Grace and redemptive relations are not in the hands of mere mortals, they are not to be manipulated. Scripture attests on several occasions (Acts 7.48; 17.24) that God does not abide in houses or other constructions built by the hands of mere humans. Yet, when he so chooses, the very appearance (tangibility) of the local church may become a sacrament. The project is his, the matter is ours, and for that reason Christians should never over-spiritualize themselves. All too lofty notions of the church are inclined to drag Christians away to docetic aberrations in unrealistic practices, speculations, and expectations, which dangerously transfer the *missio Dei* from coming into leaving.[36]

Precisely on account of its quite fragile and ambivalent humanity, the church may be considered a true *signum*, a sign "from there" drawing man "from here" to God. As Augustine writes, a visible sacrament is a sacred sign of something invisible,[37] and Thomas Aquinas concurs, a sign is a sacred thing.[38] In biblical terminology we may say that the "light" of Jesus and the "light" of the church mingle together. In the Gospel of John Jesus is addressed as the light of the world (John 8.12), whereas in the Gospel of Matthew his followers are (Matt. 5.14). However, the difference between the two is

---

[33] Fiddes, *Tracks and Traces*, 21–47; and Fiddes, Haymes and Kidd, *Baptists and the Communion of Saints*, 184.

[34] Colwell, "Church as Sacrament." Cf. Colwell, *Promise and Presence.*

[35] Hauerwas and Willimon, *Holy Spirit*, 40.

[36] Hauerwas and Willimon, *Holy Spirit*, 39–44.

[37] Augustine, *De civitate Dei*, 10.5, "A sacrifice, therefore, is the visible sacrament or sacred sign of an invisible sacrifice" (*sacrificium ergo uisibile inuisibilis sacrificii sacramentum, id est sacrum signum est*).

[38] *Sacramentum est sacrae rei signum*, see Thomas, *Summa Theologiae* III.60.2, in *Summa Theologiae*, 4:477, "Signs are given to men, to whom it is proper to discover the unknown by means of the known. Consequently, a sacrament properly so called is that which is the sign of some sacred thing pertaining to man."

evidently not of any concern, because Jesus' light becomes the church's, and so the church may want to light a candle as a symbol of this fusion and say, "Behold, the light of God." Hence, the symbol becomes a sign, a sacred sign, a sacrament pertaining to the realm of God (*sacramentum est sacrae rei signum*). As for Baptists, the mediation of grace is not in the candle or in the candlelight itself, but in the immediacy of Christ-oriented communal life, reaching out for newness.

Historically, the paradigm of new creation chiefly centered and prospered in the early rise of Anabaptist theology. Anabaptists, like Baptists almost a century later, focused their theological interest primarily on the communal dimensions of the newness in Christ. Thomas Finger underlines the peculiarity that the "content and orientation of Anabaptist faith are largely communal." For Anabaptists, "turning to Christ is inseparable from turning to his community and participating in his life, death and resurrection," which energizes them to express his life, death and resurrection outwardly in the material world in a sacramental way. "Historic Anabaptists envisioned the church itself much as a sacrament," to be sure: "an eschatological sacrament," a visible and present sign of "what God finally desires for all humanity."[39]

Furthermore, just as the incarnation plainly reflects God's readiness to operate transformatively within tangible reality, so does the church. However, faced with the spiritualists one the one hand and the Roman Catholic Church on the other, Pilgrim Marpeck (1495–1556) maintains that Christ after his ascension continues to be present and act in his unglorified body, which he identifies as the church. The church perpetuates the incarnation, inasmuch as it is oriented towards the cross, death, and newness.[40] The church is not a just state of affairs, but a life. Thence the presupposition that its authority is invested in the *imitatio Christi*, personally as well as communally, and not in clerical succession or in personal revelation. Steven Harmon, to some extent, resonates with Marpeck in propounding that Baptist sacramentalists aim at a more "robust appreciation of the Lord's presence," and a theology that understands the sacraments "as paradigmatic of the relation of God to the material order that is disclosed in the incarnation."[41] This Baptist type of sacramentalism seeks to be more open to the presence of Christ, and expects him to use the material order to make himself known. Mere matter is being transformed into signs and symbols of his coming, which, more importantly for Baptists, sustain the community to mediate grace by its intimacy with God.

Fear of community works against a proper understanding of the church as sacrament. Intimacy of communal life, resting in an intimacy with God in

---

[39] Finger, *Contemporary Anabaptist Theology*, 252 and 253.

[40] Siegrist, *Participating Witness*, 90, 91 and 93.

[41] Harmon, *Towards Baptist Catholicity*, 11–21, at 13, and 211–13.

Christ Jesus, is the heart of the mystery of sacramentality. This intimacy is grounded in the incarnation of Christ, embodied (indeed, materialized) in the community of believers who obey his commandments and share their lives together *coram Deo*. The sacraments do not define the church as church, but are "the immediate present work of the Spirit in our midst, active in our human physicality, affirming us as the very body of Christ upon earth," as Jim Purves correctly remarks. More specifically, "we should not fear the Spirit's embrace of us," because this is what the Spirit does. In his coming, he brings us into an intimate relationship with God and with one another. Moreover, this is a fearful intimacy, taking into consideration human frailty, pain and dysfunctionality.[42] However, exactly here the immediacy of the Spirit may transform mere human physicality into signs of wonder.

So, considered in detail, by itself the church is not a sacrament. As Timothy George analyses, the plain equation of the church with a sacrament is a matter of discussion even among Catholics. For example, the Belgian text of Vatican Council II adds the Latin word *veluti* ("as if" or "like as") to the assertion that the church is the sacrament of the union of men among themselves and with God. The church is a sacrament only by comparison (*veluti sacramentum*). Being church is like a sacrament or a sort of sacrament.[43] This Belgian adjustment coheres well with Baptist sacramental thinking. It is almost impossible to retain a sense of holiness of place beyond the God–human encounter, says Graham Watts. Holiness and sacramentality need experience, such as immediacy and fearful intimacy, to become apparent.[44]

Altogether, this is not an ontological approach to sacramentalism, but an epistemological one. Baptist sacramentalism is story based, rooted in narrative immediacy, and this is exactly the advantage this type of sacramentalism has at the brink of the third decade of the third millennium. Traditionally, God's coming to the world was hammered out in theological propositions and confessions, which are necessary and have, quite obviously, a merit of their own. Still, mostly due to one-sidedness and dissent, in the eyes of regular church-folk statements tend to become abstract and authoritative. They predominantly function as controllers. Being part of a narrative creates more of a balance between learned faith and lived faith. People living in the secularized West, who cannot live with or without religion, nevertheless wish to be part of a spiritual narrative. Primarily they are not really interested in endorsing declarations and policies. They look for invitation, participation, and imagination, and this is found foremost in shared narratives, in retelling

---

[42] Purves, "Sacrament of Fearful Intimacy," 43; see also 37, 44 and 47.

[43] George, "Sacramentality of the Church," 33.

[44] Watts, "Can Baptists Believe in Sacred Space?"

the gospel story as embedded in a shared story.[45] In this adventure, Jesus is expected to intervene, to impart newness, and to covenant with us. This brings me to the final section, a farewell to the powers.

A Farewell to the Powers

So far, I have argued that, for the sake of sense-making, Christian communities need to develop strong practices. Powerful practices are indispensable for being well-equipped to live a story together and to embody the presence of Christ. Here, in the shared story, the gospel story and the communal story merge. And right here, where they merge, new meanings, and newness of life and language emerge (catachresis). The porosity of words, rituals, and liturgy quite naturally enhance the opportunity for new sense-making. Moreover, here Christ, in a dynamic gospel-way, comes to make covenant with those who live involved narratives as he did when he was on earth. His presence is a storied-covenanting presence, in which he wants his people to be involved. They participate in a redemptive story by their involved communal narratives, which are lived occasions of experiential immediacy—the immediacy of things, yes, the thick of things—which prevent the church from becoming a bubble-church.

A bubble-church is all about ecclesial idealism, persistently suffering from chronic propositionalism, attitudes of moral superiority, and a lack of communicative oxygen. Its communal atmosphere is absolutist by proposition, and rather poorly established in the "thin of things."[46] Thin churches overestimate themselves in underestimating the powers and principalities surrounding them, which control them from the inside out anyhow. The church is always part of the world, its culture, its Zeitgeist. The church better be honest with God and with itself, and not underestimate the powers that be, the power of sin, self-deceit, theological projection and auto-suggestion. Let us not be impressed by theory, but by involved narrative and communal character building.

In his book on the spiritual formation of ministers, Paul Goodliff signals the necessity for pastors to generate more vision in their labors. They perceive their mission as a vocation, as something holy, and for that reason Goodliff proposes a sacramental approach to the practice of ordination.[47] Ministers should be trained in developing sustainable habits of "facing Christ in daily prayer, corporate worship and fellowship."[48] In a kind of state of the art on

---

[45] Wheeler, "Evangelical Proclamation and Teaching," 164 and 165. See also Klaver, *This Is My Desire*; and Pears, "Towards a Theological Engagement."

[46] Bakker, "Deconstructing the Dinosaur."

[47] See Goodliff, *Ministry, Sacrament and Representation*.

[48] Goodliff, *Shaped for Service*, 69.

ministerial formation, Goodliff discusses several models, settling eventually for virtue ethics and the qualities of a virtuous life. Then he closes with describing the minister as a practitioner, as a liturgist, a pastor, a guide, a missionary, an administrator, and a leader. This type of character building is highly communal, and requires a shared narrative in the pursuit of sense-making, living the story, and reaching out to Christ.

The closest to the "soft force" of the sacrament is the church, by comparison (*veluti*), when the gathered community recapitulates the gospel by re-enactment in worship. Worship displays the gospel in motion, because it recapitulates and re-enacts the work of Christ through forms and signs, says Robert Webber.[49] It may also be called a sacramental type of storytelling or just incarnational storytelling, according to Eugene Peterson and Hans Boersma.[50] Peterson writes, "Immersion in this gospel world has always been the primary way Christians have developed a sacramental imagination."[51] The text pertains to a sacrament, and accordingly communal imagination may become sacramental if it is concentrated on reconstructing the story of Jesus today, here and now, for the eyes and ears of post-Christendom people. In glorifying God, the collective imagination is filled with gospel jubilation. This may deservedly be called a "Jesus-soaked imagination,"[52] in which the congregation plays its own role in the drama of God.

Moreover, role playing in the drama of sanctified imagination—after all, this is what rituals and liturgy do[53]—makes the church partake in God's coming to the world, indeed, also in his coming to the powers and principalities of this world (*aiōn houtos*). "For we do not wrestle against flesh and blood, but against the rulers, against the authorities, against the cosmic powers over this present darkness, against the spiritual forces of evil in the heavenly places" (Eph. 6.12). God has unfinished business with these powers, and has his church be involved in defying them. In this regard, involved narrative implies that salvation is something fundamentally participative.[54] The *Christus Victor* pattern of thought in the early church was never supposed to be an easy *fait accompli* to digest. The gospel of Christ's triumph is as participative as can be. Only by involved narrative can the communal story be successful, and become a sacrament towards renewal.

In consequence, narrative identification "played out" in powerful practice may bring corporate newness, because the Lord, if he comes, will covenant,

---

[49] Webber, *Worship*, 67–70, 73–82 and 85–90.

[50] Peterson, "Foreword," vii–xii; and Boersma, *Sacramental Preaching, passim*.

[51] Peterson, "Foreword," ix.

[52] Peterson, "Foreword," ix.

[53] Ploeger, *Celebrating Church*.

[54] See D.G. Powers, "Salvation Through Participation."

help defy the powers by intervention,[55] and work his way toward renewal of practices, as Isaiah prophesies, "He will judge between the nations and will settle disputes for many peoples. They will beat their swords into ploughshares and their spears into pruning hooks. Nation will not take up sword against nation, nor will they train for war anymore" (Isa. 2.4, NIV; cf. Mic. 4.3). God's intervention results in judgments and profound modifications in terms of the industry of war and in peace-making. In order to prevent people from taking up weapons, weaponry will be done away with, and war will not be taught anymore. The Apocalypse adds to the Isaianic picture the assurance that the nations will be healed (Rev. 20:2). Some of this healing will certainly cover the natural reflexes of the Gentiles to take up armor and to pursue war, to conquer and retaliate.

Christ's intervention happens in just this way and involves just these very elements of judgement and healing, because the resurrected Christ is no other person than the historical Jesus. As he is Israel's Messiah, he fulfills the promises of old, while living on earth, and while constantly coming to earth.[56] The story is one and the same. In terms of McClendon's dictum, we could say that the Jesus of "this" is the same as the Jesus of "that," and the Jesus of "then" is the same as the Jesus of "now." So, victory then, in God's future, is no different from victory now, and "this victory" that the church experiences in worship does not differ substantially from "that victory" which can be pointed to in scripture. The frames of the stories, by Spirit-led flexibility, run into each other and cause the recipients to participate in the narrative. The sense of shared ownership makes them susceptible, by experience, to the shared storyline, and orients them towards the implicit victory the story also anticipates. The powers they see themselves confronted with, as in Jesus' day, are mainly dehumanizing powers.

Hendrikus Berkhof was one of the first to venture the notion that the "powers" in the New Testament, and in particular for Paul the Apostle, contain a variety of compelling forces which are strictly earth-bound. There may be evil spirits in the background who are in control, but this is not the main perspective in the idea of the powers.[57] Such compulsory forces are at work in traditions, in public opinion, in politics, in philosophy, in culture, which have the power to enslave people, to drag them to destructive opinions and disgraceful behavior. As such the "powers" are prone to destruct the personhood of humanity, to pull them away from God and from the high view of humanity's vocation and destiny in life.

---

[55] Immink, *Het heilige gebeurt*, 46–48.

[56] Immink, *Het heilige gebeurt*, 103–25.

[57] Berkhof, *Christus en de machten*, 15–26. Cf. Dawn, *Powers*; and Moses, "Powerful Practices."

In Christ the community of believers is summoned to say farewell to the powers that be. Moreover, the church is inspired to celebrate this farewell, and to experience it as enacted, involved narrative, wonderfully attuned to the gospel of Christ. This is no less than an act of defiance, a liberating deed of speech-act, performed in obedience to the Lord. In powerful practices the farewell accomplished by Christ is commemorated, and re-enacted by praise, prayer, baptism, eucharist, witness, conversion, anointing, exorcism, healing, sermon, education, serving. Consequently, the coming of Christ in the epiclesis of communal commitment evolves into the reinforcement and renewal of covenant, and eventually into new practices. In addressing the powers in this way, the Spirit imparts liberty to the congregation, and creative love to find ways to turn away from "those weak and miserable forces" (Gal. 4.9).

The church overcomes by storied witness of the faith, in particular by inventing new practices in this regard, new ways to tackle tough issues, and by submitting the powers to obedience to Christ. Without a doubt, confrontations of storied identity result in power encounters that test the church.[58] Indeed, despite their counter-practices, churches may still be subject to reinforcing patterns of sin and injustice. It needs christologically informed practices, such as penance and confession of sin, in order for the church to retain its transformative power.[59] No counterculture works as a true witness just by itself. Involved story may become a true witness if the confrontation with Christ works as a two-edged sword, first to the powers internally, and then to the powers externally.

By involved story a farewell to worldly powers may become a cause for renewal, not only for church practices, but also for the powers in question. Thrown into the same historic corner their separate stories definitely meet, clash and refocus. but in doing so, they offer opportunity for reciprocal catachrestic change. Sense-making goes both ways. Christians may need new words and borrow from the world in order to make sense of the newness of Christ, as non-Christians may need words, and borrow them from Christians, in order to make sense of their puzzlement in the world. This is how storied churches, storied powers, and the gospel story may become engaged in conversation. This is also how worldly powers may be subjected to Christ, as the apostle Paul testifies, "We take captive every thought to make it obedient to Christ" (2 Cor. 10.6, NIV). Sometimes worldly powers may even be dedicated to God, Christianized and sanctified.

We see some of such exceptionalities in the Lukan narrative of Acts 16–17. When Paul visits Philippi, and subsequently Athens, the Spirit has his storied, gospel-oriented life bump into the lives of others. We see Paul live an involved

---

[58] McClendon, *Witness*, 345–83.

[59] Newson, *Inhabiting the World*, 124–49, especially 132, 139, 147 and 148.

narrative by the practice of praise and preaching, and this is how he runs into conflict with, respectively, Philippian powers and Athenian powers. In Philippi he is arrested, together with Silas, and imprisoned after being severely flogged. Yet, both men start praying and praising God in the night (Acts 16.25, *proseuchomenoi humnoun ton theon*), while the other prisoners listen. Then, all of a sudden, the ground shakes, the prison doors fly open, and everyone's chains come loose. When the jailer wakes up to find the prison doors open, he takes his sword and decides to kill himself. After all, he will be held accountable for the prison outbreak and be punished in any case. but then Christ intervenes through the voice of Paul, "Don't harm yourself! We are all here!" The intervention signifies a radical change of perspective, for the very symbol of Philippian power, prison and its prison warder, are out of order, because they are being overruled by the power of Christ. Yes, even the very scene of the prison dungeon (and this is what is was), becomes a place of free choice for the apostle and his companion to stay a little longer. The dramatic change of context and meaning (prison becoming the free place of conversion) also transforms the very wording of "I must die" into "don't harm yourself!" Thereupon the jailer, who lived in the compound, opens his home, hears the gospel, and is himself baptized that very night. Christ's covenanting presence is manifest, and, if the jailer remains on duty, he is a means for change and the sanctification of worldly power (Acts 16.25–30).

A couple of months later, Paul walks in the streets of Athens, visits the market place (*agora*), and debates with the philosophers there. Luke gives a perfect characterization of Athenian philosophers in noting that Athenians "spent their time doing nothing but talking about and listening to the latest ideas." Paul, in explaining his "new teaching" to the Areopagus meeting, refers extensively to their practices, powers, and sources. He points to their statue "to the unknown god," quotes some of their famous authors, and gives the impression that the true (and only) God is not far away from them "so that they would seek him and perhaps reach out for him and find him, though he is not far from any one of us." Here, Paul executes his involved practice of preaching and finds Christ in the act of searching for ways to communicate the gospel, to bring the unknown (the *agnōstos theos*) as close as possible to what his listeners do know. At the same time, this is as close as the Jewish–Christian concept of God may come to an abuse of words (*abusio/inopia*, cf. note 14). However, such abuse, which only heightens the derision and aversion of most of Paul's opponents, somehow helps them understand what Paul is talking about. Accordingly, catachrestic encounter by involved narrative, as we see here in the forefront of Luke's narrative, could certainly be a starting point, a powerful initiative, to have the powers of Hellenist custom, culture and tradition (*stoicheia*) capitulate to the rule of Christ. This may also be a God-given means, even providence, for their preservation (Acts 17.16–28).[60]

In conclusion, powerful practices leading to involved narrative, and from there to a shared awareness of Christ's coming to covenant with us, are able to bring us to participation in an active celebration of God's farewell to the powers that be. Thinking the Baptist way through in regard to this, my observation is that it is fully sacramental.

Bibliography

Anderson, R.D. *Glossary of Greek Rhetorical Terms Connected to Methods of Argumentation, Figures and Tropes from Anaximenes to Quintilian.* Contributions to Biblical Exegesis & Theology, 24; Leuven: Peeters, 2000.

Anon. [possibly Cicero.] *Rhetorica ad Herennium.* Loeb Classical Library, 403. Translated by H. Caplan. Cambridge, MA: Harvard University Press, 1989.

Aristotle, *Technè rhetorikè.* The Loeb Classical Library, 193. Translated by J.H. Freese. Cambridge, MA: Harvard University Press, 1982.

Augustine, *De civitate Dei.* See The Latin Library online.

Bakker, Henk. "Deconstructing the Dinosaur: A Storied Example." Unpublished paper presented at the Symposium "Recovering from Ecclesial Idealism," at Baptist House Amsterdam, 13 November 2019, [n.p.].

———. "James Wm. McClendon, theoloog en grensganger." In *Andersom— een introductie in de theologie van James Wm. McClendon,* edited by Henk Bakker and Daniël Drost, 114–31. Unie van Baptistengemeenten in Nederland; Veenendaal: WoodyDesign, 2014.

———. "The Roaring Side of the Ministry: A Turn to Sacramentalism." *Perspectives in Religious Studies* 38.4 (2011) 403–26.

Berkhof, H. *Christus en de machten.* Nijkerk: Callenbach, 1952.

Boersma, Hans. *Sacramental Preaching: Sermons on the Hidden Presence of Christ.* Grand Rapids: Baker Academic, 2016.

Bradford, William. *History of Plymouth Plantation:* Volume 1. *1620–1647.* Boston: Massachusetts Historical Society, 1912.

Colwell, John E. "The Church as Sacrament: A Mediating Presence." In *Baptist Sacramentalism 2,* edited by Cross and Thompson, 48–60.

———. *Promise and Presence: An Exploration of Sacramental Theology.* Milton Keynes: Paternoster, 2006.

Cross, Anthony R., and Philip E. Thompson, eds. *Baptist Sacramentalism.* Studies in Baptist History and Thought, 5; Carlisle: Paternoster, 2003.

———. *Baptist Sacramentalism 2.* Studies in Baptist History and Thought, 5; Milton Keynes: Paternoster, 2008.

---

[60] Cf. Berkhof, *Christus en de machten,* 52–62.

Dawn, Marva J. *Powers, Weakness, and the Tabernacling of God.* Grand Rapids: Eerdmans, 2001.

Derrida, Jacques. *Margins of Philosophy.* Translated Alan Bass. Brighton: Harvester, 1982.

Fiddes, Paul S. "Covenanting Communities." In *Seeds of the Church: Baptist Ecclesiology,* edited by Teun van der Leer, Henk Bakker, Beth Newman, Steven R. Harmon. Falls Church, VA: Baptist World Alliance, forthcoming, 2020

——. *"Ex Opere Operato:* Re-thinking a Historic Baptist Rejection." In *Baptist Sacramentalism 2,* edited by Cross and Thompson, 219–38.

——. *Tracks and Traces: Baptist Identity in Church and Theology.* Studies in Baptist History and Thought, 13. Carlisle: Paternoster, 2003.

Fiddes, Paul S., Brian Haymes, and Richard Kidd. *Baptists and the Communion of Saints: A Theology of Covenanted Disciples.* Waco, TX: Baylor University Press, 2014.

Finger, Thomas N. *A Contemporary Anabaptist Theology: Biblical, Historical, Constructive.* Downers Grove, IL: InterVarsity Press, 2004.

George, Timothy. "The Sacramentality of the Church: An Evangelical Baptist Perspective." In *Baptist Sacramentalism,* edited by Cross and Thompson, 21–35.

Goodliff, Paul W. *Ministry, Sacrament and Representation: Ministry and Ordination in Contemporary Baptist Theology, and the Rise of Sacramentalism.* Centre for Baptist History and Heritage Studies, 2; Oxford: Regent"s Park, 2010.

——. *Shaped for Service: Ministerial Formation and Virtue Ethics.* Eugene, OR: Pickwick, 2017.

Harmon, Steven R. *Towards Baptist Catholicity: Essays on Tradition and the Baptist Vision.* Studies in Baptist History and Thought, 27; Milton Keynes: Paternoster, 2006.

Hauerwas, Stanley. *The Work of Theology.* Grand Rapids: Eerdmans, 2015.

Hauerwas, Stanley, and William H. Willimon. *The Holy Spirit.* Nashville, TN: Abingdon, 2015.

Immink, F.G. *Het heilige gebeurt. Praktijk, theologie en traditie van de protestantse kerkdienst.* Zoetermeer: Boekencentrum, 2011.

Kennedy, G.A. *Aristotle: On Rhetoric. A Theory of Civic Discourse.* New York: Oxford University Press, 1991.

Klaver, Miranda. *This Is My Desire: A Semiotic Perspective on Conversion in an Evangelical Seeker Church and a Pentecostal Church in the Netherlands.* Amsterdam: Amsterdam University Press, 2011.

Lausberg, H. *Handbuch der literarischen Rhetorik: Eine Grundlegung der Literaturwissenschaft.* Stuttgart: Franz Steiner, 3rd edn, 1990.

Leeman, A.D., and A.C. Braet. *Klassieke retorica: Haar inhoud, functie en betekenis.* Gröningen: Wolters-Noordhoff/Forsten, 1987.

McClendon, James W. "The Baptist Vision [Graduation Address at the Baptist Theological Seminary, Rüschlikon, Switzerland, 25 April 1985]." *Baptistic Theologies* 6.1 (2014) 23–35.

———. "The Mennonite and Baptist Vision." In *Mennonites and Baptists: A Continuing Conversation*, edited by Paul Toews, 211–24 and 258–60. Winnipeg: Kindred, 1993.

———. "Toward a Conversionist Spirituality." In *Ties that Bind: Life Together in the Baptist Vision*, edited by Gary A. Furr and Curtis W. Freeman, 23–32. Macon, GA: Smyth & Helwys, 1994.

———. *Systematic Theology:* Volume 1. *Ethics.* Nashville, TN: Abingdon Press, 2002.

———. *Systematic Theology:* Volume 2. *Doctrine.* Nashville, TN: Abingdon Press, 1994.

———. *Systematic Theology:* Volume 3. *Witness.* Nashville, TN: Abingdon Press, 2000.

McClendon, James W., and James M. Smith. *Convictions: Defusing Religious Relativism.* Eugene, OR: Wipf & Stock, 2002 [1994].

McMillan, David John. "Convictions, Conflict and Moral Reasoning: The Contributions of the Concept of Convictions in Understanding Moral Reasoning in the Context of Conflict, Illustrated by a Case Study of Four Groups of Christians in Northern Ireland." PhD diss., Vrije Universiteit Amsterdam, 2019.

Moses, Robert Ewusie. "Powerful Practices: Paul's Principalities and Powers Revisited." PhD diss., Duke University Divinity School, 2012.

Newson, Ryan Andrew. *Inhabiting the World: Identity, Politics, and Theology in Radical Baptist Perspective.* Macon, GA: Mercer University Press, 2018.

Pears, Mike. "Towards a Theological Engagement with an Area of Multiple Deprivation: The Case of the Cornwall Estate." PhD diss., Vrije Universiteit Amsterdam, 2015.

Peterson, Eugene. "Foreword." In *Sacramental Preaching.* By Boersma, vii–xii.

Ploeger, Matthijs. *Celebrating Church: Ecumenical Contributions to a Liturgical Ecclesiology.* Netherlands Studies in Ritual and Liturgy, 7. Gröningen: Instituut voor Liturgiewetenschap; Tilburg: Liturgisch Instituut, 2008.

Powers, D.G. "Salvation Through Participation: An Examination of the Notion of the Believers" Corporate Unity with Christ in Early Christian Soteriology." PhD diss., University of Leiden, 2001.

Purves, Jim. "The Sacrament of Fearful Intimacy." In *Baptist Sacramentalism 2*, edited by Cross and Thompson, 30–47.

Quintilian, *Institutio Oratoria.* Loeb Classical Library, 126. Translated by H.E. Butler. Cambridge, MA: Harvard University Press, 1986.

Siegrist, Anthony G. *Participating Witness: An Anabaptist Theology of Baptism and the Sacramental Character of the Church.* Eugene, OR: Pickwick, 2013.

Smit, Peter Ben. "Das Neue als Problem und Prinzip Neutestamentlicher Theologie." *Evangelische Theologie* 78.5 (2018) 375–84.

Thomas Aquinas. *Summa Theologiae.* Volume 4. Bibliotheca de Autores Cristianos; Madrit: La Editorial Catolica, 1958.

Tozer, A.W. *Worship: The Missing Jewel in the Evangelical Church.* Harrisburg, VA: Christian Publications, n.d.

Volf, Miroslav. *Captive to the Word of God: Engaging the Scriptures for Contemporary Theological Reflection.* Grand Rapids: Eerdmans, 2010.

Watts, Graham J. "Can Baptists Believe in Sacred Space? Some Theological Reflections." In *Baptist Sacramentalism 2*, edited by Cross and Thompson, 135–48.

Webber, Robert E. *Worship: Old & New.* Grand Rapids: Zondervan, 1994.

Wheeler, David. "Evangelical Proclamation and Teaching in the Twenty-First Century." In *Whatever Happened to Evangelicalism?* edited by Al Truesdale, 151–66. Kansas City, MO: Beacon Hill, 2017.

CHAPTER 14

Enough to Set a Kingdom Laughing: Divine Tragicomedy and Easter Laughter in a Weeping World

Jan Martijn Abrahamse

When the Lord restored the fortunes of Zion,
we were like those who dream.
Then our mouth was filled with laughter,
and our tongue with shouts of joy. (Ps. 126.1–2)

In J.R.R. Tolkien's *The Lord of the Rings*, the Hobbit Peregrin Took—or "Pippin"—looks upon the wizard Gandalf who suddenly broke into laughter just after their tragic encounter with Lord Denethor. "Pippin glanced in some wonder at the face now close beside his own, for the sound of that laugh had been gay and merry. Yet in the wizard's face he saw at first only lines of care and sorrow; though as he looked more intently he perceived that under all there was a great joy: a fountain of mirth enough to set a kingdom laughing, were it to gush forth."[1] Tolkien's description of Gandalf offers a vivid image of the theme of this article: the gift of laughter as the sacramental sensation of hope in a weeping world. By this I mean laughter as a tangible experience of another kingdom amidst the tragedy of life. But, what kind of laughter transcends our broken life?

Jürgen Moltmann, in his book *Die ersten Freigelassenen der Schöpfung* (1971), poses a similar question: "How can one laugh, if by no means all tears are wiped out, and every day new ones are added?"[2] He finds his answer in Christ's resurrection bringing forth the proleptic laughter of the redeemed as it announces the victory over death: "If you can laugh, you can cry too. If you

---

[1] Tolkien, *Lord of the Rings*, 3:759.

[2] Moltmann, *Die ersten Freigelassenen der Schöpfung*, 10, "Wie kan einer lachen, wenn doch keineswegs alle Tränen abgewischt sind, sondern täglich neue dazu kommen?" Moltmann's question is firmly embedded within his own life story, having seen the destruction of the Second World War after the bombardment of Hamburg by the Allied forces, see van Wyk, "Die heuristiese potensiaal van narratiwiteit vir sosiaal relevante Sistematiese Teologie."

have hope, you will be able to endure the world and mourn."[3] Moltmann's thesis re-joins us with the medieval liturgical practice of the so-called "Easter laughter" (*risus paschalis*) on the morning of Easter, as an appropriate celebration that God turned our tears into laughter: the celebration and joy of the resurrection manifest in a day of jokes, including also the homily, folly and laughter (cf. John 16.20).[4] Easter laughter in a broken world is somehow generated by the hope of the redeemed, precisely in confrontation with the tragedy of creation. To this end, this article intends to explore the possibility of Easter laughter within the context of the Baptist tradition. The aim is to develop our comical imagination and see the sacramental character of laughter within the "divine tragicomedy" that is Christian life. Laughter as a celebratory means of participation in God's redemptive presence in creation.[5] Yet, to discern the "real presence" of the comic in the world requires us to develop a sense of humor. For that reason, we will explore the gift of laughter as an experience of the divine through the remarkable story of Sarah in Genesis. Then, we will review John Bunyan's famous book *The Pilgrim's Progress* (1678) to help us discern a tragicomic perspective on Christian life that forms the theological framework in which we can receive laughter sacramentally. Together these stories will help us formulate a tragicomic perspective on Christian life that recognizes laughter as a celebration of the unexpected and mysterious workings of God.

---

[3] Moltmann, *Die ersten Freigelassenen der Schöpfung*, 37, "Wer lachen kann, kann auch weinen. Wer Hoffnung hat, wird fähig, die Welt auszuhalten und zu trauern."

[4] See Ratzinger (Pope Benedict XVI), *Bilder der Hoffnung*, 50–52. Cf. Bársony, "God's Clown"; Warning, *Ambivalences of Medieval Religious Drama*, 100–112; and recently Schuster, *Das Osterlachen*, 21–139. Allegedly, the ritual of *risus paschalis* goes back at least to the eleventh century. A first reference is found in a Good Friday hymn by Peter Abelard. Schuster, in his study, questions the pervasiveness of the *risus paschalis*, and concludes that it, in all likelihood, has its origins more in literary argument than as actual liturgical practice. Today, however, similar practices arise, known as "Holy Humor Sunday," "Bright Sunday," or "Holy Fools Sunday" within the English-speaking context.

[5] Following the example of Boersma, *Heavenly Participation*. I will join his broader approach to the created order as potentially sacramental in character (sacramental ontology) in order to recognize laughter as a sacramental sensation within a tragicomical vision of Christian life. Sacramental laughter should, however, not be equated with the so-called "laughter in the Spirit" associated with the Toronto Blessing in the 1990s, which featured an uncontrollable and hysterical laughter in response to a special anointment with the Spirit, on which see Beverly, *Holy Laughter and The Toronto Blessing*.

Divine Tragicomedy

Tragedy and comedy represent two major ways in which dramatic stories play out, based on their different responses to the incongruities of life, such as, notably, death, suffering, and despair.[6] Tragedies view life as a mere arbitrary result of fate and conflict, in which often superhuman heroes face various obstacles on their way to reach greatness or defeat. By contrast, comedies highlight feeble and questionable characters or anti-heroes, whose contingent lives display missteps and frailties designed to make us laugh. Comedies tend to make the incongruities of life light and more optimistic, finding pleasure even in conflict, while tragedies tend to resolve in bitterness and anger with its heroes.

Different authors have used a classic tragedy/comedy scheme to explain the comic character of Christian faith in opposition to the tragic condition of created order. Of course, we first think of *La Divina Commedia* (c.1308) by the Italian author Dante Alighieri, who used *commedia* to indicate the story's happy ending. In modern times, several authors have reconnected with the theatrical scheme of comedy versus tragedy to describe the Christian story. Harvey Cox gave an impetus for a comic approach, arguing that laughter expresses the voice of faith and hope in opposition to tragic necessity and stoic resignation.[7] More elaborate is the work of Conrad Hyers, who, in multiple books, outlined a comic theological frame of thought.[8] The comic vision, Hyers explains, allows us to recapture the awkwardness of the biblical story, featuring the nonheroic, the peripheral ordinary, and the nonhierarchical reversal of salvation itself.[9]

Of particular interest to our purposes are the contributions of Reinhold Niebuhr and Ralph Wood. To Niebuhr, humor and laughter are a prelude to faith and prayer, not part of faith itself: "Laughter is thus not merely a vestibule but also a 'no-man's land' between faith and despair … an expression of our sense of the meaningless of life."[10] Laughter, to Niebuhr,

---

[6] See Morreall, *Comedy, Tragedy and Religion*, esp. 3–40. For an introduction into Greek tragedy and comedy, see Walton, *Greek Sense of Theater*.

[7] Cox, *Feast of Fools*, 149–57.

[8] See, e.g., Hyers, *Holy Laughter*; *Comic Vision*; *And God Created Laughter*; and *Spirituality of Comedy*, containing much of what he published in his earlier *Comic Vision*.

[9] See Hyers, *Comic Vision*, 138–53. More recently, Vanhoozer, *Drama of Doctrine*, 53, who also described the whole biblical story—or "theo-drama" following Von Balthasar, *Theodramatik*—in terms of comedy, "The theo-drama is nothing less than a covenant-comedy of cosmic significance." See also Vanhoozer's *Faith Speaking Understanding*, 94–95.

[10] Niebuhr, "Humor and Faith," 115. Cf. Fackre, *Promise of Reinhold Niebuhr*, 71–74.

serves to provide an ironic perspective to human life and expose our own tragic sinfulness, but there is no laughter from the vantage point of the cross. Even the enjoyment of reconciliation does not bring Christians to laughter, except "the capacity to laugh at themselves and others" and "To know oneself a sinner."[11] As a consequence, Niebuhr diminished the significance of comedy when he stated that "when we turn life into a comedy we also reduce it to meaninglessness."[12] In the end, comic laughter fails to adequately address the incongruities of life, which only faith can, by its assertion that they will be overcome by God's power and love.

In his book *The Comedy of Redemption* (1988), Ralph Wood contested Niebuhr's tragic vision, advocating that Christian faith is rather comic by nature: "It is about eschatological laughter and joy and hope."[13] He does not deny the tragic in life, but contends that human joy and laughter can only become intelligible when motivated by the higher comedy of the gospel. For if humanity was left on its own—as Niebuhr seems to imply—"Comedy remains powerlessly encased within the same world it seeks to correct and transform."[14] In other words, Niebuhr overlooked the eschatological establishment of God's kingdom amidst the tragedy of human existence.[15] In Wood's view, true laughter is made possible through the radical grace of God's intervening advent in Christ conquering sin and death through the resurrection. In this sense, comedy is the celebration of a christological constituted assurance that the joyous God is "already" recreating the tragedy of this world into comedy (cf. Rev. 21.3–5).

Wood's perspective rightly corrects Niebuhr's dualism between laughter and faith. However, Christian faith is not only about the bigger picture of proclaimed faith, but also—as Baptists will never grow tired to emphasize—about our concrete and tangible lives. Following Christ often confronts us with the "not yet" of God's kingdom. Christians, I contend, therefore, learn to view the world's history, including their own lives, as a divine "tragicomedy." The tragic and the comical are indeed close, and yet—I contend—antithetical elements; and precisely in their opposition they denote the ambivalent character of Christian life.[16] The tragicomic vision calls attention to the

---

[11] Niebuhr, "Humor and Faith," 122–23.

[12] Niebuhr, "Humor and Faith," 127.

[13] Wood, *Comedy of Redemption*, 1.

[14] Wood, *Comedy of Redemption*, 30.

[15] See Wood, *Comedy of Redemption*, 4–22.

[16] See Berger, *Redeeming Laughter*, 117–33. *Contra* Fransen, *Het leven als tragikomedie*, 10. Fransen's general argument is, nonetheless, rather concomitant with mine; that is to say that a comical perspective offers a different look at the tragedies of

incongruity of living "between the times." The dialectical opposition between
fallen creation and the eschatological reign of God. Life's incongruity gives
rise to laughter as a tangible gift of experiencing the world anew, a perspective
that offers hope and redeems us from cynicism. Laughter, therefore, can be a
sacramental experience, the sensation of the "already" in the "not yet," not to
disguise tears or to wipe them away, but laughter through tears.

Sarah and the Birth of Divine Laughter

When and where does laughter become an experience of the divine? The *locus
classicus* on tragicomic laughter is without a doubt the story of Sarah within
the Abraham-cycle in Genesis 18 and 21.[17] Laughter is at the center of the
entire story. Before Sarah, it is Abraham who laughs when hearing the
announcement of the forthcoming pregnancy of his wife (17.17), then Sarah is
reported to laugh twice; once as expression of tragedy (18.12) and once after
the surprising birth of Isaac, expressing the joyous laughter of comic
redemption (21.6). A son who is fittingly called Isaac, "he laughs." Laughter
continues to be prominent in the story after Isaac is born, as Ishmael
ambiguously "laughs" at his brother (21.9) causing a break in the family.[18]
Sarai's own story, of course, began when Abram was called out of his
homeland, leaving his kinship to become a great nation (12.1–3),[19] having
received the promise of having a great posterity (13.15–16), and bringing forth
a son "from his own loins" (15.4)—not from Hagar—but, as it is repeatedly
stressed, through his own wife Sarah (17.15–16, 19, 21). Until now, Sarah is
already many years waiting for a promise, she may or may not have heard from
Abraham. After ninety years of childlessness all resources to have a baby have
dried out and Sarah has lost all hope. A most *fatal* situation in a context and
culture where motherhood is intrinsically connected to honor and social status.

In the opening verses, Abraham and Sarah receive three mysterious visitors
under the trees of Mamre. Three men—who together will be identified as

---

life by, on the one hand, acknowledging life's difficulties and, on the other hand,
enlightening its consequences and thereby making life more bearable.

[17] Cf. Kuschel, *Laughter*, 49–53; and Conybeare, *Laughter of Sarah*. Comic motives
are found throughout the book of Genesis, see, e.g., Whedbee, *Bible and the Comic
Vision*, 15–125; Kaminsky, "Humor and the Theology of Hope"; and Anderson, *Jacob
and the Divine Trickster*. The story of Sarah's laughter is also recorded in the Qur'an
(11 Sūrat Hūd 71), see Stetkevych, "Sarah and the Hyena."

[18] See Wenham, *Genesis 16–50*, 82; Zucker, "What Sarah Saw," 54–63; and Pinker,
"Expulsion of Hagar and Ishmael." In Gen. 21.9 the verb צחק is conjugated into the
piel (cf. Gen. 19.14), which might suggest a change in meaning to the *qal*-version in
verse 6.

[19] See extensively Moberly, *Theology of Genesis*, 141–60.

Jahweh יְהֹוָה (21.1)—suddenly appeared at the horizon (18.1–2).[20] Abraham is portrayed as an exceedingly good middle eastern host, suspending his siesta in order to offer his guests—with some sense of understatement ("a morsel of bread")—a royal meal (18.6–8).[21] After the meal, the visitors ask Abraham, "Where is Sarah your wife?" (18.9). Once more the narrator unfolds in a threefold description the despairing infertility of the couple: they are old, advanced in years, and Sarah has gone passed the menopause.[22] Though absent, being a married woman she remains a close bystander who is eavesdropping on the male conversation. Sarah now hears herself the promise that she will become pregnant. Considering the hopelessness of her own condition, "Sarah laughed to herself, saying, 'After I am worn out, and my lord is old, shall I have pleasure?'" (18.12 וַתִּצְחַק). Sarah's own words not only reiterate what the narrator has already told us, but also intensifies its meaning. She refers to tangible transformations her body went through, not only making it impossible to bare children but even to experience sexual pleasure due to the old age of her husband.[23] Tragedy has come to define her identity. Sarah's laughs cynically *at* herself, in downhearted disbelief, because of many years of unanswered waiting.[24] Yet the remarkable thing happens, though laughing inwardly, God heard her laughter: "The Lord said to Abraham, 'Why did Sarah laugh and say, "Shall I indeed bear a child, now that I am old?" Is anything too hard for the Lord?'" (18.13–14).[25] So, the tragedy of the story is suddenly being questioned by the address of God and then overturned by his promise. Sarah's barrenness and shame are, so it seems, "questioned" by God. However, when Sarah denies having done so, God's words directly addresses Sarah and for the first time God enters into dialogue with her: "No,

---

[20] Cf. Alter, *Genesis*, 77.

[21] See McKeown, *Genesis*, 103; Wenham, *Genesis 16–50*, 45; and Bolin, "Role of Exchange in Ancient Mediterranean Religion," 44–45.

[22] Alter, *Genesis*, 79.

[23] Cf. Alter, *Genesis*, 79; and Shkop, "And Sarah Laughed," 43.

[24] See Moberly, *Genesis 12–50*, 23 and 25; Wenham, *Genesis 16–50*, 48–49; McKeown, *Genesis*, 104. Cf. Shkop, "And Sarah Laughed," 42–51, who concludes, 49, that both 18.12 and 21.6 are instances of bittersweet laughter; the first instance gives expression to the irony of the situation both being elderly people, and the second a manifestation of substitute incredulity by which the message of an elderly woman giving birth to a child would be received by her context. In this way, the cynical laugher of Sarah is prophetic of the laughter of Ishmael in 21.9. Yet, she does not take the change in grammatical conjugation between 21.6 (צָחֹק, *qal*) and 21.9 (מְצַחֵק, *piel*) into account that calls for a more intensive translation.

[25] Claassens, "Laughter and Tears," 300–301.

but you did laugh" (18.15, צָחָקְתְּ). This divine visit and the promise of a son interrupts Sarah's tragedy.[26]

In Genesis 21.1 God literally "visits" (פָּקַד) Sarah herself, as she becomes pregnant from Abraham though he is still "in his old age" (21.1). It shows that the circumstances of her tragedy are not lifted, but that redemption is brought within old age. A joy that brings her the sensation of laughter, no longer something in secret, but out loud. A laughter that Sarah explains as a divine gift: "God has made laughter for me; everyone who hears will laugh over me" (21.6).[27] Sarah's words are a play on Isaac's name—*nomen est omen*—"he laughs." His name testifies Sarah's reversed situation and the surprising visit of God bringing joy.[28] Catherine Conybeare describes the scenery well: "She is consumed with laughter; she has become laughter."[29] Sarah's laugher is a sensation of the God who has visited her, turned her tragedy into comedy, reconnecting her with the drama of redemption. At the same time, as Robert Alter mentions, her laughter has also an ironic twist to it: "All who hear of it may laugh, rejoice, with Sarah, but the hint that they might also laugh at her is evident in her language."[30] The celebration of God's redemptive activity, confirms our human finitude.[31]

Divine laughter is born within a barren situation. The story of Sarah shows us laughter as a divine gift in celebration of experienced redemption. Herein lies the difference: not all laughter is a divine gift, since not all laughter is a gift constituted by a divine promise and visitation. Sarah's laughter is a bodily manifestation in response to a comic twist of tragic events overtaking her by the surprise that reconnects her with God's activity in this broken world. but in what kind of worldview can Baptists receive laughter as a divine gift?

---

[26] See Levine, "Sarah/Sodom, Birth, Destruction, and Synchronic Transaction." In the narrative structure of Genesis 18 and 19, the same messengers who announced a comic turn in Sarah's tragedy, will proclaim judgment over Sodom (cf. Gen. 18.16–33). Sarah's announcement of renewed fertility overcoming her barrenness contrasts with the fate of Sodom going from an Edenic valley to destruction.

[27] There is even some inclination of "sexual refreshment" and restoration of her menstruation cycle in Sarah's words (cf. Gen. 26.8), see Stetkevych, "Sarah and the Hyena," 33–35.

[28] See Whedbee, *Bible and the Comic Vision*, 80. Cf. Kidner, *Genesis*, 150; McKeown, *Genesis*, 112–13.

[29] Conybeare, *Laughter of Sarah*, 14.

[30] Alter, *Genesis*, 97.

[31] Cf. Cohen, *Jokes*, 41, "Thus this laughter is an expression of our humanity, our finite capacity, our ability to live with what we cannot understand or subdue."

Re-Seeing the World:
Reviewing Bunyan's Pilgrim's Progress as Tragicomedy

During his time in Bedford prison, John Bunyan (1628–88) wrote the first part of his classic *A Pilgrim's Progress*, an outcome of his own struggle with endurance and the search for joy in his tragic circumstances.[32] Though evidently fueled by personal experience, its content must also be read in close relation to his role as an organizational leader within English Nonconformity, and the persecution they experienced.[33] Designed as an allegory, Bunyan intended to convey to his audience a deeper understanding of the Christian life, investing spiritual significance to their lives in order for them to sense the presence of Christ.[34] In other words, he invited them to "re-see" the world and their place within it.

The story features a man who the reader will get to know as "Christian." In the opening of the story he is weeping and in great dismay. Bunyan describes in heavy words the tragedy of Christian. He leaves his home and with it the fate of his town—appropriately called the City of Destruction—having gained new hope through the message of the Evangelist who opened his eyes for a true destiny: "There is an endless Kingdom to be Inhabited, and everlasting life to be given us; that we may Inhabit that Kingdom for ever . . . There shall be no more crying, nor sorrow; For he that is the owner of the places, will wipe all tears from our eyes."[35] It is a road pilgrims must travel in order to reach their destiny. Every pilgrim needs to go through the Wicked Gate and needs to stop at the cross. The journey itself is never without its conflicts, doubts and struggles, coming from various angles in the form of outspoken enemies, random travelers, and society at large, all of who intend to divert Christian from his path. Noteworthy is his encounter with Mr Worldly-Wiseman who presses him not to follow the direction pointed out by Evangelist, for "there is not a more dangerous and troublesome way in the world."[36] When Christian is back on the road after having strayed a bit, he comes to the house of Interpreter, who shows him a picture of man with the

---

[32] See Freeman, *Undomesticated Dissent*, 39–83. Freeman shows the close connection between Bunyan's *Pilgrim's Progress* and the "slumbering dissent" of the mid-seventeenth century, a period in which Dissenters faced heavy suppression to enforce conformity. Bunyan, accordingly, invites his readers to mirror their lives to the pilgrimage of the main character "Christian"—what Freeman terms "eschatological imagination," 48.

[33] See Greaves, *John Bunyan and English Nonconformity*, 71–87; White, "John Bunyan and the Context of Persecution," 51–62; and Batson, *Pilgrim's Progress*, 13.

[34] Cf. Batson, *Pilgrim's Progress*, 15–16; and Davies, *Graceful Reading*, 175–221.

[35] Bunyan, *Pilgrim's Progress*, 14–15.

[36] Bunyan, *Pilgrim's Progress*, 18.

eyes lifted up to heaven and the world behind his back: "it stood as if it pleaded with Men, and a Crown of Gold did hang over its head." Mr Interpreter shows Christian its meaning: "it is to shew thee, that his work is to know and unfold dark things to sinners; even as also thou sees him stand as if he Pleaded with Men; And whereas thou seest the World as cast behind him, and that a Crown hangs over his head; that is, to shew thee that slighting and despising the things that are present, for the love that he hath to his Masters service, he is sure in the World that comes next to have Glory for his Reward."[37] It is from this new perspective that Christian is to view his journey. Two men, Passion and Patience represent two ways of relating to *this* world; the first seeks everything in the present, the second expects to receive it in the next. Not only, continues Mr Interpreter, will Patience have the best reward, but also the best laugh.

> Nay, you may add another; to wit, The glory of the *next* World will never wear out; but these are suddenly gone. Therefore *Passion* had not so much reason to laugh at *Patience*, because he had his good things first, as *Patience* will have to laugh at *Passion*, because he had his best things *last*; for *first* must give place to *last* because *last* must have his time to come, but *last* gives place to *nothing*; for there is not another to succeed: he, therefore that hath his Portion *first*, must needs have a time to spend it; but he that has his Portion *last*, must have it lastingly.[38]

To see the world differently generates a laughter that allows Christian to view the present in a different light; light that essentially brings a joy that stands over the enjoyment of transient things.[39] This does not mean that all laughter represents "the next world." During his travels, Christian meets different people who laugh at the story of the Celestial City, demonstrating "that you must through many tribulations enter into the Kingdom of Heaven."[40] Significant in Bunyan's story is the passage in which Christian and Faithful are to go through the demonic city of Vanity and notably its Fair with seductive merchandize, for "the way to the Cœlestial City lyes just thorow *this Town*."[41] Going through Vanity Fair they are made fun of, besmeared, even abused. Faithful is eventually put to death, being falsely accused, condemned

---

[37] Bunyan, *Pilgrim's Progress*, 26.

[38] Bunyan, *Pilgrim's Progress*, 28 (italics original).

[39] Cf. Bunyan, *Grace Abounding*, 89, "Sometimes, when I have been in the savour of them, I have been able to laugh at destruction, *and to fear neither the horse nor his rider*. I have had sweet sights of the forgiveness of my sins in this place, and of my being with Jesus in another world" (italics original).

[40] Bunyan, *Pilgrim's Progress*, 69.

[41] Bunyan, *Pilgrim's Progress*, 70.

and tortured. Though Christian could get away he has to be reminded of his destiny over and over again to learn how the vision of the Celestial City shapes the present reality of his journey. His faith is tested heavily once more in Doubting-Castle where they are imprisoned by the Giant Despair. Toward the end of his travels his new companion, Hopeful, entrusts Christian with a vivid account of his conversion and encounter with Jesus Christ: "And now was my heart full of joy, mine eyes full of tears, and mine affections running over with love to the Name, People, and Ways of Jesus Christ."[42]

Through his abundant use of sensory imagery, Bunyan tried to enable his readers to re-see their present condition through the lens of the eschatological vision represented by the Celestial City.[43] Significant is his entanglement of biblical texts and biblical figures with the story process of *The Pilgrim's Progress*, enabling him to construe a sacred view of Christian life.[44] Puritans, in whose lineage Bunyan writes, recognized conversion experiences as a reality of divine presence.[45] Though undertaking a journey to glory, Christian is no hero in the classic sense—neither tragic nor comic—he is a typical "saint" exemplifying the character of a true pilgrim. Much like we saw with Sarah, Christian's joy and laughter represent the proleptic experience of the hope of another kingdom provoked by the tragedies of his journey.

Travelers in Tragedy

As Bunyan's allegory of Christian life showed us, laughter in a Baptist vision does not evade the tragedy of human life and all of creation. Tragedy concerns those incongruities of life which are beyond human control, but nonetheless define our existence and become real in the experiences of loss, suffering, despair, decay, and injustice. Though tragedy is obviously related to our finite existence and vulnerability (ontology) regardless of our gender, health status,

---

[42] Bunyan, *Pilgrim's Progress*, 110.

[43] Cf. Greaves, *John Bunyan and English Nonconformity*, 25–26; and Freeman, *Undomesticated Dissent*, 55.

[44] See Davies, *Graceful Reading*, 220, "Bunyan's allegorical method, like Midrash, offers itself as both an interpretation of Scripture and instruction about belief and, mediating between the two, conventional distinctions between 'text and tradition', 'interpretation and composition' become effaced for allegorist and reader alike." Cf. Allen, "Rehabilitation of Pilgrim's Progress"; and Noble, "A Writ Good Guide," 31.

[45] Cf. Freeman, *Undomesticated Dissent*, 57, "This 'experience' was not a psychological permutation of human affection as described by William James or an anthropological feeling of absolute dependence as suggested by Friedrich Schleiermacher. It was a constellation of convictions and affections that bore the evidence of the presence and activity of God in the soul." Cf. Abrahamse, "'Dumb Dogs That Cannot Bark,'" 293–98.

or race,[46] they do not necessarily coincide. Within the Christian tradition life's tragedy is not seen as a random fate (*fatum*), but interpreted as a consequence of what is generally and theologically designated as the "fall" into sin (cf. Gen. 3.1–24) and thus can be rightfully called "evil."[47] Its narrative function is to explain the present state of creation by saying equally that evil is not original and yet unmistakably interwoven with all of existence. Sixteenth-century Baptist confessions, such as the *London Confessions* of 1644 and 1688, and the *Orthodox Creed* of 1678, all use the imagery of "Fall/fallen" in this way.[48] Within a tragic perspective on creation, sins are the tragic attempts of humanity to uphold its dignity while they paradoxically only further unveil the reality of our brokenness. The tragic condition of this world, therefore, cannot be evaded or transcended, but, as Bunyan shows us, should be confessed and suffered like the "travails" of a pilgrimage. "This Book will make a Travailer of thee," he writes to his readers.[49] We are bound to find our way in a broken world with all the incongruities that come with it.[50] Hence, the notion of tragedy is not used as an abstract theory about life, but rather calls attention to the reality of embodied existence as part of a fallen creation.[51] For Stanley Hauerwas facing tragedy is derived from the worship to a God who has taken the tragic character of our existence into his very life by the incarnation.[52] Precisely for this reason, he argues, tragedy can never have the final say.

---

[46] See Springhart, "Vulnerable Creation." Springhart argues for the ambivalent character of vulnerability having both threatening as well as enriching dimensions. Consequently, she uses "tragedy" to denote those situations in which human vulnerability faces this threatening dimension.

[47] See Van den Brink, "Should We Drop the Fall?" 761–77. There is, of course, considerable debate whether a historical "fall" fits with the discoveries of contemporary evolutionary science. Yet, as Van den Brink carefully argues, there is no decisive contradiction between evolution—describing and explaining the process of the development of life—and the theological notion of the fall to describe the dramatic change that by refusing God's call, humanity condemned itself to a life bound to tragedy. See Van den Brink, *En de aarde bracht voort*, 207–62. For a recent study on evil, see Peckham, *Theodicy of Love*.

[48] See Lumpkin and Leonard, eds, *Baptist Confessions of Faith*, 145, 242–44, and 308.

[49] Bunyan, *Pilgrim's Progress*, 9.

[50] Cf. Houtepen, *Uit aarde, naar Gods beeld*, 84.

[51] For my understanding of embodied existence, see McClendon, *Ethics*, 85–118.

[52] See Hauerwas, *Truthfulness and Tragedy*, 11–12 and 57–70, *Community of Character*, 101–108, and *Peaceable Kingdom*, 142–46. Cf. Wells, *Transforming Fate into Destiny*, 164–66. Recently Hauerwas has become more critical toward the use of the "tragedy/comedy framework" as they are open to multiple interpretations, see his *Work of Theology*, 231–32.

Facing tragedy is not the same as becoming defined by tragedy.[53] Fate is destroyed through hope made bodily present by God in Christ: "Without such a declaration, patience in the face of the tragic could as easily be but a stoic acquiescence to fate."[54] Tragedy is no fate, but, in a way, destiny for those who follow a God who lived a life of tragedy, of tears and suffering, learning obedience (Heb. 5.7–8). Therefore, Christian was destined to go through Vanity Fair for "The Prince of Princes himself, when here, went through this Town."[55]

Tragedy, it follows, "schools" our character in Christ. Rather than resolving the incongruity of existence, as Niebuhr contended, Christian's witness evokes tragedy.[56] A Christian life calls for faithfulness when facing opposition, for truthfulness when you are lied to, for patience with people who treat you unkindly, and for hospitality and generosity toward strangers. Character formation is well understood as a journey through tragedy, as vividly depicted in the story of *The Pilgrim's Progress*, when Christian and Faithful encounter heavy resistance due to their perseverance to reach their destiny following Christ through Vanity Fair: "But *Christian* and *Faithful* behaved themselves yet more wisely, and received the ignominy and shame that was cast upon them, with so much meekness and patience, that it won to their side (though but few in comparison of the rest) several of the men in the *Fair*."[57] Witness is tragic, yet not in the shape of the heroism found in Greek tragedies, which display superhuman qualities; either violently achieving victories or falling from positions of power and influence.[58] Facing tragedy is about sainthood.[59] Saints are people who have learned to embody in their lives the central theological doctrines and ethical truths of the faith, and through their example introduce the church anew in its convictions brought forth by the gospel. This

---

[53] Cf. Hunter, *To Change the World*, 173–75. Hunter notes that, at least in the Western context, outsiders define Christianity by its rhetoric of resentment and anger, or the absence of positive expressions of joy and delight toward society and its institutions.

[54] Hauerwas, *Peaceable Kingdom*, 145.

[55] Bunyan, *Pilgrim's Progress*, 70.

[56] See Hauerwas, *Community of Character*, 107, "Our character is therefore the source of our strength, as it provides us with a history of commitment, but in doing so it also sets the stage for the possibility of tragedy."

[57] Bunyan, *Pilgrim's Progress*, 73.

[58] See Morreall, *Comedy, Tragedy and Religion*, 7–8; and Walton, *Greek Sense of Theater*, 55 and 106.

[59] See the recent retrieval of Baptist "saints" in Fiddes, Haymes and Kidd, *Baptists and the Communion of Saints*. Earlier McClendon made a similar call, see "Do We Need Saints?"

means that it includes both failures as well as victories in faithfulness. The author of Hebrews, therefore, includes Sarah in his cloud of saints: "By faith Sarah herself received power to conceive, even when she was past the age, since she considered him faithful who had promised" (Heb. 11.11). Tragedy trains "saints," as Hauerwas explains, "For tragedy consists in the moral necessity of having to risk our lives and the lives of others in order to live faithful to the histories that are the only means we have for knowing and living truthfully."[60]

In the Second Part of *The Pilgrim's Progress*, Christiana finds the Valley of Humiliation where Christian fought Apollyon, a beautiful place filled with lilies, as a monument to his spiritual virtues.[61] The difference with tragic heroism is that sainthood is not self-dependent, but depends on God's grace. Christ is not only exemplary—offering an alternative pathway to be followed on one's own—but moreover reforming and enabling pilgrims to continue the journey. In the words of Mr Interpreter, "*Christ*, who continually, with the Oyl of his Grace, maintains the work already begun in the heart."[62] Hence, tragedy on its own falls short of recognizing the comic eschatology of grace "already" at work—provoking the incongruity that laughter requires.

Experiencing the Comedy of Resurrection

Christians refuse to be defined by tragedy, precisely because they have caught a glimpse of an alternate story than the rule of fate having come to see that God in Christ's resurrection changed the fate of this world.[63] Like Moltmann, Wood takes the resurrection to be the decisive turning point in human history. He makes a helpful distinction between mere cheerfulness and the "deeper comedy" of the gospel.[64] Instead of abandoning humanity to its own resources, the deeper comedy of Christian faith envisions God as acting in history through the risen Lord to establish his eschatological kingdom.[65]

---

[60] Hauerwas, *Community of Character*, 106.

[61] See Batson, *Pilgrim's Progress*, 44.

[62] Bunyan, *Pilgrim's Progress*, 28 (italics original).

[63] Cf. McClendon, *Ethics*, 96, "To be sure the world is not Christian; there is fallenness and rebellion and ruin enough here. But the eyes through which we Christians see the world are redeemed eyes; it is through these eyes that we must be trained to look if we would see without double or narrow vision."

[64] Wood, *Comedy of Redemption*, 4, "Cheer is a mere pumped-up eagerness and enthusiasm, a grinning obliviousness to the real sorrows and joys of life. Humor, by contrast, is a deep gladness of soul that does not blink the reality of evil and tragedy, but interprets them in the light of a higher and deeper comedy."

[65] See Wood, *Comedy of Redemption*, 9 and 30.

There is, one could say, a "comic already" of God's kingdom that does not hold humanity to its self-made choices. This "already" is found in God's visiting grace (Barth's "Yes") in the crucified and resurrected Jesus.[66] Christian comedy is, therefore, directly related to and dependent on eschatological hope generated by Christ's resurrection. This deeper comedy is what Pippin saw in the "resurrected" Gandalf, reversing the fate of death. It is the same joy Christian experienced when he is visited by "three shining ones" who pronounce his sins to be forgiven—"Then *Christian* gave three leaps for joy."[67] The comic perspective resounds with the apocalyptic framework of the *Christus Victor* motif that understands history as an arena of God's activity.[68] God's coming in Christ is an eschatological intervention and divine visitation that breaks into the tragic confinement of human life enacting redemption founded upon his death and resurrection. "Easter is the ultimate surprise, the punch line of God's story, turning creation on its head with the most surprising reversal of all."[69] A Christian view is, therefore, comical in so far as it sees the world from the viewpoint of the inbreaking of God's kingdom within the tragic conditions of the fall: Jesus' resurrection conquering sin and death. A "visit" that generates laughter, and can therefore rightly be called "Easter laughter."[70] It brings to expression the joy of the asymmetry of grace, overcoming a dualistic relation between God and creation.

However, comedy alone runs the risk of failing to take the "not yet" of Christ's resurrection fully into account. Where tragedy is dominant and pervasive, the comic is not so easily detected and discovered. Even the resurrected Christ is not straightforwardly recognized. The two men on their way to Emmaus, the Twelve, Mary, and Thomas, all need Christ's revelatory words to open their eyes to see (cf. Luke 24.31 and 39; John 20.16 and 27). Matthew even mentions that "some doubted" just before Jesus's ascension (Matt. 28.17). Though the fate of death lost its final say, the hope of the resurrection continues to bear the marks of tragedy (cf. John 20.27–28; 1 Cor. 15.54[b]–55).[71] In *Pilgrim's Progress*, even Christian himself carries the

---

[66] See Wood, *Comedy of Redemption*, 34–56 and 280–85.

[67] Bunyan, *Pilgrim's Progress*, 33.

[68] See Rutledge, *Crucifixion*, 348–94; cf. Wood, *Comedy of Redemption*, 18.

[69] Copenhaver, "Laughter at Easter," 17.

[70] See Schuster, *Das Osterlachen*, 107–10.

[71] Cf. Garland, *1 Corinthians*, 746, "Christ's death and resurrection signify that Christians are delivered from the fallen world under the tyranny of the triumvirate of sin, law, and death and await only the final manifestation of Christ, which will inaugurate their final transformation."

"stigmata" of his encounter with the beast Apollyon[72]—signs of his tragedy, witnessing that the laughter of redemption is never far from tears. Despair strikes Christian again just before entering the Celestial City, because there is no bridge and the water is deep.[73] It shows the comic as both mysterious and fragile, that the joy and laughter of the comedy of redemption are never in our grasp. Comedy takes us by surprise and cannot be planned, much like Sarah's unexpected visitation.[74] Peter Berger aptly writes, "At least for the duration of the comic perception, the tragedy of man is bracketed."[75]

The story by which Christians live enables them to recognize the comic dimension of existence. The comic turn is the surprising discovery that our lives are not left to fate. The comic vision is not to evade or ignore the brokenness of reality, but to express our hope for this reality. "Christ the Lord is Victor even in the midst of the suffering of his followers."[76] To experience the comedy in the tragedy of life, is to recognize God's graceful presence in created order.

The Sacramental Character of Laughter

We have seen how tragedy and comedy are two intertwined sides of the drama of Christian life. Baptists like John Bunyan, envisioned Christian life through the lens of sacred history: a divine tragicomedy playing out between the "already and "not yet."[77] A tragicomic understanding of Christian life presumes a sacramental understanding of the relation between God and creation. Not only that God is active within the created order, but, moreover, it holds that Christian life itself is a way of participating in God's redemptive

---

[72] See Bunyan, *Pilgrim's Progress*, 48, "*Apollyon* wounded him in his *head*, his *hand*, and *foot*" (italics original).

[73] See Bunyan, *Pilgrim's Progress*, 120–21.

[74] I borrowed this wording from the famous biographical account of Lewis, *Surprised by Joy*, 181. Lewis vividly describes his own search for joy and the difficulty of obtaining it, 169: "I again tasted Joy. But far more often I frightened it away by my greedy impatience to snare it, and, even when it came, instantly destroyed it by introspection, and at all times vulgarized it by my false assumption about its nature." Later on, Lewis discovers joy (as an "aesthetic experience," 205 and 221) should not be longed for by itself, 220: "Joy itself, considered simply as an event in my own mind, turned out to be of no value at all. All the value lay in that of which Joy was the desiring." Yet, 238, after his conversion he discovered that joy itself was a pointer to God, and thereby became joy—as experience—less important.

[75] Berger, *Rumor of Angels*, 79.

[76] Rutledge, *Crucifixion*, 386.

[77] In a way this is what McClendon does in his classic study *Biography as Theology*.

presence in the tragedy of this broken world. In the words of Hans Boersma, "life on earth takes on a heavenly dimension."[78] Seeing the sacred character of history and the sacramental dimension of Christian life, however, does not diminish the significance of the particular sacraments of baptism and eucharist.[79] Sacramentality denotes the participatory character of the created order as a realm of God's redemptive—that is graceful—presence. Not that we can locate God in the material, but that we, as material beings, are discovered to our finite locality within God's active presence (cf. Acts 17.28). From this perspective, sacramentality makes sacraments intelligible. Accordingly, laughter does not "mediate" grace like the sacraments do, rather they bring to expression a sacramental understanding of Christian life—that is, a participatory life in God's transformative real presence in creation.[80]

Both Bunyan's allegorical story and the biblical story of Sarah in Genesis 21, describe the wonder of the last laugh, the laugh that flows from hope as a gift of God; laughter as an expression of surprise about the reversal of expectations, that tragedy is not all there is. Within the confinements of the fallen created order Christians enjoy the reality of God's rule made tangible in the resurrection. Karl Barth writes in a sermon on Psalm 34.6 about Christian life: "Sagen wir es ruhig: er hat etwas zum Lachen bekommen und kann dieses Lachen auch dann nich ganz verbeissen, wenn es ihm um übrigen gar nicht zum Lachen ist."[81] The incongruity of Christian life—being reminded of the eschatological "already" of the resurrection in the "not yet" of broken creation—provokes laughter. Laughter is a very bodily experience and expression, overruling our physical control.[82] In this way, we interpret laughter as a divine gift in eschatological anticipation by which Christians sense the "real presence" of God's comic turnaround. Along these lines, laughter can be sacramental as it conveys the joy of redemption, the celebration of God's rule over tragedy. Of course, like the story of Sarah shows, this does not mean that

---

[78] Boersma, *Heavenly Participation*, 5.

[79] As is John Colwell's concern, *Promise and Presence*, 55. To prevent us from obliterating distinctiveness, I would differentiate between "sacramentality/sacramental" and "sacrament"; the first denoting the participatory sphere of creation in God's creative presence in which the sacraments—as means of his grace—are possible and plausible. Cf. Bakker, "Roaring Side of the Ministry," 404 n.3; and Brinkman, *Schepping en sacrament*, 167–71.

[80] Boersma, *Heavenly Participation*, 187. Cf. Pinnock, "Physical Side of Being Spiritual."

[81] Barth, *Den Gefangenen Befreiung*, 43 ("Let it be said: he has got something to laugh about and cannot completely suppress this laugh even if there is nothing to laugh about"); cf. Schuster, *Das Osterlachen*, 40.

[82] See extensively the work of Bergson, *Le Rire*; also Zijderveld, *Waarom wij lachen*, 133–97.

laughter is a continuing sign through which God's presence is experienced.[83] Not all laughter is a divine gift. but like the pilgrims in Psalm 126,[84] Christians are being trained to see the world and its history sacramentally through the lens of tragicomedy and develop a sense of humor. Hence, we can appreciate laughter sacramentally as a bodily sensation of the comic dimension of God's redeeming presence in confrontation with our fallen world.

A vivid example of such laughter is offered by Susannah Spurgeon, who tells this story of how she one time broke into laughter after praying to God because of a hurtful letter sent to her husband in the midst of the Downgrade Controversy, who himself—due to his illness—spent time in the French resort of Mentone: "and I absolutely *laughed aloud*, so little did I fear what men could do." To explain her experience Susannah used the wording of the story of Sarah and the surprising birth of Isaac in Genesis 21, as she writes to Charles: "the Lord 'had made me to laugh'," to which he then answered, "'I laugh with you.'"[85] Susannah uses the story of Sarah to understand themselves within the tragicomic experience of Christian life. She shows us sacramental laughter, echoing the laughter of Sarah, the experience that celebrates Christ's rule amidst tragedy.

Conclusion: What if God Restored our Laughter?

How could Gandalf laugh amidst the terror that was spreading from Mordor? Why did ninety-year old Sarah laugh when she received a child? What did Bunyan mean with "having the best laugh"? Could it be that by laughing we celebrate and experience the God who reigns? Baptists need to retrieve a sacred view of Christian life that allows us to laugh again. The God who made comic history in Jesus Christ's resurrection, will fulfill that history when he wipes all tears from our eyes. A Christian view of life is nevertheless tragic in so far as it teaches us to take the incongruities not only as life's unavoidable side-effect, but as the tangible context that allows us to be disciplined by Christ. The comic dimension does not dissolve the tragedy, but embraces it. In Easter laughter, therefore, like Sarah's laughter, tragedy and comedy are intertwined; a laughter through tears. Such laughter expresses a tangible experience of God's redemptive presence in our broken world. Baptists have to develop a comic sensibility that recognizes God's redemption in a weeping world, so that we may receive laughter sacramentally: the real celebration of God's presence turning tragedy into comedy.

---

[83] Cf. Colwell, *Promise and Presence*, 57.

[84] See Abrahamse, *Breekbaar halleluja*, 85–93.

[85] Spurgeon, *Autobiography*, 4:258 (italics original).

Bibliography

Abrahamse, Jan Martijn. *Breekbaar halleluja: Onderweg met de pelgrimspsalmen.* Utrecht: KokBoekencentrum, 2018.

————. "'Dumb Dogs That Cannot Bark': The Puritan Origins of Preaching Revival." In *Baptists and Revivals: Papers from the Seventh International Conference on Baptist Studies*, edited by William L. Pitts, 288–303. Macon, GA: Mercer University Press, 2018.

Allen, Diogenes. "The Rehabilitation of Pilgrim's Progress." *Perspectives in Religious Studies* 27.1 (2000) 103–15.

Alter, Robert. *Genesis: Translation and Commentary.* New York: Norton, 1996.

Anderson, John E. *Jacob and the Divine Trickster: A Theology of Deception and Yhwh's Fidelity to the Ancestral Promise in the Jacob Cycle.* Siphrut 5. Winona Lake, IN: Eisenbrauns, 2011.

Bakker, Henk. "The Roaring Side of the Ministry: A Turn to Sacramentalism." *Perspectives in Religious Studies* 38.4 (2011) 404–26.

Balthasar, Hans Urs von. *Theodramatik.* 4 vols. Einsiedeln: Johannes Verlag, 1973–83.

Bársony, Márton. "God's Clown." *Studia Religiologica* 47.3 (2015) 153–63.

Barth, Karl. *Den Gefangenen Befreiung: Predigten aus den Jahren 1954–59.* Zollikon: Evangelischer Verlag, 1959.

Batson, Beatrice. *The Pilgrim's Progress by John Bunyan.* MacMillan Master Guides. Basingstoke: MacMillan, 1988.

Berger, Peter L. *Redeeming Laughter: The Comic Dimension of Human Experience.* Berlin: de Gruyter, 1997.

————. *A Rumor of Angels.* Expanded ed. New York: Doubleday, 1990.

Bergson, Henri. *Le Rire: Essai sur la signification du comique.* Paris: Librairie Félix Alcan, 1938 [1900].

Beverly, James A. *Holy Laughter and The Toronto Blessing: An Investigative Report.* Grand Rapids: Zondervan, 1995.

Boersma, Hans. *Heavenly Participation: The Weaving of a Sacramental Tapestry.* Grand Rapids: Eerdmans, 2009.

Bolin, Thomas M. "The Role of Exchange in Ancient Mediterranean Religion and Its Implications for Reading Genesis 18–19." *Journal for the Study of the Old Testament* 29.1 (2004) 37–56.

Brinkman, M.E. *Schepping en sacrament: Een oecumenische studie naar de reikwijdte van het sacrament als heilzaam symbool in een weerbarstige werkelijkheid.* Zoetermeer: Meinema, 1991.

Bunyan, John. *Grace Abounding: With Other Special Biographies.* Edited by John Stachniewski and Anita Pacheco. Oxford World's Classics. Oxford: Oxford University Press, 1998.

————. *The Pilgrim's Progress.* Edited by Cynthia Wall. A Norton Critical Edition. New York: Norton, 2009.

Claassens, L. Juliana M. "Laughter and Tears: Carnivalistic Overtones in the Stories of Sarah and Hagar." *Perspectives in Religious Studies* 32.3 (2005) 295–308.

Cohen, Ted. *Jokes: Philosophical Thoughts on Joking Matters.* Chicago: The University of Chicago Press, 1999.

Colwell, John E. *Promise and Presence: An Exploration of Sacramental Theology.* Milton Keynes: Paternoster, 2005.

Conybeare, Catherine. *The Laughter of Sarah: Biblical Exegesis, Feminist Theory, and the Concept of Delight.* New York: Palgrave Macmillan, 2013.

Copenhaver, Martin B. "Laughter at Easter: Matthew 28:1–10." *Journal for Preachers* 30.3 (2007) 15–18.

Cox, Harvey. *The Feast of Fools: A Theological Essay on Festivity and Fantasy.* Cambridge, MA: Harvard University Press, 1969.

Cross, Anthony R., and Philip E. Thompson, eds. *Baptist Sacramentalism.* Studies in Baptist History and Thought, 5. Carlisle: Paternoster, 2003.

Davies, Michael. *Graceful Reading: Theology and Narrative in the Works of John Bunyan.* Oxford: Oxford University Press, 2002.

Fackre, Gabriel. *The Promise of Reinhold Niebuhr.* 3rd ed. Grand Rapids: Eerdmans, 2011.

Fiddes, Paul S., Brian Haymes and Richard Kidd, *Baptists and the Communion of Saints: A Theology of Covenanted Disciples.* Waco, TX: Baylor University Press, 2014.

Fransen, Tim. *Het leven als tragikomedie: Over humor, kwetsbaarheid en solidariteit.* Essay voor de maand van de filosofie. Rotterdam: Lemniscaat, 2019.

Freeman, Curtis W. *Undomesticated Dissent: Democracy and the Public Virtue of Religious Nonconformity.* Waco, TX: Baylor University Press, 2017.

Garland, David E. *1 Corinthians.* Baker Exegetical Commentary on the New Testament. Grand Rapids: Baker Academic, 2003.

Gordon. Wenham, *Genesis 16–50.* Word Biblical Commentaries. Dallas: Word, 1994.

Greaves, Richard. *John Bunyan and English Nonconformity.* London: Hambledon, 1992.

Hauerwas, Stanley. *A Community of Character: Toward a Constructive Christian Social Ethic.* Notre Dame, IN: University of Notre Dame Press, 1981.

———. *The Peaceable Kingdom: A Primer in Christian Ethics.* Notre Dame, IN: University of Notre Dame Press, 1983.

———. *Truthfulness and Tragedy: Further Investigations in Christian Ethics.* Notre Dame, IN: University of Notre Dame Press, 1972.

———. *The Work of Theology.* Grand Rapids: Eerdmans, 2015.

Houtepen, Anton. *Uit aarde, naar Gods beeld: Theologische antropologie.* Zoetermeer: Meinema, 2006.

Hunter, James Davison. *To Change the World: The Irony, Tragedy, and Possibility of Christianity in the Late Modern World.* Oxford: Oxford University Press, 2010.

Hyers, Conrad. *And God Created Laughter: The Bible as Divine Comedy.* Atlanta, GA: John Knox, 1987.

———. *The Comic Vision and the Christian Faith: A Celebration of Life and Laughter.* New York: The Pilgrim, 1981.

———. *Holy Laughter: Essays on Religion in the Comic Perspective.* New York: Seabury, 1969.

———. *The Spirituality of Comedy: Comic Heroism in a Tragic World.* New York: Transaction, 1996.

Kaminsky, Joel S. "Humor and the Theology of Hope: Isaac as a Humorous Figure." *Interpretation* 54.4 (2000) 363–75.

Kidner, Derek. *Genesis.* Tyndale Old Testament Commentaries. Downers Grove, IL: IVP Academic, 2008 [1967].

Kuschel, Karl-Josef. *Laughter: A Theological Reflection.* Translated by John Bowden. London: SCM, 1994.

Levine, Nachman. "Sarah/Sodom, Birth, Destruction, and Synchronic Transaction." *Journal for the Study of the Old Testament* 31.2 (2006) 131–46.

Lewis, C.S. *Surprised by Joy: The Shape of My Early Life.* New York: Harcourt, Brace & World, 1955.

Lumpkin, William L., and Bill J. Leonard, eds. *Baptist Confessions of Faith.* 2nd ed. Valley Forge, PA: Judson, 2011.

McClendon, James W. *Biography as Theology: How Life Stories Can Remake Today's Theology.* New York: Abingdon, 1974.

———. "Do We Need Saints?" In *The Collected Works of James Wm. McClendon Jr.* Volume 2, edited by Ryan Andrew Newson and Andrew C. Wright, 285–94. Waco, TX: Baylor University Press, 2014.

———. *Ethics: Systematic Theology.* Volume 1. Rev. ed. Nashville, TN: Abingdon, 2002.

McKeown, James. *Genesis.* The Two Horizons Old Testament Commentary. Grand Rapids: Eerdmans, 2008.

Moberly, R.W.L. *Genesis 12–50.* Old Testament Guides. Sheffield: Sheffield Academic Press, 1992.

———. *The Theology of Genesis.* Old Testament Theology. Cambridge: Cambridge University Press, 2012.

Moltmann, Jürgen. *Die ersten Freigelassenen der Schöpfung: Versuche über die Freude an der Freiheit und das Wohlgefallen am Spiel.* Kaiser Traktate, 2. München: Kaiser, 1971.

Morreall, John. *Comedy, Tragedy and Religion.* New York: State University of New York Press, 1999.

Niebuhr, Reinhold. "Humor and Faith." In *Discerning the Signs of the Times: Sermons for Today and Tomorrow*, 111–31. New York: Scribner's Sons, 1946.

Noble, Tim. "A Writ Good Guide: The Bible in *The Way of the Pilgrim* and *The Pilgrim's Progress.*" *Journal of European Baptist Studies* 12.1 (2011) 20–35.

Peckham, John C. *Theodicy of Love: Cosmic Conflict and the Problem of Evil.* Grand Rapids: Baker Academic, 2018.

Pinker, Aron. "The Expulsion of Hagar and Ishmael (Gen 21:9–21)." *Women in Judaism: A Multidisciplinary E-Journal* 6.1 (2009) https://wjudaism. library.utoronto.ca/index.php/wjudaism/article/view/15798

Pinnock, Clark H. "The Physical Side of Being Spiritual: God's Sacramental Presence." In *Baptist Sacramentalism*, edited by Cross and Thompson, 8–20.

Ratzinger, Joseph. *Bilder der Hoffnung: Wanderungen im Kirchenjahr.* Freiburg: Herder, 1997.

————. *Images of Hope: Mediations on Major Feasts.* Translated by John Rock and Graham Harrison. San Francisco: Ignatius, 2006.

Rutledge, Fleming. *The Crucifixion: Understanding the Death of Jesus.* Grand Rapids: Eerdmans, 2015.

Schuster, Benny Grey. *Das Osterlachen: Darstellung der Kulturgeschichte und Theologie des Osterlachens sowie ein Essay über die kulturelle, kirchliche und theologische Verwandlung des Lachens.* Translated by Eberhard Harbsmeier. Flensburger Studien zur Literatur und Theologie, Bd. 14. Hamburg: Igel Verlag, 2019.

Shkop, Esther M. "And Sarah Laughed. . ." *Tradition* 31.3 (1997) 42–51.

Springhart, Heike. "Vulnerable Creation: Vulnerable Human Life between Risk and Tragedy." *Dialog: A Journal of Theology* 56.4 (2017) 382–90.

Spurgeon, Susanna. *Autobiography.* 4 vols. Chicago: Revell, 1898–1900.

Stetkevych, Suzanne Pinckney. "Sarah and the Hyena: Laughter, Menstruation, and the Genesis of a Double Entendre." *History of Religions* 36.1 (1996) 13–41.

Tolkien, J.R.R. *The Lord of the Rings: The Return of the King:* Book 3. New York: HarperCollins, 2005 [1955/1966].

Van den Brink, Gijsbert. *En de aarde bracht voort: Christelijk geloof en evolutie.* Utrecht: Boekencentrum, 2017.

————. "Should We Drop the Fall? On Taking Evil Seriously." In *Strangers and Pilgrims on Earth: Essays in Honour of Abraham van de Beek*, edited by E.A.J.G. Van der Borght and P.J.J. van Geest, 761–77. Studies in Reformed Theology, 22. Leiden: Brill, 2012.

Van Wyk, Tanya. "Die heuristiese potensiaal van narratiwiteit vir sosiaal relevante Sistematiese Teologie: Jürgen Moltmann se oorlogservarings as voorbeeldstudie." *HTS Teologiese Studies/Theological Studies* 69.1 (2013). Art. #2043, 1–7. https://doi.org/10.4102/hts.v69i1.2043

Vanhoozer, Kevin J. *The Drama of Doctrine: A Canonical-Linguistic Approach to Christian Theology.* Louisville, KY: Westminster John Knox, 2005.

————. *Faith Speaking Understanding: Performing the Drama of Doctrine.* Louisville, KY: Westminster John Knox, 2014.

Walton, J. Michael. *The Greek Sense of Theater: Tragedy and Comedy Reviewed.* 3rd ed. London: Routledge, 2015.

Warning, Rainer. *The Ambivalences of Medieval Religious Drama.* Translated by Steven Rendall. Stanford, CA: Stanford University Press, 2001.

Wells, Samuel. *Transforming Fate into Destiny: The Theological Ethics of Stanley Hauerwas.* Carlisle: Paternoster, 1998.

Whedbee, J. William. *The Bible and the Comic Vision.* Cambridge: Cambridge University Press 1998.

White, B.R. "John Bunyan and the Context of Persecution, 1660–1688." In *John Bunyan and his England, 1628–88*, edited by Anne Laurence, W.R. Owens, and Stuart Sim, 51–62. London: Hambledon, 1990.

Wood, Ralph C. *The Comedy of Redemption: Christian Faith and Comic Vision in Four American Novelists.* Notre Dame, IN: University of Notre Dame Press, 1988.

Zijderveld, Anton C. *Waarom wij lachen: Over de grap, de spot en de oorsprong van humor.* Amsterdam: Cossee, 2011.

Zucker, David J. "What Sarah Saw: Envisioning Genesis 21:9–10." *Jewish Bible Quarterly* 36.1 (2008) 54–62.

General Index

160, 210, 221, 222, 223, 234, 268
local church autonomy 4
local-church eucharist online 93
congregation(s) 69, 70, 75, 84, 156, 186, 193, 196, 244, 251
local fellowship 168
online church 94 n.53
people of God 78, 164, 266
pilgrim church 23
regenerate Christian community 158, 159
renewal of the church 77
virtual church(es) 82, 84–85, 87, 89
visible church 58, 155, 177
Western Church 56
Cicero 262 n.16
circumcision 157, 225, 226
Clark, Neville xix, xx, xxvi n.30, 4, 37, 43, 73 n.19, 212
clergy 172
clericalism xxxv
co-inherence 84
collection/offertory 4 n.5
Collins, Hercules 91, 101, 102
Colwell, John E. xiv, xx, xxvii, xxviii, 90, 163, 212, 295 n.79
comedy 282, 290 n.52, 292–94
    Comedy of Redemption, The 283
    divine tragicomedy xxi, 280–96
commemoration 105, 164
commemorative signs/certificates 222
communion of saints, the xxxviii, 155
community(–ies) xxvii, 67, 94, 134, 137, 153, 172, 185, 186, 222, 225, 234, 250, 251, 260, 261, 264, 268, 269, 271
    communal imagination 272
    communions 59
    communities of faith 165, 166
    community action 193
    community acts 204, 205
    community acts of commitment 162
    community as mediator of grace 269
    community intercession(s) 3 n.2
    community of believers 17, 25, 179, 274
    community of believers 29
    community of disciples 167

community of faith 67, 181
community of God 268
community of the faithful 164
corporate 230
    in Christ xxviii
        life in Christ 98
    new humanity 78
    incorporation into the church xxiii
    transformed community xxvii
computer simulation(s) 90
Concise Catechism of the Russian Baptist Union, The 215
Concise Doctrinal Teaching, The 235
conference 111
confession 4, 70, 130, 218
    confessing sins 252
    first confession 65
    oral confession 242
Confession of Baptists, The 228
Confession of Evangelical Christians, The 228
Confession of Faith of Christian Baptists 218
Confession of Faith of Evangelical Christian Baptists, The 221
Confession of Faith of St Petersburg Evangelical Christians, The 224
Confession of Faith, The (of Odessa Theological Seminary) 221
confession(s) of faith xxv, xxxix, 36, 198, 213, 214, 217, 235, 246
confessional groups 192 n.13
confirmation(s) 123, 127, 152, 195, 225
    confirmation vows 89
conformity 287 n.32
Congregationalists 58, 59, 60
contract xiv
conversion xxiv, 38, 43, 45, 49, 220, 221, 233, 235, 249, 251, 252, 274, 275, 289, 294 n.74
    becoming a Christian 77
    born of water and the Spirit 48
    conversion process 40, 234
    instant conversion 76
    invitation of crucified, risen and ascended Lord 8
    new creation 7, 78, 98, 157
    normative conversion 44
convictional analysis 190–206
Convictions 192, 204
Conybeare, Catherine 286
Cornwell, Francis 194

Thompson, Philip E. ix, xix, xxii,
xxxi, xxxix, xxxvii, 33, 48, 147,
212
Tolkien, J.R.R. 280
Tookey, Elias xxx
Toronto Blessing, the 281 n.5
Tournier, Paul 88
Tozer, A.W. 266, 267
tragedy xv, 282, 285, 286, 289, 290,
291, 292, 294, 295
transcendent, the xxv
Treatise of Laying on of Hands, A 194
trinitarianism xxxix n.100, 87, 155,
156
    trinitarian ecclesiology 154–68
    trinitarian economy 61 n.24
    trinitarian nature of baptism 138,
    139
    trinitarian theology 154, 159
Trinity, the 15, 74, 78, 90, 136, 156
n.47, 159, 160, 168
    triune God xxii, 45, 69, 71, 73,
    82, 97, 145, 147, 150, 151,
    153, 158, 159, 160, 163, 164,
    165, 166, 168, 264
    God the Father 16, 22, 56, 59,
    60, 67, 71, 72, 73, 74,
    107, 158, 166, 243, 266
    Holy Spirit xxiii, xxvii, xxviii,
    xxxiv, xxxvi n.80, 5, 7, 8,
    9, 40, 48, 65, 73, 76, 74,
    105, 108, 111 n.54, 114,
    115, 116, 124, 127, 138,
    139, 146, 147, 148, 153,
    157, 158, 159, 163, 164,
    165, 167, 168, 172, 177,
    181, 187, 190, 193, 194,
    195, 196, 197, 200, 203,
    204, 205, 206, 214, 218,
    219, 225, 231, 232, 234,
    236, 243, 245, 250, 251,
    252, 253, 259, 261, 264,
    265, 267, 268, 270, 273,
    274
    Spirit of Christ 165
    Second Person of the Trinity
    15
    Son 158, 159, 168, 243
*True Gospel-Faith Declared According
to the Scriptures, The* 194, 195, 200
trysting-place 97 n.61, 237
    rendez-vous 97
Turner, Denys 24

typology 44

Understanding Four Views on Baptism
216
Underwood, A.C. xx, 33
unity 168, 203
    unity of Christ 57
    unity with Christ 227–35

Vanhoozer, Kevin J. 282 n.9
Varavin, I.D. 223
Verratus, Johannes Maria 26
victory 273, 280
Vins, Yakov Yakovlevich 231, 240
Virgin Mary 66
virtual world 81–98
    digital representations 82
    non-virtual church 83
    non-virtual sacraments 83
    non-virtual world 83
    virtual baptism 84, 95–98
    virtual celebration 95, 96
    virtual communion 94
    virtual community 93 n.53
    virtual congregation 93
    virtual drinking 94
    virtual eating 94
    virtual eucharist 95–98
    virtual means of grace 88
    virtual partner 92
    virtual place 83
    virtual reality 92
    virtual relationships 92
    virtual sacramental world 96
    virtual sacraments xiii, xx, 83, 94
    virtual scholars xiii
virtue(s) 148, 175, 260
visible saints 134
visitation 167
vocabulary xv
Volf, Miroslav 154–58, 159, 161
Vyzu, R. xxiii

Walker, Michael J. 102, 103 n.12, 112
n.60
Wallace, Daniel 247
Walton, R.C. xx, 33, 43
Ward, Matthew 196, 199
Wardin, Albert 210
Waters of Promise 33
Watts, Graham 270
Webber, Robert 272
weddings 152